USEFUL BULLSHIT

USEFUL BULLSHIT

CONSTITUTIONS IN CHINESE POLITICS AND SOCIETY

NEIL J. DIAMANT

CORNELL UNIVERSITY PRESS

Ithaca and London

First published 2021 by Cornell University Press

Library of Congress Cataloging-in-Publication Data

Names: Diamant, Neil J., 1964– author.
Title: Useful bullshit : constitutions in Chinese politics
    and society / Neil J. Diamant.
Description: Ithaca, New York : Cornell University Press,
    2021. | Includes bibliographical references and index.
Identifiers: LCCN 2021011483 (print) | LCCN
    2021011484 (ebook) | ISBN 9781501761270 (hardcover) |
    ISBN 9781501761287 (pdf) | ISBN 9781501761294 (epub)
Subjects: LCSH: Constitutional law—Social aspects—
    China. | Constitutional law—Political aspects—China. |
    Constitutional history—Social aspects—China. |
    Legitimacy of governments—China. | Sociological
    jurisprudence—China. | China—Politics and
    government—History.
Classification: LCC KNQ2070 .D53 2021 (print) |
    LCC KNQ2070 (ebook) | DDC 342.51/02—dc23
LC record available at https://lccn.loc.gov/2021011483
LC ebook record available at https://lccn.loc.gov/202
1011484

To the memory of my mother, Arline Diamant-Gold, ל"ז,
and stepmother, Rachel Halevi-Diamant, ל" ז

Contents

ACKNOWLEDGMENTS

This book is the product of two disappointments for which I am very grateful.

Around 2010, after publishing *Embattled Glory: Veterans, Military Families, and the Politics of Patriotism in China, 1949–2007*, I became interested in the issue of vaccination campaigns in China from the perspective of those receiving the shots in their arms. Always fascinated by questions addressing political legitimacy—which the current book is also concerned with—I reasoned that an interesting way to go about this would be to look at how people reacted to the governments' efforts to enforce a variety of public health campaigns. I dutifully conducted background research on vaccination campaigns around the world, and over the course of two summers did some preliminary archival research. Unfortunately, there was scant material from the perspective of ordinary people asked to roll up their sleeves. Archivists indicated that if any organization possessed these materials, it would be the People's Republic of China's (PRC) equivalent to the United States' Centers for Disease Control and Prevention, but on a separate trip to China with Dickinson College students I was informed by officials there that vaccination records were mainly charts with names, locations, and marks indicating when an injection was provided; how people reacted was not particularly interesting to the authorities. As it turned out, and unbeknownst to me, the historian Mary Augusta Brazelton was researching a similar topic (*Mass Vaccination: Citizens' Bodies and State Power in Modern China*, 2019), which was also published by Cornell University Press.

So much for that project. I was at loose ends for a while, trying to come up with a new project that fit three criteria: data from a popular level; concern with political legitimacy; and of interest to historians and social scientists. At some point during this period, I recalled reading a document I found in a keyword search for "veteran" (*fuyuan junren*) at the Shanghai Municipal Archives when researching *Embattled Glory*. It was not about veterans per se but mentioned the fact that during the 1954 "National Discussion of the Draft Constitution," veterans were one of the only groups in that city that did not discuss this document. My interest piqued, I began my research in Hong Kong and

Shanghai, finding—much to my amazement—not only that there was abundant documentation of how ordinary people reacted to the draft constitution and what they thought about the Chinese Communist Party but also that this subject had received scant attention among constitutional scholars in China or the West.

The second disappointment occurred very soon after I dove into this new topic. I was invited to give a talk as part of a job interview for a senior position in a well-known history department. Excessively excited by some of my findings from the archival research that I had completed only a week prior to the interview, I rashly decided to present these along with some tentative arguments about what they might mean. Trained in political science and "law and society," I failed to anticipate that someone in a history department would ask about the history of Chinese constitutions. As it turned out, the very first question was something along these lines: "Why does China even have a constitution?" I had no clue—and did not get the job—but over the course of the 2010s I have come closer to an answer, which I share in this book.

Institutionally, this project would not have been possible without a travel grant and research assistance funded by Dickinson College's Research and Development Committee.

I also have benefited enormously from the advice and support of many excellent colleagues in the China field, law, Soviet history, philosophy, and English literature. My heartful appreciation goes out to Jennifer Altehenger, Jeremy Brown, Alyssa DeBlasio, Janet Chen, Nara Dillon, Douglas Edlin, Jacob Eyferth, Feng Xiaocai, Mark Frazier, Mary Gallagher, Keith Hand, Gail Hershatter, Nico Howson, Thomas Kellogg, Chauncey Maher, Sarah Niebler, Elizabeth Perry, Siobhan Phillips, Karl Qualls, Dave Strand, Eddy U, and Felix Wemheuer. Jeremy Brown, one of the expert readers for Cornell University Press, was especially helpful identifying the manuscript's weaker spots and providing excellent concrete suggestions for corrective measures. Emily Andrew, senior editor at the Press, was again a source of excellent advice as well as a wonderful guide during the publication process. My uncle, Bob Rothenberg, an engineer with the soul of a writer and editor, was kind enough to proofread the manuscript before it went to press. I, of course, remain responsible for all remaining errors.

I also benefited from the opportunity to present some of my ideas and receive helpful feedback from audiences at the University of California, Los Angeles, the Australian National University, the University of Michigan, Harvard University, Nanjing University, the University of Pittsburgh, and a panel discussion at the Annual Meeting of the Association for Asian Studies.

I am also grateful for the highly capable research assistance provided by Pauline Bu, and Joanna Wang.

As someone who has made a career using archival materials, I am especially appreciative of the assistance provided by archivists at the Shanghai Municipal Archives, the Guangdong Provincial Archives, and archives in Shanghai's Baoshan, Huangpu, Songjiang, and Yangpu Districts. One of my most importance sources, *Neibu cankao* (Internal Reference), was made available thanks to the staff at the Universities Services Centre for China Studies in Hong Kong. I am also grateful to librarians at Dickinson College for their help in gathering numerous materials from libraries around the world. A special thanks goes out to Haihui Zhang, Head of the East Asian Library at the University of Pittsburgh, who worked tirelessly and selflessly on my behalf to secure copies of rare sources in the PRC through interlibrary loan.

Some materials in this book were first published in Neil J. Diamant and Xiaocai Feng, "The PRC's First National Critique: The 1954 Campaign to 'Discuss the Draft Constitution,'" *The China Journal* 73 (January 2015): 1–37 (© University of Chicago Press); and Neil J. Diamant, "What the [Expletive] Is a Constitution?! Ordinary Cadres Confront the 1954 Draft Constitution," *Journal of Chinese History* 2 (Fall 2017): 1–22 (© Cambridge University Press, reprinted with permission). I am grateful to these presses for permission to reuse these materials.

Finally, as always, I am grateful to my immediate and extended family, whose support over the last decade made this book possible.

Introduction

Constitutions, Legitimacy, and Interpreting Popular Commentary

> [For the liar] it is correspondingly indispensable that he considers his statements to be false. For the bullshitter, however, all these bets are off. His eye is not on the facts at all . . . except insofar as they may be pertinent to his interest in getting away with what he says.
>
> —Harry G. Frankfurt, *On Bullshit*

> [The government] is always coming out with some verb or noun but never explains what that word means. You're not to be counterrevolutionary, it says, for instance, without defining counterrevolutionary. You can't be a hooligan, it says, but it won't tell you what a hooligan is . . . if we say you're guilty, you're guilty.
>
> —Han Han, *This Generation: Dispatches from China's Most Popular Literary Star (and Race Car Driver)*

"There's no point researching that useless document" was how a colleague in China, a comrade in the social sciences, shot back when I told him I had turned my attention to studying the 1954 Constitution. Even though that 1954 document formed the basis of all subsequent constitutions (1975, 1978, and 1982) and on this basis alone would seem to be somewhat important, his frustrated voice is far from a lonely one: Chinese citizens, including officials, have long critiqued politicians' long-standing preference to govern by way of administrative policy, utterance, phone call, speech, and proclamation rather than "rule of law" or "rule by law" standards, as well as for their willingness and ability to flagrantly violate rights that appear to be very clear on paper.[1] Correspondingly, scholars have been reluctant to invest scarce resources to studying a document that, although tenacious in terms of its long-term survivability across political turmoil since 1949, does not seem to matter much at all, at least in the sense of shaping political, legal, and social behavior they deem to be meaningful.[2]

This book challenges this perspective. Profiling the voices of ordinary Chinese participants whose constitutional comments, queries, musings, and deliberations have been preserved in archives, I will make the case that the study of Chinese constitutions—as written and audible texts, as a form of interaction between officials and citizens, and as a political process—provides powerful insights about how people understood law and assessed the legitimacy, meaning, and consequences of the Communist Revolution, as well as the variety of emotions stirred up by law and revolution.[3] Substantial evidence demonstrates that many state officials did not understand constitutions, did not accept their underlying rationale, or even cursed them—but still found these documents useful as words that could easily induce feelings of terror, jealousy, uncertainty, and confusion among citizens and other officials; intensify social divisions; and help push through unpopular policies. Constitutions were also useful as brute displays of political power: despite knowing that people at home and abroad knew that these documents had a problematic relationship with truth, the government promulgated and discussed them anyway.[4] Evidence also shows that ordinary citizens who did not believe a wide variety of constitutional claims nevertheless found constitutions useful as a mechanism to defend rights and as a convenient platform for criticizing the government for a variety of transgressions, commenting on current and past policies and their experiences of them, or requesting better enforcement or abrogation.

This book will also make the case that Chinese constitutions must be understood beyond their textual forms. Constitutional texts sometimes became country-wide constitutional conversations that were initiated by the state but not entirely controlled by it. Largely ignored in the legal and political science literature, these constitutional discussions allow us to explore—for the first time—various dimensions of popular constitutionalism in China, or what ordinary people thought and felt about this document.[5] Talking about constitutions was the product of the state's efforts to enhance citizens' legal knowledge but (probably unintentionally) opened a surprisingly safe political space for people from all walks of life—including officials—to talk about law and politics and raise fundamental questions concerning the nature of Chinese Communist Party (CCP) rule, its governance practices, interpretation of history and understanding of class, and their role as citizens. Within this space, people also defended their status in ideology, promoted Han ethnic superiority, sought out enhanced material and symbolic benefits, caught officials in flagrante delicto about policy and legal knowledge, and mocked, ridiculed, critiqued, and rebutted them, all well-established features of Chinese political culture that predated the CCP and continue to survive its humorless politics.[6]

The perspective on Chinese constitutions offered in this book, I suggest, requires a major adjustment of the more commonly used lenses through which they have been understood in scholarship and among nonspecialists. The first, which can be best described as *disappointment*, is largely the result of constitutions consistently failing, for a variety of reasons, to match their words with real-life functions (e.g., a "legislature" that does not do much legislating) and to live up to their idealized definition of "constraint" on the coercive power of the executive in a democracy, a feature achieved through inclusive and effective popular participation in the constitutional drafting process and clear separation of powers in the final product.[7] The second, but still related to the first, is *insignificance*, a perspective shaped by the idea that constitutions are important if and when they shape politics, culture, and society. Considered disappointing and insignificant, it is unsurprising that Chinese constitutions have been dismissed as documents unworthy of the paper they are written on.

Among these two perspectives, the disappointment position is easier to critique. While many contemporary observers are disheartened by the failure of Chinese constitutionalism—the oft-noted arbitrary and ruthless behavior of officials—we cannot assume that those who experienced the rollout of the constitution in 1954, or in 1982, felt the same way. This fallacy, which the intellectual historian Quentin Skinner awkwardly called the "mythology of prolepsis," occurs when "the historian is more interested—as he may legitimately be—in the retrospective significance of a given historical work or action than in its meaning for the agent himself."[8]

The view that constitutions are insignificant is a tougher rival largely because it runs counter to the popular notion that the most important questions in the social sciences are of a causal nature, whose answers can be measured and replicated. Echoing political scientist John Gerring's critique, I would argue that this approach is mistaken both in principle (describing something well is as important as establishing cause and effect) and in practice; in authoritarian or revolutionary regimes, we frequently lack the data to make strong causal arguments.[9] While state intentions might be possible to figure out, the impact of any law, ideology, or policy is harder to assess, particularly when trying to account for mentalities or emotional states of large social units. Many scholars try to work around this data problem simply by asserting unsubstantiated claims about citizens' "subjectivity" and the existence and power of hegemonic "discourses," but this is a road I would rather avoid.

Rather than make deductions based on limited information, this book adopts an inductive approach that is rarely applied to studies of constitutions, even in "law and society" scholarship that privileges the voices of ordinary people. Discipline-wise, this book is situated at the intersection of legal and social history, a fairly well-trod space in studies of the Ming and Qing dynasties (1368–1644; 1644–1911, respectively) and the Republican era (1911–1949) but still off the beaten track in studies of the history of the People's Republic of China (PRC) and nearly nonexistent in studies of constitutions in the legal academy and political science.[10] Focusing primarily on China's first constitution of 1954, I look closely at the constitutional text—the words, grammar, concepts, phrases, and the many things that were omitted but remained cognitively present through memory, association, connotation, and metaphor—and describe how these were understood and emotionally absorbed by a wide variety of people, including Buddhists, businessmen, Christians, ethnic minorities and Han, men, officials, policemen, university faculty, villagers, women, and workers. For example, how did officials think about law as a source and tactic of public order? How did ordinary people "sense the state" in conditions of widespread misinformation, confusion, and general unfamiliarity with key concepts in constitutional law and Marxist-Leninist ideology? More generally, how did people understand and interpret the Communist Revolution in Year Five, ignorant about how things would turn out politically or constitutionally even several years later? Beyond 1954, was China's first large-scale constitutional moment relevant to politics and law in the subsequent decades? The answers to these questions will speak to the historiography and governmentality of the Mao era while also providing a colorful view of Chinese society during the formative stages of a new political and legal order.

This book contributes to legal and social scientific study of constitutions in another important way: the quantity and quality of data it provides.[11] Between April and September 1954, the Chinese Communist Party, apparently following the model of the 1936 Soviet constitutional process, promoted an "all-people national discussion" (*quanmin taolun*) of its draft constitution, encouraging hundreds of millions of people to suggest amendments to its articles, propose corrections to wording and grammar, and ask questions to clarify its meaning. These discussions, often led by poorly trained propaganda officials (*baogaoyuan*) and lasting anywhere from several hours to days, ranged widely, covering the preamble (six pages dealing with revolutionary history, ideology, and policy); "General Principles" (chapter 1, consisting of twenty articles addressing the identity of state, power, class relations, economy, ethnic minorities, and the military); state structure (chapter 2, the largest, at sixty-three articles); citizens' rights and obligations (chapter 3, eighteen articles); and state symbols such as the flag, the national emblem, and the location of the capital (chapter 4, three articles).[12] This constitutional verbiage produced a massive paper trail that has been preserved in archives, compiled in the classified political newsletter *Neibu cankao* (Internal Reference), a regularly read source in the highest echelons of the Communist Party, or gathered in the multivolume *Collected Suggestions about the Draft Constitution from the All-People Discussion* (*Quanguo renmin taolun xiancao yijian huibian*) in the National Library in Beijing.[13] Despite the abundance and accessibility of these materials, law school–based legal scholars either have not utilized *Neibu cankao* or the *Collected Suggestions* in any analysis of the PRC constitutional process or perhaps worse have praised it based on biased official statements.[14] Those few who have used nonpublic sources, such as Han Dayuan, have also argued that it was a very well-received document everywhere it was discussed that (causally) contributed to political legitimacy.[15]

Fortunately, this extensive documentation about the constitutional process provides us leverage to address the issue of legitimacy, as well as two others that have long preoccupied China scholars: the origins and functions of constitutions, and how people experienced the Communist Revolution (which overlaps to a certain extent with legitimacy). As we will see throughout this book, when people read the constitution or heard others read it to them, they often asked questions, and offered what they claimed to be helpful suggestions. But many of these were in fact critiques of the state, law, the revolution, policies, the economy, and ideology, frequently expressed from the standpoint of their own personal and family experiences. For many, insinuating by questioning mitigated the risk in confronting authority—the more vagueness and ambiguity, the more deniability. But if we assume that the authorities were not easily bamboozled and that they were aware of widespread skepticism as people talked about their experiences, why did they promulgate constitutions and even celebrate them (under Xi Jinping, Constitution Day is every December 4)? Exactly how did this serve state interests (often called "instrumentalism")? On the flip side, why would ordinary people invoke the constitution knowing that the authorities do not take it seriously?

Constitutions and Legitimacy

Why have PRC leaders bothered to write constitutions in the first place? This was by no means preordained. Most Chinese dynasties, after all, functioned for centuries without them, and many countries manage to conduct political life in their absence.

To date, scholars interested in this issue have focused on the concepts *modernity* and *legitimacy*. Since the late Qing, the argument goes, political reformers associated some form of constitutional government (monarchal, democratic, or authoritarian) and political rights as necessary to make China a modern state that enjoys domestic and international legitimacy, as well as to strengthen China against foreign powers; Japan's post-Meiji resurgence was a case in point.[16] By 1911, when the Qing dynasty fell, most influential politicians accepted the idea of constitutional rule. In accordance, the Republic of China (1911–1949) emerged with three constitutional documents (a "provisional constitution" in 1912; the 1913 Draft Constitution [also known as the "Tiantan Constitution"]; and the 1947 Republican Constitution), as well with a tight-knit circle of legal professionals well versed in constitutional theory and practice. Not a few articles in the Republican constitution, including important parts of its administrative structure and many political rights and obligations, carried over to the PRC's, whose leaders were immersed in late Qing and early republican discourse causally linking constitutions with political legitimacy. Tom Ginsburg and Alberto Simpser call this alleged connection scholars' "standard answer" about why authoritarian regimes (as a more general category of analysis) have adopted constitutions that they then proceed to ignore.[17]

Mao Zedong's early views on constitutions are not entirely in focus. As a youth Mao avidly read Liang Qichao, the famous constitutional monarchist and political reformer.[18] In the 1940s, when the CCP was a severely weakened party and at war along several fronts, he appeared receptive to at least the concept of constitutional government but mainly on tactical grounds. As part of the wartime "United Front" strategy (building a coalition between the revolutionary classes and progressive intellectuals, so-called patriotic businessmen, and relatively well-off segments of rural society), he reasoned that a constitution could help attract "all possible democratic elements to us" and help achieve "our goals of defeating the Japanese bandits and building a democratic country."[19] In November 1948, as the CCP neared victory in the Civil War, a small group of its leaders drafted a document intended to have this coalitional appeal and calm fears of Communist rule, much along the lines of Mao's logic from 1944.[20] After some discussion with nonparty intellectual elites in a CCP-led Constitutional Draft Committee, an interim constitution, called the Common Program (*gongtong gangling*), was promulgated in the name of the Chinese People's Political Consultative Conference, an important body in the CCP's United Front.

Several articles in the Common Program would seem to support the view that the constitutional enterprise was, at least in part, motivated by the desire to bolster legitimacy. For example, it incorporated, rather than excluded, based on class status. Its preamble stated that "New Democracy" would be the "political foundation" of the state; Article 1 recognized the leading role of workers in alliance with peasants but also that "uniting all democratic classes and all nationali-ties in China" was a political priority. The document also protected private property and explicitly recognized "peasant land ownership." It offered the same political rights—including freedom of thought, speech, press, assembly, associa-tion, correspondence, person, change of domicile, religious belief, and the free-dom of holding processions and demonstrations—that had been included in the Republic of China's 1947 Constitution. These were provided to *renmin* (the people), which included the working class, peasants, the petty bourgeoisie, CCP-supporting capitalists, and some "patriotic democratic elements" without spe-cifically excluding the "reactionary" classes (landlords, "bureaucratic capitalists," and the like). While the Common Program had punitive elements (for example, Article 7 dealt with either "suppressing" or threatening counterrevolutionary war criminals, traitors, and others "who oppose the cause of people's democ-racy"), it was, on the whole, a conciliatory document.

The second major approach toward constitutional origins has emphasized the historical role of the USSR in Chinese Communist Party history, and Sta-lin's ability to persuade Mao that constitutions were a useful way to generate legitimacy for the new state. The CCP's United Front strategy—of which doc-uments such as the Common Program and the 1954 Constitution were a part—had been a central plank in the Soviet Union's effort to foment revolu-tion in semicolonial and colonial contexts, which included China. When the CCP took power in 1949–1950, the United Front having done its job, Mao wa-vered about the necessity of a constitution even for political legitimacy pur-poses.[21] But according to Chinese constitutional historians, Stalin was adamant that the CCP, having unified the country in a military conquest, adopt a con-stitution as a prerequisite for political legitimacy domestically and internation-ally, as well as a marker of modernity.[22] The critical role of the USSR was recently noted by the historian Jennifer Altehenger, who argued that the PRC promulgated a constitution, and the all-people discussion about it, to demon-strate that its law "was among the superior kinds of law in the world because, like its socialist brethren, it made constitutional thought and language acces-sible and a weapon of the people."[23]

As a result of this convergence of interests and ideas, Stalin dispatched, at China's request, senior legal experts to help draft a new constitution modeled on its own (from 1936) as well as several Eastern European countries, in addi-tion to other laws and regulations (this was the early stage of what would be-come a wave of Soviet experts visiting China over the next several years). Their advice was apparently taken seriously and incorporated into the final version.[24] Between 1953 and 1954, Soviet experts worked alongside top CCP leaders and senior Western-trained constitutional scholars who had worked under the

Kuomintang, resulting in a hybrid document recognizable to Leninists and to liberal officials.[25] One scholar even deemed 1954 a "Year of Hope" because of the promulgation of the new constitution.[26]

The tension between Mao's more radical plans for political and economic transformation, which did not require obeisance to constitutional niceties, and Stalin's effort to push the CCP toward a constitution on legitimacy grounds, can be discerned in the 1954 Constitution.[27] For example, as was the case in the Common Program, the proletariat was designated as the leading class in alliance with peasants. Chapter 1 announced the CCP's transition from its wartime United Front policies to socialism and communicated China's national and "class" identity to its citizens and the rest of the world.[28] The constitution also excised the United Front–style language that had been included in the Common Program's preamble: "uniting all democratic classes" went missing; the bourgeoisie was removed from the class alliance represented by the CCP; and threatening terms to describe the socialist transition were added. For example, the "rich peasant" rural economy would gradually be eliminated (*xiaomie*), and the state reserved the right to expropriate (*zhengyong*) private property.[29] In what might have been an effort to balance this out, the list of rights grew longer. In addition to those in the Common Program, the 1954 Constitution included work, education, rest, and judicial due process—but limited them either to "citizens" or, in the case of rest, to "laborers."[30]

In this book I will argue that these legitimacy-centered explanations for constitutions are unpersuasive because they downplay or fail to include the second, more important, part of China's constitutions—the discussions about their content and the reporting of people's often-problematic reactions to political leaders—as well as the economic and political context that developed in 1954. If the most important goal was political legitimacy generated by a formal legislative process and the resulting constitutional text, why would the CCP also adopt a Soviet-style, months-long national discussion about its draft? The prevailing wisdom is that CCP leaders rather uncritically copied the Soviet example from 1936, when it also held such a discussion, presumably through the conduit of the Soviet advisers in Beijing, and by doing so joined the family of other socialist countries articulating an alternative version of legality.[31] But I have not come across any substantial discussion of precisely who among the Soviet advisers took the lead on this, if the Chinese leadership weighed the pros and cons, and who among them voiced opposition. More importantly, from a legitimacy perspective, why would the CCP open up political space for a broad discussion of challenging historical, ideological, political, legal, economic, and social issues (simultaneously!) only one year after a difficult war in Korea (1950–53) and years of traumatic political campaigns, such as those targeting former Nationalist officials and anti-Communist religious organizations ("Suppress Counterrevolutionaries," 1951), businessmen ("Five Antis,"1952), university faculty ("Thought Reform," 1950–51), and even elderly people ("Marriage Law," 1953)? Given that such a discussion was unprecedented, the risks would seem to outweigh the benefits. In contrast, in the USSR the national discussion occurred nearly two decades after the Bolsheviks seized power, and the 1936 Constitution was supposed to symbolize the end of class struggle, not its beginning or middle.

The economic and political context in 1954 also militated against adopting a constitution for legitimacy purposes. Economically, 1954 was a busy year, as factories and farms transitioned toward a socialist economy. Why would the CCP ask the Chinese people, 80 percent of whom were illiterate or minimally so, and its millions of harried officials, many of whom were young and poorly educated, to spend their valuable time talking about a *xianfa* (constitution), a "return graphic loan" word (derived from Classical Chinese, it was used in Japanese *kanji* to translate modern European words and then reintroduced into modern Chinese) that had not been used in this context before, let alone talked about in everyday life?[32] In contrast, in the USSR literacy rates were nearly the mirror image, and convening discussions over law and policy were very much a part of Bolshevik and Russian intellectual culture.[33] The political context was also problematic. Stalin's behavior toward China during the Korean War did not leave a positive impression; Mao and his colleagues thought that the Soviets seemed "more like arms merchants than genuine proletarian revolutionaries" because they requested payment for the military support they provided.[34] Furthermore, in March 1953 Stalin died, removing whatever direct political pressure Mao was under to enact a constitution. According to Liu Shanying, Mao supported the constitution anyway to fulfill a bequest and raise his status in the socialist camp after Stalin's death, but given the costs to political legitimacy that soon became apparent through the national discussion, these reasons strike me as overly sentimental and politically unnecessary after China fought the United States to a stalemate in Korea two years earlier.[35]

In this book I propose a different explanation of the origins and functions of Chinese constitutions that avoids any causal relationship between constitutions and legitimacy. Drawing on Mao's wartime view of constitutions as a political tactic shaped by fear of subversion and the need to build alliances, I suggest that, at their core, CCP constitutions are a legal dimension of what Sebastian Heilmann and Elizabeth J. Perry have called "guerilla style" policy making (tactically oriented, flexible, experimental, and ruthlessly pragmatic about alliances).[36] Politically, constitutions served the purpose of "controlled polarization"—a Bolshevik-Maoist divide-and-rule tactic—because the text explicitly divvied up the population into friends and enemies and offered particularistic rewards and punishments.[37] The national discussions that took place around constitutions were less a product of Soviet intervention than (as Mao noted in his *Selected Works*) another example of the CCP's cherished, quasi-populist "mass line" governing strategy in which officials in direct contact with people gain an understanding of their basic desires and concerns, report these to higher-level leaders who, with their superior understanding of the laws of history, decide what policies to implement.[38] They were not designed to provide legitimacy, which historian Feng Xiaocai argues is not difficult to "counterfeit," but rather provide the CCP with an even more valuable weapon: data.[39]

As many scholars have noted, authoritarian rulers, like their democratic counterparts, need techniques to "read" their population to understand sources of potential threats to their rule and, to a more limited extent, people's preferences. In China, this need was especially urgent. Coming to power as a rural-based insurgency, the CCP hungered for information about what people were thinking about issues such as law, political institutions, ideology, class, identity, and symbols; in a broader sense, the CCP wanted to know how people assessed the Communist Party and the revolution. A months-long national discussion about these subjects, therefore, could yield valuable social and political intelligence, particularly from sectors of society that had always been skeptical, if not antagonistic, to Communist rule. This had been the case in the USSR and may have been communicated to the CCP leadership during their discussions in the early 1950s.[40] In the Soviet Union much of the discussion was conducted by the secret police, which sent copious documentation about people's opinions to central leaders, and in China there was also a mechanism for reporting people's views to the highest levels of the state. I propose— but cannot prove definitively—that as leaders became readers of constitutional commentary during the spring and summer of 1954, they learned that a document, if carefully worded and called a fancy name (*xianfa*), could be tactically deployed to achieve several desired effects.

So, what did they learn about the usefulness of such a document that convinced them not only to promulgate a constitution in 1954 but also to continue writing and revising them for the next sixty years? Now that we can read what Chinese citizens said and what their leaders likely read, we can propose more plausible explanations about constitutional origins and functions. These do not assume that a constitution helps generate popular legitimacy because of its high status in the legal hierarchy, regardless of its content.[41]

The Constitution and the Revolution

Much like legal scholars, historians and political scientists working on the early history of the PRC have also focused on the issue of legitimacy, but have done so primarily by exploring how ordinary people experienced the Communist Revolution. Scholars have debated whether the revolution was a "liberation" (and if so, for whom?), if there ever was a honeymoon period between the CCP and the population in the early years of the PRC, and the extent to which the Communist victory ushered in a new form of political domination based on Marxism-Leninism merged with traditional forms of authority.[42] Answering such questions became even more complicated as a bounty of "grassroots" materials—local archives, diaries, and private collections—have become available to scholars working on how state power was experienced by ordinary people in the foundational years of the PRC. As noted by the historians Jeremy Brown, Paul Pickowicz, and Matthew Johnson in the edited volumes *Dilemmas of Victory: The Early Years of the People's Republic of China* and *Maoism at the Grassroots: Everyday Life in China's Era of High Socialism*, the diversity of people's experiences revealed by new sources makes it impossible to provide a definitive answer about the nature of the CCP's relationship to citizens in the early 1950s.[43] While this reluctance to draw broader inferences and paint a more comparative picture connecting the dots between the early years of the state and future developments has frustrated some, from my perspective this dispute is mainly the result of the publication format (edited volumes) and source materials.[44] It is very challenging for editors to create a coherent tapestry from essays that are often complex, colorful, detailed, and often biographical in content.

The primary source materials used in this book help resolve some of these substantive and methodological debates and hopefully bridge the gap between grassroots PRC historians, social scientists, and law school–based research on constitutions. First, unlike documents dealing with discrete political campaigns or case histories of people who experienced some sort of legal or political trouble, our constitutional materials usually dealt with the entire polity, covering issues as disparate as "who governs" to the images on the flag and the national emblem; the substantive and symbolic are baked into the sources. In scale, many millions across all sectors of society participated. Thanks to their wide scope, topical diversity, and high level of abstraction, what ordinary people said about a variety of constitutional articles—what I have called popular constitutionalism—merges with the broader question of legitimacy.[45] During the 1954 discussion, for example, *Neibu cankao* reporters fanned out to large cities such as Shanghai, Beijing, Chongqing, Xi'an, Chengdu, and Shenyang, as well as to remote areas of Yunnan Province, Inner Mongolia, and Shanxi. At the local level, state investment in education about the constitution was impressive.[46] County-level gazetteers, institutional histories, and *Annals of Important Events* (*Dashiji*) mention that people heard, read, and offered comments on a variety of constitutional articles.[47] Shanghai's industrial sector alone generated some 15,000 comments and questions, while at the national level, the National Draft Constitution Committee considered 1,380,000 comments.[48] Many of these were straight-up legal questions, but people also wanted to know about politics, history, society, culture, and military topics as well, in other words, subjects bridging law, the humanities, and social sciences.

This extensive, constitution-driven documentation—cutting across popular sectors, topics, and disciplinary silos—allows us to provide a reasonably panoramic account of how people experienced the Communist revolution. When reading or listening to various articles of the constitution, how did specific groups talk about what had happened to them and their families before 1954? How did they react to discussions of class, political power, gender, and military service, and how did these, in turn, shape the way they assessed the meaning of constitution and the Communist revolution and its legitimacy?

Since several of this book's chapters examine specific populations that reacted to the draft of the 1954 Constitution, I will leave the specific arguments about those groups to their own chapters. Here I will only make a broad-brushed assessment of what constitution-based documents tell us about legitimacy, the meaning of the revolution, and class and institutions: neither the state nor the revolution was particularly legitimate, and only a few groups evaluated the revolution as "liberation." At the same time, evidence does not show that people interpreted the CCP as a thoroughly oppressive regime. Instead, in the still relatively open political space surrounding the constitution, two years before the conventional dating of widespread critique of the CCP during the Hundred Flowers Campaign in 1956, we hear a cacophony of voices.[49] While some people expressed hope and satisfaction, many more felt confused, angry, worried, anxious, jealous, frustrated, bitter, and fearful. Assessing the constitution, they had a strong sense that the CCP was "up to something," but what this was could not be easily discerned. Looking at the revolution at year five, the verdict on its impact and meaning had yet to congeal. However, given the continued challenge of laying down a broadly understood and acceptable political and legal vocabulary, and the social and political devastation that proceeded apace after 1956, we can reasonably infer that whatever thin layer of legitimacy had been established by 1954 became more tenuous in the middle and latter parts of the decade.

Constitutions as Useful Bullshit

Bringing together elite goals in promulgating and talking about constitutions with how these documents were often perceived by ordinary officials and people is the important concept *bullshit*. I use this term neither as a term of derision nor as a deductive assessment of state and popular views but rather as an inductive, data-driven distillation of the role of the constitution in Chinese politics and society and how it was viewed. That is, I argue that in promulgating a constitution the CCP was engaging in a form of bullshit, and many people understood this even as they, too, participated in this behavior. They did this because even as bullshit the constitution was useful, for reasons we will see throughout the book.

Although widely seen as an insult, albeit of the very tame variety, the concept bullshit acquired more scholarly legitimacy when the esteemed philosopher Harry G. Frankfurt published *On Bullshit* to wide acclaim.[50] In this work, Frankfurt takes bullshit seriously, expending considerable intellectual effort figuring out the definitional boundaries of this popular word. He pays special attention to the ways in which lies are different from bullshit, a critical distinction in the study of Chinese constitutions because many have categorized them as the former. In Frankfurt's view, when someone lies they deliberately misrepresent the truth. For the liar, he argues, there is, at minimum, a concern for truth, even if a decision is made to assert its opposite. Frankfurt's bullshitter, on the other hand, is "unconstrained by a concern with truth"; thus the "essence of bullshit is not that it is *false* but that it is *phony*," and "closer to bluffing . . . than to telling a lie."[51] In this perspective, it is possible that what a bullshitter says about facts, or what the bullshitter takes the facts to be, might be true, but this could be entirely incidental. Instead, Frankfurt's bullshitters' "only indispensably distinctive characteristic"—what distinguishes the bullshitter from the liar—is that "in a certain way he misrepresents what he is up to," is "trying to get away with something," and is "attempt[ing] to deceive us about . . . his enterprise."[52] To the bullshitter, facts "may be pertinent" only insofar as they affect the bullshitter's "interest in getting away with what he says."[53]

Several examples should suffice to make this a bit more concrete. Take, for instance, the fantastical constitutional claims that China's National People's Congress (NPC) was "the highest organ of state authority"; that capitalists' production resources would be protected; that ethnic minorities could decide through a "majority" about their own self-governance; and that citizens enjoyed a long, generous list of political and socioeconomic rights. Throughout the history of the PRC, but beginning in earnest in 1954, citizens and even officials called out these claims as bullshit in the sense not only that they were untrue but also that the CCP knew they were lies (Frankfurt's "unconstrained by a concern with truth") and that people were aware of this as well, but the party remained unbothered and did not respond to questions or engage in significant revisions of the draft. Why not? Frankfurt's analysis of bullshit suggests that we focus our attention on what that "enterprise" was, what the CCP was "trying to get away with" by engaging in a variety of constitutional projects, and whether the attempt at deceit actually worked, without presuming success. To the extent that it did not, and the CCP was aware of this, we should consider the possibility that drafting and promulgating constitutions were intended as a raw demonstration of the power to proclaim and promulgate bullshit, not to convince people of it. Methodologically, Frankfurt's perspective encourages us to examine sources that give a reasonably good sense of state goals, as far these can be discerned, and popular reactions to constitutions. As they read or heard constitutional articles, what did people ask? What did they suggest revising? What "back of the envelope" analyses did they construct? In what ways did both state officials and ordinary citizens consider constitutions as bullshit, but *useful* bullshit nonetheless?

How to Read Unusual Constitutional Commentary

What sort of social science methodology is appropriate or, more accurately, even available for a study based on primary sources mainly consisting of brief comments and analysis, snippets of longer conversations, unanswered questions, and suggestions for textual or grammatical revision, most of which were disregarded? This is neither a trick nor a trite question. In the ongoing conversation between researchers and their human subjects, or between researchers and their documents (or "texts" in the field of literature), scholars always ask the questions, and the sources occasionally answer them. For example, scholars engaged in survey research invest considerable resources thinking of good questions, trying to get their wording exactly right to elicit responses that speak most directly to their overarching concerns. Like the episode on *Seinfeld* when Jerry asks a telemarketer what his home phone number is so he can call him back and the telemarketer refuses, respondents rarely get to ask researchers about their views. Likewise, researchers who go to "the field"—a court, a village, a local government—prepare in advance at least some of the questions they want answered. Probably without many exceptions, research subjects are not asked to provide data in the form of questions and suggestions but rather direct statements, feelings, ratings on a scale, or dichotomous answers about the issue at hand.

In both political science and law, only one subfield of American politics comes close to answering the methodological challenge posed by China's constitutional data. Scholars of public policy studying federal regulations have paid attention to "public comment periods" after a new or revised regulation is proposed. During such comment periods, which last sixty to ninety days, people can offer comments (these days, usually online), propose changes, or criticize a proposed regulation—a practice that does have a family resemblance to what Soviet, Chinese, and other citizens of socialist states did during their constitutional discussions. Ostensibly a democratic and equal opportunity form of political participation, such public comments have favored organized interest groups, particularly business. Despite this, people who pen letters to regulatory agencies believe, inaccurately it seems, that they have a lot of say (on average). However, in a reflection of the quantitative orientation of American political science, researchers arrived at these findings mainly through innovative statistical methods, not reading the actual comments, suggestions, or questions more interpretively or ethnographically to get at underlying meanings and citizens' political values, or to discern larger critiques of the political system. For this reason, their value to this project is limited.[54]

More promising vistas can be discovered if we take a brief trip outside the social sciences. Our first stop, befitting a study that looks at citizens as readers whose emotions are galvanized by textual encounters, is a study of romance novels (you know, those with the images of beefcake, long-locked men and attractive women on their jackets). Considered a classic in the field of literary criticism called "Reader-response theory," Janice A. Radway's *Reading the Romance: Women, Patriarchy, and Popular Literature* (1984) contested the conventional view that romance novels unduly reinforced traditional gender roles and patriarchy.[55] In Radway's view, the established wisdom, while not entirely inaccurate, was methodologically flawed largely because literary scholars never bothered to ask the women who read romance novels why they read them, which books were popular and why, and what they thought about as they read. Instead, she proposed that the "analytic focus . . . shift from the text itself, taken in isolation, to the complex social event of reading."[56] Her research, which used anthropological methods such as field work among romance novel readers, found that contrary to the expectations of text-driven theories, only four percent stated (or admitted?) that they "like to read about the strong, virile heroes."[57]

Although far removed in topic, time, and space from constitutional discussions in China, Radway's analysis provides substantial explanatory leverage. First, in the constitutional discussions the Chinese government engaged ordinary Chinese officials and citizens as readers and listeners of texts read to them.

Even though this identity was temporary, it is worthwhile asking how these texts were understood, which words grabbed people's attention and why, what emotions were conjured up by certain phrases, and what chapters were brushed aside for lack of interest. Radway shows us that even when a book is purchased based on free will and read with interest, we cannot assert a claim about readers' understanding of it based on the text; scholars need to gather evidence about how readers reacted as they read. Even if an image of a hunky Mao had adorned their front covers, Chinese constitutions are about as far as one can get from hot romance novels in narrative structure, language, or heroic figures and are not happily purchased, but comparable questions can be raised. For example, did an ordinary official who read about a constitutional article dealing with the "dominant classes" in socialism understand it as such? Did citizens get the message about "exploitation" the text intended to convey? Did they read carefully or browse to find the juicy parts? The Radwayian answer is "Perhaps; let's find the data."

Second, Radway stressed the critical importance of knowing a lot about the context of reading—is it done in isolation? in groups?—as well as the context from which readers come to a text in the first place, including their family situation, gender, life experiences, and expectations. In the case of the constitutional discussions, variables such as gender, occupational status, and previous experiences with state texts come to mind as potentially important variables, as well as the structural settings within which the text was read or heard (a room? a conversation among colleagues or family members? an offhand comment?). Reading by oneself, for example, can produce a very different interpretation than reading with others, whether a book club or a state-organized study session, as was the case in China. In short, contexts matter, and we must do our best to situate readers in them insofar as the sources allow.[58]

The second methodological stop of our excursion outside the social sciences (or perhaps the third if we include Frankfurt's study of bullshit) is "Speech Act theory" in philosophy, a field in which scholars pay a great deal of attention to what people mean to say beyond the words they use, as well as to speech acts that do not involve language at all (such as bidding, resigning, or not speaking at all). Their most basic contention is that since grammatical sentences composed of meaningful words express more than those sentences' contents, it is best to focus on "speaker meaning," or what a speaker means in uttering a sentence.[59] Speech Act theorists argue that a fairly clear distinction could be made between what is said and what J. L. Austin called an illocutionary act—the "performance of an act *in* saying something as opposed to performance of an act *of* saying something."[60] Whether one asserts or merely suggests, promises or just indicates an intention depends not only on the literal meaning of one's words but what one intends to do with them and, critically, the institutional and social contexts in which the linguistic activity occurs—variables we have also seen in Radway's account of romance readers. "The occasion of an utterance," Austin writes, "matters seriously, and the words used are to some extent to be 'explained' by the 'context' in which they are designed to be or have actually been spoken in a linguistic interchange."[61]

For Speech Act theorists, the conversation is the primary unit of analysis. Whether it is Australians chatting about rugby or Chinese citizens discussing a constitution, illocutionary acts have various sorts of force, as in ordering, warning, assuring, promising, and expressing an intention, all of which produce "certain consequential effects upon the feelings, thoughts, or actions of the audience, or of the speaker, or of other persons."[62] In the Chinese case, for example, officials used official and unofficial language, as well as studied silence, to impress on the public the serious nature of the document called a constitution, while ordinary people used their own words to convey a variety of complex feelings about it, as well as silence to indicate fear or apathy.[63] But perhaps most relevant for our purposes, Austin considered asking a question to be a distinctive type of illocutionary act in itself ("an utterance with interrogative force"), and therefore no less substantial a conversational move than making an assertion. Another theorist, H. P. Grice, identified particular words or phrases to be part assertion and part question—a "quessertion"—defined as putting forward an idea while stressing that it is questionable.[64] Others have noted that rhetorical questions also have the force of assertions ("Is not Switzerland a peace-loving nation?") and that "why" questions are intimately linked to requests for explanation. There are also embedded or indirect questions that serve as requests for answers. For people trying to criticize somebody in a position of power, and who are afraid of retaliation, asserting through insinuation has served as a useful linguistic devise because it includes the possibility of deniability.[65]

Getting a firm grip on the context in which a question is asked, figuring out the assumptions and shared understandings behind it, and unearthing its tonal quality and wording can help explain what a question or other illocutionary acts convey to another person (or, in our case, the Chinese Communist Party) or imply to them. In one of Grice's examples of these "conversational implicatures," if someone asks you to lunch and you reply, "I have a one o'clock class I'm not prepared for," you have conveyed that you will not be coming even though you haven't literally *said* so. According to Grice, one distinctive element of implication, which is also directly related to the authoritarian context in China, is its "cancelability"—all one needs to do is state, "I do not mean to imply that . . ." In other words, stating something as implying an understanding, or implicitly stating something in quessertion form, can, like insinuation, provide speakers with an element of deniability, and therefore more safety, while at the same time opening space for broader political commentary.[66] Whether a conversation partner or institutional authorities react to an illocutionary act does not matter; what does is that the hearer is aware of the utterance and understands it in a certain way. Such shared understandings—which can also apply to jokes—can create what Hans Steinmüller has called a "community of complicity" based on a "shared experiential horizon."[67]

To make these methodological excursions a bit more concrete, as well as to provide a bit of a preview of the book, let us take just one question as an example. First, let's establish the structural context: a room somewhere in Shanghai, with a dozen businessmen, a CCP official, and a note taker. The prior relationship between the participants is also important (the closest notion to this in Speech Act theory is a "common ground," a sort of shared scorecard of who believes what).[68] In this case, several of the businessmen had been interrogated by the CCP for embezzlement two years prior. After reading the last section of the constitution, which deals with state symbols, one businessman asks, "Will there be five stars on the flag in the future?"[69] Conventional political science methodology provides little guidance about how one can use this sort of data point, or hundreds like it, but Radway would encourage us to learn more about his family situation, state of mind, motives for reading that section, and his relationship with colleagues, whereas Speech Act theory pushes us to ask, "What's implied in this question?" What did the official hear in this question?" Was this even a real question, or more of a sly assertion about the prior history of the CCP's interaction with the business community, or both? While it is often difficult (but sometimes not) to get inside people's heads, asking questions about the questions, comments, and suggestions is a very useful approach to these data or, more modestly, the most productive among the various alternatives.

How the Sources Cooperated . . . or Not

This book takes most of its organizational cue cards not from a hypothesis but from the content and organization of the documents.[70] That is, the chroniclers and archivists of constitutional issues in China—all associated with the state as propagandists, investigators, gazetteer compilers, law professors, and archivists—"pre-organized" most of the book according to the populations and topics they considered important over the years. The CCP, for instance, was far more interested in the business community than women, in workers more

than villagers, in abstract rights more than concrete benefits or holding officials accountable, and state institutions more than political symbols. In an ideal
world, I would have preferred an "all-people" organizational format or one
based on topical themes (rights, symbols, class, etc.), but the large disparities
in level of documentation would not allow for this.

Nor did the sources cooperate with a more straightforward chronological
account. Official reports in China, adhering closely to the conventions of
Soviet-style documentation, did not follow this narrative convention. Instead,
they usually included a beginning section reveling in the CCP's successes and
accounts of popular enthusiasm (which, Sheila Fitzpatrick notes in the case
of the USSR, even the leadership "surely skipped over") followed by "problems," the latter often preceded by "but," or "however."[71]

As we will see in chapter 6, after 1954 constitutional issues mainly emerged
in particular political moments, not as a product of journalist reporting, scholarly research, or even official investigations. Often, this was somewhere in the
cycle of political relaxation, public mobilization, and state reaction. For example, constitutional rights were mentioned by CCP critics during the 1955
purge of Hu Feng (a liberal-learning literary critic) and the 1956 Hundred
Flowers Campaign. Legal officials brandished "fundamental obligations" in the
constitution as part of the Anti-Rightist Campaign a year later. Liu Shaoqi cited
the constitution as he was purged during the Cultural Revolution. After the
economic reforms began in 1978, the party authorized yet another discussion
of its draft constitution, which was based on 1954 but revised in key parts.
However, as we will see, ordinary citizens, less bound by official events and
calendars, had their unscripted say about it as well. Unsurprisingly, state-
centered events occupy more space in state-run newspapers, journals, and
internal party reports than casual mentions of the constitution by ordinary
people in ordinary settings. Even so, archival access to materials from 1982 is
more limited than the early 1950s.

This is the nature of our constitutional beast. While certainly unwieldly,
the vagary of sources in terms of organization and content is not altogether
different from my own intellectual predilections and location in the academic
universe. Neither a social historian nor lawyer but writing about people and
law, I have chapters that zero in on distinctive communities, those that are more
law thematic, and another that is roughly chronological. For instance, chapter 1, chapter 2, and chapter 5 examine how officials, the business community,
and ethnic minorities and religious figures understood the constitution; chapter 3 focuses on popular constitutionalism (covering ordinary people but not
easily distinguishable groups); and chapter 4 is about rights and obligations.
The last substantial chapter (chapter 6) addresses the long "afterlife" of the

constitution in the post-1954 period. As such, it draws on a more eclectic array of sources, including *Neibu cankao*, archives, surveys, the official press, and the Internet.

While most of the book is decidedly China-centric, readers will sometimes notice references to comparative cases in the notes. In the conclusion, however, I place the Chinese experience with constitutional discussions in more explicit comparative context, focusing on the USSR and Vietnam.[72] In what ways is China's experience with constitutional discussions different from these cases, and what does this tell us about legitimacy? In engaging with comparison, I hope to encourage PRC historians, who can sometimes be reluctant to see their work in comparative perspective, to consider the potential of comparative research. This is not comparison for comparison's sake. Instead, narrow and focused comparisons can help train our eyes to see outside the documents toward the big, longitudinal questions in PRC history, as well as the comparative history of communism as a worldwide movement, much as Alex Cook and his collaborators have done recently with another seminal PRC document, Mao's "Little Red Book."[73] Big questions answered with intriguing documents and focused comparisons strike me as a reasonably good recipe for future work in PRC history.

Running through these chapters are several threads that are tightly interwoven with the argument. As you read about people's questions and comments about the constitution, please keep in mind the "big picture" questions the book sets out to address: How did people "sense" the state? What did they think about their new polity and their role in it? Just how legitimate was it? And perhaps the biggest one of all given all the upheaval of the years preceding the 1954 Constitution, as well as the current one of 1982, what meanings did people assign to the revolution itself?

CHAPTER 1

Officials Read the Draft Constitution

Viewed from the standards of Western constitutionalism, which emphasize that "politics must be conducted in accordance to standing rules and conventions, written or unwritten, that cannot be easily changed," it is tempting, following the political scientist Giovanni Sartori, to dismiss China's constitution as a "nominal" one—it organizes political power but does not restrain politicians in how they exercise it or protect individual freedoms.[1] This temptation should be resisted. As Graham Maddox has noted, the word *constitution* originally derived from *constituere*, "to set up, establish, erect, construct, arrange, to settle or determine"—not to restrain or limit.[2] Since constitutions have been most closely linked to states, one might argue that this "settling" function has been more politically significant than how states interacted with their citizens or addressed their political aspirations within the context of a constitution. For other constitutional scholars as well, constitutions are best seen as "public 'texts' that organize and empower a political regime . . . for certain clearly defined aims or goals," thus helping it "acquire legitimacy."[3] In these respects, the PRC's five-decade-long history of writing and revising constitutions seems reasonably consistent with Western constitutional history (even though there are no data demonstrating that it has contributed to legitimacy) as well as with the legacy of Chinese states that were more concerned with the absence of power than with its potential abuses. For example, it devotes large sections to the role of function of state institutions, informs readers about state symbols such as the flag and emblem and the location of the state capital, and includes cannot-be-missed statements about what the government expects from its citizens. Citizens' rights vis-à-vis the state are also there, but with minority status in the text. In other words, like many others, the Chinese constitution is preoccupied with the state and its officials in relation to each other, not individuals trying to protect or advance their interests against the state by using its words. The collection of essays in Tom Ginsburg and Alberto Simpser's *Constitutions in Authoritarian Regimes* (2014) rightly emphasize the diverse role of constitutions beyond state restraint and citizens' rights.

But in their helpful corrective to implicit or explicit biases in assessing the role and function of Western and non-Western constitutions, constitutional scholars have neglected a critical facet of constitutions. Mainly trained either in law schools or in "public law" in political science departments, and concerned primarily with rights claims, constitutionalism as a matter of jurisprudence, and appellate courts as the key site of judicial interpretation, legal scholars have not paid enough attention to how ordinary officials in charge of the political order at the center of constitutionalism—a broad category encompassing politicians, street-level bureaucrats, educators, and policemen—have understood constitutions and their role in them.[4] Historically, these sorts of officials had more frequent contact with ordinary citizens than senior judges and constitutional framers, and their understanding of the political order arguably had more impact on political life than the more high-minded discussions about constitutions in law journals, textbooks, and policy speeches. What does constitutionalism look like if we focus our attention on the mid-to-lower levels of the state? Rather than deducing constitutional understanding from the constitutional text, elite discourse about it, or scholars' models and concepts—an understandable scholarly tactic but methodologically flawed—I propose to listen carefully to what officials *said*, in real time as it were, about the document and to leave the answer open-ended.[5]

This is challenging. During the Mao era, Chinese legal scholars did not survey ordinary officials about their views of the constitution (unlike the post-Mao period), nor could officials submit frank "Letters to the Editor" to newspapers or the few legal journals that survived the consolidation of the media in the early 1950s.[6] Contextually, Chinese officials did not arrive at their understanding of the constitution, or convey their opinions about it, in colleges, universities, or dedicated seminars in air conditioned rooms led by eminent law school faculty, nor were they tested about its principles or have their misunderstandings corrected in a systematic manner. Instead, officials were forced to squeeze the national discussion of the draft constitution into a packed political and administrative schedule stuffed to the brim with mandated political study sessions and meetings, all while managing everyday tasks. Since the constitution was often referred to as a "foundational" or "basic" law, it made more political sense for officials to opine by way of asking questions or offering helpful suggestions for improvement—this was far less risky than providing their superiors with detailed expositions of their views. The task before us, then, is to patch together these questions, comments, and suggestions to create a rough quilt within which the meaning of the constitution—and, by implication, the revolution—will be embedded. This certainly does not provide the same texture or "flow" of constitutional explication based on elite sources—the *Federalist Papers* would be a good example here—but there is much to be gained by shifting our perspective. In the American case, Pauline Maier's *Ratification: The People Debate the Constitution, 1787–1788* is an example of how much can be gained from shifting our gaze downward.[7]

The 1954 constitutional discussion provides an unprecedented and, given the current research environment in China, unlikely-to-be-repeated opportunity for this sort of "constitutional anthropology." During this discussion period, ordinary officials were not only allowed to offer commentary but encouraged to do so. They spoke up without knowing the precise boundaries of admissible questions, but with the knowledge that they were watched and recorded by a party, their party, with a long history of internal purges. Even though their training was short-lived, lasting from several hours to several days, its scope was wide-ranging and required substantial investment in resources.[8] Officials were asked about constitutional history ("Where did the constitution come from?"), role ("What is a constitution?"), ideological foundations ("Whose interests does the constitution represent?"), and institutional underpinnings ("Who is the premier?" What does the National People's Congress do?") and how China's constitution was different from those in capitalist countries. These questions were not easy to answer; even Mao Zedong seemed unclear about how a "president in a capitalist country" was different than the PRC's state chairman position.[9] Focusing primarily on the Shanghai area, with several other areas sprinkled in, I look at the state from the inside out, beginning with officials' political and sociocultural concerns, and then to the process by which they got educated about the constitution. I then turn to officials' reactions to two key elements in the constitution that were critical to their work: public order and ideology.[10]

Who Was the State?

The state that reveals itself to us in the discussions surrounding the draft constitution shares occasional similarities to its well-known image of a ruthless organization, but only on its outer edges. Faced with an unprecedented mass campaign to teach ordinary people about its complicated ideological and political plumbing, dealing with matters as large as its class basis (workers, in alliance with peasants) and seemingly insignificant as the state emblem, it should not be all that surprising that many officials did not feel quite up to the task, for a variety of reasons.[11] Politically, owing to the Communist Party's lack of expertise in managing cities, chronic shortage of qualified and loyal personnel, and ideological flexibility during years of rural insurgency, many officials gained party membership despite unfavorable class background (*chushen*) or problematic political history (such as fathers, uncles, mothers, or grandfathers who belonged to the "exploiting" classes or who had served in the Kuomintang (KMT). With the official end of the United Front with the national bourgeoisie, some CCP officials were described as "panicked" (*konghuang*) about their future.[12] In Shanghai, for example, a policeman from "rich peasant" background read the constitution and became "very concerned" about the CCP policy of "elimination" (*xiaomie*) toward them; another official from "bourgeois" background worriedly asked whether people in China's "democratic parties" were included in the bourgeoisie; and an official who had been in the KMT but retained in his former position was concerned about the United Front policy.[13] This reaction was apparently triggered by their group leader's description of the constitution as "the expression of the will of the dominant classes."[14] In Jiangxi, some officials with historical "blemishes" (*wudian*) mostly stayed silent, fearing that saying something wrong about "the basic law of the country" would result in criticism for being politically backward and having a "wavering political standpoint."[15]

More prosaically, hunger could also become an obstacle to proper constitutional education. In Inner Mongolia, Zhou Zhuomin, a post office official, asked his wife to study the draft constitution. Her status as a low-level official did not stop her from lashing out: "What's the point? Are they going to give us any more oil rations?"[16]

Age also seemed to matter. In Wuhan, younger officials were said to be diligent, perhaps sensing this to be an opportunity to demonstrate their political aptitude and good memory—important qualifications for promotion—but older officials, probably in their thirties and forties, were decidedly less so. Every article, they claimed, "is correct" because the CCP drafted it.[17] Whether this view of CCP infallibility represented officials' true beliefs is difficult to know, but their alleged lack of enthusiasm could also be explained by that other benefit of rising age—seniority—which made their positions more secure. Among officials in Zhejiang Province, officials ranked section chief and above were said to be terrible students of the constitution.[18] On the other hand, in

Shanghai there were young officials who mocked constitutional education as useless. Focusing on Article 39, which stipulated that one had to be thirty-five years old to be chairman of the People's Republic of China, they said "it doesn't matter if we study it or not—we're too young to be chairman anyway."[19]

But far more so than hunger or claims of CCP infallibility (which superiors occasionally dismissed as excuses for not wanting to study), the text's turgidity and lack of accessibility ran headlong against the low literacy level among officials, many of whom felt uneasy dealing with legal matters that historically had been the purview of educated elites, not people of their social class. In Guangdong Province, discussions of the constitution petered out before the scheduled denouement because officials, claiming that "our cultural level is low," did not raise questions or suggestions.[20] This might have been a convenient excuse, much like someone might claim to be too tired or ill to work, but multiple sources suggest that for many, the constitution was too heavy an intellectual load to lift. In Chongqing, one noted that "the more [of the report] they heard, the more confused they became."[21] In Shanghai's working-class Zhabei District, Women's Federation officials complained that even after training the material was "too deep" and they "didn't understand it." District-level officials in upper-class Xincheng District were also frustrated, saying they "could not get it" (wufa jieshou) even after hearing a report, and union officials complained that the constitution was hard to understand because it had "very many words."[22] One report noted that a widespread reaction to the constitution among midlevel officials, including those at the CCP's General Office, was "I don't understand it" (tingbudong). The main problem, they noted, was its high level of abstraction—they spent two out of three allocated hours reviewing a single phrase: "foundation and superstructure."[23]

Because of the heavy reliance on good memory to pass along state policies to ordinary residents, retention was also an issue. One official complained, "I understood it when I heard it but forgot half on the way home. Only a couple of sentences were left by the time I arrived."[24] Women's Federation officials in Shanghai's Shuishang District "all shouted 'We don't understand it!'" with some offering the explanation that the constitution was meant for "new brains, not old ones." "Does the constitution mean that we've liberated someplace else?" they wondered.[25] As a result, many very important questions about the nature of the CCP and its relationship to society remained unanswered. In Shanghai's Jing'an and Penglai Districts, such questions included, among others, "What's public ownership"? and "What's a production resource?"[26] One did not understand the term "ruling class" (tongzhi jieji).[27] In the Shanghai suburbs, officials complained that they really did not understand what they were being asked to do; some from the Communist Youth League refused to attend study sessions because they thought it dealt with a new "Theater Law" (*xifa*), a near homonym to *constitution* (*xianfa*) in local dialect.[28] In Cao Village in Hebei Province, officials "could not say for certain" (*shuobu qingchu*) what the articles of the constitution were about, only that it was "written in martyrs' blood, lawfully protects laborers . . . and suppresses counterrevolutionary activities."[29]

Even though officials sometimes cited their "low cultural level" to excuse their less-than-adequate understanding of the constitution, a view seconded and thirded by their better-educated superiors writing up summary reports about the constitution, there were other forces at work producing shorthand conceptualizations of what the document was about, its "spirit" in CCP propaganda.[30] The pell-mell pace of politics in the first decade of Communist rule took a serious toll on officials' ability to absorb new materials and accurately convey them to colleagues and ordinary people. In factories, just in the previous year officials had been kept busy with the Marriage Law Campaign (March 1953) and with the campaign to study the CCP's General Line about the transition from New Democracy to Socialism (early 1954) while simultaneously pressured to ramp up production. In Harbin, officials wondered why the draft constitution, a "major national issue," was going to be discussed by workers of all people, who were presumably not qualified to do this. Instead, they prioritized production, with study of the constitution "only after this, if there's time."[31] In the countryside, the decision to conduct the constitutional discussion during the summer months (mainly July and August) proved particularly unconducive to proper learning. Even though the summer was the slack season in farming, village officials were still unhappy that constitutional education coincided with their work, especially flood prevention, which required mass mobilization of labor.[32] It also coincided with so-called democratic reform (a purging of "bad class" and problematic officials from local leadership positions), which took many officials away from home to study sessions located at the township and county seats. As a result, officials and villagers sometimes studied the constitution on their own, with very poor results according to a report from the Shanghai suburbs.[33]

The lack of fans during the summer heat did not help. Harried officials sometimes convened meetings in spaces too small for large sweaty crowds, making it very difficult for propaganda officials to properly convey their answers to basic questions about the constitution (such as "What's a constitution?").[34] Perhaps most critically as far as audiences were concerned, officials were themselves unclear about why they had been forced to congregate in the first place. Rural officials, according to transcripts of meetings and subsequent reporting, could not understand why the constitution was relevant to farming (judges and legal officials were a different story).[35] Nor could they grasp its language, which was not translated into more colloquial forms by speakers who resorted to dry recitation of the text.[36]

As one might imagine, officials did not welcome the prospect of reading out constitutional articles in front of crowds large and small in the summer heat, a problem they called attention to by unfavorably comparing the constitution to "normal propaganda" which used political essays.[37] Many considered the constitution a boring document. Its language was abstruse (*shen'ao*) and excessively theoretical. Critically, it was disconnected from officials' everyday experiences, and therefore difficult to discuss, let alone speechify about, in settings where audience members, tired from work, dozed off.[38]

But remedies were available! Some officials resorted to humor to lighten the atmosphere ("Those guys [National People's Congress representatives] really have a lot of power. Even more than me!") or, like bored people pretty much everywhere, found other ways to entertain themselves, such as reading the more entertaining classic *The Dream of the Red Chamber* (which, perhaps coincidentally, also dealt with the practices of power and authority), playing poker, or satirizing the new "Mother Law" (*mufa* 母法) of the country, as the constitution was sometimes called: "Blah blah and it's done, and then there'll be a Children's Law."[39] Union officials played guessing games about who is where in government: Who's the vice chairman? Is it Liu Shaoqi? Song Qingling? Who's the premier?[40]

"Birds without a head don't fly" (*niao wutou bufei*) was how local authorities described ill-prepared rural officials in the Shanghai suburbs when trying to pass on their constitutional knowledge to ordinary citizens.[41] In Dongchang District, for example, people emerged from a meeting about the draft constitution understanding that its promulgation was a "joyous occasion" (*da xishi*), but otherwise most did not understand anything else about it and required supplemental study.[42]

While this may have been technically true in the sense that audience members could not define key legal terms, restate the political ideals articulated in the preamble, or understand the role of the new State Council, some understood all this constitutional brouhaha as something perhaps even more important: a useful opportunity or space, a political platform of sorts, within which they could air other grievances, a theme which will be developed in the next chapters. In Cao Village, for example, villagers struggling to comply with state grain requisitions complained about the government not purchasing enough cotton after mobilizing them to grow the crop, its failure to supply contracted goods in a timely manner, the lack of fertilizer, and the operation of mutual aid teams—instead of talking about the constitution.[43] Local officials shared this opportunistic view of the constitution as well, but with a statist twist. In

Jing'an District, a female official, apparently prompted by mention of the Soviet Union during the discussion, asked (with not a small dose of critical insinuation) about misplaced state priorities: "Why is the Sino-Soviet Friendship
Mansion getting built and not schools?"[44] An official in the industrial sector
asked, perhaps innocently but probably not, whether the CCP's goal was to
"enlarge democracy" (*kuoda minzhu*), implying that the party was less democratic before.[45]

The opportunity to use the constitution as a political platform worked in
the other direction as well. Officials found it quite useful in expanding their
power over local society. Not far away from the acerbic woman in Jing'an District was someone in Huangpu who was reprimanded for saying that the government would sue people who violated the constitution.[46] In the suburban
district of Dongchang, the Public Security Bureau investigated an official who,
during discussion of the constitution, drew lines on the ground in the shape
of a prison and told people that he could make the lines/prison as long or short
as he pleased whenever citizens misbehaved (*bu xingle*).[47] In rural areas, *Neibu
cankao* reporters criticized local officials for saying that because collectivization is in the constitution, it would be a "legal violation" to not participate in
a cooperative and that their villagers "will not dare to be uppity and brash"
when such a document could be wielded in their faces.[48] In Gao'an County in
Jiangxi, some officials—said to be a minority—thought that the constitution
was a useful tool to "deal with" (*duifu*) people.[49] In these cases, there was really
little practical difference between the constitution as a document and the discussion of it because officials could interpret and talk about the text pretty
much as they pleased without worrying that villagers could offer countervail-
ing text-based arguments, a situation that would change in the reform era.

The Constitution in Context

As we can see, context, as well as readers' background, is critical to figuring
out the meaning of the constitution in China (both were centerpieces of Radway's analysis of romance novels discussed in the introduction). This context
variable, however, must be understood in the plural and should include the
welter of other policy documents officials heard, read, or discussed, usually
without knowing which was more important, as well as past and future historical events and even rumors, all of which shaped the way they learned about
the constitution and conveyed its contents to people.[50] Put more straightforwardly, the constitution cannot be properly understood at any remove from
other official actions and officials' understanding of them. Below I focus on

three "contextual dialogues" that formed the cognitive infrastructure for constitutional interpretation among officials: (1) how the constitution was viewed as an authoritative text, (2) its relationship to other political documents and history, and (3) its place relative to foreign constitutions.

The Constitution as the Dominant Textual Authority

Probably in anticipation of questions about what a constitution was and its relationship to other sorts of laws, regulations, and policies, propaganda about the constitution often focused on two elements of its status in China's emerging legal regime: its role as a "foundational law" and Mao's vital role in its creation (some in the city of Kunming suggested calling it the "Mao Zedong Constitution," perhaps in homage to the 1936 Soviet Constitution, widely known as Stalin's Constitution).[51] From the perspective of ordinary officials, this designation (and the colorful status-oriented analogies it inspired, such as "the Large Wormwood" [hao zi 蒿子, a tall flowering shrub], the "Elder Brother Law" to the younger siblings' Labor and Marriage Laws), and personalized attachment to Mao was highly problematic, particularly because the CCP did not publish an official interpretive textbook with model cases, while the popular media, which could have served as an alternative, often made mistakes (and sometimes came under withering criticism for these).[52] First, officials faced the daunting task of explaining at least part of the constitutional text, and therefore, by dint of their status, interpreting it in an authoritative way in an ambiguous and risky political environment. What would happen if an explanation was wrong? Second, the national discussion of the constitution called for political participation in the form of raising questions and suggesting improvements, and officials were expected to take the lead. But in practical terms (and consistent with Speech Act theory), for both speaker and listener the line separating raising questions, suggesting revisions, and outright criticism—a dangerous proposition in Leninist regimes—was opaque if not invisible at times, something many more Chinese would learn during the Anti-Rightist Campaign (1957–59).

In this politicized context, many officials attempted to avoid talking about the constitution altogether. As one explained, "The draft constitution was written by Chairman Mao himself and very many nationally famous people, so we don't want to discuss it."[53] Others adopted the Leninist tactic of stipulating that because it had been written by Mao, it could not be anything other than 100 percent correct.[54] All that was necessary, according to another official, was "to just do what it says," implying that the constitution was similar to implementing a "policy" which required unquestioned obedience, or a "campaign."[55] Factory officials in Shanghai put this succinctly: "It was Chairman Mao who drafted this anyway so there can't have been a mistake; we guarantee to enforce it—that should be enough."[56] Others begged off by referring to themselves as "minor officials" for whom studying a document about higher-minded "principles" was inappropriate, or noting that the constitution was irrelevant to their jobs ("We don't do constitution work"), and therefore could ignore it.[57] Both of these positions were criticized and said to have been rectified: "Now they understand that the constitution is a weapon of class struggle, and if they do not study it they cannot grasp this weapon."[58] Some officials' we-couldn't-care-less attitude was said to stem from their view that knowing that the constitution was "the foundational law," that "all laws stem from it," and that "it's the fundamental law of the state" (dafa) was enough.[59] Some evasive tactics were a bit more innovative, like officials who, after noting that Mao drafted the constitution, confined their discussion to the safer area of "theory" while disputing the premise that the constitution had anything to do with their own political thinking or job, or who quipped, "That guy spoke really well—I was going to say the exact same thing so there's no point repeating it."[60]

But fear was lurking just below the surface of these justifications for avoiding discussion or framing the constitution as just another law that they will implement. If not the original intention, it was something CCP leaders quickly learned reading *Neibu cankao* over their morning tea or noshing in the afternoon. "Foundational" was broadly interpreted as a threat or insinuation that those violating it would be dealt with more seriously than those in transgression of an ordinary law. And since the constitution was vague about what it meant to "abide by the constitution," local officials had even more reason to avoid trouble. It also meant they would be all the wiser to not flap their lips or, if they asked questions, to weigh their words very carefully.[61] In Guangdong, for example, officials said that because the constitution was nothing less than the state's "foundational fundamental law" (*genben dafa*), they "cannot speak out carelessly" or do anything wrong. Mistakes, they worried, would not only result in people criticizing their political standpoint but, equally seriously, violate the constitution as well.[62] In Inner Mongolia, officials were afraid of being on the receiving end of questions lest they provide the wrong answer ("whoever explains incorrectly will have to take responsibility"), so when they educated people about the constitution, they made sure to read the document without using any of their own words.[63] At the Red Star Car Factory in Shanghai, officials' fear of committing an interpretive error was triggered by their traumatic experiences during the Three Antis Campaign several years earlier, which targeted corruption, waste, and bureaucratism. Some claimed illness to avoid participating in it. Their general take on "political work" and the Party Committee was to "respect it but keep your distance."[64]

Referring to Political Documents and History

This intrastate constitutional dialogue did not only take place within the confines of legal terminology or, more accurately, within the framework of ideas triggered by the unexpected proliferation of these terms in early to mid-1954. Officials also brought to this conversation their understanding of a temporally proximate event far more important than the constitution: the victory of the revolution in 1949. In their (accurate) narrative of recent political history, law and constitutions were simply irrelevant; the CCP did not rely on law to achieve victory and therefore could manage the transition to socialism in its absence. According to a "top secret" report about midlevel officials in Shanghai,

> It's common for these officials to downplay the significance of drafting a constitution. At the beginning of the discussion they were unenthusiastic, but this was mainly because they did not possess basic knowledge about the constitution and did not understand its critical function. But this also reflected officials' satisfaction with their recent experience and lack of awareness of newer ways of doing things. Many are not familiar with the functions of the state, political power, and law. Some say, "We conducted revolution for so long and managed to win without a constitution."[65]

Others just could not stomach the rather bombastic claims in official propaganda that the constitution was both a capstone event in the history of the party and a turning point in the development of socialism. The legal drama somehow did not measure up to officials' self-conception as actors in a particularly moving production. Officials who were said to be "uninterested and cold" toward the hoopla surrounding the constitution explained: "We didn't have a constitution and still beat the Japanese devils and Chiang Kai-shek, so I don't really care if we have one or not."[66]

Officials who peered into the future also did not see much need for a constitution. Presented in utopian terms redolent with militaristic terminology, socialism was connotatively disconnected with *law*, a more technocratic and bureaucratic field of knowledge associated with expertise, jargon, paperwork, cleverness, and ambiguity. Many officials simply did not buy into the notion that the constitution was an indispensable part of this process. In Shanghai's Xinjing District, for instance, one official asserted, "Even if we don't have a constitution we can build socialism," while another half questioned/half asserted, "The General Line is advancing socialism—why do we need a constitution for this? [*hebi hai yao xianfa ne*]."[67]

As suggested by this reference to the General Line, officials' understanding of the role of the constitution in CCP history was another critical component of their context-driven engagement with the text. From their perspective, the constitution was but one document fluttering down from Beijing vying for their attention, which was already in short supply, and not necessarily the most important one. In various assessments of how the constitutional discussion proceeded, officials were critiqued for complaining that the constitution was "nothing new" because its content had already been discussed in the Common Program, Marriage Law, the General Line, and the Election Law, which had taken place in the previous years, and it was therefore "irrelevant" (*you meisa daguanxi*), "no big deal" (*meiyou shenma liaobuqi*), "none of my business" (*xianshi*), excessively prescriptive or just a repetition of previous "turning around one's life" (*fanshen*) propaganda campaigns in which the authorities "want us to remember the past, look at what is happening today, and express hope for the future."[68]

The position of the constitution in relation to other laws and policies was not the only problem. Officials were also perplexed by the constitution's status in the CCP's ideological universe. Did it supersede ideology? Was it a guide to political action in the same way ideology was? Officials mostly concluded it was not. "Some comrades," a Shanghai report noted, "say that the constitution has no relevance; we just have to abide by Marxism-Leninism to debate," and in the "question and suggestion" part of the discussion asked, "What's a state?" and "What's the definition of the state in relation to Marxism-Leninism?"[69] These were not entirely abstract questions: Marxism-Leninism was a revolutionary ideology that was quite comfortable with the deployment of targeted violence to achieve its objectives, whereas the existence of a "state," "law," and "constitution" all connoted institutions, constraints, and formal processes—none of which were particularly appreciated by Mao (or more recently by Xi Jinping, who pushed through a revision to the 1982 constitution that effectively allows him to serve as president for life).[70]

Even high-level officials had a difficult time reconciling these ideas. In Guangzhou, some feared that they would soon be called to implement socialism in one fell swoop, which would presumably involve mass executions of rich peasants and capitalists, much as had been the case with rural landlords. In fact, provincial authorities became aware of rumors to the effect that "after the constitution, rich peasants and then middle peasants will be eliminated."[71] Likewise, propaganda guidelines in Songjiang County fingered rich peasants for various crimes and preventing an alliance between poor and middle peasants who were afraid of socialism.[72] Yet the constitution also invoked specific procedures for arrests, "protections" for capitalists' property, citizens' rights, and a "gradual" elimination of the rich peasant economy. Officials in Inner Mongolia, for example, were unable to explain the CCP's policy toward rich peasants, a difficulty which was said to open space for such villagers to argue that "cadres said so—it's not allowed to violate rich peasants' interests" and "the government protects people's rights, and rich peasants are people."[73] Which framework would prevail in the end? Unable to figure out a solution to these conflicting imperatives, some factory officials in Shanghai used the Confucian concept of *tianxia weigong* (the whole world as an egalitarian community under Heaven) to explain that socialism was the economic foundation of the country. The CCP Party Committee of the Heavy Industry Bureau deemed this an "error of principle."[74]

But more officials than not had their feet planted firmer in the ground and concerned themselves less with ideology than the practical impact the constitution would have on them personally. Here, again, they found the constitution rather lacking in relevance. As party members, they pointed out, they were already subject to the "Party Program and Party Constitution" (*danggang dangzhang*); their rank and salary were based on the cadre management system (*baogan zhi*), and their "accustomed" method for discussing matters of policy and ideology were meetings devoted to "inner-party democratic life," not a constitution.[75] Even though officials praised the constitution to the heavens because it allowed opportunity for public participation and because they were well aware of what they were supposed to say during such events, when the constitution was placed alongside other documents relevant to their lives, it was not seen as particularly important.[76]

There was an exception to this general pattern. This was not the consequence of the concept *constitution* (*xian*), but only its second character, *fa* (law). Very many officials, as we have seen, were not familiar with or had never heard of *xian*, but all knew *fa*, and often framed their understanding of the constitution within a broader interpretative framework of the duty to "obey the law."[77] That is, no matter what they were told about the constitution in terms of its laying out the functions of the state, articulating rights, and describing the symbols of the state, its beating heart was compliance (*shoufa*). This could mean that the constitution had little direct relevance to them "so long as I obey the law" (*bu fanfa jiuxing la*), or that all the articles in the constitution had the status of "law" (*xianfa yibailingliu tiaotiao shifa*) and therefore could be used to get people to do things they otherwise would resist. Some district-level officials, a report noted, "think that now that there's a constitution they can use it as a substitute for complicated and detailed educational and orga-nizational work."[78]

Critical comments aside, it is unlikely that the CCP leadership was terribly bothered by the meta-notion of the constitution as a framework for obeying the law among its own officials. After all, gaining the compliance of millions of officials in a vast bureaucracy and geographically dispersed empire has al-ways vexed Chinese leaders, so if the constitution was interpreted as being about obedience, so much the better. Indeed, as Jennifer Altehenger has noted, the state pushed this conception of the constitution well after 1954.[79]

The Constitution in Comparative Contexts

Far more problematic was officials' tendency to further stretch the boundaries of constitutional interpretation to other countries, particularly the USSR, Re-public of China (ROC), and capitalist countries such as the United States and then finding the CCP's constitutional claims deficient, contradictory, or just false. This was a problem of the CCP's own making: by 1954 China's alliance with the Soviet Union was common knowledge, and constitutional propa-ganda was not shy about claiming that "people's constitutions" were superior to Western bourgeois ones which only benefited the rich. For example, in the city of Fuzhou in Fujian Province, female officials pointed out that the Soviet constitution instituted welfare payments to mothers caring for many children as well as to single mothers, so "our draft constitution should have the same rule."[80]

References to the Soviet Union, however, were less ideologically problem-atic than officials who referred positively to the KMT's ideology or the ROC's constitution, or to capitalist ones. In Guangdong, officials who worked for the provincial radio station (who may have been holdovers from the previous re-gime) boldly stated that the CCP's draft constitution was "not as good" as Sun Yatsen's "Three Principles of the People" and that the main problem with Sun's was "enforcement," not its basic ideas.[81] In the Shanghai suburbs, township officials avoided praising the US electoral system, but they implied that just as the "fake" US elections awarded power to only "several people," future elec-tions in China would produce a similar result at the highest level of political power.[82] Another official, in response to the CCP's assertion that capitalist countries (and therefore their constitutions) are grounded in selfishness, slyly asked whether the fact that US president Franklin D. Roosevelt's sons served in World War II and General James van Fleet's served in Korea "shows that there's unselfishness in imperialist countries," a view that was said to have been "corrected" during the discussion.[83] In the city, there were officials who spoke positively of both the United States and the KMT or noted that constitutions in capitalist countries also provide "freedom and equality."[84] Even at the CCP's East China Bureau, officials pointed out that in China people "cannot say anything reactionary or read reactionary books or pornographic literature even though there's the right to free speech," but in the United States, "even though they do not have freedom, it's possible to buy Communist publications."[85] In Guangdong, radio station officials had a similar observation: there were only "two party-led newspapers in Guangzhou (Canton), but in Hong Kong there were all kinds of different ones." In another critique of CCP censorship, someone noted that under Chiang Kai-shek literary forms such as sentimental poetry and essays could be published—an "incorrect view" according to the report writers. These officials also took issue with the way "freedom" was presented in constitutional propaganda, which unfavorably depicted the freedom enjoyed by citizens in the West as highly restricted by their class and racial status. In China, they semi-noted, semi-critiqued, "freedom is not limitless," and "in the whole world there's no such thing as absolute freedom."[86]

Constitutional Theory to Practice

Many of the officials who participated in the constitutional discussion correctly pointed out that the constitution had little to no bearing on their everyday work. Village officials working the soil, factory leaders meeting production quotas, and Women's Federation officials dealing with marriage disputes and health issues understandably found the constitution irrelevant and boring. While propaganda officials charged with educating them about the document critiqued this view, and often claimed, using the standard trope in Communist officialese (seen above in the fix to the General van Fleet comment), to have "turned them around" by reading a report, it is more likely that officials grinned, nodded, said "Sure," and hoped that this odd constitutional seminar would soon end.

This luxury of boredom and disinterest—asking a wrong question during constitutional education rarely resulted in adverse consequences—did not apply to all Communist officials, however. If we ranked those most vexed and perplexed about the meaning of the constitution, policemen and others in the security apparatus were surely at the top. Like its predecessor the Common Program, the constitution stated in black and white that PRC citizens had rights, including freedom of assembly, speech, privacy, and press. It also told officials that arresting citizens requires approval from judicial authorities. As officials had claimed victory after a bloody revolution only five years earlier and now were dealing with a population dissatisfied with many state policies (particularly collectivization), constitutional freedoms and procedural rules had concrete implications for those responsible for maintaining political order.[87] Given that constitutions have historically focused on the constituent elements of the political order, with "rights" a relatively modern addition, this is hardly surprising, but to date we know little about the people charged with managing this order in everyday life. This stands in marked contrast to a growing literature about the Republican period and recent ethnographic research on contemporary policemen in the PRC and Taiwan.[88]

Even though the word *police* does not appear in the draft constitution, an omission noticed during the discussions, the Chinese government was keenly interested in security personnel's understanding of the provisions dealing with the legal apparatus, the legal process, and everyday police work.[89] Except for one provision in the draft constitution unrelated to security matters—the establishment of a national emblem, which some thought would look just dandy on their uniforms, give them an official rank (*jibie*), and help them get married—ordinary cops were not pleased.[90] Beyond personal fear of being purged because of their bad class background or having served previously in the KMT, several disturbing scenarios came to mind as they contemplated the impact of the constitution on their work.[91]

The first was the fear of providing constitutional rights to disgruntled citizens who would then use them to stage a counterrevolution. In Shanghai, some officials used the historical precedent of the CCP's own rise to power by taking advantage of the relative freedoms allowed by the KMT to warn against supplying a basic law that would provide a political opening for dissent: "If we have the same rules [as the KMT], won't our enemies also take advantage?" some critiqued through this innocent wondering.[92] In the city and countryside, the right to privacy in communication was a particular worry because it would allow various counterrevolutionaries, members of underground sects, and "secret agents" to organize against the CCP.[93] The concern over constitution-based resistance was shared among their counterparts in the CCP party organization, who also opposed the right to demonstrate, the requirement of judicial authorization prior to arrest, and a "grand pardon" (*dashe*) and "special pardon" (*teshe*) for the same reason: "These people are enemies, counterrevolutionaries, and criminals."[94] To correct this, some officials in Shanghai's Penglai District wanted to add the adjectives *legal* and *correct* to the articles about citizens' rights. Without these, they argued, Catholics and "bad elements" would be able to stage anticommunist demonstrations, while students who could not move up a grade and had to stop their education would create disorder (*luan*) by petitioning the government for redress.[95]

But considering that the CCP had been entrenched in power for nearly five years, during which time it conducted harsh campaigns against political enemies real and imagined, fear of a constitution-facilitated counterrevolution does not appear to have been the majority sentiment among the police.[96] Instead, there was more of an inchoate anxiety that because of the constitution, routine police work—questioning suspects, arrests, checking household registration documents, and the like—would become more challenging, and more dangerous for them personally. In their view, reduced police powers, in combination with citizens' rights, could embolden people to give them guff, refuse orders, and resist in other annoying ways. "It will be more difficult to get things done," some noted, because "people will raise more objections than they have in the past."[97] In Guangdong, a report summarizing the views of officials from the police, judiciary, and procurators' offices noted their consensus that because the constitution protects human rights and arrests require the approval of the director of the procurator, and because people will become "extremely democratic" (*jiduan minzhu*), security work will become more difficult (*nan gaole*). Having relied for so long on virtually unchecked despotic power, they were now unsure how to conduct investigations in this new environment.[98] In the Shanghai suburbs, for instance, cops wondered how they could catch a criminal in the act if Article 89 stipulated that arrests required prior authorization from a court or procurator, and whether arrests without obtaining a warrant were no longer possible now that citizens' "personal liberty could not be violated."[99] In the city, some were baffled by what seemed to be the government's "catch and release" policy (the police catch the criminals, but they are released via a constitutional pardon) and questioned how they would have managed to catch counterrevolutionaries during the Campaign to Suppress Counterrevolutionaries had they been required to seek court approval prior to arrest.[100]

The fear of enhanced accountability was usually expressed in terms of greater exposure to prosecution if they made a mistake in rounding up and arresting suspects. In Lianhua County in western Jiangxi, for example, policemen were afraid that any future error would be "on our heads" should a citizen appeal.[101] In the Shanghai suburbs, a policeman said, "After the constitution is promulgated our job will get tougher—make a little mistake and you've violated policy and will be punished by the law."[102] And in Beijing a beat cop remarked, "From here on in if you make a mistake the law will punish you—it won't be as easy to do things as it was in 1949."[103] They wondered: With the constitution offering various rights and "protections," even to capitalists' property, who would be there to protect the police when citizens became more assertive and courts, sometimes staffed by "Democratic Party people," back them up?[104] The constitution, some complained, "protects everyone except the police."[105] As a result, some cops were accused of "not wanting to bother" with tasks such as investigating household registration, inspecting mail, and summoning suspects for fear of committing a mistake and going to jail for them, while others were criticized for "impatience" (*jizao*): "If we want to arrest someone let's do it right away, and if we want something done, now's the time."[106] Some, arguing that the Public Security Bureau was under the "absolute control" of the Party, said that they would just flout the constitution's articles about court and procurator approval.[107] "In the past we suppressed counterrevolutionaries and now we'll suppress counterrevolutionaries," another noted straightforwardly and presciently.[108]

Citizens who felt constitutionally empowered to voice their complaints or file appeals to judicial authorities was one thing, but even worse from the perspective of the police was Article 97, which stipulated that "people suffering loss by reason of infringement by persons working in organs of state of their rights as citizens have the right to compensation." Fear of making a mistake—perhaps the most common trope in reporting about low-level officials—was supplemented by dread of having to cough up money to pay for it: "When we detain peddlers we'll have to pay compensation for their loss of business, but we won't have enough funds for this."[109] However, Article 97 did not make clear exactly who "we" was—individual cops? The police station? The Public Security Bureau as an institution? Nor was it clear how much would be paid, so policemen worried they could not afford it. As might be expected, anxiety and fear produced questions, but there is little evidence they were answered.[110] Was this silence deliberate? From a governance perspective, leaving police in the dark, in a somewhat anxious state, could be a viable method of deterring bad behavior. In other words, the constitution was useful less for institutionalizing rules and procedures—the "settling" function in the language of constitutional theory—than for keeping officials psychologically unsettled.

Further complicating matters was how the compensation issue intersected with state policies that contradicted constitutional rights. Policemen, who in their everyday jobs inspected citizens' household registration status, were unsure whether this violated Article 89 ("freedom of the persons of citizens of the People's Republic of China is inviolable"). What would happen, some wondered, if a citizen filed a claim against the police based on this article? Would lawyers become necessary? Who would pay the compensation if they won?[111] As it turned out, citizens who feared the police were thinking the same thing. At the constitutional discussion at Jiaotong University, participants asked what they should do if the police could not afford to pay compensation to those who suffered at their hands. Sharp critiques masqueraded as questions: If the government pays, and the government gets its money from the people, doesn't this mean that the people are compensating themselves? If the person has died (presumably in state custody), is compensation offered as well?[112]

Cultural concerns added another layer of anxiety. Many policemen were not born into families with advanced degrees or substantial wealth, both of which were manifested culturally by possessing a certain personal bearing, mannerism, and facility with oral expression, broadly labeled as "civilized." Until the Communist Revolution, high social status was strongly associated with these characteristics, but after 1949 the CCP had made it quite clear, in policy if not personal preference when seeking out spouses, that the old social hierarchy was no longer acceptable.[113] Nevertheless, from the perspective of the ordinary policeman charged with implementing this revolution, the constitution tossed in an unwelcome wrench. As they imagined it in Tianjin, unlike the recent past when they could get away with shoddy (*diaoer langdang de*) police work and "two hour talks about minor issues," upper-class people would now have the gumption to argue with them, or just refuse their demands on constitutional grounds. If citizens argued *well*, how should policemen respond? Fearing getting tongue-tied and losing face, they admitted to the difficulty of investigating upper-class people. What should we do if a bourgeois person in a multistory building refuses to let us in, one Shanghai household registration inspector asked.[114] This was not entirely a product of an overactive imagination. In a constitutional discussion elsewhere, a man who had been a high-ranking KMT officer (therefore, a "reactionary") told a propaganda official that he would complain the next time a household registration officer checked up on him just because he felt like it.[115]

But there was also apprehension about dealing with those from the other side of the cultural divide. Somewhat ironically given the dangers and disorder typically associated with the poor, this concern was mainly the result of empathy, perhaps a reflection of similar class origins.[116] In Guangdong, for example, officials criticized the constitution, and by insinuation the CCP, for representing the views of the exploiter class because of its demands for compliance with all sorts of obligations they considered too difficult to fulfill. High unemployment, they argued, made it difficult to avoid theft or "harming social ethics" (*pohuai shehui gongde*), a constitutional violation. Likewise, it did not seem appropriate to accuse people who were just trying to survive by peddling wares or food of "undermining social order," another constitutional violation. Rather than deploy the language of the law—viewed as a top-down state mechanism for imposing order—they suggested that it would be better to talk to the poor and desperate "from the standpoint of a citizen" (*zhan zai gongmin de lichang shuohua*).[117]

Officials and Ideology

While policing (and, in a broader sense, "public security") is a nitty-gritty job mixing blunt coercion with paperwork, investigation, and dispute resolution, in China it could not avoid matters of ideology and class as well. All officials needed some measure of clarity about which sort of people were the "enemy," "exploiters," "traitors," "counterrevolutionaries," and the "dominated classes" to conduct their work. They also had to have some grasp of which of the *Homo sapiens* in their jurisdiction should be considered "people," who were "non-people" (*fei renmin*), and what protections the status of citizen provided, if any. Before 1954, the Communist Party persecuted millions based on their class status (landlords, rich peasants, capitalists, and others) with no regard for quasi-constitutional protections in the Common Program of 1949. Most officials would surely have been happy to never talk about their understanding of class status and its relationship to this new document called a constitution, but the months-long national discussion, which specifically asked officials to pose questions about these matters, put many on the spot. What sort of questions did they ask, and what do these reveal about the relationship between class and the new constitution? Sometimes officials' questions can be interpreted as straightforward requests for clarification because of confusion over terms and the apparent contradiction between different articles. Other questions were personal: officials wanted to know more about how the constitution would affect them. Some questions, however, were, as the Speech Act theorist H. P. Grice would have characterized them, quessertions (see the introduction to this book), laced with a sharp interrogative tone that questioned the premises of ideological order articulated in the draft constitution. Since few if any of these questions were authoritatively answered, we could reasonably deduce that confusion about class, and its relationship to law, remained well into the decade, if not longer.

There were good reasons officials would scratch their collective heads about the constitution when it came to class matters. Becoming a member of the Communist Party, or working on its behalf, involved attaining a certain level of class consciousness and understanding of modern Chinese history interpreted through the lens of class struggle. The constitution was an educational document of this nature: its preamble was a short history lesson about the rise of the Communist Party, and it articulated which classes wielded power. At the same time, however, it failed to resolve an obvious tension in socialist conceptions of law that had practical implications for their work: If law is a product of class domination, how is it possible for citizens to have a neutral or equal position within its jurisdiction? Midlevel officials in Shanghai hit the nail on the head when they asked, "Doesn't equality under the law [in Article 85] contradict class consciousness?"[118]

The constitution's rearticulation of the standard Marxist classes (proletariat, bourgeoisie, and others) also failed to provide answers to questions that seemed more technical, but still had far-reaching political ramifications. For instance, an official in Jing'an District asked about the class status of a worker should he inherit real estate when his father passes away. Would this property make him a member of the bourgeoisie (and therefore a potential target of the revolution)? This question was probably not hypothetical; his family in Ningbo owned some forest land, so he worried the state could expropriate it as "state land" in a way consistent with the constitution.[119] A local neighborhood official had class issues closer to home. An owner of a barbershop, he asked, "What class am I?" Some people, who themselves were likely spitballing, informed him that he was "bourgeois," but he pushed back using a "sweat of the brow" principle: "In truth my life is harder than a worker's." Because the constitution excluded the national bourgeoisie from the ruling alliance, he wondered whether he would be "wanted under socialism?" (*dao shehuizhuyi yaobuyao wo*).[120] Other officials, however, questioned whether the constitution would produce a sort of class leveling that could be felt in everyday life: "In the end, it's still a more comfortable life being a capitalist," said some female officials.[121]

These sorts of questions and the philosophical and practical complexities they brought to the surface were not entirely unanticipated. During constitutional training sessions for midlevel officials, for example, topics of discussion included who were the dominant and dominated classes.[122] But even if officials got crystal clear answers to questions of this nature in their ad hoc classrooms, other authoritative voices in the state muddied the waters. The Shanghai Party Committee Propaganda Bureau criticized some newspapers for turning a blind eye toward the topic of "working-class leadership" and the "worker-peasant alliance" to focus instead on "New Democracy" (according to which the national bourgeoisie was included in the ruling alliance), even though it was effectively ended by the new constitution. Nor did enough articles include testimony by capitalists acknowledging that they have "accepted working-class leadership" and how they promise to reform.[123] High-level politicians were equally if not more to blame. According to a report from Luwan District, three top leaders, including Mayor Chen Yi, provided varying answers to the question, "In the end, are the bourgeoisie our friends or enemies?" (Chen Yi said they were not friends).[124]

In the absence of what modern public relations or advertising specialists would call consistent "messaging," it is not surprising that the constitutional discussion prompted a wide range of questions about class among officials. Unlike many others, they were relatively secure in their status but were perplexed by how the constellation of "social forces" (a term used in the constitution but confusing because the word *society* was not always understood and because it could include rich peasants and capitalists) around them fit into the new political order.[125] One midlevel official in Shanghai's Civil Affairs Bureau was under the mistaken impression that the dominant class included workers as well as peasants (the latter were not included) and that the bourgeoisie were still "people," just not in the ruling class (an error as well). Blame for this was mainly placed on poor training, which apparently did not pay much attention to the actual articles of the constitution but instead to its "spirit" and "basic content."[126] Other midranking officials asked whether "our constitution also expresses the will of the bourgeoisie and the peasants" and if the United Front will "include the bourgeoisie, or only the progressives among them?" (It included neither).[127] In Luwan District, officials did not know which class was "dominated" or understand why capitalists had political rights if they are the dominated class. They also did not know what class rich peasants belonged to, how it was possible for workers and capitalists to be equal before the law as dominant and dominated classes, respectively, what *economic base* and *superstructure* meant, and whether the worker-peasant alliance was the same as the United Front and which people were included in it.[128] In the Shanghai suburbs, officials were said to be unclear about which classes were dominant and dominated. If workers were the former class, they asked, did this include peasants as well? Or are peasants dominated?[129] Elsewhere, officials asked why the constitution proclaims that the PRC will eliminate poverty (*xiaomie pinkun*) but did not apply the same verb to class, and why rich peasants were targeted for gradual elimination (officially they were not; the rich peasant *economy* was) but not capitalists, who will only be replaced (*daiti*).[130]

In this constitutional fog, many officials fell back on more familiar modes of political action. These were usually revolutionary—aggressive and involving violence or potential violence—and lacked the sort of legalistic subtlety and occasional nuance in the constitution (how, in practical terms, on human bodies, would "gradually eliminate" differ from "eliminate" or "replace"?). Not a few documents called attention to excessive "leftist" tendencies among officials when it came to class, and in particular their refusal to accept the constitutional language of equal citizenship under the law and protections for ideological enemies. In Jiangmen City in Guangdong, for instance, officials were said to be displeased by a section in Article 10 stating, "The state protects the right of capitalists to own means of production and other capital according to law" because they did not consider capitalists "people."[131] In Shanghai, low-level officials in Jing'an District asked why the CCP expropriated and distributed land belonging to rural landlords but was not redistributing the homes of "big landlords" in the city.[132] In Luwan District, a detective reportedly told the wife of someone under investigation that when the constitution is promulgated, "all property belonging to the bourgeoisie will be nationalized, and the class will be eliminated."[133] Around the country many officials thought that the PRC would have to eliminate one star on the national flag because the national bourgeoisie, who were represented in a star, would soon be eliminated by the Communist Party.[134] On the other hand, there were some who may have been criticizing the CCP for its ever-growing urban bias, or perhaps its betrayal of rural interests, by quessertioning why the constitutional wording about the capitalist economy used the words "utilize, limit, and reform" (*liyong, xianzhi, gaizao*) but "limit and eliminate" (*xianzhi, xiaomie*) when dealing with the rich peasant economy (Article 8).[135] In this perspective, capitalists had less to worry about than the rural elite."

This harsh approach to elites, however, was not universal, in part because it was leavened by competing political ideas in other constitutional articles. There were, for example, officials who took the constitution and its more gradualist language toward capitalists seriously, as the new "Party line," which absolutely could not be violated.[136] Judging by the number of questions about this, others were uncomfortable with the idea that the state could just expropriate private property whenever it wanted to.[137] Someone also questioned why the CCP lumped together "traitors and counterrevolutionaries" as subjects for punishment in Article 19, arguing that "traitors were surely counterrevolutionaries but counterrevolutionaries are not necessarily traitors," probably in reference to KMT members who fought the Japanese but opposed the Communists.[138] There was also pushback based on the principles of equality under the law and fairness, particularly between the countryside and city, a cleavage that could overshadow Marxist class analysis. Officials working at the Hangzhou Cultural Bureau, some of whom were probably non-Communists, wanted to know why the constitution was especially harsh on capitalists if, constitutionally speaking, people were equal under the law.[139] In the Shanghai suburbs, someone asked whether there was a contradiction between the constitutional promise to protect "the right of peasants to own land and other means of production according to law" and those that gave the state the right to nationalize or expropriate it "in the public interest" (Article 13).[140] Assuming that the person asking the question already knew the answer to be "yes," the insinuation was that there was something wrong about this. Industrial-sector officials in Shanghai also accused the government of discrimination against the countryside by wondering why it did not allow peasants to come to the city "to enjoy labor rights" without making any distinction between poor, middle, or rich peasants, as did officials working in the South China Party Committee in Guangdong.[141] In Jiangxi Province, representatives to local people's congresses were upset about the constitution's focus on workers' rights to the total exclusion of peasants' and requested that the government reexamine this issue.[142] In short, *class* was a central concept to the CCP, featured prominently in the constitutional text and the propaganda surrounding it, but it was not the only language, or even the most dominant one, circulating in officials' minds as they tried to make sense of its various provisions. Usually officials were left to figure out for themselves which language was the most appropriate in any given context.

Of course, these reactions, including apathy, critique through implication and insinuation, obedience, militancy, skepticism, seriousness, and barely hidden mockery were of the "for-your-eyes-only" sort among CCP officials; they were not raised in mixed audiences in constitutional discussions which were segregated by class status, occupation, gender, religion, and ethnicity. When the so-called capitalists and bourgeoisie met to talk about the constitution, for example, they could not have been aware of officials' own doubts and confusions—they could only rely on the text in front of them, newspapers, and what they heard from local officials as the voice of the PRC. How these groups reacted to the constitution will be the subject of several chapters in this book, but we will begin with the urban business elite.

CHAPTER 2

The Draft Constitution in China's Business Community

The meanings assigned to the constitution were context dependent. As Reader-response theorists such as Radway would expect, they were shaped by the words in the text but even more so by more macro variables, such as how officials interpreted the revolution and their past and future role in it, their own status vis-à-vis the party and society, and the significance assigned to the constitution in relation to other documents and policies. As victors in the Civil War, they approached the constitution as a weapon that could be useful in implementing policy; simultaneously, as party members, some feared it could be mobilized against them by their superiors should they make a mistake, while also trivializing it because it was unnecessary to realize socialism; as people with roughly the same level of legal knowledge as ordinary citizens, not a few found it difficult to translate the complexity of life into the legalist categories in the constitution, particularly when other documents vied for their limited attention.

Burrowing into the context in which the constitutional text was read, interpreted, and experienced is probably even more important in the case of China's wealthy urban stratum (the "bourgeoisie" in Marxist terminology), encompassing medium and large "capitalists" as well as store owners and managers (*laoban*, or bosses) who lacked significant capital but had power over several employees and were thus in a position to "exploit" their labor. As central players in China's robust commercial sector and industrial development in the early to mid-twentieth century, China's business community was not a trusted ally of the Communist Party in its decades-long rise to power. This was partly ideological—there is no Communist Party in the world that takes a favorable view of the bourgeoisie or capitalism, seeing both as necessary evils on the way to reaching a Communist utopia—and partly the result of political circumstances.[1] Although the CCP was born in Shanghai in 1921 and spent the first six years of its existence trying to recruit industrial workers into its ranks, it became a rural-based insurgency from the late 1920s to 1949 (unlike its Soviet counterpart), during which time the KMT governed cities and their wealthier denizens. While the KMT did its best to gain control of the industrial sector (including owners of capital and unions) as one might expect of a Leninist party that was also a late industrializer, and extracted substantial capital from industrialists as part of its wartime mobilization against Japan from the early 1930s, it was wary of but not ideologically hostile to capitalism as an economic system or to capitalists as a class.[2] As it became clear that the KMT was going to lose to the Communists in the Civil War (1945–1949), wealthy Chinese and their families were forced to make agonizing decisions, such as whether to leave China with their entire families (and usually go to Hong Kong, Taiwan, Southeast Asia, or the United States, sometimes taking money and equipment with them), depart China but leave some family members behind, shuttle between the mainland and Hong Kong in a "wait and see" mode, or remain in place and hope for the best; the history of postwar Asian capitalism was shaped by thousands of these choices.[3]

Anxious about an imminent confrontation with the bourgeoisie and concerned about massive capital flight, the CCP made strenuous efforts to convince China's business class, and its top industrialists, to remain in China. By offering material inducements (such as retaining some level of ownership) and official positions in the new regime (by way of the Chinese People's Political Consultative Conference [CPPCC] and other CCP-led associations), ideological flexibility (the concept of New Democracy, which included the "national bourgeoisie" as part of the ruling coalition), and restraining demands from officials and workers to strip capitalists of their assets, the CCP managed to persuade quite a few to stay put.[4] However, many others, probably the majority, lacked the wherewithal to move and did not receive any of the patient cultivation that characterized CCP policy toward the top tier of the business community (which continues in the reform era in the "Three Represents" policy, initiated under former party secretary Jiang Zemin, which allowed private entrepreneurs to join the CCP).[5]

After its victory, the CCP's approach toward the business community retained its element of co-optation toward the capitalist elite and especially their progeny, producing a critical mass of "Red Capitalists," but soon added a strong dose of coercion to the mix.[6] In 1952, the party launched its Five Antis Campaign. Aimed at "the bourgeoisie as a whole" and the business community in particular, it subjected many to denunciation, interrogation, confiscation of assets, and arrest for tax fraud, evasion, theft of state property, cheating on government contracts, and illegally passing along secret economic data.[7] Encouraged by CCP party organizations, in stores, small-scale enterprises, and large factories across China, workers exposed their managers' alleged crimes, occasionally inflicting corporal punishment to satisfy quotas. In many instances, the party used businessmen's wives and children as leverage to obtain confessions and revelations of wrongdoing; faced with political and economic persecution and isolation from their families, there was a "wave of suicides" among businessmen.[8] This harsher approach to the bourgeoisie—alongside a broader tightening of class categories—was confirmed in the draft constitution two years later, which omitted the national bourgeoisie from the ruling coalition of "workers, in alliance with peasants" as part of the state policy of transitioning to socialism. At the same time, however, the draft also offered conciliatory language, such as maintaining inheritance rights and protection of private property (at least on a temporary basis) and political status (by not labeling them "non-people," the CCP implied that they enjoyed the rights of citizens).

How did the Chinese business community react to these developments? How did they read the constitution and come to understand their place in the new polity? To date, the voices of Chinese businessmen and their families during the constitutional discussion have been skipped over (for example, in Xiaohong Xiao-Planes's and Cheng Zhengqing's respective accounts of the famous businessmen Li Kangnian and Wu Yunchu), or obscured by abstractions in the concepts *nationalization* and *transition to socialism.*[9] Bergère, for example, claims that by the end of 1956, "rural collectivization and the nationalization of urban commercial and industrial enterprises had been completed *without major trauma*" but does not provide evidence from those who experienced these events.[10]

Intentionally or not, this assessment tracks not a small amount of state-produced documentation. Newspapers frequently reported on elite capitalists' exuberant responses to the draft constitution, as did accounts that appear in archival documents not intended for public consumption.[11] In the archives one can find statements of support from Rong Yiren of the famous Rong family (whose fortunes came mostly from textiles) as well as lesser-known businessmen (mostly in district-level archives).[12] Others heaped praise on the constitutional process, in particular the CCP's willingness to listen to their comments ("We never talked about a constitution before") and the abundance of rights and the small number of constitutional obligations. Some expressed appreciation for the opportunity to "get educated" and "reform" themselves. "In general," one report noted, "people in industrial and commercial circles understand that class is not yet eliminated, they have appropriate status, their private property is protected, and the government pays them an undue amount of attention; they are very satisfied and pleased with themselves."[13]

But even among those offering praise, this summary whitewashed (red-washed?) all sorts of more nuanced reactions, many of which hinted at deeper problems. One businessman, for example, exclaimed, "The constitution is very good—it protects the industrial and commercial circles" but also noted that he had not paid much attention to other articles.[14] Others differentiated between the constitutional document and the discussion, praising the former but saying that there was "no need to discuss it" or were indifferent, stating that keeping factories running and not engaging in tax evasion were all one needed to do.[15] Drawing on previous experiences in the early 1950s, some argued that there was little new in the draft constitution, having encountered similar language about their class in their education about the General Line and the Election Law.[16]

The CCP's broad-stroked and influential narrative unravels further if we dig deeper and look at members of the business community who were not well known or co-opted and at the microcontexts of rooms within which conversations about the constitutional discussion took place (as Radway encouraged us to do in the case of American romance novel readers). Indeed, in the voluminous documentation about "capitalists' reaction" to the draft constitution, those purporting to show enthusiastic support are in the minority. While this is surely a reflection of the biases of the reporters, it makes intuitive sense: After experiencing a Communist Revolution undergirded by a rural-based insurgency, why would monied urban interests feel comfortable? Why would people familiar with the travails of elites in the USSR not be apprehensive? Why would vague terms such as *the transition to socialism* not be disconcerting? After being targeted in the Five Antis Campaign, why would businesspeople trust a state that instructs them to gather at their workplaces, in the confines of small rooms and offices, to both comment on and offer revisions to a document said to be of utmost political importance? These questions were hardly rhetorical; in fact, they supplied the broad and narrow contexts within which people understood the constitution. These anxiety-infused understandings, in turn, were reported to the leadership in *Neibu cankao* in early May 1954, while the first version of the draft constitution was being hammered out in Beijing.[17]

Reading and Responding to the Draft Constitution

Media reports about the draft constitutional discussion invariably cited "red capitalists" who showered praise on the document and the CCP. These wealthy individuals hitched their gilded wagons to the Communist Party, accepted official posts, and even chaired meetings in "industrial and commercial circles." Whether positive comments about the constitution were genuinely felt is difficult to ascertain, but even if they were, we should treat them skeptically: they tell us about what was said at meetings that took place, and therefore documented, but not about those who decided to vote with their feet by not attending, sat on their chairs but remained silent (and in doing so, speak to us as well), or were more indirect in their critiques. In Shanghai's Jing'an District, for example, a meeting that was supposed to bring together 512 people had an attendance rate of 50 percent. Those who were expected to lead the discussion were said to be well prepared, but audience members did not say much, failed to engage in any topic that might be controversial, and did not ask many questions. When the discussion leader, a chemical industry executive, asked a seemingly straightforward question, "Why should we call this a 'constitution' and not something else?" one participant quickly issued a stark warning to the others: "Our discussion today should be very serious—don't bring up any matters of principle lest we distort the words of the constitution, and that would be wrong." When asked if they supported the constitution, most answered positively, but the lack of enthusiasm was noted.[18] In other meetings, there were awkward silences, and people sometimes asked questions without even bothering to read the draft. According to a report, the business community, much like CCP officials we saw in chapter 1, did not feel qualified to comment on a document that had already been reviewed by experts: "It's like trying to find a bone in something as perfect as an egg," one quipped in Suzhou dialect.[19]

From within such perfect-as-they-are eggs, however, critiques hatched. In Jiangsu Province, some refused to utter a word because the constitution was said to have been drafted by Mao, but others took the effort to explain that offering suggestions for revision was pointless because the constitution was drafted "only for appearances" or that it would not change anything: "You say you're going to change a ruby into an emerald, but that's impossible."[20] Likewise, in Chongqing, business elites refused to "directly expose" their oppositional stance to three key concepts in the constitution—reform, restrict, and utilize (capitalist industry)—but conducted a wordplay with the *xian* of "constitution," since it is a homophone for "restrict." Saying "The constitution comes and goes" could imply and mean, "This is restricted and then that is restricted." This was followed by a warning and critique: "As soon as you're not careful you've done something illegal."[21] And in Inner Mongolia, most businessmen publicly stated that they supported the constitution ("but in their hearts they hate it," noted the report writer), but there was "no point study-ing it." In their view, the constitution was not law but an advance warning that we "will slowly die" (*yibu yibu si*), as well as a weapon that will make it "easier [for the CCP] to deal with us" (*hao nongle*).[22]

In other cases, businessmen (and their families) gauged how (and how much) they should speak based on their assessment of the political status of the text, the reactions from their discussion leaders, and contextual cues hinting at what sorts of topics were broachable with officials. In Chongqing, for instance, the owner of a small business recommended to "offer sacrifices" to the draft constitution much like one would do with a spirit tablet: "read a few lines a day to avoid getting punished."[23] A report on Shanghai's Yimiao District noted that businessmen did not even do this, preferring to avoid talking about it or asking questions. This high level of reserve, however, was the consequence of having raised suggestions in a previous meeting only to have them rejected. Others attributed their silence to a recent execution (probably of someone of their class) that they thought was unjustified. They declined to say anything about state law. They reasoned, "If you make a mistake discussing it, it's a legal viola-tion; if it's a legal violation, you'll get executed" (*tan cuole yao fan fa; fan fale yao pan sixing*). Insinuating their displeasure, some businessmen expressed unequiv-ocal support by bullshitting: "The constitution is always correct; there's no need to talk about it."[24] In Shenyang, bullshit praise included the adjective "flawless" (*tianyi wufeng*), which officials knew was not the case, since many of them also noted problems in it.[25]

Given the complexity of the constitution and its length at over 100 articles, not a few people took advantage of the opportunity to utter quessertions about it within the general framework of "expressing support" or veiled critique. In Shanghai's central Xincheng District, some said that the draft constitution did not have any "taste" (*weidao*) upon first read, but "the more one bit in the more bitter it got," and "the more carefully you read it, the more questions there are." Focusing on the ownership of capital and machinery, these questions went to the heart of the transition to socialism enshrined in the constitution: "What's a 'production resource'?" "What are the other kinds of production resources?" Correctly anticipating decisive shifts in state policy, someone said, "When ownership becomes collective, capitalists' profit allocation system [*sima fenfei*] will disappear."[26]

Some credited the constitution with providing greater clarity but not in lan-guage that suggested much gratitude. In Laozha District, someone in adver-

THE DRAFT CONSTITUTION IN CHINA'S BUSINESS COMMUNITY   51

tising said, "Things are clearer after the promulgation of the constitution; the tail [of the capitalists] will be snapped off and we'll also surrender," and a man in the warehouse industry remarked that he had been "somewhat suspicious" about the issue of "exploitation" during the period of transition (that is, he was worried about the fate of those who were accused of exploitation), but "now, with the constitution, it's clearer: during the transition period exploitation is still safeguarded," but he expressed support for its "gradual elimination" in the constitution.[27]

The handwritten report cited above provides clues as to why at least some people in the business community could have been enthusiastic, or moderately supportive, of the constitution. One noted that they had spirited discussions of its preamble and the articles dealing with political and economic interests and offered many revisions to the text but had little interest in the rest of the document. That is, their enthusiasm was confined to certain parts of the text. Another critical variable was status within the business community, which shaped the depth of their experience dealing with the new government and level of legal and policy knowledge. According to this analysis, business elites had the opportunity to study the constitution as it was being drafted, they learned about the General Line, and their industries had already been transitioning to "state capitalism." Their views toward the constitution were said to be "stable" and their mindset only a little anxious. In meetings, they made the case for the "special qualities" of Chinese capitalists, emphasizing just how useful they can be in the transition to socialism. These qualities, they suggested, were disturbingly dismissed in Article 1, which ended the United Front and declared the PRC a state "led by workers, in alliance with peasants." However, "middle and small capitalists" were less conciliatory. Because their businesses were doing well, they were "nostalgic" about the period of New Democracy and hoped it could continue for a longer period. Many could not figure out how to manage their businesses with the transition to socialism.[28]

Central to this question of management, of course, was how managers would deal with workers now that the latter's position as the leading class was firmly placed in the constitution. Well before 1954, and certainly after the Five Antis Campaign, managers had to deal with a restive and often feisty working class, but the end of New Democracy and the removal of the national bourgeoisie from the document seemed to herald even more profound changes. Complicated workplace interactions shaped the way China's managers viewed the draft constitution. In reports describing the discussions about it, not a few were said to be hostile to the idea of working-class leadership, in part because workers were "oppressing capitalists" and "seeking revenge," even as some of them were "taking the capitalist road" by faking illness, refusing to work, and producing shoddy products. In Fujian, a manager said that in conflicts between labor and capital in a People's Democratic Dictatorship it is "democracy for workers [rather than the 'people'] and dictatorship toward capital."[29] Without mentioning its name, managers argued that the CCP abetted this behavior by not punishing workers who had murdered their managers, and that the legal cover the constitution was providing would make it impossible for them to manage their firms. They expressed hope that the constitution would include a method for dealing with "unreasonably contentious workers," probably because the existing article requiring citizens to "uphold labor discipline" (Article 100) was not having its intended affect. In Tianjin, for instance, a businessman asked, "Is it a constitutional violation if workers come late, leave early, and violate labor discipline? Is producing substandard goods and not completing a job on time a crime?" and in Chongqing a small business owner insinuated through his question that the CCP was at fault for workers' dissatisfaction: "Isn't it forcing us to exploit" workers by not allowing employers to lay them off?[30] Others had the temerity to ask the CCP to conduct an education campaign among workers after the transition to socialism was complete, as well as to complain that they should enjoy the same "labor protections" as workers because they were citizens and "participated in labor" (both statements that were worthy of reprimand but not carried out, according to the report writer).[31]

Businessmen's family members, also stung by their sharp decline in status after 1949 and skeptical about the leadership abilities of ordinary workers, took a similar position on the issue of class. Workers, they argued, did not behave "democratically" now that they had power, and it was a mistake to apportion political power based on what class one belonged to; instead, "Whoever has the ability should lead." Unsurprisingly, they also opposed the fundamental principle in socialist constitutionalism that constitutions should empower previously oppressed classes and promote their interests at the expense of former elites. "Class," they suggested, "should not be too clearly differentiated."[32]

Faced with workers contesting their authority and fearful of class-based discourse about exploitation and oppression, some managers tried to prevent workers from hearing about the draft constitution in the first place. They did this, according to the report, while publicly proclaiming their support for it—thereby providing the grist for CCP propaganda—while mocking it on the sly in private.[33]

Displays of active subterfuge, however, appear to have been rare. Instead, anxiety, entirely absent from popular media reporting but seen in entrusting mockery only to friends and colleagues, cast the longest shadow over discussions in the business community.[34] In the city of Shenyang, businessmen worried that the constitution made them "a target of the revolution."[35] In Shanghai, they quailed that everything they possessed and worked for their entire lives would soon be "eliminated" by the Communist Party. Describing them as "having the jitters," these businessmen were accused of unwarranted nostalgia "because they don't get the plight of the working class" and of failure to understand the necessity of revolution: "Why does the government want to eliminate us?" "Couldn't the government just let us quietly do business?" they pleaded.[36] Anxiety was said to be particularly pervasive among businessmen who lacked the sort of political connections of the "big capitalists" who had been courted by the Communist Party. "Can we not get on the socialist road?" some asked in what was probably either a humorous or despairing tone. Others viewed the constitution as a prelude to, or perhaps preparation for, a broader crackdown: "Today we talk about the constitution; tomorrow maybe someone will be in Tilanqiao [a Shanghai prison]."[37]

Whether these views reflected an actual reading of the constitution or rumors about it is not clear. One report noted that all sorts of "nonsense" (hushuo badao) about the constitution was bandied about among those who had not studied it or understood its content. But most of this nonsense did not focus on potentially good news, only deep concern about their future income and livelihood. Described as worried and suspicious about the CCP's intentions, businessmen were observed "frantically pacing back and forth" (panghuangde lihai).[38]

As per usual in CCP documents, there was nary a problem that could not be resolved by "education" or "hearing a report," and reports about the constitutional discussions did not deviate much from this script. Businessmen and their families who were described as nervous and anxious prior to their study predictably regained their composure after hearing reassurances from party officials. A district-level report from Yangpu, issued at the tail end of the constitutional discussion in September, called the business community "hostile," but gradually "coming around."[39] Elsewhere, some of those who had been quite suspicious "say they can relax now." But this was hardly the universal sentiment: in the very same report, "be careful" was the advice.[40]

In the space between constitutional literacy and partial or total ignorance, and between officials who breathed fire and those who offered reassurance, the business community—much like the officials they feared—interpreted the constitution through other cognitive devices, most notably locally grounded analogies and metaphors. Of these, the most prominent by far was land reform. This was probably inescapable: like landlords in the countryside, members of the business community were designated exploiters and, New Democracy platitudes aside, the bogeymen of the Communist Party. Confronted with barely contained leftist radicalism, businessmen compared themselves to landlords—a

community anxiously waiting for the ax to fall on their heads. In their suggestions for constitutional revision, they proposed reinserting into the preamble
both the "national bourgeoisie" and "rich peasants," a proposal quickly dismissed on account of their "lack of understanding the worker-peasant alliance."[41] In Tianjin, a businessman interpreted the constitutional guarantee of
protecting private enterprise as a "means to an end" or, to use the term in the
introduction, a wartime tactic. During the war, he explained, landlords had also
been "protected" but "eliminated" soon afterward. The same fate awaits capitalists, he warned. Like their Shanghai counterparts, Tianjin businessmen scanned
the constitutional text for potentially hospitable phrases and zeroed in on "All
power in the People's Republic of China belongs to the people" in Article 2.
Since they considered themselves part of the "people," perhaps the CCP would
not seek to eliminate them after all.[42] Others, however, had a less charitable take
on how the CCP treated landlords but still concluded that a similar fate might
await them. In the countryside, they noted, the party's policy toward landlords
had been "first attack, then be courteous" (xianbing houli), but toward the business community it was "first be courteous, then attack" (xianli houbing). To gain
greater clarity, they wanted to know "if they are among the people or outside of
the people."[43]

Comparisons to the fate of landlords also appeared in reports that emphasized how the party had successfully allayed these fears. Among very many
"relatively poor capitalists" (xiaohu zibenjia), the draft of Article 10, which stipulated that "the state protects the right of capitalists to own means of production and other capital," produced much-needed relief: "We used to think
that socialist transformation would be the same as the confiscation of landlords' property. Now that we know that the constitution has an article about
protection, we can relax." According to the report, some who had wanted to
sell their real estate thinking it would soon be confiscated had changed their
plans, while others were said to "welcome socialist transformation" and hoped
to join the working class.[44]

Rural analogies did not end with measuring their fate against that of the
landlord class. CCP policy toward somewhat wealthier peasants—"rich peasants" in official parlance—also caught their attention. In Shanghai, a businessman compared state policy toward capitalists and rich peasants and found the
latter to be quite harsh—elimination for them but reform for us.[45] Similarly,
in Changsha in Hunan Province, businessmen acknowledged that they were
better off than rich peasants who would be gradually eliminated. At the same
time, they worried that the CCP "says one thing but then does another" and
was just being coy about its intentions, in contrast to its blunter approach to
rural elites.[46] Bourgeois sympathy for wealthier peasants was noted as an emo-

tion worthy of mention in reports sent up to the leadership. In Jiangsu, one said, "The state has already paved a clear path for industrial capitalists—state capitalism—but the draft constitution says nothing about the future road for rich peasants; it looks like the state will be more serious (*yanzhong*) toward them than capitalists."[47] In the city of Guiyang in Guizhou Province, one male resident saw the policy toward rich peasants and said, "You see—they want to eliminate them again."[48]

Political experiences, whether personal or empathetically imagined, were not the only analogic or metaphoric reference points for getting a firmer sense of what the constitution meant, or would mean, in the near future. Drawing on a musical metaphor, a Tianjin businessman did not think the constitution would be very significant. He compared the constitutional text to a musical score, CCP leaders to the composer, and everyone else to a choir: "As soon as the center publishes the lyrics everyone sings it in unison, and then it's finished."[49]

Others used analogies rooted in a variety of hierarchical arrangements. In Shenyang, a manager of a shoe store, classified by the report writer as part of a group that was dissatisfied with the constitution, mocked the notion that the CCP was genuinely interested in gathering people's honest opinions about the constitution. "What's there to study? Who will dare not support it?" he asked incredulously. "If the government was really interested in our suggestions for revisions it would have already sent a car for us to become senior officials." Others used a family-based analogy, comparing the study of the constitution to adults telling children how things will be: "From here on in, if you violate that article we'll spank your ass."[50]

Analogies to various hierarchical relationships were complemented by metaphors of impenetrable, hard objects that produced exclusion and pain. In Shanghai, a businessman surnamed Zhu compared the constitution to the government not only shutting two out of four "windows"—one representing the petit bourgeoisie, and the other the national bourgeoisie—but also boarding up the remaining ones so that they could not get through. Another said the constitution was like a lead plate used in printing and he a wooden nail: "How can I get through?"[51] In Songjiang County, this came up in a conversation between two supposed members of the bourgeoisie who were summoned to a meeting to discuss the draft constitution. One warned the other: "You're in the bourgeoisie and about to be wiped out. Going to the meeting is like taking a rock to smash your own foot."[52]

Rocks squashing feet were rather tame compared to some other objects and the damage they might cause. In the northern city of Taiyuan in Shanxi Province, the business community was described as generally not satisfied with the constitution, comparing it to "a noose that's getting tighter." "With the constitution I've become a counterrevolutionary," one lamented. "Just look at Article 10 [the state will "utilize, restrict and reform private capital"]: to the left there's a 'restriction' [*xianzhi*] and to the right the same thing. Make a mistake and you're punished, so be careful what you say, and especially what you do."[53] Similar images were invoked by some Guangdong businessmen who compared Articles 10–14, which dealt largely with income and property, to leashes and capitalists to dogs. The more capitalists resist, they said, the tighter the leash gets, leaving them little choice but to be "good little pups and obey."[54]

As metaphors for discipline and domination, tightening nooses, or slipknots (*huokou*), were certainly evocative. But within this menacing constitutional imaginary, some businessmen conjured up even worse fates. In Guangdong, some compared the CCP's wartime United Front policy vis-à-vis capitalists to a "postponed death sentence" and the draft constitution to a "death sentence for immediate execution."[55] The manager of a private enterprise in Harbin asked why there was no mention of the bourgeoisie in the CCP's articulation of the social basis of the government, taking this to mean that their end was quickly approaching.[56] In Shanghai, the constitution was intentionally renamed (misnamed) "Ways of Killing" or "Death Law" (*sifa*), a provocative act lightened by the coincidence that "constitution" and "death" are pronounced in a roughly similar way in Shanghainese, and *fa* can mean "law" or "method."[57] Few seemed to trust that CCP promises (even those made by officials as senior as Zhou Enlai) would take them off this "road toward death."[58]

Contradictions

Confronted by a document described by the authorities as possessing foundational significance to the state and with the status of "law," many in the business community were not content to rely on hearsay, rumor, or a rough understanding through analogy or metaphor. Instead, consistent with the long legacy in Chinese civilization of taking written words seriously, they read very carefully for telltale clues, using the draft constitution as a heuristic device, or perhaps weathervane, to gain a better understanding of the fledgling Communist state—then only five years old—and their place in it. In Harry Frankfurt's blunter terminology, they used the document to figure out what the CCP "was up to," an integral part of the definition of bullshit.

However, this eyeballing did not take place in isolation, person versus document, but rather in a churning environment that blended knowledge of international politics, other political documents, random conversations, and previous political experiences. Take, for example, the constitutional discussion at a Shanghai brewery. After the revolution, the CCP arrested many of its employees as counterrevolutionaries, and as a result many feared saying anything about the draft lest they utter the wrong thing and get into political trouble. Instead, many went to the source, shelling out one mao to purchase the document "for their personal interest" (at this time a young worker would make 1.5 yuan per day, an older worker three; there are 10 mao to each yuan). It was a tough read: some could not understand or read it until the end; others grasped the characters but not the meaning. But even with these obstacles, people asked good questions. For instance, family members of counterrevolutionaries wanted to know if the constitution, with its clear language about "pardons," would help their relatives get sprung from prison; a man who had participated in a counterrevolutionary organization after 1949 bought a copy and concluded that the document would not help him; workers read about their rights; officials carried around copies. Nearby, an owner of a tofu store happened to see someone immersed in his reading. She asked him what it was about, but his answer did not help. Still, her post-1949 experiences in the neighborhood and the official's answers provided enough context for a reasoned judgment: in the USSR, she noted, the Russians had used all sorts of "tricks and ruses on people and killed them." The constitution, in her view, was part of a Communist conspiracy to get rid of Chinese business owners.[59]

Perhaps it was this combination of a conspiratorial mindset (whether prompted by campaigns against counterrevolutionaries in 1951–52 in China or Soviet campaigns of terror during the previous decades) and learning how to read and speak in the language of the new state that primed the Chinese business community to peruse the draft constitution and point out "contradictions" (*maodun*) between it and other CCP documents, and internal contradictions in it.[60] Of the former, the most relevant were those related to the CCP's United Front policy, which found its clearest (quasi) constitutional expression in the 1949 Common Program. The members of the business community were unlikely to have read the Common Program in its entirety, but years of political education made them aware of the classes to which they had been assigned, or with which they now identified (national bourgeoisie, capitalist, petit bourgeoisie) and the rights they had been given. But these words went missing in chapter 1 of the constitution ("Statement of General Principles"). In Changsha, businessmen noticed, and worried what this meant.[61] In Shanghai, some simply said, "In the past the classes were there, now they're not" (*guoqu you, xianzai mei youle*).[62] Family members panicked: "If we are not added there, what does the government consider us as? In the future we won't even have the right to talk"; "China has four different types of ownership systems," so why "weren't four classes written into Article 1?"[63] Some also noticed that "freedom of thought" had been in the Common Program but was not in the draft constitution.[64] In industrialized Huangpu District, a reporter noted that businessmen "feared that the government no longer wants their class" and that their class would soon be designated an "enemy." Many of them registered strong objections to Article 1, comparing it unfavorably to the Common Program. They were also confused by the mixed messages they received from a variety of official statements and documents about whether they were friends or enemies of the Communist Party.[65]

Whether included to appeal to the widest range of businesspeople, the result of the CCP's being of two (or more) minds as to what course to pursue, or just indifference to their audience's desire for a predictable environment, such messages—contradictions—were built into the constitution itself. Some businessmen in Guangzhou in Guangdong Province concluded, accurately in my estimation, that these were intentional since using the words "protect" and "eliminate" in reference to capitalists could not be a coincidence.[66] In Fuzhou City in Fujian Province, a businessman pointed out the contradiction between Article 5, which "recognized capitalist ownership," and Article 10, which proclaimed the state's intention of replacing capitalist ownership with collective ownership (*quanmin suoyouzhi*).[67] In Shanghai, reports claimed that businessmen, comparing the constitution to a compass informing them about the direction of the state, were concerned about the contradiction between the words "expropriate" and "protect" in different articles dealing with property.[68] Others drew attention to Article 17, which stipulated that the government must "rely on the masses of the people" (*yikao renmin qunzhong*). Did this mean that members of the business community were "of the people?" The constitution, they claimed, sent conflicting messages: Article 10 referred to them as "capitalists" (and therefore "not people"), but Article 11 gave the distinct impression that they were "citizens" (*gongmin*): "Do we have two types of status?" "Will we become citizens only after socialism?" they wondered.[69]

Members of China's business community were also concerned about the mechanisms through which socialism would be achieved; as potential targets of the Communist Revolution, they tended to view the transition to socialism as a threat to their livelihood and even survival. Here, too, they found the constitution's phraseology contradictory and therefore worrisome. Many focused their attention on the phrase "in a peaceful way" (*heping daolu*) in the first paragraph of the preamble: "The system of people's democracy—new democracy—of the People's Republic of China guarantees that China can in a peaceful way eliminate [*xiaomie*, translated as *banish* in the English version] exploitation and poverty and build a prosperous and happy socialist society."

They also noted that its fourth paragraph stipulated that the "democratic people's United Front will continue to play its part in mobilizing and rallying the whole people," stressing "will continue" as a sign that the Communist Party will treat the business community with a relatively light touch. In Chongqing in the southwest and Shenyang in the northeast, businessmen were described as much relieved and pleased with these word choices.[70] But they could hardly shrug off words that insinuated a far darker future, such as *struggle*, *eliminate*, *suppress*, *punish*, and *deprive*, taking these as unsubtle hints that "peaceful way" and "will continue" did not necessarily imply that the Communist Party had abandoned political struggle as its weapon of choice. In line with previous assessments of the constitution as a sly document, a wide variety of businessmen in Shanghai believed that the CCP was just "being thorough" (*zhaogu zhoudao*) with the more pacific language or included it accidentally. If it were genuinely interested in continuing the United Front, it could have easily avoided mentioning the word *struggle* in such an important document.[71]

Voluntarily (*ziyuan*) was another member of this family of contradictory concepts. Used in the context of the Korean War to describe an often involuntary draft process, it was introduced in Articles 8 and 9 in the context of the collectivization of individual peasants and handicraft workers.[72] The concept, called a "principle," suggested that at least some people had a choice whether to join the collective economy. In Shanghai, some businessmen were upset that *voluntary* was not used in any of the articles dealing with industrial transformation and asked, "Why does the CCP favor one and discriminate against the other [*houci bobi*]?" But this was a problem of not only omission, they argued, but also "contradiction": they had read a speech by Li Weihan, one of the drafters of the constitution, who articulated the principle of voluntary reform as an option for some firms in what remained of the private economy (the others being "possible reform" and "required reform").[73] The "internal contradiction" of the constitution was thus complemented by the "external contradiction" between it and a major policy statement, which they had learned to view as an authoritative text equal to law or policy, much as officials had. Reports called the business community's understanding of this issue "chaotic" (*hunluan*) but without attributing responsibility.

Keywords

In addition to their focus on contradictory phrases and concepts, both within and external to the text, the Chinese business community also paid attention to particular words, viewing them, as a fortune teller might, as indicators of their political, social, and economic status in the new state. Among many of concern, three stood out: *law, labor,* and *class.* The fourth, bundling together words and symbols, was the PRC flag.

Law

Concepts related to law appeared frequently in the draft constitution. *Lawmaking* was the most obvious, since it fell under the jurisdiction of the National People's Congress, whose functions were articulated in chapter 2. The business community, however, was not particularly interested in the functions of the NPC. Instead, they engaged in considerable rumination and asked serious questions, many of which were outright assertions and criticisms, about the terms *before the law (zai falü shang), in accordance to law (yizhao falü), by law (you falü),* and *following the constitution and law (fucong xianfa he falü). Law* appeared in multiple articles in the context of the state promising to treat people equally, protecting something citizens valued (land, livelihood, inheritance) or something the government did (claim ownership of mineral resources, water, forests), demanded (compliance), or reserved the right to do (expropriate land for the public interest, deprive "feudal landlords" and "bureaucratic capitalists" of their political rights).[74] The business community, already wary of the CCP for many good reasons, worried about all of these: What, exactly, did the government mean, if anything, by stating that they were equal under the law, or placing "in accordance to law" before the verb "protect", or demanding compliance to law?

Much like many of the officials with whom they spoke about this, few in the business community took equality under the law seriously. Given their political experiences and political study sessions during the previous years, it would have been quite surprising if they had. Equality before the law, it was argued, was distinct from the more meaningful standard of political equality for the simple reason that "in China there is a dominant class and a dominated class." But acknowledgment of this reality was quite different from agreement with it, and to the consternation of officials, who labeled these views "confused" (*mohu*), some held that legal equality should apply to everyone without considering who is the dominant class: "It's OK that we cannot stand up to the working class as equals [*fenting kangli*], but giving workers rights is giving rights to 600 million people; if they won't share them with us they've lost the virtue of impartiality."[75]

But this issue of equality, while disturbing to some, was generally not considered as worrisome as *in accordance to law.* In Nanjing, for example, a textile factory manager, in what appears to be an implicit rebuke, cleverly suggested removing this phrase to better differentiate the CCP's constitution from the Republic of China's provisional one (1947). The KMT, he argued, used the same phrase to restrict the very rights it was providing, which led to their curtailment. In Articles 8, 9, and 10 (those dealing with "capitalists"), the CCP was doing the same ("the right hand gives freedom while the left takes it away").[76] In Shanghai, businessmen did not evoke the KMT in this regard, but insinuated that *in accordance to law* was just a disguise for lawlessness, much as the constitution, with its intentionally ambiguous phrases, masked totalitarianism. Among small and medium-sized businesses in particular, *law* was said to be worryingly elastic or flexible *(tanxing; linghuo; shensuo)*, used to suit the circumstances of time and place *(yindi zhiyi yinshi zhiyi)*. (In Heilongjiang, some called it a "plaything" *[wanyi]*, just like the Qing [Dynasty] Code.)[77] Even within a large field of constitutional arbitrariness, *in accordance to law* was said to be too imbued with elasticity: law "is written by the Communist Party, which can change it at any time, so it looks like we have protection and also looks like we don't have protection."[78] In a question that probably masqueraded as a pointed critique of how the CCP used law, a businessman's wife asked, "What's the difference between 'the state in accordance to law protects' and 'the state protects'?" insinuating that the former was added for no other purpose than to provide useful ambiguity.[79]

Seemingly unlimited legal flexibility, and the forecast it provided about the absence of legal protections, was still not as dangerous as the notion of "following the law," simply because its opposite—not following it—could mean prison or worse. In the eyes of many in the business community, law's ambiguity was easily equaled by its expansiveness; much like Michel Foucault's understanding of the concept *discipline*, it touched everything but could not be situated in any one place. In the constitution, "following the constitution and the law" was placed in Article 100 alongside other obligations such as upholding labor discipline, respecting social ethics, and maintaining public order.

But were these separate obligations in practice? Businessmen, singed by investigations and arrests, worried that the vague terms "public order" and "social ethics" (and, in Article 10, "endangering the public interest, disrupting the social economic order and undermining state planning") provided the CCP cavernous space to charge them with constitutional offenses alongside not following the law. In Beijing, one businessman said to another one, "Let's compare what we've done to the constitution *[dui yi dui xianfa]* and check out which article in it we've violated."[80] In Shanghai, most businessmen were not particularly concerned about their ability to be patriotic in supporting the CCP, deeming this easy, but noted the difficulty of following the law "especially after the promulgation of the constitution" because law's realm was too wide (*tai guangle*): "It's hard not to do something that isn't illegal," they complained.[81] In what seems to have been a preemptive defense of some future crime, they told officials, "No one breaks the law on purpose."[82] Businessmen in Huangpu District echoed this sentiment. As individuals, they could follow the law, but because of the vagaries of rules and regulations governing business, enterprises had little chance to successfully comply: "Abide by the law today, but tomorrow there's another law."[83] Elsewhere in Shanghai, a businessman, taking advantage of the opportunity to suggest revisions, boldly proposed to delete the entire clause in Article 10 that warned capitalists about inflicting damage to the public interest and social-economic order.[84] In Heilongjiang, one provided a succinct summary of the sentiment in some parts of the business community about the constitution and law: "Before the constitution, the Communists used persuasion to educate bad people and executions were held in public places [but] now that there's a constitution there's no longer any need to use persuasion to educate. Whoever violates the law will be dealt with based on an article."[85]

Labor

What activity counted as labor, which type of income was derived from it, and who was imagined as a laborer were questions that came up frequently among members of the business community as they read the draft constitution. Much like their relationship with the concept *law*, they understood that how the CCP answered these questions would affect their futures, and they used the opening provided by the constitutional discussion to express their views, concerns, and questions.

Adding to their already long list of reasons to be anxious, the deliberate ambiguity baked into the constitution, the unintended conceptual confusion in related authoritative sources, and the word *lawful* (*hefa*) made it difficult to pin down where the CCP stood on these issues. Not a few businessmen, but particularly large-scale industrialists who were members of the party-led Industry and Commerce Association, were aware that in the initial drafts of the constitution—before it was sent out for the country-wide discussion—the CCP promised to protect "income derived from labor" (*laodong shouru*). In Shanghai, a report noted that a businessman said that his colleagues were very shaken (*zhendong*), worried, and suspicious about this wording, since few could credibly claim that their lifestyle was funded through labor rather than investment dividends, bonuses, profits, and other sources. In response to these concerns, the subsequent draft revised the wording for the final text: the government would protect capitalists' legal income (*hefa shouru*). While report writers claimed that this revision calmed capitalists' anxieties, the addition of the politically-infused adjective *legal* probably had the exact opposite effect since it sent an ominous reminder of the state's discretionary power.[86] Those more favorably inclined toward the CCP, such as a businessman in Beijing who suggested (quite presciently, given the current class coalition in the PRC) that they should "unite with the government and form a ruling class with it," found little problem accepting this formulation, but for others the arbitrariness of law made cooperation too risky a proposition.[87]

While this word shift was deliberate, other sources of legal information appear to have unintentionally complicated all concepts about labor. Unlike the issue of income, the CCP never mentioned the bourgeoisie or capitalists as worthy of benefits, instead deploying vague terms such as *citizen* (for the right to work and education, for example) or *laborer* (right to leisure). However, in Shanghai, and probably in other cities as well, in the days immediately following the national rollout of the draft constitution, many newspapers changed the wording: *everyone* enjoyed the right to work, leisure, and education. Just how firm the CCP was about class and who counted as a citizen—topics about which many CCP officials were also confused—could have easily remained contested long after 1954 even though the draft constitution's language on these issues was not revised.[88]

These sorts of definitional ambiguities provided the space within which the business community could push back against the constitution's implicit argument that only certain kinds of laborers deserved state benefits and that they, by virtue of their ownership of capital, should automatically be excluded. In Shanghai's Jing'an District, for example, they claimed rights on two grounds: that they were, in fact, citizens and therefore equal to workers in the eyes of the state as articulated in the constitution; and that they participate in labor as well. Drawing on the classical differentiation between those who labor with their hands (the ruled) and those who labor with their minds (the rulers), they asked, "Is it only physical and not mental labor that counts?" "Why do only workers get labor rights?"[89] Elsewhere, they brashly ridiculed the notion that they do not labor (*laodong*)—"If what I do isn't considered labor I'll just put my feet up on the office desk and have the workers support me"—and warned that they would lose their motivation to work if the category *laborers* did not include them.[90]

As summarized in a report from Shanghai,

Some capitalists still emphasize that some of their activities constitute "labor." For example, the elite capitalist Yan E'sheng (严谔声) says:

"Capitalists are citizens who have the ability to work. Can you say that everything they do now is for the 25 percent profit they get under the current profit allocation system? Isn't capitalist labor included in the other 75 percent?" There are others who say that even though capitalists cannot become "laborers," it should be recognized that they are in the process of reforming themselves, that their lives have already changed, and that at the end of the process might become "laborers." Managers of small and medium sized enterprises vehemently disagree with the notion that they do not labor [laodong] since everything they do is run around dealing with their business. A manager of a textile factory said that, "capitalists today are characterized by two things: producing wealth for the state, and generating legal profits, so how can it be said that they do not engage in any labor?" As the owner of a watch factory said, "It was only possible to set up the factory by working hard; not recognizing this means that labor is 'exploitation.'"[91]

In Beijing, some businessmen took this argument further by objecting to the standard Marxist generalization that owners of capital, as a class, exploit their workers. The situation, they argued, was more complicated: "Not all capitalists eat without working; they wash their own hands and are involved in day-to-day management." Moreover, while it might be true that in some cases owners derived much of their income from bonuses, "workers also share in these," which makes them beneficiaries of the capitalist system. Furthermore, when it came to those who managed enterprises on owners' behalf, the so-called capitalists' proxies, the case for classifying them as an exploitative class was even weaker (because they worked hard and did not own majority shares).[92] While leftist radicals were hostile to this argument, the masses they falsely claimed to represent could be more sympathetic. Some agreed that there were capitalists who work as well as those who exploit but also said that their work should be considered "labor that is glorious" and that the situation was "complicated."[93]

Factory managers' wives enjoined this definitional battle. Like their husbands, they disputed the notion that people in their class did not work, but with a twist drawing on their management of household affairs: "Don't we move our hands and feet?" Adding another body part, they claimed, "Our mouths are always moving," presumably giving instructions to staff and helping their husbands.[94]

Reflecting these views, members of the business community had some very practical questions and suggestions about how to revise the draft constitution. The word laborer, they suggested, should be replaced by citizen, and capitalists should be considered citizens when rights are provided to them.[95]

Class and the Flag

Reports emerging from the draft constitutional discussion painted a complex picture about how the business community addressed the concepts of class, class domination, rights (or lack thereof), and the relationship between class and citizenship. While some expressed befuddlement and skepticism about the CCP's larger claims that constitutional law reflected class relations ("The previous constitution was bourgeois? I didn't know that"; "It is enough to have $5 in your account and you can meet the head of a bank" in the United States, in contrast to China where you can't meet him even if you have more money) many noticed specific items related to class in a variety of constitutional articles.[96] In addition to Article 1, which excluded the bourgeoisie and petit bourgeoisie from the CCP's ruling coalition and prompted strenuous opposition on the grounds that "working-class leadership was not democratic," and the "very harsh" Article 10 ("use, restrict, and expropriate"), the business community also focused on the image presented in Article 104, basically a simple description of the PRC flag as "a red flag with five stars."[97] Since many knew that the big star symbolized the CCP and each small star represented a class, they had to figure out how to interpret this article in the context of their exclusion in Article 1.

As with many constitutional articles, the business community gazed at the stars and tried to divine the CCP's intentions and policies toward them. The same contradictions that kept the business community divided, on edge, worried, and panicked applied to the flag as well. If Article 1 excluded the bourgeoisie and petit bourgeoisie, why were they still on the flag? Answering this, some looked on the bright side, arguing that Article 1 did not matter because the flag still had five stars; if the CCP was serious about eliminating two classes, surely it would have changed the flag as well. Others did not go quite so far about the proletarian basis of the state but were still optimistic: "Even though Article 1 does not include us, the flag still has five stars, so the bourgeoisie is still in; we can rest easy [*duding*]"; "The flag's five stars mean that the bourgeoisie still exists."[98] This relief apparently came against the backdrop of a rumor circulating that the CCP would soon rid the flag of two unwanted stars. That it still included five and was included in the draft constitution surely meant that the "People's Democratic United Front is still useful."[99]

Others, however, did not place such confidence in the quantity of the stars on the flag when weighing the relative significance of Articles 1 and 104. In Tianjin, for example, the deputy manager of the China-UK Trade Company said that it was "true enough that the flag has five stars, but it's only a flag." More important to him was the absence of clear protections in law.[100] Taking advantage of the opportunity to ask questions about the draft constitution, members of the business community pushed for more clarity: "What does it mean that Article 1 only has two classes, but the flag has four?" "Do the five stars on the flag mean that the national bourgeoisie are included or excluded?" Since the propaganda officials assigned to teach them about the constitution were themselves in the dark about the future of the capitalist class, the discussion did little to reassure them. It also widened the space for more pessimistic views: Article 1 was the key piece of evidence for the CCP's "change in policy."[101]

Peering into the Future

As texts, constitutions can exist in three overlapping time dimensions: they are read in the present, interpreted in light of the past, and used to predict politics in the future. As they read the constitution in 1954, members of China's business community were justifiably worried about their place in the new constitutional order considering CCP policies in the early 1950s while also looking for silver linings from the wartime United Front. Looking at the "how many stars" query as a proxy question about their fate, optimism was mixed with uncertainty and pessimism in unknown proportions. However, if we look more broadly at how the draft constitutional text, images, and propaganda were interpreted, their assessments fell mainly in the negative camp. While propaganda about the business community's enthusiastic support for the constitution was not entirely fiction, since at least some of its elite members found the state's embrace hospitable (or pretended to), the overwhelming sentiment, captured in archival sources and *Internal Reference*, was anxiety about their future.[102]

This sense of impending doom was triggered by a variety of textual cues and ideological sources. In Hunan, for example, businessmen noticed a small difference in wording that spoke volumes about their future relationship with the CCP. Unlike other groups who were given proper pronouns such as *theirs* (*tamen* 他們), in Article 10 drafters selected its homophone that had a very different meaning—*its* (*tamen* 它們). They wondered why others were referred to as 他們 but not them: Does this mean that the government sees us as "less than people?"[103] In Shanghai, some called their prospects bleak (*qiantu mangmang*) because Article 13, which gave the state authority to purchase, expropriate, or nationalize "land and other means of production both in cities and countryside according to law," would completely overturn (*wanquan tuifan*) the protections offered to businessmen in other articles.[104] Others, worried that the CCP would not give them an opportunity to earn a living or recognize what they did as labor worthy of state rights, and foresaw a future of poverty.[105]

Since the constitution and the media reporting about it linked its promulgation to the transition to a socialist economy and society, members of the business community were forced to envision themselves in that future society. For some, this was not easy. A Shanghai businessman praised the constitution as "good" but predicted that "when socialism comes, we'll be goners" (*women yiqie dou wanle*). He predicted that the constitution would become wastepaper within four years after the CCP eliminated his class. Not all were so dramatic, merely anticipating a future full of lawsuits filed against them, or just "even more bitterness" than they experienced up to that point.[106] The prospects for managing a business were also dim. In Guizhou, a businessman forthrightly stated that even with a knife on his neck he would not invest any more resources in his businesses, including plans for expansion, because of the uncertainty in the political environment.[107]

But beyond their concerns about the future of their class and enterprises, members of the business community also worried about their individual fates during the draft constitutional discussion. Even though report writers were instructed to accentuate the positive, at a factory in Shanghai's Huangpu District there was not much positive to say: "Even though there is a little improvement, their thoughts about the future are chaotic, as they were in the past." Factory managers, the report noted, "are worried about what happens in the stage after socialism. . . . They say, 'After the nationalization of industry what direction will the flag blow in, and what will that mean practically? Will the individual have any status under socialism? What's the way out (*chulu ruhe*)?'"[108]

For at least some portion of the business community, the answer to this question was clear: there was no way out. In Huangpu, a businessman said that the constitution's language of "gradual abolition of systems of exploitation" in Article 4 meant that "capitalists have no future."[109] "No way out" was also used to describe the end of capitalists after they read Article 10: "Sooner or later they will be eliminated."[110] Elsewhere in Shanghai, businessmen lamented, "We'll soon be gone and workers will be well liked; it's only bitterness for us"; "Those of us who stayed in China and did not go to Taiwan only want to retain our profits and have no interest in usurping power. Why does the government want to eliminate (*xiaomie*) us?"[111]

Such emotions, many of which proved to be accurate reads of what the CCP had in store for many people in the private sector, stood in stark contrast to the propaganda about the enthusiastic reception of the draft constitution among businessmen and by implication of the legitimacy of the Communist

Revolution and CCP policy. As an internal report in Shenyang noted, the business community felt hopeless, depressed, and "waiting for death" while trying to get along day by day; in Shanghai, bourgeois women said their class was done for (*wandan*).[112]

Whether this sort of reaction was intended by the drafters of the constitution or the unintended result of complicated wording still awaits a conclusive answer. While we wait for the Communist Party to fall and its archival collections to become accessible to all, I'll place my bets on intentionality. Considering the already available evidence, we know that the CCP took pride in how hard drafters had worked on the constitution's wording, how it benefited from the input of experts, how Mao himself had intervened to change particular words (using, for example, the more colloquial character 和 for "and" instead of the more literary 与), and how the input of regular people was taken seriously.[113] We have every reason to believe, and (so far) fewer reasons not to, that each word was carefully considered and that the internal contradictions in the constitution were apparent. It was, as some noted at the time, a cunning rhetorical tactic, instilling fear, panic, and hopelessness while also offering carrots to some and vague hopes to many. Top CCP leaders were aware of these reactions, reading about them over the course of several months in *Neibu cankao* and in documents generated by the normal bureaucratic process. Producing these emotions in large numbers seems to have led to some crowing among officials.

Take for example a 1955 speech by Rao Zhangfeng (饶彰风), the head of the Guangdong Provincial United Front Department, to municipal and town-level party secretaries. Critiquing officials for treating the bourgeoisie as either an undifferentiated mass ("all black, like crows in the sky") or rural landlords, or for mechanistically deducing their politics from whether they belong to a large, medium, or small enterprise, he urged his audience to focus instead on provoking tensions and anxieties among them as the CCP sped up the socialist transformation of industry. He provided two examples of just how effective this tactic could be. In the elections for the National People's Congress, he argued, there were CCP officials who interpreted "making socialism" (*gao shehuizhuyi*) as "strengthening dictatorship and eliminating the bourgeoisie." However, the CCP center advocated the opposite: "broadening unity and strengthening leadership," resulting in an increase in the number of non-CCP officials. Rao noted that even though many officials did not understand or were unhappy, the bourgeoisie were "taken by surprise" by this move but quite pleased and presumably much relieved.

The second example, taken from the discussion of the draft constitution, also demonstrated the virtues of alternating fear with conciliation. Not only did the constitution provide a legal basis for promoting joint-state ownership in industry—an effort Rao compared to the Huaihai Campaign during the Civil War—it sowed internal divisions among the bourgeoisie, caused them to betray their class interests, and generated substantial deference to the CCP through fear. In a particularly evocative analogy, Rao compared the constitution to the magic golden hoop that was used to restrain the legendary Monkey King in the literary classic *The Journey to the West* (resisting it caused the Monkey King considerable pain). Using the scary pronoun *it* (*ta* 它) in reference to the bourgeoisie, Rao told the assembled officials that should they "resist reform," the golden hoop, that is, the constitution, will "crack their heads open."

Recalling the reactions from the constitutional discussion the previous year, Rao said that the bourgeoisie clearly understood what was implied by such language. In Beijing, one capitalist enthusiastically supported the draft constitution in a meeting, but after it was over told someone that "although it's good, it's like a chain around the neck of the bourgeoisie." This person, Rao stated, "is very smart—he knows it's a chain, but still supports it and casts his vote in favor." Among Guangdong capitalists, however, co-optation produced louder opposition. At a national meeting of the Industry and Commerce Association in Beijing, some shouted out loud (the Guangdong delegation was the loudest, according to Rao), and others cried or remained mute. In smaller groups, they mostly mumbled to themselves (clearly a tactic to avoid accountability). Faced with the combination of constitution-induced outbursts and fear, the CCP's United Front Department dispatched someone to talk to some of the delegates individually, getting some of them to promise that they would express support for the draft constitution at a larger meeting. When the time came to speak up, however, they stayed mum.[114]

Before 1954, how the bourgeoisie would react to a document called a constitution was unknown to top-level CCP officials; there had never been a national discussion about the 1949 Common Program, its closest equivalent. As officials observed meetings and read documents from the spring and summer of 1954, they learned just how useful having such a document could be—not for generating legitimacy, order, stability, and "institutionalization" but for their near opposites: uncertainty, anxiety, and confusion. This assessment of the functions of the constitution lasted well into the Mao era and continues today.

CHAPTER 3

Popular Constitutionalism

As documents establishing the basic rules and procedures of a political regime authored by highly educated elites, constitutional texts often lack a broad lay readership. From the perspective of most ordinary readers, constitutional texts, unlike the romance novels devoured by Janice Radway's subjects, are rarely page-turners and have the same limitations as any other textual encounter, such as readers' attention span, incentive, interest, time, and distractions. Given that popular constitution-reading was a state project in China, this uninteresting language was surely intentional. It was, however, a problematic decision considering the CCP's objective of teaching ordinary people, many of them minimally literate, about the new constitution. Perhaps propaganda officials were exhausted: in 1953 the party invested considerable resources educating people about the 1950 Marriage Law, making extensive use of ordinary language, interesting drama, and graphic illustrations.[1] In chapters 1 and 2, I examined populations who, other things being equal, were incentivized to be more careful and attentive readers, officials because they were told it was important to their jobs and identity and businessmen because the constitution could provide clues about their fate under socialism. Recalling harrowing experiences under CCP rule in the years prior, both groups gravitated toward matters pertaining to institutions, ideology, law, and class. But what did the constitution mean to those with less of a stake in the text, to those readers who were told it was the fundamental law but were otherwise fuzzy about what it was? As with any other text—literary or journalistic or a blogpost—we should do our best to avoid deducing readers' understanding and instead try to look, in real time, at what questions were asked (and, through this mechanism, assertions made), what comments were proffered, and what sorts of things were getting called out as important even if they were not in the text. While it might be trite to argue that constitutions mean what people make of them, figuring out who the people are and what they say (beyond the most attentive audiences) is not easy, particularly in the context of meetings where *Neibu cankao* reporters and officials were listening in.

In this chapter I shift focus to more casual readers' understanding of the constitution—what I will call popular constitutionalism—and, by implication, their political experiences over the previous decade and how they assessed the legitimacy of the CCP. Although there has been much scholarship on concepts such as constitutionalism, citizenship, and nationalism during the Republican era and PRC, such studies have relied primarily on elite voices, even when using the concept *popular*.[2] What did ordinary people say about the constitution as they confronted it in 1954? What questions were raised about political and legal institutions, practices, and concepts? For example, did people understand what a constitution was and why it was important? Were the terms *citizen, congress,* and *social* understood? Considering that many of these were return graphic loans from Japanese *kanji*, and rarely used in everyday life, it would hardly be surprising that many people would be bewildered.[3]

In what follows, I begin by looking at general assessments of the constitution and the concepts that were particularly befuddling, covering institutions, law, society, the economy, and the military. I then turn to a variety of understandings that were officially deemed mistakes or "deviations" but were sometimes accurate and politically savvy or, as Czesław Miłosz put it, "cases of accidental unmaskings" of those who had only pretended to follow the party line.[4] Some of these errors were traceable to language and dialect, others to pre-1949 political experiences, and the rest to what I have called elsewhere "policy blending"—a tendency for political campaigns to overlap, sometimes temporally and sometimes in people's minds.[5] The concluding section focuses on constitutional omissions: When prompted for their suggestions for revision, what additional articles did people recommend? Assuming that these were not random utterances, what political, legal, and social stories were behind them?

Examining confusions, mistakes, and omissions places us at a good vantage point for the next chapter in this book, which considers citizens' "fundamental rights and duties." While some did not quite understand the text, many questions addressed the nature of CCP rule, what had happened to them during the revolution, and the meaning of rights and obligations in the Communist state.

General Impressions and Feelings

If law is said to have a "radiating effect," to use Marc Galanter's terminology about courts, it does not radiate in a uniform manner—obstacles like mountains surrounding a village might get in the way, for example.[6] Similar to their counterparts who became officials during the CCP's rural insurgency and takeover of the state, many ordinary people were not exposed to constitutional education or to civics lessons in which mainstream political and legal concepts would be taught. But this did not deter the CCP. As documented by Jennifer Altehenger, having come to power at least in part by providing rudimentary education to the poor, it considered radiating legal knowledge into working-class districts, remote rural areas, and regions with many ethnic minorities as well within its wheelhouse. Exactly how this would be done, however, was not well thought out. Considering the many practical problems facing ordinary people, getting a legal education about a state constitution could hardly be a priority. Nor did the party appear to have rigorously analyzed how constitutional propaganda would fit into other just-finished, ongoing, and soon-to-be-launched campaigns.

In this context, one dimension of popular constitutionalism was a collective shrug of the shoulders occasionally tinged with resentment. This remains the case in the reform era as well. In the city of Wuxi in Zhejiang Province, for example, "very many" workers complained that the constitution and the propaganda surrounding it had "too much content," and as a result they "didn't know what was important to remember," were "very confused" (naozi hen luan), and "remembered the first part but forgot the latter." Some could not hear the report very clearly but said, "It's all the same whether you heard it or not."[7] In Guangdong, city residents did not see the connection between the constitution and their lives: "Life's about work, sleep, putting on clothes, and eating—this will be the same with or without a constitution."[8] In Beijing, a worker at a printing factory also noted that the constitution was irrelevant to his life: "Work's OK, so I'll be fine." Another focused on the law (fa) part of constitution (xian fa), which to his mind was associated with criminal behavior. Since he personally had not committed a crime, he argued, "it doesn't matter if I know about the constitution or not."[9] Similar sentiments were expressed among workers in Anshan ("The constitution is the state's and has nothing to do with us"), Dalian ("The constitution's a matter for the higher ups"; "we'll just follow whatever it says. In any case, it's OK for us to just earn an honest living") and Shanghai ("It's irrelevant to working people. I can pull a rickshaw my whole life and never get to live in a Western-style house").[10] Some workers could not fathom why the government would ask them, the lower class, to comment about the constitution, since it was a "major national issue," and even after hearing officials talk about it, they "still had no idea what they were talking about."[11]

Frustrated apathy—generated by the accurate understanding about the provenance of constitutional law as an elite affair and officials' failure to convince them otherwise—was not limited to workers. In the city of Taiyuan in Shanxi Province, the city and suburbs of Xiamen in Fujian, and Nanchang in Jiangxi, teachers, store employees, and medical workers noted with annoyance that the constitution was an issue for the courts and government. As wryly observed by a medical worker in Nanchang, "Leninism cannot cure illness; the theories of Pavlov can," and therefore the constitution had nothing to do with him. Similar antipathy was noted at Jiangxi Provincial Hospital, where a physician refused to participate on the grounds that it "would give him a headache" and was a waste of time.[12]

Villagers also called attention to the gap between "constitution law" and their everyday lives—the same one the government was trying to close with its large-scale legal education campaign. In Pingshun County in Shanxi, some pointed out their inability to manage (*guan*) constitutional matters and that their primary duty was farming. Constitutional knowledge, even in basic forms, was unsurprisingly spotty. According to one investigation in Liu Family Village in Xigou Township, among twenty-four village women who frequently attended community schools (*minxiao*), only eight understood "something" about the draft constitution's content; in another township, for every ten people there were "at most two or three who understand its content."[13] But what was this vague something? A report from Xibei Township in Anhui's Su County provides some clues. After hearing their officials read them a report about the draft constitution, a villager had the impression that it was about stopping exploitation by rich peasants. A local official did not fare much better. After hearing two reports he said, "The constitution is the fundamental law of the state [*dafa*]; the fundamental law of the state is the constitution; and the constitution is a development of General Line on the way toward socialism."[14]

Emotionally speaking, popular constitutionalism could be angry as well as apathetic. The disjuncture between abstract, highfalutin political-legal concepts and people's struggles to survive generated a high enough level of resentment to be noticed by those tasked with writing reports for central state leaders. In Guangzhou, for example, some unemployed workers harshly criticized local officials, and by implication the CCP, for misplaced priorities: "You eat the imperial family's rice and wear their clothes—that's why you can speak with those lofty words [*gaodiao*]—you don't get the bitterness of the unemployed person"; "You only bother to fix up fancy buildings like Nanfang Dasha [an architectural gem constructed in 1922] and Cultural Centers [*wenwu guan*], and don't open enough factories to hire the unemployed."¹⁵ Resentment of the CCP's abuse of language bled into outright mockery among both "leading-class" workers and those categorized as "bad elements" because of their service with the KMT. At a Beijing candy factory, a worker surnamed Ji, who was said to "always make trouble," said, "So now we can make suggestions! How 'bout this one? During the next campaign to suppress counter-revolutionaries how about we suggest to *not* suppress them? Is that OK?"¹⁶ And in Inner Mongolia, a "bad element" asked, in what was surely a feeling many shared, "Damn it! What's all this about a constitution? There's nothing to eat to fill my empty stomach!"¹⁷

Not everyone had the chutzpah, or perhaps the sense that there was nothing to lose, to criticize CCP officials and the constitution so openly—albeit lightly wrapped in the safer language of a question. Instead, a common impression about the constitution generally—without delving into specific articles—was that it was fearsome. This was the case among officials, many in the business community, and villagers in whose name the revolution had been partially waged and who were in the ruling coalition, if one can speak in these terms. Proving state intentionality here is difficult, but it strikes me as plausible that CCP elites, their kvetching about confusion notwithstanding, were pleased with reports about this general impression as they came up the media system. For example, in early August in Heilongjiang Province, constitutional propaganda workers in the experimental area of Hailun County were criticized for using intimidation (*xiahu*) tactics to rouse indifferent villagers about the constitution. The issue was taken up by the Provincial Draft Constitution Discussion Committee, which led to instructions to avoid this sort of policy error.¹⁸ However, in late August, village officials in the province were criticized for violating policy by using the constitution to push for collectivization. In meetings, officials arranged their discussion topics so that the constitution came first, followed by the formation of agricultural cooperatives. The result, not surprisingly, was policy blending: villagers got the impression that "the constitutional draft *is* collectivization" with no light between them.¹⁹

Intended or not, evidence suggests that this overlap had an impact. In Pingshun County in Shanxi, villagers were both irritated with officials for talking about the constitution when they were hungry ("Don't bother calling me to discuss the constitution! We have nothing to eat so I don't care") and suspicious that the constitution was yet another state campaign to impose policies detrimental to their interests. Some said, "We did propaganda for the Korean War, mobilized youth to join the army, told people to contribute money for bombs and airplanes, did the General Line and grain requisition, and now there's the constitution. What's next?" The answer quickly came into view: after the promulgation of the constitution, not a few households that had refused to enter cooperatives clamored to get into one, fearing that not doing so would result in getting labeled "backward." When asked why, they responded, "The screw's getting tighter and tighter; we could hide from the General Line, but not from the draft constitution."[20] The constitution seemed to generate even more fear in the Seventh District of Wudong County in Inner Mongolia. There, most villagers were said to not understand the constitution because they claimed it "restricts people." According to the report, villagers told one another to be more careful about what they say, because if they misspoke, the constitution would "have you sitting in the slammer." They feared that the constitution was just a cover to requisition more grain and was yet another campaign to arrest "bad people." "Who knows what will happen?" they worriedly quipped.[21]

Nevertheless, it would be misleading to portray popular constitutionalism on a spectrum ranging only from indifferent (for various reasons) to fearful. Like many legal documents, the constitution was a grab bag of different measures, policies, and potential loopholes, some of which might even inspire encouragement and hope. Among these was the mention of "special amnesties" (teshe ling) and a "general amnesty" (dashe ling) in Article 40 (in the chapter on state institutions, under the powers of the chairman of the People's Republic of China). While many did not quite understand what these words meant, a report from Inner Mongolia noted that wives of counterrevolutionaries—presumably many former KMT officials and officers—were quite interested in these and made sure they attended a meeting when this topic was being discussed.[22]

Questions about State Institutions

Given the combination of widespread popular ignorance and apathy about constitutional law and the generalized fear and apprehension about it, particularly in the context of unpopular and not-well-understood policies, it made sense for the CCP to tailor its content to what was perceived as audiences' primary interests: material on property and class was appropriate for businessmen, sections on marriage and family for women, and the like. Chapter 2 in the constitution, on state structure, was largely geared to officials who worked in it.

This constitutional playbook notwithstanding, many lay readers perused chapter 2 as well. Many found it difficult to comprehend. In Shanghai, for example, a report on ordinary residents noted that they did not understand the state institutions laid out in the draft constitutional text—the role of the State Council, state chairman, the Supreme People's Court, the National People's Congress (NPC) and how they operate in relation to one another.[23] At a printing factory, workers asked, "What's the 'state social system and political system'?" Farther out in the suburbs, some asked, "What's a legislature?" Apparently they had never heard the term before.[24] Catholics and Protestants, who may have been somewhat more educated because of missionary schools, also found themselves lost in an institutional fog: "Are the state chairman and the National People's Congress the same thing? Do they have the same authority? Why is the leader called 'Chairman' and not 'President'?"[25]

Outside Shanghai, *Neibu cankao* reporters noted a rising swell of questions about government institutions. Like those in Shanghai above, some of these were of the "What's this?" variety, while others were sharper, aimed at getting answers about where political authority was located, who had it, and how it was exercised. In Taiyuan, Shanxi, for example, questions included, "What's the relationship between the state chairman and the State Council?" "What's a 'state institution'?" "Are we a state institution?" but also, more deeply, "Why do the constitution now?" and "What's the difference between our State Council and the US cabinet"?[26] In Fuzhou, some residents asked, "As a 'people's democracy,' why does the article say you have to be over thirty-five to be elected chairman?" and in Xi'an someone wondered why the chairman had to be that age to be elected "if people have the right to vote at eighteen."[27] Residents of Xi'an also tried to figure out what, exactly, the state chairman did, since it seemed to be nothing ("Isn't it an empty position?"), why only certain high-level jobs were subject to elections ("The head of a court is elected, so why isn't the head of the procurator's office?"), and, in another jab at inequality, why lower-level people's representatives served shorter terms than their provincial counterparts.[28] Somewhat similar questions and assertions were raised in Wuhan, where people asked whether Mao's limited role in opening the meeting of the "Supreme State Conference" (*guowu huiyi*) meant that the CCP, concerned about his health, was allowing him to "go behind the front line in order to think about more important issues." They also tried to figure out what sort of problems the State Council took care of, and which issues the National People's Congress dealt with, hypothesizing that the former did "concrete" problems and the latter larger issues.[29]

Given the problems with officials' explanatory skills, it is unlikely that constitutional propaganda officials provided helpful answers to these questions. In one example from Chongqing, one of them, after using the adjectives "rigid," "soft," "written," and "unwritten" before "constitution," vaguely told his audience that "NPC representatives can control other people [*guan bieren*], and the chairman can too, but other people cannot control him." Resembling Hans Steinmüller's "community of complicity," his poor performance became the grist for jokes afterward.[30]

The bullshit-quality of the assertion that the National People's Congress had real power (Article 21) alongside the relative quiet about what, exactly, the chairman of the PRC did politically beyond ceremonial, diplomatic, and military roles opened political space for even more probing questions, many of which surely bordered on sly mockery. In Sichuan Province, for example, people who belonged to "democratic parties" (nominally allied with the CCP but not CCP party members) compared the CCP's constitution to the one promulgated by Yuan Shikai in 1914 and to Chiang Kai-shek's in 1947, both of which included powerful roles for legislatures that were known to all as nominal. Surely knowing the answer was no, they nonetheless asked, probably with a dubious tone, "Is our political system [really] based on a tripartite division of power?" "Is there [really] an independent judiciary?" But to lower the potential risk for speaking up, and to demonstrate their loyalty, they cleverly added, "Will this cause problems?"[31]

Others, however, used this space to call out bullshit and tell the truth about power. Deemed "impure political elements who seek to mislead people," a *Neibu cankao* reporter provided an example of someone who worked in a commodity inspection bureau in Shanghai who said that the constitution's claim that the NPC had a great deal of power was "bogus" (*jiade*). "All power is in the hands of the CCP," he proclaimed.[32] This, of course, was hardly factually misleading; it was the goal of the Communist Party since 1921. Saying this publicly (in front of officials, neighbors, and reporters) in the context of a constitution that tried to hide the CCP's real power appeared to be the problematic issue.

People, Citizens, National

Given that national-level institutions such as the National People's Congress or the State Council were far removed from most people's lives, lack of familiarity with institutional nomenclature was both understandable and inconsequential to their futures. The concepts that attracted more questions from officials, the business community, and the lay public, and which remain unresolved today, were the threesome *citizen* (*gongmin*), *national* (*guomin*, which was also used as *citizen* in the Republican era), and *people* (*renmin*) considered separately and, even more confusingly, in relation to each other.[33] Officials, for their part, needed to know who would be targeted ("non-people"), while businessmen desperately wanted to know if they were "people." But the prevalence of these terms in the constitution (*citizen* was used more frequently than *people* or *national*), the shift in language between the Common Program and the Constitution (the former used *national* more extensively), the names of political parties (the *Nationalist* Party), states (the *People's* Republic of China), documents, propaganda, and campaigns surely influenced others to inquire as well.[34]

First, there was the simple matter of categories and definitions. If political status was so important to one's prospects, if not survival, it was natural that people would want answers to basic "what" or "who" questions. For example, in Shanghai, teachers in private primary schools straightforwardly asked, "Who are people?" while other women wanted to know "what's a citizen, national, and people."[35] In Guangdong, people asked officials: "What's the definition of 'citizen'?" and "Are children citizens?" since audience members could not figure this out from the text or from the legal education campaign.[36]

More common than who or what questions, however, were those that placed the terms in relational context, perhaps because these were more likely to produce concise and useful answers than the legal or political definitions of each in isolation. However, with three concepts, there were numerous complicated possibilities: citizens who were nationals but not people; Chinese nationals who were not citizens or people; people who were nationals but not citizens, just to name a few. Whereas *people* was largely understood as a political concept, *nationals* could have an ethnic component or be merely residential (a Chinese national is someone who lives in China). *Citizenship*, on the other hand, was legal, political, and to a certain extent ideological because modernist Chinese political parties, like their Western counterparts, sought to transform imperial subjects into modern citizens. Given these complexities and the dangers of losing people or citizenship status, there was widespread consensus that the differences between them were not clear in the draft constitution or in the constitutional discussions. In nearly every report, cutting across region, gender, education level, class, and official versus nonofficial status, the same questions were raised: What is the difference between a citizen, a national, and people, and how can we make this distinction?[37] In effect, people were asking the authorities to provide a civics lesson that would help them navigate new political and linguistic terrain.

Requesting more information about distinction, however, could also be a platform to express a variety of concerns about one's position in the state. A worker at a Shanghai printing factory (who was "among the people") complained that the draft constitution mentioned citizens more often than people.

Does this mean that "people have fewer rights than citizens?"[38] For those closer to the opposite side of the political spectrum such as intellectuals, questions about the difference were linked to the very real possibility of becoming a counterrevolutionary, or perhaps knowing someone who was. At Jiaotong University, for instance, a faculty member asked officials whether counterrevolutionaries, who were already understood not to be people, could remain citizens.[39]

Legal Concepts

Another broad category of constitutional concepts that proved difficult to understand were those specifically related to law. Chinese, to be sure, used law and judicial institutions for centuries, but suing or defending oneself in a lawsuit is not quite the same as understanding law as a discrete field of knowledge, which constitutional education seemed, at least on the surface, to encourage. To the extent that ordinary people learned about law, it was more likely to be either criminal law or various parts of civil law—both of which were elaborated on by dynastic leaders and by the KMT in the 1930s and 1940s with the promulgation of their Civil Code. While the terms *constitution* and *constitutional government* had been bandied about by elite Chinese reformers since the late Qing, few people had ever come into direct contact with a constitution or tried to sue using its provisions, let alone learned what functions they served. This gap in knowledge surely would have gone unremarked and unmentioned had it not been for the massive effort to teach ordinary people about the draft constitution in 1954, whereupon it became unescapably evident that the basic building block on which a rudimentary understanding of constitutionalism would be built—knowing what a constitution was—was either missing or had serious cracks in it. That is, an important part of popular constitutionalism in the PRC in the 1950s and today was highly fragmented knowledge of what a constitution was and what it was supposed to do.

During the constitutional discussion, the question "What is a constitution?" was part of the curriculum constitutional propaganda officials were expected to cover.[40] Their answers, provided to them in propaganda materials, largely focused on class (it was a "people's constitution," not elites'), its function as a basic law and role in the transition to socialism, and its symbolic function as the fruit of victory of the revolution. To what extent was this basic education successful?

In the PRC, much like the USSR from whom it learned how to write "officialese," reports about such transformational campaigns tended to follow a fixed pattern: noting widespread ignorance, an official gives a report or speech which is then followed by evidence of change or ideological awakening, with "remaining problems" at the end. Reports about the constitutional discussion, however, skewed, surely realistically given the state of knowledge at the time, toward describing problems in the pre and post phases, while offering vague evidence about new officials, model workers, and old workers to support claims of gained knowledge. For example, in Shanghai, a record of one meeting noted that "before the report," very many women and workers "did not know what a constitution is," and more disconcertingly could not "even explain what the two characters [*xian* and *fa*] mean." After their study, report writers did note transformation, but only to the extent that people now knew that the constitution was the state's "biggest law" (*zui da de fa*), "Basic Law" (*genben fa*), or the "Mother Law" (*mufa*).[41] Likewise, residents of Shanghai's working-class Yulin District and suburban areas "did not understand what a constitution is, and even after hearing a report could not explain what's good about it (*haochu zai sa difang*)."[42] In Foshan in Guangdong, residents learned about the benefits of having a constitution and could, on request, say "It's good." However, on further questioning, they could not explain why.[43]

Not all people, to be sure, were this inarticulate or, perhaps with equal probability, unwilling to reveal to officials what they really thought. Representing another strand of popular constitutionalism, some offered their own interpretation based on contextual clues, such as their general impressions of what the CCP was doing in politics, and probably from what they heard from other people (who were likely in the semidarkness as well). Workers in Shanghai's Luwan District, for example, opined that the main reason for the promulgation of the constitution was to correct mistakes that transpired during the land reform struggle—a view not offered in any official document.[44] Another report noted that many workers "fought war for many years and had never heard of a constitution" but "now understand that the constitution is a weapon of class struggle."[45] In the suburbs, some residents thought that it was a "Suppress Counter-revolutionaries Law" (a campaign which had occurred several years prior) that had no relevance to them, only to officials.[46]

This assessment was not entirely off the mark. An ordinary worker could be blasé about a constitution cloaked as a law against counterrevolutionaries and was right to think that if this were the case, officials should know more about it. But the situation could be quite different in the countryside, as well as among the urban lower-middle classes. Sichuan Province, for example, was controlled by several warlords between 1927 and 1938, and the ROC moved its capital to Chongqing, the province's largest city, during the Sino-Japanese war. Also known for its robust opium trade, it was one the last provinces to be "liberated" by the People's Liberation Army in 1950–51. According to a report on peasants' "misunderstanding of the content of the constitution" in some regions, reaction to the constitution was strikingly negative, which was pinned on officials' "unclear explanations." In Liangping County, some villagers said that the constitution was a law targeting those who violate a ban (*weijin fa*) and that its basic purpose was to punish people. Whether this issue of a "ban" was triggered by opium suppression is not certain, although plausible, but other CCP activities in the area solidified this conception. For instance, in Jianyang County, two "corrupt elements" had been executed by a firing squad during July and August 1954, so villagers there said that the constitution "is a law for prosecuting cadres who have violated discipline, a law to punish bad people."[47]

Since the criteria for who was "bad" were always fuzzy, fear of what the CCP was up to with this new "constitution law" quickly spread. One Sichuan villager said that it was unlikely that the constitution would only impact landlords and bypass peasants; another, after hearing propaganda about the draft constitution, went home and told his family, "Let's enter a cooperative right away—it's in the constitution, so not joining one is a violation of the law." Others reportedly thought that with the constitution, "the government is giving itself yet another way to punish people. If you make a mistake, they can say you've deliberately broken the law, and you'll be doubly guilty." Another said that the constitution is a government-laid trap (*quanquan taotao*): "first the mass line, and now the constitution comes along." Fears of being caught in this trap, and thus resistance to it, seemed to be particularly acute among villagers who were a bit wealthier than the poor—so-called middle peasants—and those with more resources. One "relatively well-off middle peasant" used language similar to that of the business community: "The constitution has 106 Articles, and each one has a trick inside it." In this respect, it was just one more CCP policy designed to deceive them: "First the General Line, then Unified Purchasing, then the 'Worker-Peasant Alliance' and Buying Bonds for the Korean War. We still don't know what they're up to [*yao gao shenma ne*]".[48] Another report, from Shanxi, also drew a line between the constitution and the impact of extractive policies. In Xigou Township, Nansai Village, some called the constitution a "reduction law" (*jianfa*) and "grass law" (*caofa*) because the state was taking away too much of their grain, reducing them to eating grass. "Those lacking grain," report writers noted, "unintentionally revealed their dissatisfaction."[49] However, since the character for grass (*cao*) is the same for "draft" (as in a draft of a document), villagers might have heard "grass law." Perhaps *Neibu cankao* reporters, looking for dissent, misinterpreted this. But even if they had not, it's fairly clear that the concept law (*fa*) within the two-character *xian fa* was associated with punitive measures, which was an accurate assessment of how Mao understood the role of law in this period.[50]

Popular imagery of the constitution as a mechanism for punishment was also noted among urbanites. In Beijing, for example, a man who worked in a barbershop understood the constitution as a fundamental law (*dafa*) whose primary aim was to control people: it locks them up, and the government has the key. A Beijinger who worked at a printing press said that the constitution was the same as the "announcement of a death sentence; the transition period [to socialism] is a suspended sentence." This outburst, which was apparently not isolated, got categorized in the report as "bad elements using the opportunity [of the constitutional discussion] to stir up trouble."[51]

Constitution, however, was not the only legal concept that raised eyebrows and opened mouths. There was widespread interest in understanding another trio of characters, like citizen, national, and people, that conjured up images of state power: *falü* (law), *faling* (decree), and *mingling* (order). Members of constitutional discussion groups in Shanghai, Beijing, Wuhan, Guangdong, and surely many other places asked for both the definitions and the differences between these concepts, but officials only noted down the queries without answering them.[52] In this same family of intimidating political concepts was *social power* (*shehui liliang*). First, there was the issue of definition: *power* was relatively straightforward, but *society* was a return graphic loan word from Japanese *kanji* and not universally understood.[53] Second, what social power referred to was unclear to many people irrespective of region and class status—neither the origin nor content ("What does this include?") nor object of this power was explained.[54] Finally, how social power was different from other forms of coercion was fuzzy. In Xi'an, some asked, "What's 'social power'? What's the difference between this and 'state institutions'"?[55]

Direct references to law, power, and the state were not the only constitutional concepts that grabbed people's attention. If these were at the core of people's law-related anxieties and curiosities, others circulated just outside. In Shanghai, a report on heavy industries noted that people wanted to understand the differences between a traitor and a counterrevolutionary and the verbs *suppress* (*zhenya*) and *punish* (*chengban*). Others asked for the definition of a feudal landlord and wanted to know if it included all landlords.[56] In Wuhan, people inquired about the term social ethics (*shehui gongde*), and *public enemies of the people within the nationalities* (*minzu neibu de renmin gongdi*).[57] In Anshan, some workers sought more clarity about class power, in particular the relationship between workers and peasants. Calling attention to the phrase *worker-peasant alliance*, they noted, perhaps with a skeptical tone, that in the past the CCP often used the term *peasants' role* or *function* (*zuoyong*), but that this concept was missing in the draft constitution when referring to them. Did this imply that the idea of "peasants conquering the country [*da tianxia*] but workers ruling the country [*zuo jiangshan*] is established in the constitution itself"?[58] Other "softer" political-legal questions included "What's a *huaqiao* [overseas Chinese]?" "What does 'protecting the family' refer to in Article 96?" "What's the difference between a demonstration and a procession, and between mainland [*dalu*] and territory [*lingtu*]?"[59]

Economic Issues

The Chinese constitution, like all others in the larger family of socialist constitutions, was not just a legal document. Because it was grounded in Marxist ideology where law was placed in the "superstructure" and the means of production in the "base," the constitution could not avoid economic issues. This meant that those who read, heard, or were encouraged to raise questions about the constitution had to (1) contend with the abstract causal argument that the constitution, or law more generally, was related to the economy and (2) grasp economic concepts, many of which were infrequently used in ordinary speech. In a discussion in Shanghai, for example, people said that they did not understand how the constitution moved the country toward socialism and how the two were related at all. Even though this was supposed to be a cornerstone of their legal education, reports noted that people at some group meetings either talked very little about it or disregarded it completely. Instead, the discussion about the economy focused on an easier subject: the good life under socialism people would soon enjoy.[60] In the Shanghai suburbs, discussions of economic matters were further complicated because of more basic questions such as "Why do workers lead?" and "What's the difference between a 'worker' and a 'proletarian'?" One worker argued that "peasants and workers are the same."[61] This absence of class-based understanding of constitutionalism is also prevalent in the reform era, as we will see in chapter 6.

While constitutional propaganda officials preferred to stick to vagaries, people demanded more specificity, in particular about those parts of the economy that directly impacted them. This sort of request—for clarity, precision, and clear-cut definitions—is yet another important feature of popular constitutionalism we will see frequently; it was prompted by, and ran in opposition to, the state's clear preference for obfuscation. For example, socialism was confusing (since the term *society* was not universally understood) and abstract, but who got to own things in this system mattered a great deal to their future well-being. Seeking greater clarity, many questions focused on the term for ownership (*suoyou*), concepts related to it such as *ownership system* (*suoyouzhi*) and *ownership rights* (*suoyouquan*), ownership categories, and what sort of activities belonged to each of them. Low-level officials in Shanghai—many of whom were said to not understand a lot—asked "What's an 'ownership system'?" and "What does an 'all-people's property system' mean?"[62] At a silk factory in the city of Wuxi in Jiangsu Province, some workers, "not understanding the term 'ownership system'" asked whether the 1950 Marriage Law was one of these.[63] Workers in Shanghai's Luwan and Baoshan Districts also tried to understand these concepts through comparison, in particular what distinguished an ownership system belonging to the entire people (*quanmin*) and "state ownership" in a socialist system, as well as what "national economy" (*guomin jingji*) meant.[64] As with many legal concepts, in the absence of authoritative answers, some people relied on familial analogies: at a Shanghai brewery, state ownership was called the elder brother which leads the younger brother ownership systems toward socialism.[65]

Figuring out who benefited from this new thing called, interchangeably, a socialist or state economy was another way to peel away layers of abstraction. Here the most important concept was *laborer* (*laodongzhe*), since some of the economic benefits provided to people in the draft constitution, such as the right to leisure time, were provided to them, not department store workers, farmers, journalists, or even workers as a category. Since most everybody thought they labored for a living, including so-called capitalists, it is not surprising that people wanted to know who these lucky people were. From Shanghai's working-class Huangpu District to Shanghai Finance College, constitutional discussion attendees wanted more clarification: "What sort of people are 'laborers'?"; "Who are the laborers who get the right to rest?"[66]

As with questions posed about legal issues, propaganda officials are not on record as having provided answers to these questions. Whether people even expected them to is not clear. But perhaps more important than this thwarted conversational Q&A about the economy was the broader context within which this talking took place. For many, the draft constitution and the education surrounding it were useful because they allowed people to raise economic-related grievances in an officially sanctioned platform outside the usual structure of rectification campaigns. This constitutional bandwagon effect, in which people used the constitution to complain about all manner of things while being fully aware that many articles were basically bullshit, was yet another thread in popular constitutionalism. A worker in Anshan, for example, complained that after the CCP's General Line came out, "whenever workers didn't have work to do we only received 75 percent of our salaries, and that after the constitution it was changed to 55 percent." What the constitution was up to, its basic "enterprise" in Harry Frankfurt's terms, he insinuated, was saving the government money: "Does the constitution control [*guan bu guan*] workers' [ability] to eat and drink?" An employee of the bus station in Lishan also complained about salaries, fingering the constitution as a culprit in excessive regularization of the salary structure: "Since the constitution everything has become regularized [*guding*]—even salaries cannot be changed now." Others asked a more general question, which not so implicitly called into question the CCP's commitment to represent the working class: "If the constitution gives workers labor rights," he wondered, "why are there still people unemployed in Anshan?"[67]

Clear Mistakes

Thus far we have seen that popular constitutionalism was characterized in roughly equal measures by indifference, fragmentary knowledge, anxiety, fear, contextuality (guided by recent history), demands for greater clarity, and a propensity to raise nonlegal grievances, particularly about practical concerns. Many had good reasons not to care at all (or know much) or to be quite concerned about their status and how power and privilege were structured. While many questions existed in the border region between lack of knowledge and criticism, some tilted more decisively toward ignorance. Since the CCP devoted considerable resources to legal education, we should spend some time examining what, exactly, was a "mistaken" understanding of the constitutional text. For example, the workers whose comments appear above were categorized by the CCP's National Draft Constitutional Discussion Committee as having a confused understanding of rights and obligations, since the party was not constitutionally committed to full employment and was silent on the topic of salaries and rank in the industrial workforce. But workers were not entirely off the mark—what was the point of labor rights, after all, if many could not get jobs? Since officials could not admit to this possibility, the easier route was to label such views as wrongheaded. While politically correct, this categorization was overly simplified. Looking at a wide range of these so-called confusions, we can observe a spectrum ranging from out-and-out mistakes (largely caused by the tonal nature of Chinese, high levels of illiteracy, people's historical associations with the word *xian*, and the tendency to use contextual clues) to a grayer area in which mistakes were both lexical and an accurate description of the CCP policies and people's experiences with them.

To the misfortune of state officials and ordinary people struggling to understand new legal concepts, the word *xian* in Chinese, like many other words, has many different meanings depending on the tone in which it is pronounced. Since Mandarin Chinese—the dialect spoken in north China—was not universally understood or spoken, it should not be surprising that quite a few people either did not understand at all or mistook the *xian* in the constitution (fourth tone) for other tonal or dialectical variants.[68] In Wuxi, for example, a report on factory workers' understanding of the draft constitution found that some thought the constitution was, improbably given the CCP's atheism, the Law of the Immortals (*xianfa* 仙法, *xian* in first tone), a deities with superpowers in Daoism, as well as Theater Law, since *theater* began with *xi*, which was apparently close enough to *xian* in Wuxi dialect for people to understand it in this way (a phenomenon noted in Shanghai as well, a city with many residents from the Wuxi region). Report writers blamed these mistakes on poor propaganda work.[69] In Beijing, dialect was not an issue, but homophones were: fourth tone *xian* for "constitution" happened to be same word and tone for *county* (县) and, when used as an adjective, for *current* or *present* (现) as well. During the discussion, one worker asked, "What's the meaning of the *xian* in *xian fa*? Why not use the character 县, as in Wanping County [which is close to Beijing]?" Another misunderstood *xianfa* as "the current law" (现法) rather than "constitution."[70] Similar misunderstandings were also noted among some villagers in Liangping and Jianyang Counties in Sichuan who were under the impression that the constitution had been promulgated by their county rather than the national government and was the current law of the land.[71] Yet another mistake, noted in Shanghai among "uneducated women," was interpreting *xianfa* as the Before Law (先法), with *xian* in the first tone rather than the fourth. This prompted an interesting question: If the constitution was the Before Law, what would be the After Law? Like those in Wuxi, some also thought the constitution was a Theater Law (*xi fa*), as well as the "Western Law" (*xi fa* 西法) and, again, County Law.[72] In this case, officials blamed the "lack of understanding" on illiteracy and the low "political level" among the "broad masses of workers."[73] Perhaps the most intriguing misinterpretation, however, was in Heilongjiang Province, where a worker mistook the fourth tone *xian* in *constitution* for the similarly toned *xian* in *restrict* (限), and the *fa* for "law" as "France" (*fa guo* in Chinese), thereby rendering the constitution into the Law that Restricts a French Invasion, probably invoking France's colonial legacy in Asia.[74]

Other correctly diagnosed cases of misinterpretation were less about language than the intermingling between historical and contemporary politics and constitutional education. Drawing on history, in Shanghai's Luwan District, a worker asked whether "state law" was the same thing as the Emperor's Law (*wang fa* 王法), which, while not entirely inaccurate in terms of its general function as "the law of the land," nevertheless did not appreciate the fact that China had not had an emperor since 1912.[75]

Closer to people's historical consciousness, however, was the Republic of China (1911–1949). Triggered by the *xian* of constitution, people all around the country were alarmed that the PRC government was reviving the KMT's reviled military police, known, unfortunately for constitutional propaganda, as the *xianbing*—the Constitutional Police. In Shanghai, for example, a man surnamed Zhang was quite worried about the constitution because the swaggering (*yaowu yangwei*) xianbing left a negative impression.[76] Workers called them bastards, and were sufficiently concerned to ask officials, "In the constitution are there any xianbing things?"[77] and "Will the xianbing come back with the constitution?"[78] Elsewhere in the city, someone said that he "heard about the constitution and immediately thought about the xianbing."[79] Both in the suburbs and in the nearby city of Wuxi, people were said to misname the constitution (*xianfa*) as the *xianbing fa*, or Military Police / Constitutional Police Law.[80] Farther away in Shenyang, the manager of a textile factory said, "Did you see how much damage those xianbing guys did? They were soldiers who restricted people (*xianzhi ren de bing*). If there's a constitution, there will also be xianbing."[81]

In addition to these not-so-distant memories, contemporary events both international and domestic weighed on people's minds, and the welter of political news brought to people in CCP-organized political study sessions could make it difficult to compartmentalize each item. For example, in Shenyang a report noted that "some city people are not clear what a constitution is," believing it to be either an issue related to the Geneva Convention [the Geneva Peace talks were taking place] or "brought to China by the delegation from North Korea," a meeting that occurred in mid-November 1953.[82] In the city of Foshan in Guangdong, the constitution was misunderstood as an election law, the name of a country, a resolution, state planning ("the Five Year Plan is 'doing the constitution'"), an order, and elected by the National People's Congress.[83]

Many other misinterpretations, however, were significantly less clear-cut than these. Even though they shared similar conceptual and linguistic roots as the outright errors, they were mostly accurate reads of the constitution, official criticism of faulty understanding notwithstanding. In Shanghai, for example, the "uneducated women" who erred in thinking that the constitution was a Theater Law also "misunderstood" the document as "generally about capturing counterrevolutionaries," which was not so far from the truth of the matter and was seen this way by many in the security forces.[84] In Foshan in Guangdong, some perceptively said the constitution was only meant for criminals: "Good people do not need legal supervision. . . . If someone's a criminal the constitution will be used to punish them."[85] In the Shanghai suburbs, a man surnamed Yang called the constitution (*xianfa*) a similar-sounding *bianxifa*, a "magic performance that keeps us guessing" (*gei woni qingmi*) and "prescribes what you and I can eat"; the government, for its part, "had a lot of tricks" (*huayang duo*) with "many different policies, one after the other."[86] In Beijing, a man in Qianmen District said that the *xian* in constitution is "restrict" (*xian* 限 in fourth tone), and *fa* is for *falü* (law), so *xianfa* is about "restricting bad people."[87] In Shenyang, the draft constitution was called a Restriction Law (*xian fa*), an accurate understanding of it but not one the government could admit was basically correct.[88] And in yet another tonal variation of *xian* that can be placed somewhere on the spectrum between error and truth, in Jianyang County in Sichuan, many villagers took it to mean "danger" or "risk" (险), which was *xian* in the third tone in Mandarin but likely pronounced in the same fourth tone as *xian* for "constitution" in Sichuan dialect, in which that tone is dominant.[89] Was this a linguistic error, the product of recent executions of "corrupt elements" in the area, or both?

Perhaps most comically given the long held stereotype associated with residents of the Guangzhou (Canton) region of Guangdong Province as willing to eat anything, among the "mistaken views" (such as the constitution being the name of a country) was this semimocking, semireal query from workers at a toothbrush factory: "What on earth is a constitution? Something you can eat?"[90]

Were these workers confusing *xian* in Mandarin for a certain food item in Cantonese cuisine? Was the last phrase spoken sarcastically? That is, was it a quessertion about hunger? Among many household-based (female) spinners and their neighbors in the area, it was. Deemed both dissatisfied and hostile to the draft constitution, they said "Constitution whatever—to hell with it! We can't even get sugar and fish, so what good is it anyway?" According to the government's report, these women were not happy with the lack of provision of nonstaple foodstuffs, and this "affected their views of the constitution."[91]

Sounding off on Constitutional Silences

As political documents, constitutions are important for what they include as well as for what they exclude: groups with claims to power can be brushed aside; issues that the population considers important can be dismissed. As noted by the legal scholar Ran Hirschl, constitutions can "provide an ideal platform for 'locking in' certain worldviews, policy preferences, and institutional structures, and for disadvantaging, limiting, or precluding the consideration of others."[92] So far, I have only addressed the former: people responding to words and phrases understood or not so much. Shifting course, below I look at what people said about what was missing from the constitution. As we will see, another key component of popular constitutionalism was figuring out the answer to the classic political question "Who gets what?" By identifying what was missing, people also commented on who they thought should be included. What topics did people think were important enough to raise in comments and letters to local and national-level Discuss the Draft Constitution Committees?[93] These touched on the presentation of history, national policies, and symbolism, as well as personal and occupational complaints. While these comments were expressed in the context of the 1954 draft constitutional discussion, many of the topics raised in them proved prescient, emerging as points of contention into the reform era as well.

History

The 1954 PRC constitution, much like many of its brethren around the world (especially the socialist world), included a short, ideologically stylized, history lesson. In it, the Communist Revolution was placed in the much larger context of China's far longer history of "heroic struggle" (*yingyong fendou*) which began, according to the constitution, "over 100 years" ago, a reference to all events after the Opium War (1839–42) until 1949, when victory was achieved. As with the legal topics, members of discussion groups had the opportunity to ask questions about this timeline. Questioning the veracity of the causal linkage between nineteenth-century history and the rise of the CCP would have been risky, but pointing out missing elements (through the mechanism of questions) in this narrative was less so. Depending on the stated omitted events, this small speech act could have been an act of resistance or a way to score points with discussion leaders—a way to demonstrate loyalty in a cost-free way (whether these were genuinely felt is difficult to say, but surely possible).

   Questions about history tended to take on one of three topics: timeline, events, and people. In Xi'an, for example, some people wanted to know why the constitution did not include the history of struggle before those hundred years, while others requested greater clarity about when, exactly, those hundred years began; the precise date was not included in the constitution.[94] This lack of specificity also bothered some in Jiangxi, who wanted the phrase "especially in the last thirty years" to be added to the constitution to emphasize the decisive role of the Communist Party in Chinese revolutionary history.[95]

   More frequently, however, complaints about historical omissions focused less on periodization than on specific events that were excluded in the constitution.

Probably reflecting editorial discretion as well as a sizable number of officials writing in, these comments focused on events of very recent vintage. In the Shanghai suburbs and industrial districts, and Xi'an in Shaanxi, for instance, people asked why the Three Antis and Five Antis campaigns were not included in the CCP's list of great revolutionary victories after 1949.[96] According to a questioner in Xi'an, the constitution should also have included some mention of "victories in culture" since the establishment of the PRC instead of focusing exclusively on politics and economics.[97]

Beyond the omission of these events, or nonevents in the case of cultural victories, not a few people wanted the constitution to correct an obvious omission: Mao was not in it. In subsequent revisions, it was suggested, the phrase *Chairman Mao's courageous leadership* should be added to the text as a corrective.[98]

Policies and Symbols

In addition to history, people also had a lot on their minds about missing policies. Constitutions rarely articulate domestic and foreign policies, but many Chinese citizens, told that the constitution was the country's fundamental or "Mother Law," thought that it was strange that it did not. If a policy was in the constitution, they seemed to reason, it would be taken far more seriously, a position the CCP took regarding family planning in the 1982 Constitution, albeit with some reservations, as we will see in chapter 6.

Some of these policy-oriented comments about constitutional omissions told larger stories. For example, women asked why there was no specific prohibition against footbinding and gambling in the document, and they recommended that the government consider including one in the final draft.[99] They did not specify male gambling, but the link between gambling, domestic violence, and larger-scale social unrest was probably well known enough not to be mentioned.[100] Relatedly, other people—unclear whether male or female—wanted the constitution to add a rule banning stepfathers and stepmothers from abusing their stepchildren.[101] Another suggested punitive measure, proposed by a public health official in Tianjin, appears to be directed at women who deferred marriage until they were older, temporarily placing themselves out of the marriage market. Not only should the constitution include an obligation to wed by a certain age, he suggested, citizens who do not should "have to pay a tax by law."[102] To be sure, not all proposed correctives to constitutional omissions were punitive. One included adding a provision that would place the policy of "substitute cultivation" (*daigeng*) on a constitutional basis.[103] Designed to assist women whose husbands or sons were in the military by re-

POPULAR CONSTITUTIONALISM   91

quiring other villagers to pitch in during busy seasons, it was often poorly implemented, leaving many military families impoverished.[104]

Other proposals to fix omissions also had a very practical bent to them. Many rightly distrusted legal vagaries, which opened too much space for slipshod implementation or ignoring the national state altogether. In this strand of popular constitutionalism, the main function of the constitution—its use beyond the clearly identifiable bullshit—was to provide greater heft to state policies, or even replace them, to ensure greater compliance; in this respect, the more specific the text, the more likely people—officials and ordinary citizens alike—would take it seriously. For instance, officials in the Shanghai suburbs who struggled collecting taxes noticed that the constitution did not include a law about paying taxes. Instead, taxation was only mentioned once, in Article 102, as an obligation, which was apparently too vague.[105] In Shenyang, a factory manager wanted the constitution to include a specific provision for factories with employees who had many children requiring additional financial assistance. Factories in this position, he suggested, were worse off than farmers who had many children because at least they could rely on the land to produce food.[106]

Politics, and political stories, were also behind several callouts about missing pieces in the draft constitution. In Taiyuan, for example, members of China's democratic parties—non-Communist allies of the CCP who often held symbolically important but politically powerless positions—pointed out that the document did not have enough articles focused on education. Moreover, concerned that there were no educational requirements to be the state chairman, they wanted a specific provision stipulating that whoever occupies this position be well-educated, and another one that would raise the age requirement for people eligible for election to political positions.[107] But this probably insinuated something else: the Communist Revolution was a rural-based insurgency that installed very many young people with minimal education in positions of authority. These speech acts strike me as implicit critiques of the Communist Revolution.

History, demand for greater specificity, and politics combined in another prominent critique. In contrast to the ROC's 1947 Constitution and the PRC's 1949 Common Program (chapter 13, section 6 in the former; Article 2 in the latter), the 1954 draft constitution was silent about territorial boundaries or policies (an ironic contrast, considering the CCP's criticism of the KMT as insufficiently nationalist during the War of Resistance against Japan). Given that one dimension of Chinese nationalist discourse has been the return of territories lost to Western powers and Japan from the mid-nineteenth century and that "political cartography" was an important component in Republican-era nationalist education curricula, this constitutional omission did not go unnoticed.[108] In Sichuan, for example, *Neibu cankao* noted that among "democratic personages" (among them some were probably former KMT members) there were many questions about this issue. They asked if borders were omitted because "there are still many problems there, which would make them harder to solve if they were in the constitution"; "Is it because of problems with Hong Kong and Macau or because of a plan to return Inner Mongolia to the USSR?"[109] In Hunan, representatives from Hengshan County thought that the constitution would establish national and provincial boundaries and would clarify that Taiwan and Hong Kong are part of Chinese territory; in Beijing, someone asked why there was no provision about liberating Taiwan.[110] Farther south in Guangdong, people also wanted to know why there was no mention of sovereignty (they guessed: "Is it because it's not easy to explain the issue of Hong Kong and Macau?"), "eradicating remnants of Chiang Kai-shek's bandits," or the liberation of Taiwan. When this happened, someone asked, "Will the name of the People's Liberation Army have to change?"[111] This was a frequent topic of questions in the Shanghai region as well, where people from all walks of life and occupations wanted to know why there was no mention of borders, why previous constitutions included these and not the PRC's, why the liberation of Taiwan was missing, and why China's foreign and defense policies were not included in the document.[112]

Interestingly, these questions about sovereignty and Taiwan, unlike millions of others, provoked the leadership to respond. In his post-discussion "explanatory remarks about the basic content of the draft constitution" provided as part of the official *Report on the Draft Constitution of the People's Republic of China*, Liu Shaoqi, the newly installed chairman of the National People's Congress' Standing Committee, not only chose to focus on topics that did not figure prominently in the national discussion as they appeared in *Neibu cankao* and in routine bureaucratic reporting, but dismissed these specific concerns, arguing that an additional article establishing boundaries was unnecessary because the "fundamental task of a constitution is to set down the social and state system in legal form," not "describe the countries' territorial boundaries." He also rejected popular calls for an article about Taiwan: "That Taiwan is China's inviolable territory has never been questioned," and so "the constitution does not need articles to be added for this purpose."[113]

Other features that might have allowed people to better imagine the state (its place in space, policies, and prominent people) were also targets of people's questions. Compared with the extensive preamble, the long section about state institutions, and the enumeration of rights and obligations, the draft constitution said little about the symbolic dimensions of state power—only the flag, the national emblem, and the location of the capital (Articles 104–6, or 3 percent of content). Probably as a result, people commented extensively on items they thought should be omitted, as well as those not there. The flag was in the former category. Predicting that the CCP would soon eliminate the bourgeoisie and petty bourgeoisie, each of whom was thought to be represented by a star, officials and ordinary folk were convinced that the flag had two too many stars.[114] Turning an abstraction into something very literal, people asked whether the party would issue new flags with three or four stars after one or both of these classes were gone, if it would be a problem printing new ones, and how the government could explain the removal of stars to ordinary people.[115] Never resolved in 1954, the CCP, probably unknowingly, finally addressed this "too many stars" problem in the spring of 2004, when the Three Represents policy, allowing businessmen into the party, was inserted as an amendment to the 1982 Constitution. In the "missing" category, another nearly universal sentiment—cutting across occupational, religious, regional, ethnic, educational, and gender divides—was that the constitution was deficient because it lacked a permanent national anthem (one that was "solemn, dignified, upbeat and bright") alongside the other state symbols mentioned in it. (Despite popular demand, raised in 1982 as well, this only was addressed fifty years later, in 2004, as an amendment to the 1982 Constitution). Would the CCP or National People's Congress put one in place soon? Why have a state symbol and flag but not an anthem?[116] There were also requests to have a single flower represent China (which China still lacks amid ongoing debate).[117] Finally, much like during the Republican era, in the early 1950s many did not understand why the capital should be in Beijing or even be called Beijing and not Peiping or Beiping. Beijing, after all, was the former imperial capital (associated with the much maligned Qing dynasty) and was considered backward by many. In this sense, the capital was "missing" from other places. Citizens proposed better locations, such as Shanghai for its economic significance and central location, as well as the Shaan-Gan-Ning border region, a CCP base area in the 1940s.[118] There were also pointed questions about the national emblem: Why was one necessary if there was already a flag? What was the significance of Tiananmen (pictured on the emblem)? There was also critique. A worker in Shanghai, for example, said that the emblem should have a worker, a peasant, and a soldier rather than Tiananmen, which he considered inappropriate.[119] Along these lines, someone suggested that Tiananmen itself should change to Xinzhonghuamen (新中华门), or "New China Gate."[120] Countering these revolutionary sorts were traditionalists who thought that the PRC should have reign titles, as dynasties had in the past, as well as a national Daoist master.[121]

People

The desire to "people" the national emblem reflected a broader trend in ordinary Chinese citizens' constitutional analysis. This document, said to be the most important in the land, neglected to mention entire categories of people or understated the urgency of their needs (and therefore entitlement to benefits). In the first category were the large number of people associated with the People's Liberation Army; in the second were people marginalized by rapid economic changes, natural disasters, and family-based crises (women were at the center of many of these).

Considering the critical role the People's Liberation Army (PLA) played in the Communist victory, the omission of military populations—veterans, disabled soldiers, martyrs, military dependents, and orphans—was an extraordinarily glaring one. At the same time, it was not very surprising: the PLA was not mentioned in the draft constitution; its veterans, unlike almost every other occupational group, did not participate in the national discussion; and Marxist-Leninist ideology (reflected in the articulation of the state as "led by workers in alliance with peasants") did not leave ideological space for military-based identities. This legal neglect was part of a broader trend, which I documented in *Embattled Glory*, of rampant discrimination against veterans and military families in politics, society, and culture.

Much like veterans who protested mistreatment at the hands of local officials and their meager welfare benefits, military personnel and their allies among CCP officials frequently expressed their concerns about being left out of the draft constitution. In Jiangxi Province, for example, reporters for *Neibu cankao* noted that military families noticed that there was no provision for their care in the draft constitution "and are worried that from here on in they will not receive any more preferential treatment [*youdai*]."[122] In Anhui, officials noticed this omission as well, and they proposed to the National Draft Constitution Committee a new article that would oblige citizens and the state to support the military and military dependents.[123] The Tianjin official who worked in the public health department suggested a rule about protecting soldiers who had been injured on the battlefield because the draft constitution did not list them among populations deserving of benefits.[124] Others were concerned, accurately as it turned out, that soldiers' marriages were being violated while they were at their bases and suggested a constitutional revision to solve this problem.[125]

This concern extended to military families and others whose fathers or mothers died valiantly for the revolutionary cause, so-called martyr families. Because many soldiers were recruited from the countryside, and often forced to return there after their demobilization, the chances for upward mobility for their children, particularly through obtaining higher levels of education, were quite limited given the poor enforcement of state affirmative action policies. The constitution, in this view, was the appropriate place for the government to make a stronger commitment. Suggestions for constitutional revision in different regions of the country included a provision for the "special care" for children of revolutionary martyrs, boundless glory (*wuxian guangrong*), preferential treatment, commemoration and burial ceremonies for martyr families, lifetime assistance for those disabled as a result of service to the public (such as disabled soldiers), and a guaranteed right to education for sons and daughters of military families and martyrs.[126] Here, again, these pleas fell on deaf ears. However, in 1982, after decades of social unrest and complaints about their treatment, the PRC government finally included a limited version (veterans were still slighted) of such a constitutional provision ("the state and society ensure the livelihood of disabled members of the armed forces, provide pensions to the families of martyrs and give preferential treatment to the families of military personnel"). While symbolically important, it was not much of a change. Not only did the CCP not deem it worthy of a separate article—it is tucked into other benefits distributed to the "old, sick and disabled" in Article 45—this clause is still not supported by a statute.

Other populations also called attention to gaps in the constitution to make claims for their worthiness and seek benefits. Unable to frame suggestions for revision within the framework of state discourse about military heroism, they resorted to the cultural tradition of requesting state benevolence for those who suffered misfortune through no fault of their own. For example, someone proposed that the constitution include an obligation to provide care for citizens who are widows, widowers, orphans, blind, and mute, as well as free medicine to those who were sick.[127] Another advocated including the right to material assistance to those who suffered from flood and drought, a long-established feature of imperial governance.[128] Some people asked for constitutional consideration in advance of man-made misfortunes they expected to experience. Workers in private stores, worried about being laid off after the economy transitioned to socialism, suggested a constitutional guarantee for employment.[129] Street peddlers, noticing that the draft constitution did not mention them (unlike peasants, private businesses, and handicraft workers), were anxious about their future. They asked drafters of the constitution for some guidance about state policy toward them. Would they have to "reform" like the other groups?[130]

To be sure, not all comments about constitutional omissions fit into neat categories, but they all told larger stories about nineteenth- and twentieth-century history. Invoking late nineteenth- and twentieth-century discourse of social Darwinism and eugenics, for instance, someone proposed a constitutional article that would require the state to build sports stadiums in order to improve people's physique.[131] Other proposed amendments reflected modernist suspicions of religious practice and faith, such as one that would require citizens to report reactionary sects and secret societies and another stipulating that freedom of religious belief should not include Buddhism, Daoism, and Catholicism.[132] However, in anticipation of constitutional critique during the Hundred Flowers Campaign and today, some people focused on limitations to state power, rights, and freedoms. Article 97, which gave citizens the right to complain about state officials, prompted quite a few questions even though it was not an authorized topic of discussion (comments about this mostly appear in the National Draft Constitution Committee's compilation of comments, not archives or *Neibu cankao*). Some asked for clauses that would guarantee protection for those making a legitimate accusation against officials (including privacy of personal information such as names and addresses) and punish those who violate constitutional rights and "use their official powers to take revenge upon those who file complaints against them." Some requested a clarification of the word *compensation* should someone be falsely charged: Would this be material or spiritual?[133] At the Shanghai Finance College, faculty ominously pointed out that "freedom of thought," which appeared in the 1949 Common Program, went missing from the draft constitution, and called out the CCP for violating it during the "Thought Reform Campaign" in universities several years prior.[134] Elsewhere, citizens wanted the constitution to include the freedom of "entertainment and leisure" (*yuele*), a comment on political repression and general prudishness.[135] Others appeared to critique the long-standing fixation on youth in CCP revolutionary discourse. The constitution (Article 94) stated that "the state pays special attention to the physical and mental development of young people." Affronted by this generational bias, a Shanghai worker asked, "Does this mean that the state does not want to develop older people?"[136] A businessman, however, was more concerned with the development of business than bodies and minds. The Chinese constitution, in his view, would do well to include patent rights like capitalist countries did.[137]

In many of these comments, the constitutional discussion provided an opportunity for people to use history to assess and critique the present, as well as to envision the future. These critiques could be liberal as well as conservative; after all, there is nothing inherently liberal or liberalizing in engaging in constitutional discourse. Because this was a state-sanctioned process brushed with a patina of dry legalism, people could express many discordant views, so long as they were disguised as mere questions or suggestions for revision.

Even though the authorities rejected almost all popular suggestions in the 1950s, they did indicate areas of popular discontent that the CCP did eventually address in the reform period. The national anthem, as mentioned, is finally in the PRC constitution; Taiwan is as well; disabled veterans' rights are there too. More broadly, albeit not constitutionally, the CCP has effectively recognized people's right to leisure, cares far more about citizens' organized behavior than individual private thoughts, and has spent a fortune building sports stadiums. On the other hand, the CCP has also cracked down on religious belief and practice, as not a few people suggested in 1954. People's questions about limitations to state power in 1954 would come up with even greater frequency in the 1982 draft constitution discussion (in part because of the Cultural Revolution and the post-Mao regime's efforts to legitimate itself), but this is still a highly problematic area. These tensions between rights and obligations articulated in the constitution and a more conservative approach to political order will be discussed in greater depth in the next chapter. Reading about their "Fundamental Rights and Duties" (chapter 3 of the constitution), what did people have to say?

Chapter 4

Reading about Rights and Obligations

Unlike the chapter on state symbols in the 1954 Constitution, the articles dealing with political and socioeconomic rights (chapter 3) attracted extensive commentary by political scientists, legal scholars, and lay constitutionalists. This is hardly surprising: that chapter articulates a wide variety of rights and freedoms (including, among others, speech, press, assembly, religious belief, privacy in communication) that are neither enforced by the government nor considered justiciable by China's Supreme People's Court as part of its normal work routine. For academic observers and China's critics, the hollowness of constitutional rights has provided an easy access route to expose the PRC's lack of seriousness about its stated commitment to "rule by law" as well as a handy shorthand to critique authoritarian rule. As such, constitutional rights have been the mother lode for a sort of "gotcha politics": easy, convincing proof of constitutional bullshit and hypocrisy.

The preoccupation with rights, and the ridicule it has invited from disparate parties, raises an interesting question. When the first constitution was promulgated in 1954, were Chinese leaders aware that their citizens and people around the world would call attention to, and mock, the gap between rights on paper and state repression in practice? If not, perhaps the inclusion of so many rights can be explained as a case of political naiveté; after all, CCP leaders had never promulgated a document called a constitution. However, if the leadership was aware that its political message was not getting through in the way it intended, that it did not serve the instrumentalist goal of increasing state legitimacy, why would it invest substantial resources to teach this content around the country? As noted in the introduction, Stalin, who strongly encouraged Chinese leaders to draft a constitution and dispatched legal advisers to help, died over a year before the constitutional discussions took place. It would have been politically plausible, and in many respects politically logical, to use the constitution to lay out the basic functions of government institutions and symbols and just leave it at that. American constitution framers had initially done just this, adding the Bill of Rights as amendments several years later.

Evidence from the 1954 discussion of rights in the draft constitution puts to rest the first proposition—that Chinese leaders were unaware of widespread critique of many rights provisions in chapter 3; thanks to extensive reporting in *Neibu cankao*, "Situation Updates" about the progress of constitutional propaganda, and the usual bureaucratic channels, leaders had extensive knowledge of public skepticism. Evidence shows that few people ever expected the CCP, much like its KMT predecessor, to fulfill its constitutional promises, and that many citizens, including officials, "called BS." Knowing that people were aware of the many gaps between rights on the books and rights in practice but not caring one whit, the CCP plowed forward, and in the process violated one of its core principles of governance, the mass line, which required some level of policy adjustment in response to popular resistance. On the face of it, the benefits of producing a constitution with robust rights (and therefore laying claim to membership in the family of socialist law countries, for example) do not appear to outweigh the costs of exposing the state to decades of ridicule, particularly if increasing legitimacy was a primary motivation, as many have argued. A strong case could be made for this in 1954, when a variety of constitutional options were still open (including, among others, not formalizing a constitution, limiting its scope, or reducing the number of rights to those that were somewhat plausible), and an even stronger one for the twenty-first century as public knowledge of the constitution has increased alongside blatant violations.

So why did the leadership include chapter 3? Assuming that in matters of this significance they would try to be rational from a cost-benefit calculation, as well as rely on tried-and-true governance tactics, we should look for the pragmatic upsides to governance in at least some of the words and provisions of this chapter, as well as listen as best we can to its overall tone. These, I suggest, can be located through an inductive approach, by listening carefully to the comments uttered by those who experienced rights talk at the time and whose views were conveyed to the national leadership though the media. Not knowing that the CCP would disavow the constitution only several years later or that it would be revived in another large-scale campaign in the early 1980s, what did readers surmise about the CCP's goals at that historical juncture? Equally important, as far as it is possible to discern, what emotions were brought to the surface by engaging in a discussion of chapter 3?

Evidence shows that many Chinese understood chapter 3 in ways similar to their takes on the preamble and chapter 1 ("General Principles"), but with an interesting twist. In addition to interpreting this chapter as a state effort to induce uncertainty, fear, and intimidation through deliberate textual ambiguity, they also understood rights as a mechanism to induce jealousy. As CCP leaders read about constitutional readers' fear and envy in *Neibu cankao* and other sources, they learned that even though constitutional rights were widely understood as bullshit, they successfully sowed politically exploitable social divisions (controlled polarization, a key wartime mobilization tactic). This was not difficult to do. For example, chapter 3 gave certain rights to *citizens*, but as we have seen in the previous chapters of this book, many did not know who qualified as one (was a "capitalist"?); it also provided rights to some but not to others. Most significantly, the chapter included three articles dealing with citizens' obligations, such as paying taxes, upholding the law and labor discipline, respecting and protecting public property and "social ethics," "defending the homeland," and "perform[ing] military service according to law." Constituting only 20 percent of the chapter, these articles effectively nullified many proffered rights and benefits. Officials understood these as a tidy boost to their power that outweighed whatever reputational costs were incurred when people pointed out inconsistencies between law and practice.

But this is only half of this constitutional story. Citizens' side, like the state's, also has little to do with constitutional law or rights as we usually think of them. Instead, in an elaboration of the constitutional bandwagon tactic, the discussions around fundamental citizens' rights and duties served as an all-purpose platform to complain about a wide range of problems, including personal and family predicaments, related and unrelated CCP policies, laws, and governance practices. In a broader context, people used the constitution to speak candidly about their lives under the KMT and CCP governments. Moreover, since fear of detention and arrest was not uncommon under both regimes, and many dangers lurked inside Articles 100–103, many citizens understood rights as a flimsy (and likely to fail) defensive shield should they be detained or formally arrested.

General Impressions

To illustrate the key importance of timing and context, let us first consider the more general impressions about constitutional rights and obligations as they appeared in the constitutional discussion before examining citizens' perspective on specific articles. Many of these were shaped by international comparisons and recent historical experiences under the KMT and the CCP during the years preceding the constitution. For example, in Shanghai, high school teachers and staff members openly stated that constitutions in capitalist countries, as well as those in Germany and Japan, were superior to China's because they were enforced.[1] Those who experienced persecution in the early 1950s were skeptical about all rights-based commitments made by the CCP, considering them unenforceable as well. During the Three Antis Campaign, some intellectuals complained, schools "locked people up" without any formal arrest process, and during the Five Antis Campaign, the same thing happened (for over twenty-four hours) without being transferred to the courts. Real power (*shiquan*), they said, is in the hands of officials, not a document or formal institution.[2] In Guangdong, constitutional rights were also viewed with skepticism because the CCP (intentionally) did not say who had the power to interpret the constitution (and did not allow private publishers to offer commentary) and because people did not believe the initial premise, articulated in the General Principles, that people were equal under the law: why not write "politically equal" or "economically equal" they wondered.[3] The National People's Congress, said to be the highest authority in the land and the source of rights and obligations, was just for show—all representatives have to do is raise their hands.[4] Some businessmen in Luwan District understood rights in the context of their problematic class status, not citizenship: the constitution was an opportunity "to reform themselves and receive education." Not having contributed to the revolution, they were happy to discuss the constitution and "even have rights."[5]

Rights as something inherent to citizenship, or to personhood in the natural rights variant, was also lost on many officials. In his study of a segment of elite Chinese opinion, Andrew J. Nathan finds that the purpose of constitutional rights was to "enable the individual to function more effectively to strengthen the state," but this also does not quite capture how rights were understood on the ground.[6] Policemen mainly saw them as troublesome because some people might take them seriously, making their work more difficult. Officials outside of the security field, however, had other problems with more liberal interpretations of chapter 3. Consistent with long-standing conservative political ideology in China that placed individual rights in the context of the greater social good, the general will, and the needs of political order without prioritizing them, the constitutional text implicitly linked rights to the fulfillment of political obligations by situating them in the same chapter when they just as easily could have been separated; this was less a matter of "effective" political participation than maximizing social control and discipline.[7] During the draft constitutional discussion, they were explicitly connected: only by fulfilling obligations (paying taxes, for example) could citizens expect to realize proffered rights (such as welfare) or activities labeled as such. Rights are produced from obligations, it was argued.[8] Even local officials, whom we might have expected to possess a somewhat more entitled view of their rights, said, "Now we have our duties, and we'll get rights only when socialism comes" or even more narrowly conditioned their rights on personal performance: "Doing our work [in Shanghai's lanes and alleys] is fulfilling an obligation [*yiwu*]; if we do this well we can enjoy the right of hearing a report or watching a play," none of which, of course, were rights as we usually think of them.[9] During a meeting whose atmosphere was described as tough (*qiangying*), officials in Cao Village in Hebei Province told villagers, "Now that the country has given you so many rights, why aren't you fulfilling your duties?" Asked to speak up about the draft constitution, villagers stayed quiet.[10] In a Shanghai suburb, on the other hand, officials largely brushed off rights to focus almost entirely on Articles 100–103 in order to "push collectivization."[11] Here the wording of the text and the ratio of rights to obligations were less important than the conceptual linkage between them, which gave officials the latitude to impress upon the public the importance of obligations in either tone or content.

The connection, if not conceptual overlap, between obligations and rights was not lost on ordinary citizens. By 1954, many had experienced, or at least knew about, the often arbitrary and despotic nature of authoritarian rule under both the KMT and CCP—the fear of the Constitution Police drew from this deep well—and read the vague language about citizens' obligations in chapter 3 with heightened anxiety. These fears proved to be a powerful motivator for people, including members of China's "leading class," to reach into their pockets for one mao and buy a copy of the document. Not only did it describe some rules of the legal process and give names to legal institutions, it also listed rights that might be uttered to officials should one get into trouble (assembly, free speech, etc.). In Shanghai's Luwan District, one worker told another to "go buy a constitution—it will explain things after you're arrested for committing a crime."[12] There was also a rush to buy constitutions among employees of department stores and shops for "self-study" in Foshan in Guangdong Province.[13] In Chengdu, however, so-called bad elements were dubious about spending money to learn about rights, arguing that citizens can enjoy them if and only if officials are committed to enforcing them, and these did not exist.

In their view, the CCP's larger enterprise in promulgating the constitution—what it was "up to" in Harry Frankfurt's terms in *On Bullshit*—was to calm people down (*anding renxin*) by persuading them otherwise.

Spending money to buy copies of the constitution was not limited to those workers anticipating trouble with the authorities. At a Shanghai brewery, quite a few workers, swallowing their frustration that they had to spend their hard-earned money while officials got free copies, went out to get theirs, but on their return, they found that they could not understand it or easily get to its end where chapter 3 was located.[14] Other workers, perplexed by their comrades working so hard to figure out this legal document, asked why they had bothered. Their response, "To learn about workers' rights," might have referred to a defense against danger.[15] But it also could have been about positive rights—the benefits *certain* workers, called laborers in the text, were entitled to. In the case of the brewery workers, the challenging reading might have paid off, at least in the sense that they would be better informed. On the other hand, store employees who bought the constitution were either disappointed—they surely knew their work was different from those who worked on an assembly line—or just perplexed. We can imagine them thinking, "Are *we* entitled to rights?" Not only did the constitution fail to answer these questions, its deliberate ambiguity appeared designed to produce envy among them, pitting worker against worker and the countryside against the city; farmers, after all, were "peasants," not laborers or workers. As state policies such as unified state purchasing of grain and collectivization generated widespread hardship among villagers and as sympathy and anger about their plight spread to their urban-based relatives, anything driving a wedge between workers and farmers could be politically useful.

Many forms of inequality-induced tensions, such as those based on gender, status, class, and region, frequently surfaced in discussions of chapter 3. Below I focus on three rights in which people tended to complain about what other people received (Articles 86 and 96, which deal with gender; Article 94 about citizens' right to education; and those articles dealing with work-related benefits). Sandwiched between these, I will delve into what people said about their political rights. Finally, I will turn to people's reaction to two of the more onerous obligations in the constitution: observing "labor discipline" and "perform[ing] military service according to law."

Articles 96 and 86: Gender Equality

Gender equality, most always framed as women's rights, received the least amount of attention among other topics. *Neibu cankao*, among the most helpful sources of reporting on the draft constitution, did not have articles specifically dedicated to women's reactions to the draft constitution but rather included these voices in more general accounts about how "people from different circles" (gejie renmin) felt about it. This was surely the result of lack of interest, not sources. Women's Federation branches around the country organized women (mainly workers, housewives, and low-level officials) and transcribed their reactions, and these found their way into local archives. Furthermore, women and men wrote to the National Draft Constitutional Discussion Committee to tell them what was on their minds. The CCP leadership surely knew about gendered reactions but did not prioritize them.

There are several reasons for the relative absence of gender-specific content in Neibu cankao. First, Neibu cankao was often fixated with potential threats to the CCP, and women, as many as there were in China, were not considered a threat. Second, the historical context was not conducive to reporting on this topic. In 1950, and again in 1953, the party mobilized to enforce its new Marriage Law, which had been reported on in Neibu cankao, the official press, and many other outlets.[16] Around the country, party and government organizations were dealing with divorce cases, mostly initiated by women.[17] Third, quite likely many male officials thought such discussions were superfluous because the CCP, in addition to the Marriage Law, signaled its strong commitment to gender equality in the draft constitution. Article 96 proclaimed that women "enjoy equal rights with men" in all spheres of life (political, cultural, economic, and in the family) and that the state "protects marriage, the family, and the mother and child"; a clause in Article 86, which dealt with voting rights, stipulated that women enjoy "equal rights with men to vote and stand for election." As far as the CCP leadership was concerned, many women were considered sufficiently "liberated" by the time the constitutional discussion took place.

Much of the documentation about how people talked about gender rights in the draft constitution was shaped by this post-1949 emancipatory discourse about women. In many respects, the discussion was a Marriage Law Campaign redux, which is unsurprising given that it was a script readily available to harried officials and had already proven effective in mobilizing women. Women who convened to learn about their constitution rights either "spoke bitterness" about their low status in the "old society" or listened as other women did so. They heard women praising the CCP for improving their lives and were taught that they were now "masters of the country" and did not have to tolerate men's abuse.[18] As in the past, they learned that a critical source of their suffering was KMT law, which protected elite male interests and denied ordinary people, and women in particular, a voice. This contrasted with the CCP's constitution which, thanks to the discussion period, reflected popular needs and desires.[19] A new society, constitutional educators taught, required new law, one that undoes past injustices inflicted on women.[20] In Songjiang County outside Shanghai, for example, women were told that "old law" was controlled by landlords, much like Marriage Law propaganda focused on the evils of the "feudal marriage system" that worked to the advantage of the dominant class and against the interests of the poor.[21]

Most of the women whose voices can be heard in these reports expressed strong support for the draft constitution, using Marriage Law–esque language and emotions. Some "cried as they recalled the bitterness of the past"; others appreciated it because of its focus on equality and rights and the benefits it provided.[22] A report from Shanghai's Luwan District noted that one woman named her baby Welcome the Constitution (*Huanxian*), and one from a printing factory included testimonials about how their lives had been turned around thanks to the revolution and its new laws.[23] In Guangdong, some women were happy to talk more about equality between the sexes because "in society there are still very many male comrades who are chauvinists, ordering their wives to wash their clothes," and were especially pleased with the clause providing state protection for marriage, family, mothers, and children.[24] This support cut across classes: university women said that the constitution gave them legal protection, and wives of businessmen, long targeted by the CCP to push their husbands into a compliant stance, enthused about the state's concern for women and tried to persuade their husbands to "accept reform."[25]

Given the genuine strides that had been made in three years, if not in gender equality than in freedom of marriage, urban employment, and relative peace, it strikes me as plausible that the CCP earned substantial credit among many women before the discussion of the draft constitution, support that was consolidated with the addition of an entire article on women's status in this "fundamental law." This broad-stroke picture, however, concealed not a few sources of discontent among women, as well as a backlash among men. In addition to providing ballast to CCP policies toward women, the discussion of the draft constitution also brought to the surface dissatisfaction with the state of gender relations and, through its divide-and-rule tactics, contributed to social polarization along gender lines.

While reports describing the extensive support among women for the draft of the new constitution tended to focus on high politics (revolution, history, law, and ideology), those that revealed gender-based fissures found their outlet in the discussions about concrete benefits. Concerned as many women were with everyday practicalities in caring for families, they called attention to the gap between the constitutional promise to protect the mother and child in Article 96 and the absence of state-provided assistance. According to the constitution, benefits were awarded to laborers, but who labored and received privileged entry into this category was unclear; only full-time workers in large factories seemed to have an untrammeled path. In Shanghai, someone asked if "our household labor" makes us laborers, and if so, "do we get the rights in Article 93?"[26] Other housewives asked propaganda officials why they didn't get the right to time off, since they worked "all day without rest." They also wanted to know if doing housework well could be considered labor that gets glory. Looking comparatively at the USSR, they asked similar questions: Are Soviet women laborers? Do they enjoy those rights? Others noted, inaccurate textually but correctly in spirit, that the constitution has an article about "protecting women." If this was the case, why were women who wanted to work still unemployed? "It seems like we'll never be able to enjoy those rights," they groused.[27] In Shenyang, there was similar pessimism: a housewife said that the constitution was no help to women like her and only marginally useful to female officials.[28] In Fuzhou, Fujian Province, some female officials were on the same page. In contrast to China, they critically noted, the USSR's constitution included provisions for state aid to mothers caring for many children as well as for single mothers. "Ours should have something like this," they suggested.[29]

Women whose identity was also shaped by their class designation had even more reasons to be skeptical about the CCP's legal commitments to gender equality and the benefits that would result from achieving this. Teachers in a literacy class, for example, also wanted to know who laborers were: "We do housework and then go teach literacy class. Are we [laborers]?"[30] Another woman, said to be a member of the bourgeoisie, complained that even though the firm she worked for had been nationalized, "we still cannot get any labor rights." The constitution, she observed, "does not really protect us," and she predicted that in the future she and members of her class would "not have the right to speak." Those with worker status, on the other hand, would be able to enjoy a very comfortable life.[31]

Men who participated in the constitutional discussion, however, did not differentiate between those women who benefited from the constitution and those who were less likely to. Having experienced several years of women asserting their rights to divorce and free choice marriage, often with the support of courts and local governments, many objected to Article 96. In Kunming, for example, some argued that the constitution, in general terms, should not have included a separate article on women's rights; in Xi'an, men asked why, if women were citizens and thus covered by other provisions of legal equality, there was "specific mention of them in Articles 86 and 96."[32] Some officials in Shanghai's Luwan District did not mention specific articles or rights but asserted that the constitution's "care for" (*zhaogu*) women was both excessive (*guofen*) and repetitive.[33] Male Jiaotong University faculty also commented on the special treatment (*tebie youdai*) women received in the constitution and jealously wondered whether in the future men would get this treatment.[34] Some men also felt that the constitution unfairly placed the state in women's camp. In Huangpu District, a man asked if the state's protection of women meant that "men are not protected," and in Luwan District workers wanted to know why the constitution provided rights to women and not obligations, without noting that because women were citizens, women's obligations would be the same as men's.[35]

Recent political changes also figured into men's objections. The presence of increasingly large numbers of women serving in political positions, even though at relatively junior levels, probably prompted workers at a smelting factory to propose omitting the clause in Article 96 that gave women equal rights to vote and stand for election.[36] Reflecting the prevalence of divorce in the early 1950s, some Luwan District men complained, with some justification, that rural women divorced their husbands because they considered them too poor, and the government allowed this to happen. Women, they argued, are already very equal, and the government already favors them. Given these circumstances, why should mothers get specific rights?[37]

Also getting men's goat was the draft constitution's omission of fathers as worthy of the state's protection and concern (and language, since the word father is not in the document). Whether this sort of complaint was motivated by an effort to reassert patriarchy or by indignation that fathers did not receive credit for their contributions and sacrifices to their families is not clear, but the sentiment appeared to be widespread. In Shanghai, the question of why women and children received the state's protection but not fathers was asked by students at Jiaotong University as well as by factory workers.[38] In the suburbs, a man asserted that the principle of equality between men and women in the constitution meant that both sexes should receive equal protection of the state. If this was the case, "Why doesn't the draft constitution include fathers?"[39] This "missing fathers" problem was posed in similar terms by officials in the South China Party Committee as well.[40]

Even though men took advantage of the opportunity provided by the constitutional discussion to push back against several years of women's political and social gains after the revolution, women were far more assertive in suggesting detailed textual changes to gender-related topics in the draft constitution; men seemed content to raise their hands to complain, but not write in. Women's comments and questions focused on three broad areas: education, family, and work. Proposals about the former included giving women priority for educational access (rather than just equal opportunity as citizens), the expansion of K–12 education, and a constitutional commitment to stamp out illiteracy, arguing that even four to six years of schooling is insufficient.[41] Those related to the family either were intended to reinforce provisions of the Marriage Law (such as prohibiting polygamy, concubines, and interfering in marriage freedom) or recommended improvements to it. Men, someone suggested, should not be allowed to make up any sort of reason to force a wife to divorce, and the constitution should prohibit women in their twenties from marrying "codgers" (*laotouzi*) over fifty years old. And since the Marriage Law was also silent about maternal benefits even as women were exhausted by high birth rates, women proposed constitutional clauses that would grant fifty-two days' paid postpartum vacation, the title "Heroic Mother" for any woman who gave birth to twelve children, and honors for mothers with more than four.[42] Someone else proposed an article stipulating that men who passed a certain age and remained bachelors or those who had married but after an established period still did not have children pay an "assistance fee" to mothers who had many children.[43] Concerned about the status of children, they used the constitutional discussion period to request state protection of orphans, economic assistance to help raise children, equal protection for children born outside of wedlock, and the right for children to take their mother's or father's surname.[44] Looking out further in the life cycle, they quailed that children would not care for them in their old age and thought that a constitutional clause dealing with children's responsibilities toward their parents would increase their sense of obligation. "What if they don't and we still don't have labor rights?" they asked.[45] Work-related commentary was less frequent but just as far-reaching in its implications. Women called for "equal labor rights as men," a ban on discrimination against women who did not work, a right for housewives to get part-time work, and better childcare and dining facilities "so that women can enjoy their rights."[46]

Not one of these suggestions was included in the final draft of the constitution, nor were these questions answered by local authorities. In 1982, however, two of these 1954 recommendations were adopted. Unsurprisingly, these were not expansions or clarification of rights as most people wanted but a new constitutional obligation (children were required to "support and assist" their parents [Article 49]) and the inclusion of family planning, which would lower the birth rate and make it easier to care for children, as something that the state "promotes" (Article 25).

Article 94: The Right to Education

Unlike the constitution—which many people are surprised even exists in China—the significance of education in Chinese civilization is reasonably well known. And for good reason: for centuries, attaining higher levels of education was a critical, though by no means exclusive, means of achieving upward mobility, even though the chances of success for ordinary people were very limited.[47] Chinese who passed exams based on classical Confucian learning, the official Civil Service examinations, attained higher social status in local society even if they were not assigned a government post. Education in Confucian texts was also an important measure of "civilization" (or, more precisely, "barbarianism") of various ethnic groups as well as Westerners.[48] Around the world Chinese people are well known, often for good reason but sometimes not, for stressing the importance of educational credentials.[49]

The Chinese Communist Party, for all its commitment to social leveling through revolution, was far from immune to educational elitism. Like its Leninist counterparts, the CCP attracted highly educated people to its ranks at the formative stages of development (most of its top leaders were radicalized left-wing intellectuals who conveniently granted themselves the title "proletarian revolutionary"), and after the revolution it continued to recruit senior high school and university students to implement its modernist (industrialized) vision and reduce its reliance on poorly educated peasants and workers.[50] The party's ability to recruit new members from both elite and lower-class strata through a wide variety of inducements—including "food borrowing," land redistribution, rent reduction, power, ideology, and educational opportunities—was a key ingredient in the mobilizational prowess that led to its eventual victory.[51]

After 1949, the CCP mounted campaigns against illiteracy and supported community-based schools (*minban xuexiao*) to encourage a populist education curriculum while simultaneously saving the state money.[52] The right to education in Article 94, therefore, reflected its significance in culture and politics and was consistent with both the ROC constitution and other socialist constitutions. At the same time, we must assume that CCP leaders, having led a rural-based insurgency, knew very well that educational opportunities had always been in very short supply (particularly given China's large population) and that this right could not stand up to even minimal scrutiny. It was, in short, legal bullshit, and thanks to reporting on the draft constitutional discussion, officials knew that citizens knew this. Nonetheless, the CCP did not revise the document in light of this information. They could have, for example, simply qualified the right to education with the adjective *elementary* much like the 1947

ROC Constitution (Article 21) did. Since the 1954 Constitution had already borrowed from that earlier one, why not do this? The answer, I suggest, was that this right proved politically useful in generating confusion, social antagonism, and, for some, demoralization as well, as Ginsburg and Simpser noted as a possibility in their discussion of constitutions in authoritarian regimes.[53] As a political sentiment, widespread demoralization can easily produce political apathy, a common feature in such states.[54]

Throughout the country, citizens of all walks of life, including officials, responded with what can best be described as incredulity to the expansive language in Article 94. Rather than conferring legitimacy because of high-minded aspiration to provide universal education, people instead sounded off at the CCP's apparent cluelessness about basic demographics and terminological vagueness. In Shanghai, for example, people asked whether peasants had a right to education and how the government would manage to educate so many of them.[55] Whether these questions were prompted by mistakes in propaganda (some media outlets wrote that "everyone" had a right to education, not just citizens) or a straightforward empirical observation is not clear, but the lack of clarity about the definition and boundaries of citizenship, which the CCP knew about, did not help. At a printing factory, for instance, a worker voiced his confusion about the age of citizenship: "The constitution says that 'citizens' have education rights. Do people under the age of 18?"[56] In the Shanghai suburbs, workers were said to be very pleased with legal protections in the constitution but also pointed out that the right to education was untethered from reality because of the lack of opportunities to get one.[57] In Taiyuan, an official working in a finance office advised that the constitution should only include "things that can be done; things that cannot should not be put to paper." Among the things that the official thought should be excluded was the right to education, because many do not have the chance to study.[58] So disconnected from reality was this right that it caused suspicion among rural people's representatives (perhaps because they knew higher authorities were aware of a crisis in rural education but included this article anyway), and teachers did not want to tell students about it.[59] Some people requested that the CCP add more provisions to this article, such as gradually increasing the number of cultural institutions for officials and workers to go to in their off-duty time, a right for people in their twenties and thirties to take tests for intermediate technical schools, and a right to free primary school education (since the constitution said nothing about costs).[60]

For many people, the constitution's blanket promise of education was both oblivious to reality and personally irritating because it flew in the face of their experiences as parents. This was a cross-class emotion. In Shanghai, factory workers were very unhappy with Article 94 because their children could not get into schools ("Don't children of workers have preference to attend school?").[61] Officials who had children in school but who could not graduate to a higher class asked sarcastically, "What right to education? My kid can't move up a grade."[62] Another quipped that Chinese citizens are said to be equal under the law, but in politics and in their characters (*renge*), they aren't. Children of workers and peasants, they complained, "get preference in school," but CCP members "hear reports that we cannot."[63] In the countryside, however, few were aware of these alleged preferences. In Cao Village, for example, farmers said that while they supported the constitution generally, they took issue with Article 94 because it was toothless. They told reporters that the village had over ten middle school student graduates but not even one could move up a grade. Perhaps even worse, of the 250 elementary school graduates in 1953–54, only 110 were able to go to the township middle school; the rest had to stop their education. Villagers "raised objections" to Article 94 because "it connected to their own situation."[64]

Educational access was not the only problem. For the right to education to have any impact on the ground, school materials—books, pencils, paper—were also necessary. More important than the objective fact of limited supply of these items was the government's apparent lack of awareness of this reality. Shanghai workers feistily complained that the government "only talked in high principles, especially when it comes to education rights and the material support necessary for this." At the same time, they envied brawny peasant children in Shandong Province because, unlike their physically slight Shanghai counterparts, they could work in the fields to help their parents if they could not continue their education. What were urban parents supposed to do with middle schoolers who could not move up a class and were too young to work?[65] Poor mothers and parents who operated businesses and were members of China's democratic parties wondered why there were elementary school students who lacked books.[66] Others issued condemnations as broad as Article 94: "The government makes promises that cannot be enforced . . . they're all empty."[67]

But not fulfilling promises, as politicians know, is hardly a fatal critique. Promises can be made and broken for many reasons, and politicians are often adept at wriggling out of them by offering ex post facto rationalizations or claiming they were misunderstood. In China, however, the government did not bother with these niceties because the promises in and of themselves achieved their objective of causing politically useful social tensions. Language was at the heart of this: rights were given to citizens, but benefits, punishments, status, and power were infused with a more important concept—class status—and whether one was among "the people." Lacking clarity about the relationship between citizen, national, and people, the conceptual foundations on which rights (and duties) were established were too weak for any serious challenge to state authority. The government, for its part, was content to leave these conceptual issues murky as people looked at each other with jealous eyes.

Members of China's more vulnerable political classes, whose political antennae were already raised high thanks to years of persecution, noticed the problematic role of political status in the implementation of Article 94. A report on the business community in Shanghai offered a summary of their predicament: "The draft constitution says that citizens have an equal right to education but in practice this isn't the case—when it comes to school admissions, the bourgeoisie and the working class are not the same."[68] In Huangpu District, they were quite upset that their children were being rejected from schools, their slots supposedly taken by children from worker and peasant backgrounds. They understood that the CCP wanted to "take them down a notch" but still claimed this was unfair because they were citizens just like the other groups.[69] Love and concern for their children led some to bitterly complain that it was problematic to "separate children into classes," and "not fair" that their children needed 90 percent on their exams to enter school but working-class kids only 80 percent. It was also unfair on a second account: children cannot choose their class. "They are not bourgeoisie," they argued, and parents' class predicament should not be passed down to them (similar arguments about inherited class status became a major point of contention during the Cultural Revolution). There was also the constitutional argument: if citizens were equal under the law, why did the state prioritize worker and peasant children? The perception that children of capitalists were being replaced by worker and peasant children was widely held but not universal. Some acknowledged that children of businessmen could still pay for private schools even if they were discriminated against by city schools and that many children of workers, peasants, and military dependents could not attend school either—that a lot depends on "individual talent and achievement, not only class status [chengfen]."[70] Businessmen in Yangpu District, in a similar vein, could accept schools admitting children of worker and peasant background but strongly resisted special treatment: "Why should they have priority for education rights?"[71] Others took a glass half-full approach, comparing their situation to a school where only some students go up a grade: "We remain left behind, but this is better than getting kicked out."[72]

The conflict between the constitutional right to education for citizens and education policy and practice caused no small amount of distress and conflict within elite families, pitting families against the government and children against their parents. One Shanghai businessman, alluding to the government's law-fueled divide-and-rule tactics, criticized education rights as an "empty promise *for some*"; in his view, "If rights cannot be completely fulfilled, they should not be introduced in the first place." Bitter that children as young as seven were being investigated ("What is there to investigate about a seven-year-old?"), he accused the government—through a question—of violating the constitution: "Isn't it a constitutional violation of Article 94 to prevent the kids of landlords or capitalists from attending school?"[73] Within business families, some reported that children got angry at their parents when they could not test into a higher-level school. This, in turn, prompted fathers to complain to the state about this problem while also expressing hope that Article 94 could help his situation.[74]

Businessmen's critiques loom large here mainly because available sources focus on their predicament more than on others. There is evidence that other groups whose views also interested the CCP, such as Catholics and Protestants, expressed similar worries ("Our kids cannot get into schools despite the right to education").[75] Unfortunately, there is little documentation about the situation of landlords and rich peasants. But considering that even "bona fide" proletarians in Shanghai's Luwan District asked officials, "Why haven't our children received education rights?"[76] we can reasonably infer that "non-people" in the countryside also had a difficult time claiming this "citizen's" right.

Not surprisingly given the harsh assessments of Article 94, many people wanted the CCP to further clarify its scope to make it more enforceable—a thread of popular constitutionalism I noted in the previous chapter. In Zhejiang, for example, there was a suggestion to change the wording of the article to "Chinese citizens have the right to four years of compulsory elementary education."[77] Neither this practical revision nor others that offered reasonable proposals to increase the level of clarity were accepted, however. Why not? For the government, I would argue, rather than being inspirational, the conflicts, resentments, and anxieties this article generated were at the heart of the provision; it was not a serious legal effort to enhance state legitimacy or to remedy social inequality. Moreover, given the magnitude of the promise and the deficits that existed at that time, it was not interpreted as an inspirational goal either.

Article 90: Mobility through Space— Humans and Mail

Changing one's status through education was a hallmark of Chinese civilization, at least as it came to be defined by the elites who passed the Civil Service examinations and came to compose the core texts of Chinese culture. Since successful examinees tended to live in wealthier areas of the empire (mostly the Lower Yangzi Delta region), upward mobility usually meant vertically through the state hierarchy. For most Chinese, however, moving up often required moving out—through internal migration or immigration. Historically, Chinese governments lacked both the inclination (light government was the Confucian ideal) and the resources to ban such movement, and the 1954 Constitution, like its predecessors, included this "freedom" as a "fundamental right."[78] Chinese citizens, noted a clause in Article 90, "enjoy freedom of residence and freedom to change their residence." Nonetheless, it was well known to all—from drafters of the constitution to officials, intellectuals, and ordinary people—that the police, through the emerging household registration (*hukou*) system, attempted to restrict the flow of poor villagers into cities on public security grounds, as well as to limit the numbers of these "consumers" of urban resources.[79] At Jiaotong University, for example, faculty noted that "in the countryside police inspect *hukou* as they wish. They come and you have to answer; it's illegal otherwise."[80] Put another way, the drafters of the constitution knew that people knew that this article was, like some others, textbook bullshit (à la Frankfurt). Many said as much, and even CCP officials pushed back, but the clause remained. The logic behind this was not legal consistency, reality, or enforceability, but something entirely different.

The clue to understanding the physical mobility clause lies in its sibling clauses in Article 90: that homes of citizens are "inviolable" and that "privacy of correspondence is protected by law." Logically, as clauses that addressed entirely different rights, they should have received their own articles—this would have been very easy to do—yet the framers grouped them together. Why? One plausible explanation is that all were institutionally associated with the police and other security forces (some during KMT rule, some between 1949 and 1954), which many citizens experienced either directly or indirectly. Taken together, invoking nonexistent freedoms, and then making them staples of political-legal propaganda while knowing that citizen-readers understood them as bullshit, were inexpensive reminders of the power of the state over the individual; this was somewhat similar to what the political scientist Timothy Mitchell called the "effect" of the state.[81] This power operated on the level of memory as well as language, since leaders understood they could not be held accountable for bullshit (which could be politically intoxicating and lead to disastrous policies) and citizens understood they had no recourse to align language with obvious truths. This was, in Applebaum's words, the "power to proclaim and promulgate a falsehood ['bullshit,' in Frankfurt's terms], not to convince people of a falsehood."[82]

This explanation strikes me as plausible because Article 90, unlike Article 94, which provided education rights, did not provoke much "what-about-me-ism." Even acknowledging biases in the sources toward suspect populations, there is little evidence of people asking why others were able to move, or receive a letter unopened, and they were not. In fact, the opposite was sometimes the case—some expressed solidarity with other classes because of freedoms denied. Article 90 also generated tensions within the state, as rural officials objected to its provisions.[83] But there were some similarities to Article 94: both generated a mixture of bewilderment and memory-induced anxiety and fear.

Somewhat unexpectedly considering intellectuals' reputation for elitism and disdain for villagers, quite a few not only paid attention to Article 90 but also raised questions about it. Whether this was motivated by a desire to call out the CCP for hypocrisy, put befuddled officials on the spot, or express sympathy is not known, but the outcome was the same: sharp-edged questions (that remained answered). For example, some asked why peasants were not allowed to live in cities.[84] At Shanghai's Finance College, readers of the draft constitution wanted to know whether the CCP was violating that document by not allowing peasants who want to come to Shanghai to move there.[85] In Guangdong, questioners used the word *contradiction* to describe the constitution and the policy of "not allowing peasants into the cities."[86]

An even more critical stance toward Article 90 was noted among officials in the Shanghai suburb of Dayi. Rather than just call attention to the gap between reality and the legal fiction, some suggested doing away with the article altogether, and even invoked the KMT to support this critique. Freedom of residence and mobility, they argued, also existed during the KMT period as both a legal matter and popular practice and was not a problem. Because of this, they proposed, "it was not necessary to stipulate this again in our constitution."[87]

Residents of working-class districts did not go so far, but they raised a broader question about movement through space: if the constitution allowed the freedom to change one's residence, does this mean that Chinese can move abroad?[88] Given Shanghai's status as one of China's primary commercial centers, Hong Kong came up as one of those cities to which Shanghainese should be able to move. Some factory women took advantage of the constitutional discussion to ask why emigration was not protected by the constitution.[89]

At Jiaotong University, faculty and students noted a different contradiction between Article 90 and state policy. Surely known to drafters of the constitution, citizens were given the freedom to change residences but could not decide for themselves to change jobs in the state's system of unified labor allocation (*tongyi fenpei*), thus rendering their constitutional right moot. They asked, "How can we speak of the right to change residence when there is no freedom to change jobs?"[90] By merely raising the issue of state power over jobs, which the clause implicitly did, the state effect was successfully generated; whether this was hypocritical was less important.

But not all were unhappy with Article 90 because it provided a right that was not enforced. In some poor areas, where outmigration to wealthier regions was a standard survival strategy, the opposite was probably the case: some feared that many villagers would use it as a justification to leave home. In Jiangxi, for example, some people's representatives were pleased with some parts of the constitution because it gave them a tool to "deal with" peasants they deemed backward but were opposed to the provision granting mobility. They argued that it would cause villagers to "blindly move" to cities, and as a result, land, without its tillers, would become barren. In the past, they noted, township and district officials managed to prevent this, but the constitution would "make it difficult" for them to continue this practice.[91]

It is not known whether these villagers learned about Article 90 or used it in their encounters with officials, but such fears were probably overblown. The article was less about freedom than a sticky-note reminder that the state had the power to deny it. This view was particularly evident in the clause about "freedom of privacy in correspondence," since state censorship of the written word was a long-standing political practice in imperial and Republican China. As was surely expected, people raised critical questions about the clause. An official in Shanghai's Jing'an District who had a reputation for asking "strange questions" pointed out that the KMT investigated mail and asked, incredulously, "Is it really true that we're not doing this now? This is hard to believe."[92] Workers wanted to know if they would be able to send letters to Hong Kong and Taiwan without government surveillance and whether communication between special agents and counterrevolutionaries is allowed; some university faculty conveyed these same questions.[93] In Guangdong, people invoked lower-level state organizations that might inspect letters ("Are there work units [danwei] and other institutions that can still inspect letters?") and wondered whether letters and packages sent from abroad—Guangdong Province had a large diaspora, and many lived in Hong Kong—would be allowed in the country without getting confiscated.[94]

It was in the countryside, where CCP social control had yet to be firmly established, where this clause of Article 90, like its "freedom of mobility" sister, caused the most consternation. Worried that enemies would take advantage of it to communicate with one another to engage in destructive activities, officials proposed ridding the clause of the word "private" (mimi), which they interpreted, not unreasonably, as secret (so that the constitution protects "secret communication").[95] As with the other concerns raised by its officials, constitutional authorities were not particularly worried about this scenario, most likely because they were aware that their enemies, no fools, would recognize it for the bullshit it was and not take its assurances seriously.

Article 87: Political Rights

Article 87 was the CCP's—and other Communist regimes'—primary constitutional rebuttal to Western critiques of rampant political persecution of ordinary citizens and political dissidents. It included six separate freedoms under its wide umbrella (speech, press, assembly, association, and participating in processions and demonstrations) and guaranteed that it would provide the "necessary material facilities" so that citizens could enjoy them. The CCP, of course, never intended to allow any of these—even at the initial drafting stage Mao preferred not to include "procession and demonstration," and aggregating them in such a manner so that no one could ever cite a numbered article corresponding to a specific violation more than hinted at a lack of commitment—and people were not fooled.[96] It did, however, prove quite willing to tolerate tough conceptual and hypothetical questions, "callouts" for blatant violations and contradictions, suggestions for revision, and even satire.[97] All this was well and good: hypocrisy was as good as truth in getting people to conjure up the separate domains of CCP power.

Telling millions of people that they had a constitutional right to free speech after having recently presided over the execution of between two to three million people was an impossible sell, and many, including officials, did not buy it.[98] This, however, did not prevent people from asking questions, perhaps in the hope of catching bumbling officials in policy or ideological in flagrante delicto or simply giving voice to pent-up anger over previous experiences; either way, it was too juicy an opportunity to pass up. In Guangdong, some asked the most obvious question: Does freedom of speech, implausibly unrestricted in the constitution, have any limits, or is it allowed only within a certain scope (*fanwei*) of official boundaries?[99] Asking hypothetical questions was a clever way to play "gotcha" with propaganda officials. A wag of an official at the Nanchang Medical School in Jiangxi Province wondered if a future communication on his part with another man's wife would be legally protected.[100] Moving from the private sphere to the public, in Shanghai some wondered whether someone who shouted that they opposed the CCP would remain free.[101]

More often, however, people stuck with real-life examples of how the CCP violated its own free speech provision. In Shanghai, someone pointed out that both the KMT and CCP had provisions for free speech that "sounded great, but in reality, were restricted."[102] In the suburbs, a man told propaganda officials that some of his coworkers had been locked up for complaining (*fa laosao*). "What sort of freedom of speech is that?" they asked.[103] Policemen, many of whom had spent several years cracking down on various regime enemies real and imagined, asked the same question from their perspective: "The constitution protects freedom of speech and the press but in practice aren't these restricted for the bourgeoisie?" Which newspaper could give them the freedom to publish?[104]

Among these (state-defined) members of the bourgeoisie, whose status as citizens entitled to this right was still unclear to many, questions about freedom of speech were infused with cynicism and disbelief as well. At Jiaotong University, there were far fewer questions about citizens' rights than about political institutions (at a ratio of 1:4), and those that were asked had an acerbic tone: What's the definition of *freedom* when it comes to speech and publishing? they queried. Is it freedom when what you write has to undergo review? What about the accusations of "irresponsible" (*luan*) writing and speech? Does the right include counterrevolutionaries who spread rumors? To better align the constitution with reality, some suggested that the word *legal* (*hefa*) be placed before "speech" ("people have the freedom to *legal* speech"). They also voiced their dissatisfaction with the clause in Article 89 that stipulated that "freedom of the person" of PRC citizens is inviolable, pointing out that during the 1951 Three Antis Campaign, "some universities detained people." Isn't this a violation of personal freedom?[105] Businessmen also were prompted by the discussion of Article 87 to reflect on their experiences. The constitution provides for freedom of speech, they noted, but "in practice cadres have put [political] hats on others [for speaking incorrectly]."[106] Some drew on comparisons to bring their point home. A man who worked at a Shanghai radio station said that, unlike the United States, where one can buy Communist publications, in China "we cannot say anything 'reactionary' or publish these sort of books" even though we have "freedom of speech and the press."[107] An official in the CCP's East China Bureau raised this same issue, also by drawing on the US example.

Despite widespread skepticism about the authenticity of the CCP's willingness to protect freedom of speech, the mere fact that it was in the draft constitution injected an unpredictable element in political struggle. A news item about Shanghai businessmen warned, probably with some exaggeration, that some of them were taking advantage of Article 87: "When reading the constitution to workers the businessmen loudly say 'freedom of speech'; they think that from here on in they'll be able to say whatever they want, and workers, unlike the past, will not be able to respond [*fanying*]. They told workers:

'Now we have equal status.'"[108] Workers, for their part, wondered whether the constitution should be revised to account for the possibility of counterrevolutionaries spreading rumors. With freedom of speech, what could be done about this?[109] Others suggested including a footnote to this clause in Article 87 because "you cannot write freedom of speech and then say that 'bourgeois thinking' is illegal."[110]

Even after reading intelligence reports about these reactions to the promise of freedom of speech, CCP leaders did little to square the constitutional definition of citizenship, which was based on legal equality, with class, which was purposely discriminatory. Nor did the party attempt to provide more clarity to those who raised good questions about just how free "free speech" could be, preferring instead to retain a broad zone of uncertainty (as it does today as well). These tensions also surfaced in the discussions about Article 87's freedom of the press clause. During a constitutional study session in Hangzhou, for example, an official at *Zhejiang Daily* asked whether the members of the capitalist class could publish their materials and "put their views out there." If not, he continued, "isn't there a contradiction with the constitution's clause about freedom of the press?"[111] Writers and others whose living depended on the printed word also took notice of this clause and immediately recalled previous experiences with state power. In Guangdong, for example, one said, "In the past anything that was published had to undergo censorship. Is this still the case after the constitution? If so, doesn't it conflict with the constitution?"[112] In Shanghai, a writer complained that he had submitted a manuscript to Xinhua Publishing two years ago but had not heard anything back, apparently because of censorship.[113] Readers were also irritated over CCP censorship policies, which covered more ground than any other regime until that point. The absence of erotic literature seemed to be a sore spot, at least among male participants in the constitutional discussions. Some wanted to know why it was banned—a question that, according to the report writer, revealed their willful neglect of "CCP and working-class leadership" and their extreme views about democracy.[114]

But even leading class workers found themselves stymied by censorship in the years prior to the promulgation of the constitution and took the opportunity of the draft constitutional discussion to voice their irritation while being simultaneously reminded that such policies had not changed. In a report written by a union at a printing firm, workers pointed out the contradiction between freedom of the press and the restrictions (*xianzhi*) they encountered when they tried to publish an internal history of their industry.[115]

The right to demonstrate, assemble, and stage processions in Article 87, perhaps more so than freedom of the press, cut more extensively across class lines.

This was not particularly surprising given the long history of collective action among intellectuals, workers, officials, and many others. In CCP propaganda there was much hoopla about this (and other freedoms), which were said to be authentic, unlike the "fake freedoms" (the only real ones were given to the rich) provided by the KMT and capitalist countries.[116] But this line of argumentation was challenged by ordinary people, officials, and, more predictably, "non-people" on historical and political grounds. For example, a Shanghai resident surnamed Qian contended, "In the past the reactionaries didn't give us the freedom to demonstrate" but also stated, accurately but problematically, that "we don't allow the reactionaries to have the freedom to demonstrate either—it all depends on who wields the knife." Report writers attributed his (clear-eyed) assessment to Qian's lack of understanding of class, which blinded him to the differences between the CCP and the KMT.[117] A report on officials in Penglai District also disputed the CCP's claim to have clearly differentiated itself from its predecessor. Fearing demonstrations and unreasonable (luan) petitioning by "bad elements," Catholics, and "students who could not move up a grade," they suggested that the words legal or correct be included in all clauses dealing with rights.[118] Bad elements, however, were hardly on the precipice of protest. In Qianmen District in Beijing, a former KMT official who was now the manager of an oil business told his associates that "Article 87 is useless—who would dare?" He also disputed the CCP propaganda on historical grounds: "Is it OK to have demonstrations like during the KMT era?"[119]

Recalling their experiences with assemblies and processions in the four years prior to the constitution also prompted people to ask questions of this sort. In Shanghai, one worker was upset because the police not only busted up a Labor Day dance party but also confiscated his record collection. "What was the reason for that?" he wondered aloud.[120] Intellectuals were similarly cynical ("What freedom of procession?") and asked why processions under the CCP for May Day and National Day were mobilized from above, and only certain people in specified numbers could participate. If they decided to march, they asked, would the police "really not intervene?"[121] Jiaotong University faculty members were also skeptical: "Is it now allowed to march in processions and demonstrate against the government?" Like officials, they also suggested that the word legal be placed before "freedom" in the clause to better align reality with words.[122] Even junior high school students pushed back. In Beijing, a youth surnamed Wang said, "The draft constitution says that citizens have the freedom to demonstrate and march in processions, so can I get a big flag and protest in front of the central government now?" For this line of questioning, or perhaps because of problematic family background, he was labeled a "backward element."[123]

While it is tempting to view such comments as acts of popular resistance cloaked in satirical or mocking questions, the larger story here is that they reinforced feelings of political impotence. As young as he was, Wang likely knew he could not protest in front of the central government, and it was probably not a large imaginative leap given recent CCP history to answer the question, why not? The CCP was willing to absorb these questions so long as the "state effect" conjured up by them was achieved.

Article 88: Religious Belief

The PRC draft constitution stated, in seemingly straightforward language, that its "citizens . . . enjoy freedom of religious belief." But much like other freedoms granted in the constitution, Article 88 was anything but straightforward. The first hint of this was in its first word: unlike the KMT's 1947 constitution (Article 13), which gave this right to *the people*, exactly who was a deserving *citizen* in the PRC was ambiguous to officials and ordinary people alike; multiple political campaigns between 1949 and 1953 had created many non-people, bad people, class enemies, bad elements, alien class elements, reactionaries, and other such dehumanizing terms. Moreover, it was hardly clear (and unsurprisingly so) what the definition of *religious* was. Furthermore, the history of the CCP's efforts to suppress religion (like the KMT's before it) was not exactly a well-kept secret.[124] Given this context, the wide latitude of freedom in this article just did not smell right. In chapter 5, I will delve into Article 88 in greater depth, focusing on the reactions of officials and faith adherents (Protestants, Catholics, Buddhists, and Muslims). Here I want to preview chapter 5 by noting in more general terms how this article was perceived in the context of the larger discussion of fundamental rights.

Much like the rights to change one's residence and demonstrate, discussion group attendees zeroed in on the contradictions between constitutional rights and political practice. More colloquially, and truer to the spirit in which these comments were made, they deemed Article 88 legal bullshit. In Shanghai, for example, someone who worked at the library asked whether the fact that the CCP prevented villagers from burning incense for the Bodhisattva Guanyin contradicted the constitution's right of religious freedom.[125] In Luwan District, workers—many of whom hailed from rural areas—wanted to know why they were prohibited from attending religious meetings in the countryside if they had freedom of religious belief.[126] Other workers pointed out that many rural temples had been destroyed, and they asked whether this contradicted the constitution.[127] In Guangdong, someone asked whether Article 88 conflicted with long-standing CCP policy of opposing superstition (*fandui mixin*) and the constitutional clause that promoted scientific thinking (in Article 95).[128] Not surprisingly, CCP members asked whether they also enjoyed the freedom of religious belief. In other words, could they act as citizens, or did their party membership matter more?[129]

Others pointed to the problematic nature of the words *religious belief* (*zongjiao xinyang*). Anyone familiar with religion as it existed in the real world— and this included top CCP leaders who spent years in the countryside—knew that people practiced religion in the form of rituals; in other words, it was a matter of *behavior*, not only belief. The CCP, however, committed itself only to belief. In Shanghai, faith adherents wanted to know whether religious activities came under the umbrella of belief and whether people under the age of eighteen could practice legitimately (since it was not clear if they were citizens). Some were suspicious about the constitution's lack of clarity in these matters.[130] In some villages in Jixi County in Heilongjiang Province there was confusion about the difference between "freedom of religious belief" and the policy of "opposing superstition": "In the past we didn't allow people to believe in spirits; now the constitution allows it, and temples can be repaired too." In one village, religious activities had already restarted.[131]

Whether this happened or reflected local rumors is not clear; both scenarios are plausible, given that these spread quite easily and that religious groups remained active throughout the Mao era. What matters here is that the draft constitution enhanced uncertainty, and therefore anxiety and fear, among officials and ordinary people alike. In Guangdong, for example, high-ranking officials (municipal level and higher) were afraid that that a written provision of freedom of religious belief would encourage the revival of religious practices such as fortune-telling and using horoscopes.[132] More often the case, however, the right to religious belief in Article 88 was an exercise in controlled polarization because it invited antagonism between secular and religious people—a worker in Shanghai, for example, asked whether it was all right to not believe in any religion—and among members of religious groups who had to figure out what to make of this provision and how to respond to it.[133] This was a key outcome of the discussion of Article 88, as it was with many others.

Articles 91, 92, and 93: The Right to Work, Leisure, and Age-based Benefits

Returning to the bottom part of our sandwiched discussion of rights, aside from the right to education, nowhere else was the generation of uncertainty, anxiety, and antagonism more apparent than in the other concrete benefits promised by the draft constitution as fundamental rights, most notably the right to labor (*laodong de quanli*) for citizens in Article 91 (Article 16 proclaimed labor to be "glorious") and the right to rest and leisure time provided to laborers ("working people" in the official English translation) in Article 92. Such workers, as well as "office employees," could also expect that the government would limit how many hours they could work, set aside time for their vacation, and "gradually expand the material facilities to enable working people to rest and build up their health." Article 93 gave the right to "material assistance in old age, and in case of illness or disability" through state-provided social insurance—but only to working people. These sorts of benefits—fixed working hours, vacations, disability insurance, and pensions—were staples of socialist constitutions written in the name of the downtrodden proletariat but had little precedent in the level of their specificity in the KMT era; its 1947 Constitution, following the "right to livelihood" in Sun Yatsen's Three Principles of the People, promised to "the people" the right to existence, work, and property (Article 15).

These provisions inspired wide-ranging comments. Among workers in Dalian, chapter 3 was said to be the most interesting one in the entire draft constitution, but within that chapter some only focused on the welfare provisions.[134] Benefits also drew disproportionate attention among officials. In Guangdong, they were supposed to focus on the preamble and the description of institutions, but some immediately fixated on chapter 3, and "especially the right to rest"—an understandable concern given how hard the CCP worked its officials in those years.[135] The right to labor, however, proved conceptually problematic and less popular. Across occupational strata, working was not viewed as a government-given right but an obligation that one had to fulfill to survive. At Jiaotong University, faculty asked constitutional educators, "How is there a right to labor? Isn't this a duty? What is the meaning of 'right' in this case?"[136] Out in the suburbs, the fact that people were obliged to work was considered a simple fact of life: "Why's it called a 'right'?"[137] Workers in the city ribbed officials: "Labor is glorious, but we don't get much money for it"; "Is working in cultural entertainment (*wenyu*) and sports glorious?" "Is working as a dancing girl?"[138] "If a counterrevolutionary is a good worker, is that glorious?"[139] Skilled workers critiqued those who performed manual labor as "crass": "What's the big deal about this?" they half-asked, half-mocked just before they were educated and realized the error of their ways.[140] Even officials, from whom we might expect a bit more conformity, were irked and perplexed by the draft constitution's language: "Everyone works for a living," some noted in Shanghai. Equally problematic from officials' perspective, criminals were often sent to perform "reform through labor." If labor is used as a form of punishment, they argued with logical precision, it means that "people don't like to work, so work is an obligation, not a right."[141]

Most comments, however, focused on the large gap between the status and benefits associated with labor and China's bleak economy at that time; as always, and as emphasized by reader-response literary theory discussed in the introduction to this book, context mattered a great deal. As with other promised but unfulfilled rights, the constitutional discussion provided a relatively safe platform to raise many other, often nonlegal, problems. But unlike, say, the right to move one's residence or demonstrate, work, connected as it was with survival, social status, and marriage prospects, concerned almost everyone, and as a result it prompted the highest volume of cynical remarks, mockery, and outright astonishment. Urban unemployment was probably the issue that bothered people the most. Middle-aged female street-level officials in Jing'an District in Shanghai, for example, assured their superiors that the constitution was "good" before complaining about the large numbers of unemployed people and age restrictions imposed by employers. Since "nothing could be done about this," there could be no "guarantees" about rights. Because they did not work, they continued, "how can we even talk about the right to rest?"[142] Unemployed workers in the city appeared to be particularly displeased. One wanted the government to replace the adjective "gradually" (zhubu) with *immediately* to describe the time during which the state would expand employment in Article 91, and another man, described as an ordinary city person, was "dissatisfied" with the article because he did not have work even though the constitution said he had labor rights.[143]

Having a job, however, was not necessarily enough to close the gap between rights and reality, since the government also promised leisure time and regulated work hours. In Luwan District, a worker described by propaganda officials as "backward," commented that even though Chairman Mao had promised "pay according to work," he had worked hard and was paid little and was not provided any time to rest despite working twelve consecutive hours. "There's no future as a worker," he concluded, contradicting the draft constitution's description of the working class as the country's leaders.[144] Other workers were grumpy because the government abolished holidays that were specific to certain trades (gongxiu), which they believed should have been folded into their class-based right to rest as "laborers."[145] Some were convinced that the right to rest would only be provided to "model workers." Propaganda officials characterized such comments as cynical (guaihua) and the product of weak class consciousness rather than accepting the worker's observation that he consistently worked twelve-hour days without a break.[146] Soldiers of the People's

Liberation Army (or perhaps their family members), most of whom worked more than twelve hours a day, also commented that they deserved constitutionally mandated leisure time of "several days" per year.[147]

In Guangdong and many other provinces, people across a wide variety of occupations were dismayed by the lack of alignment between the constitution and their everyday work lives. In Guangdong, for instance, officials at the provincial radio station were irritated that the CCP exploited their constitutionally promised rest time to force them to engage in political study.[148] While some workers praised the CCP for its concern (*guanxin*) because they had been exploited and looked down on by their wives, those who were unemployed were left empty handed.[149] Like their Shanghai counterparts, they complained that the CCP was taking too long to right China's economy: "Now the constitution has a provision that gives us labor rights, but we wait and wait and there's no work and no way to get by. I graduated primary school and can't go higher, but I can't work in agricultural either."[150] In Fuzhou in Fujian Province, people associated with China's democratic parties also jabbed officials: "Why are so many people unemployed when there were so many labor rights?"[151] Some students at a lower-status preparatory school (*bu xuexiao*) in Chongqing (who appear to have come from the countryside) joined the criticism: "The draft constitution guarantees citizens' labor rights but we didn't get land, don't have work, can't join a production unit and don't have a place to study—so what's this about labor rights? The center says one thing and what the lower levels enforce is something else." This situation and others like it, the report noted, led "some" ordinary residents and unemployed people to be unhappy with the draft constitution.[152]

Upset with promissory overkill, many people went beyond calling out inconsistencies by requesting greater clarity and proposing revisions that would serve this end. Lurking just beneath the surface of these suggestions, however, was the practical and emotional matter of who would benefit from state policies, under what conditions, and how the constitution might be used to advance these. For example, at Jiaotong University, students wanted to know if having tests on Sundays—a day off for them—violated Article 94, which provided leisure time.[153] Faculty at Shanghai Finance College pushed back against the broad promise of labor rights by pointing out that, due to variables such as the size of a population, level of mechanization, supply of fertilizer, and other factors, only some people were positioned to enjoy these.[154] Gender equality was another issue. One man pointed out that his wife could not find work that would make her a laborer, but she was still working from morning to evening—shouldn't she get the right to rest?[155] For the sake of obtaining benefits, officials also considered themselves laborers or office workers ("After eight hours of work can I not participate in meetings?").[156] In Shanghai, owners of small and medium-sized businesses said that it was not fair that they were not included in the right to rest or to get material assistance when they became sick or old or lost their capacity to work; "capitalists with skills," they argued, should also get rights, noting that in handicraft shops "the boss also works." They, too, proposed exchanging the concept "laborer" with *citizen*.[157]

In letters submitted to the National Draft Constitutional Discussion Committee, many proposed revisions aimed at improving the living conditions of populations pushed aside by the draft constitution's focus on laborers and office workers. Working hours for handicraft workers, some wrote, should be limited to eight hours a day, and nine to ten hours for those who worked in commercial enterprises. More generally, the document should precisely say how long rest lasts and how many hours work can continue in the absence of extraordinary circumstances and should clearly state that salary would be provided during rest breaks, vacations, and convalescences.[158] Other suggestions for revising the draft constitution included giving the children of workers and low-level officials priority for employment, government assistance for unemployed people "until unemployment problems are solved," and adding descriptors to the right to work, such as the right to *choose* work.[159]

Reports filed by *Neibu cankao* reporters were also full of requests for clearer constitutional commitments. In Nanjing, a member of a democratic party asked why the draft constitution did not specify an eight-hour workday system, and in Beijing some officials wanted the constitution to "solve their personal problems," including obtaining a higher salary.[160] Not many had high hopes for such interventions, however. In Harbin, some workers thought that factory officials would successfully thwart any top-down mandate to limit working hours even if they were in the constitution, and in Beijing a store worker surnamed Jiao said, "What labor rights? It's the same with a law as without one—workers still don't have enough to eat." His skepticism was explained by noting his rich peasant background.[161] This might not have been entirely off the mark. Even though labor rights were awarded to citizens, people were aware that class status mattered as well. In Shanghai, some people, who defined themselves as bourgeoisie, said that it was going too far (*guohuo le*) to give these rights to us [as citizens] while "knowing that we cannot enjoy them" [as bourgeoisie] and that even though they might work, they could not be considered laborers either.[162] From their perspective, humiliating them was what the CCP was up to in promulgating the constitution.

The awareness that constitutional benefits would be selectively distributed was not limited to politically problematic classes such as the bourgeoisie or those whose family backgrounds were tainted. Even among the state's favored classes, the constitution's combination of vague language ("laborers," "office workers," "citizen") and silence about how and when benefits would be distributed created feelings of jealousy and resentment, which poked through the questions they asked during the draft constitutional discussion. In Shanghai's Luwan District, for example, workers asked whether young and middle-aged people would also get material support from the state if they lost their ability to work, a not uncommon occurrence given the poor safety conditions in many factories, implying that this should not be based only on age.[163] They also asked why workers in small firms do not get labor insurance—a topic not covered by the constitution directly (but indirectly through the mention of benefits) but rather the Labor Insurance Law, which also had divide-and-rule elements to it.[164] In the suburbs, construction workers were upset because they did not get labor insurance. In their view, they were the same as factory workers who did enjoy this benefit, only mobile.[165] Peasants, despite their designation as allies of the working class and having formed the backbone of the CCP and PLA during the 1930s and 1940s, were left out of the constitution's benefits articles entirely. This did not go unnoticed. As noted in chapter 1, in Jiangxi Province, people's representatives were said to be unhappy that the government was only concerned about workers' and office employees' leisure time and working conditions while ignoring peasants.[166] Shanghai workers, many of whom came from the countryside, also found this strange and asked, "Why don't peasants have the right to rest?" as did officials in the CCP's South China Bureau.[167]

Constitutional propaganda officials did not answer these questions, thus avoiding difficult historical, ideological, and even moral questions about who deserved to benefit from the revolution. They certainly could not have pointed out the underlying political logic at work in the constitution and the discussion around it. Like many other CCP policies, the constitution's drafters deployed divide-and-rule tactics to pit classes and genders against one another. Not only did this prevent the formation of a united front against the CCP, it also, in the absence of any meaningful market mechanism, enhanced the CCP's power as the arbiter of who gained benefits and status.

Obligations

Whatever reputational risks the CCP took on by promising many benefits that might take some time to be realized (if at all) were decisively outweighed by the inclusion of several obligations laid out in the last several articles of chapter 3: to pay taxes, observe labor discipline, serve in the military, and uphold social ethics. As we have seen in the discussion of officials' take on the draft constitution, many people did not view rights independently of obligations but rather as a quid pro quo arrangement: citizens get rights only because they fulfill obligations. By this logic, awarding more rights was a useful mechanism to achieve greater *discipline*, not personal freedom. During the constitutional discussion, officials did not mind discussing rights because it opened space to talk about, or even focus on, citizens' obligations, which were conveniently placed in the same chapter; tough questions from attendees were a secondary concern, since they did not have to answer them anyway.

Among citizens' obligations, two were particularly useful in generating the "state effect" that the CCP found so useful in controlling the behavior of potentially problematic lower-class citizens: labor discipline (*laodong jilü*) and military conscription (*fubingyi*). While people such as businessmen, rich peasants, and intellectuals were constitutionally terrorized through the frequent use of words such as *abolish* or *eliminate* (*xiaomie*), or the ambiguity in concepts such as *people* and *citizen*, workers and villagers required a different vocabulary, one drawn from their own well of fears.

Labor discipline proved an extremely useful legal concept in this respect. In part, this was because of its inherent vagueness—as a faculty member at Jiaotong University asked, "What's labor discipline? What aspects does it include?"[168] Even considering the subjective nature of assessing discipline, the range of possible infractions was vast, potentially including time of arrival or departure from work, how one interacted with people and machines, how one spent leisure time, and more. It was also useful because some workers could not satisfy their superiors' expectations about appropriate conduct in and out of the workplace, a common occurrence in the early stages of industrialization.[169] In Shanghai, for example, managers complained that workers gambled, had extramarital affairs, made false reports about production, and even "mistakenly thought that they will become bosses and forgot about labor discipline," all of which they duly promised to change after receiving party education.[170] Other complaints included workers disrespecting public property (taking factory items for personal use), leaving work without permission, seeking status (*nao diwei*), sleeping on the job, seeking to start their own business, chasing fame and fortune while disparaging manual labor, not following factory plans, and "pretending to be CCP members to attract women" (although not stated, these reports suggest that these workers were male; the Shanghai workforce included many women). Workers were also accused by their superiors of "economism," whose symptoms included fear of low salaries in state-owned enterprises, dissatisfaction with their current standard of living, complaining that they got the same no matter how hard they worked, and grumbling that private firms were under "capitalist exploitation" but their salaries were higher.[171] Any of these could come under the rubric of disciplinary problems.

Within this context—whether real or partially concocted—workers were very alarmed by the inclusion of labor discipline in a document as grandiose as a constitution. Their status as China's leading class notwithstanding, workers clearly understood the totalitarian aspirations of constitutional discipline because it linked their personal, work-based transgressions (or accusations of such transgressions), to law, which was widely seen as punitive, rather than campaigns, which were understood as short-term efforts to raise production through discipline. Workers all around the country expressed deep reservations about this obligation but, more importantly from the state's perspective, their fear of it as well. In Shanghai, reports noted that workers were "not happy" with the concepts *labor discipline* and *obeying the law* and wondered how it happened that "discipline" got included in the constitution. One worried: "Will violations of labor discipline be legal violations?" Courts, he argued, should not treat labor discipline problems as criminal offenses, which he associated with counterrevolutionaries, not ordinary workers like himself.[172] Another proposed to omit the clause from the constitution because he feared that "leaving work a couple of minutes early will be a legal violation"; others called its inclusion too harsh (*tai lihai*), and a "small issue" that, should it be considered a violation of state law, would be hard to swallow (*chibuxiao*).[173] These sentiments were not restricted to workers. Since it was unclear what labor was, and therefore who exactly laborers were, labor discipline could be applied to other sectors as well if this proved useful. An official in Luwan District mocked the CCP's intrusiveness into minutiae such as labor discipline, asking a comrade, "There's no article that allows you to eat, so why are you eating?"[174]

Similar reactions were recorded outside Shanghai, and as a matter of course were made known to central state leaders. In Anshan, a worker surnamed Guo, categorized as someone with a "confused understanding of rights and obligations," was astonished that the constitution "even has a provision for the small issue of workers' labor discipline": "That's far too strict!" he complained. Another, apparently impressed by how far the constitution went in dealing with small matters, asked his union chair whether the constitution would take care of (*guan bu guan*) his youngest son if he could not continue studying or find a job.[175] Officials at *Nanfang Daily* in Guangzhou suggested that authorities excise Article 100 because it had too many demands.[176] At a silk factory in Wuxi, some workers feared that if their labor discipline was not up to snuff they would be punished. "Now there's a law for everything now" (*yangyang youfa*), they complained, and added mockingly, "It's raining now—why isn't there a law to stop it?"[177] Such fears were not entirely unfounded. As seen in chapter 2, in Tianjin, "capitalists" wondered whether it was a constitutional violation if workers came late, left early, and violated labor discipline, and if producing substandard goods and not completing a job on time were criminal offenses, perhaps thinking that this would give them more leverage against their workforce.[178]

Whether employers or officials invoked Article 100 to fine, arrest, or otherwise discipline workers is not known (but probable). However, evidence does suggest that it induced anxiety and fear. At Jiaotong, an employee of the engineering department wrote in a self-criticism, "Only after I studied the constitution did I realize that leaving work early violates the constitution," behavior that he promised to change.[179] Some workers also got this message. In a textile mill in a suburb of Shanghai, workers who saw the phrase "labor discipline" in Article 100 told each other: "It's in the constitution, so we'd better observe it!"[180]

Such comments could have been hyperbole; report writers had to include statements attesting to the effectiveness or popularity of certain provisions of the constitution. Whether out of fear or respect (or a combination of these), both could be useful in inducing compliance. But in the end, none of the expressions of astonishment, fear, mockery, or respect made any difference to CCP leaders who read these reports. Not only did Article 100 remain unchanged, the 1982 Constitution (Article 53), which was largely based on the 1954 version, also included labor discipline in its long, vague list of citizen obligations: "Citizens of the People's Republic of China must abide by the constitution and the law, keep state secrets, protect public property and observe labor discipline and public order and respect social ethics." After years of social instability induced by the Cultural Revolution, having this article in the state's legal arsenal was as useful as it was in 1954.

Article 103 added yet another layer of anxiety by stating that it was the "sacred duty" of every citizen to "defend the homeland" and their "glorious duty" to "perform military service according to law." Much like the provision of rights and labor discipline, the sources of popular stress lay just beneath the surface, and thus easily triggered by words such as *defend* and *military service*; the War of Resistance against Japan (1937–45), the Civil War (1945–49), and the Korean War (1950–53) all occurred in the ten years prior to the promulgation of the draft constitution and were fresh in people's memories. Thanks to the constitutional discussion, social anxiety about conscription, requests for clarification, proposals for revision, and criticisms of wording were conveyed to China's leaders in *Neibu cankao* and other documentation from May to August 1954, but the article remained unchanged. Even a suggestion as politically correct and easily revised as eliminating the word "sacred" (shensheng) was ignored.[181]

Anxiety about military service cut across social class, region, and political status but was particularly acute among workers, villagers, and officials since they, more than politically suspect but less numerous capitalists, were likely to be drafted. In Shanghai, for instance, a report documenting the reactions among its commercial class noted that the use of the word "obligation" in the draft constitution meant that, unlike the past when military service was voluntary, "from here on in conscription will probably require coercion" (jinhou dagai yao qiangpole).[182] In Neibu cankao, young Shanghainese were described as very worried about conscription, and asked propaganda officials why conscription existed if the constitution's preamble stated that China was "fond of peace."[183] Perhaps reflecting the harsh toll of warfare in the Northeast from the early 1930s, in Anshan many workers and villagers were described as panic-stricken (jingkong) about their glorious obligation to serve in the army. Villagers said, "From here on in all youth will have to serve three years," an exceptionally long time for a young male villager to be away from his home.[184] In Shenyang, very many people were concerned about enlistment; workers said that their families would have a hard time getting by should this happen.[185] Farther south in Beijing, a worker who had family in the countryside had similar worries: "What will they do if I have to join the army?" and in Taiyuan in Shanxi, a worker in "Work Area 109" said that he feared the conscription system would rely on a draft (choubing).[186] Moving farther south to Jiangxi, a province with a robust military tradition which furnished many soldiers to the KMT during World War II, officials said that they would rather not even tell people about Article 103 lest they get scared.[187] In Foshan in Guangdong, some expressed their fear of enlistment because of the possibility of a war in the near future.[188] In Xiamen, Fujian Province, a rumor of a war between West Germany and the Soviet Union sparked fears that all youth over the age of eighteen would be forced to enlist. In Fuzhou, merely reading the draft constitution produced the same effect. A factory manager read Article 103 and "anxiously asked, 'How do we follow this law?' 'Do we have to serve in the army?'"[189]

Many people who asked questions about conscription either directly or implicitly critiqued the CCP for failing to live up to its revolutionary history. In much of its propaganda, including the hoopla surrounding the draft constitution, the CCP sought to differentiate itself from the KMT on the one hand and capitalist countries on the other. But conscription made this a hard sell, and people did not shy away from confronting harried propaganda and other officials with challenging questions. In Beijing, for example, an "old worker" at People's Printing Factory said that people had been press-ganged into the KMT military (*zhuabing*) and seemed skeptical that CCP conscription was much different.[190] In Shanghai, a young official, naturally described as "backward," said with alarm: "We'll have to enlist! Isn't this the same as under the KMT constitution?"[191] Other remarks were deemed "cynical" because they compared China to capitalist countries: "So military service is a citizen's glorious duty. So what's the difference between this and the draft in capitalist countries?"[192] Even worse from the CCP's perspective, villagers in China's northeast compared China to World War II Japan: "In Manchukuo [Japan's puppet state in northeast China] people were conscripted into the army—and now the government wants to do the same"; in Shenyang, some "backward city people" said that Article 103 "is just like in Manchukuo."[193] Historical memory even burrowed into rumors that came to the attention of officials (and thus into the archives). In the Shanghai suburb of Chuansha, a mother was overheard by one telling her son over the telephone that she had heard in a mass meeting that "the law has called for a press-gang [*chou zhuangding*]" and advised him to be careful.[194]

Wide-scale anxiety, whether based on bad memories, rumors, or a textually correct reading of the draft constitution, led to many requests for clarification. In Gaoqiao in the Shanghai suburbs, for example, someone wanted an explanation about why military service was necessary, and local officials in the city asked whether conscription meant that "we have to fight in a war" and how conscription would be implemented.[195] Most questions, however, asked for more specifics about the boundaries of Article 103—in particular, which citizens were expected to fulfill this glorious duty and for how long. In Luwan District, ordinary people—said to be in a panic about the article—asked officials about age limits, and at Jiaotong University someone wondered whether people under the age of eighteen would have to serve.[196] Officials also asked why the constitution did not include age limits, as did CCP members at the Kunming Machine Tool Factory in Yunnan Province who proposed that the final draft of the constitution include limitations on service time.[197] In Nanjing, people from one of China's democratic parties pointed out, inaccurately, that, unlike the constitution of the KMT "reactionaries" that specified age limits, the CCP's did not. As a result, they noted, during times when the country requires protection, "it won't matter if you are old or young—everyone will have the duty to join the army."[198]

This scenario, however, was quite unlikely, as some of these people likely knew. No military in the world wants to draft "everyone," but rather those who are not too old to fight, in good enough health, expendable, and in cases of party-armies like China's in the twentieth century, politically reliable. On one side of the class spectrum, these broad criteria suggested that "good class" party officials, veterans, workers, and poor and middle peasants were the PRC citizens who would have the glorious duty to fight a war. During the discussion about the draft constitution, these groups followed the well-worn script for campaigns and praised the CCP and PLA for liberating the country but also sought out more information about exemptions from service. In Anshan, for example, veterans asked officials, "Do we need to return to the army?" Workers wondered, "Can we get an exemption?" and "some officials" said, "We've been cadres for several years now—can we be exempt?"[199] In Dalian, where there were very many misgivings about military service, workers wanted to know if the government would draft single children.[200] In Shanghai, officials wondered if the government would exempt them on the basis of "having already participated in revolutionary work."[201] On the other side of the good class/bad class spectrum, some in the business community were afraid that the CCP would use Article 103 to press-gang them into service, perhaps thinking that this would be a convenient way of "eliminating" them.[202] From a constitutional perspective, the CCP had the discretion to label them as citizens for the purposes of conscription while also designating them as members of a class that would soon be wiped out.

In addition to questions about length of service, age, and possible exemptions, many people—but men in particular—sought out greater clarity about the role of gender in Article 103's articulation of citizens' obligations. The CCP made it clear during the Marriage Law Campaign in the spring of 1953, as well as in the constitution, that women should be treated equally. Many men—probably out of self-interest, since more female conscripts could mean fewer males, and with more than a whiff of resentment—wanted to know if women, now their supposed equals, would be required to serve as well. In Guangdong, for instance, men asked, "If military service is a glorious obligation for citizens don't women have to serve too?" and "Why aren't women allowed to join the army? Are they exempt?"[203] In Zhejiang, someone asked whether "citizens" in Article 103 "includes female citizens too," as did Jiaotong University students in Shanghai.[204] Residents of a suburban district there asked why female military service was not specifically written into the constitution.[205] Exposed to both the text and men's reactions, women worried. While praising the constitution generally, some asked whether they would have to serve, when they would go, the age requirements, and whether service would be coerced or done on a volunteer basis.[206]

As with all the other readers' questions about rights and obligations, the state exercised its power by not bothering to answer, leaving CCP intentions vis-à-vis its subjects hazy at best. But by simply raising rights and obligations to the surface of the national discussion, the CCP generated uncertainty, fear, anxiety, resentment, and envy. It also polarized already existing tensions between and within classes: Who would get the most benefits? On whom would most obligations fall? Would the CCP take any rights seriously? Rather than providing clear answers, the CCP preferred, as someone said in the Shanghai suburbs, to keep people guessing. In chapter 5, I will examine two other groups who tried to figure out what game the CCP was playing in the constitution: religious adherents and ethnic minorities.

CHAPTER 5

Christians, Buddhists, and Ethnic Minorities

The early PRC state, still insecure in its domestic power and international status, invested significant resources—including the constitutional discussion and the promulgation of the constitution—toward strengthening itself on these fronts. Facing overlapping threats from multiple directions, it had to prioritize: What are our own officials thinking? Which groups were the most threatening? Based on the volume of materials in *Neibu cankao* and local archives about the draft constitutional discussion, the leadership was primarily concerned about the reactions of people in the business community ("capitalists"), officials, and intellectuals and to a more limited extent workers, villagers, and ordinary people; chapters 1 and 2 in particular reflected this first tier of state concern. In this chapter, I turn to the second tier: ethnicity and religion, with the focus on the Hui and Catholics.[1] What was the reaction of ethnic minorities to the clauses in the draft constitution dealing with their education, culture, and political autonomy, and what was the reaction of religious groups to the constitutional guarantee of "freedom of religious belief" in Article 88? Might the political logic that was central to Chinese constitutionalism—using law not to "settle" or institutionalize the state but rather to sow confusion, fear, doubt, uncertainty, and jealousy—be found in these cases as well?

Religion and Ethnicity: Background

As with all the populations we have examined so far, the context within which the CCP engaged ethnic minorities goes far in explaining their reactions to the draft constitution. As far as the CCP was concerned, ethnic minorities not only constituted an alternative world view to the CCP's version of modernity and Marxism-Leninism, they also occupied strategically important territory along China's borders (Xinjiang, Tibet, and Yunnan) and constituted demographic majorities or significant minorities of some villages. Like almost all religious adherents whose faiths were deemed "superstitions" (in contrast to "scientific" Marxism-Leninism), the CCP considered Buddhists ideologically backward at best. Although Muslim delegates were present at the 1949 Chinese People's Political Consultative Conference which drafted the Common Program, the PRC government, in contrast to the USSR, could not accept the idea of federation of ethnic-based republics, and from the 1950s had a "head-on collision" with its Muslim minority.[2] Protestants and Catholics, although far fewer in number than Buddhists or Muslims (one and three million respectively), were connected to the KMT and Western powers (and in the case of Roman Catholics, the Vatican), and were known for their anticommunism.[3] Nevertheless, as a rural insurgency fighting for survival, the CCP frequently tempered its high modernist ideology, forging tactical alliances with some popular religiously-inspired groups (sects, secret societies) to gain entrée into the unions and villages where it might find potential supporters.[4]

In its dealings with religion and ethnicity, the PRC state did not start with a blank slate; ideologically and tactically, it drew on the legacies of the imperial state, its KMT predecessor, and their experiences as a rural insurgency. For example, for centuries, Chinese states had sought to co-opt leaders of ethnic minorities by granting them official titles and power over territory in the native headman (*tusi* or *tuguan*) governance system, which derived from the Tang-era vassal state (*jimi*) model but with varying degrees of success.[5] Ming Dynasty (1368–1644) emperors restricted early Christian missionaries such as the Jesuits to the imperial court and traders to distant outposts, a policy that continued under the Qing (1644–1911) until the unequal treaties signed with Western powers after the Opium Wars (Treaty of Nanjing, 1842; Treaty of Tianjin, 1858), which allowed the establishment of treaty ports and inland missionary activity. Like the PRC, leaders of the Republic of China were at odds with groups whose otherworldly views they considered obstacles to China's enlightenment and progress. With the exception of Christianity, these were pejoratively called "superstition," a broad but unclearly defined category that included "nonscientific" understandings of the body and healing practices as well as beliefs in local deities, fortune tellers, and others who claimed otherworldly insight and knowledge. Tellingly, one of the first acts of the new republic was the introduction of the Gregorian calendar (starting January 1, 1912), which strove to eliminate "numerous festivals and deity birthday rituals punctuating the traditional calendar . . . all of which were occasions for 'hot and noisy' crowds and unbridled 'superstition'—and replace them with a new set of civic rituals."[6]

The CCP also seems to have inherited many of the Republic's legal and bureaucratic approaches to ethnic and religious matters. The first provisional constitution of the Republic of China (proclaimed in March 1912) provided for freedom of religious belief (*xinjiao ziyou*) but not protection against destruction of temples to deities. Republican elites failed to see any contradiction between these, since such wrecking was beneficial to the "eradication" of superstition.[7] Bureaucratically, the story was similar. In a June 1912 blueprint authored by a bureau in the Ministry of Religious Affairs, the state announced its goal of reforming (*gailiang*) existing religions "so that they might continue to social progress." In practice, this meant that the government accepted religions as doctrinal, ethical, and spiritual systems but on the condition that they rid themselves of "superstition," including most of their rituals, and demonstrate that they were "patriotic and contributing to welfare and progress."[8] In the early republic, the state recognized Roman Catholicism, Protestantism, Buddhism, Islam, and Daoism, and national associations were set up for each. However, some faiths, such as Islam and Tibetan Buddhism, were subsumed under the government's ethnic nationality policy because they were historically identified with minority groups (including the Hui, Tibetans, Manchu, and Mongols).[9] In the case of the Hui, state discourse became highly assimilationist during the 1930s, and as a result those who advocated for a distinctive identity for Chinese Muslims "retreated into silence, either under duress or due to shifting priorities." Only when the war was over could these advocates regain prominence and call for specific articles in the constitution guaranteeing autonomous rights to all Muslims of China as a distinct community.[10]

Upon taking over power in 1949, PRC leaders deployed a variety of offensive tactics against "mainstream" (Christian, Muslim, Buddhist Tibetan, and other) and "superstition"-based organizations perceived to be, generally correctly, as anti-Communist or even counterrevolutionary. The CCP ousted Western missionaries and gradually confiscated their properties. As Xiaoxuan Wang noted in his recent study, in the city of Rui'an in Zhejiang Province, police surveilled Catholic activists and collected detailed information about them.[11] At the same time, following the same United Front tactics it used with businessmen and intellectuals, the CCP cultivated ties with leaders of the major faiths (giving some official positions in People's Congresses and the Chinese People's Political Consultative Conference) in the hope of using them against those who were not inclined to support the party. According to Goossaert and Palmer, these religious leaders operated within the system and acted as spokesmen for the government vis-a-vis their followers but also "tried to defend the interests of their communities within the system itself."[12] Designated the religious sector (*zongjiao jie*), they were brought into meeting rooms to raise questions and offer comments and revisions to the draft of the 1954 Constitution.[13]

Uninvited to these United Front–inspired meeting rooms but instead hauled by the security forces to prisons, execution grounds, and reform-through-labor camps were leaders of various religious sects and secret societies whose activities before 1949 and immediately afterward earned them the status of counterrevolutionary. As part of its Campaign to Suppress Counterrevolutionaries between 1950 and 1953, the CCP arrested 2,620,000 people, imprisoned 1,290,000, and executed 712,000 while subjecting 1,200,000 to "control" by local authorities.[14] Among these were many members of various "reactionary sects" (*huidaomen*) operating around the country but especially the Yiguandao, seen as a wartime ally of Japan and a supporter of the KMT.[15] The Shanghai Public Security Bureau's *Gazetteer* adds local flavor to these national figures. Its officials classified roughly one-fourth of what it called reactionary sects as "counterrevolutionary." Said to be active in factories, schools, government institutions, and even the CCP and democratic parties, on April 27, 1951, in a twenty-four-hour sweep of counterrevolutionaries, the bureau claimed that it arrested roughly 9,000 people, among whom were 1,200 "heads of secret societies." Two days later, 285 were executed in three separate places, with nine after public trials.[16]

Though certainly a dramatic show of state power, state terror largely failed to destroy religious organizations. In large part, this was because the CCP forced through a variety of dramatic changes to rural society in the early 1950s (such as land reform, collectivization, and unified grain procurement) which, according to Steve Smith, "created conditions of fear and uncertainty highly conducive to the revival of the societies."[17] By the mid-1950s, CCP religion policy became more patient and nuanced. Each religion, it was argued, had its own unique problem that needed to be solved. For Catholicism and Protestantism, it was their relationship to imperialism; for Buddhism and Daoism, "feudalism"; and in the case of Islam and Tibetan Buddhism, ethnicity and "feudalism."[18]

It was into this fraught context that the PRC dropped the 1954 draft constitution on religious and minority communities. Below I examine how they responded—their comments, questions, criticisms, and statements of support—to the primary constitutional clauses dealing with religion and minority policy. These include the freedom of religious belief, the establishment and operation of autonomous ethnic minority political regions (chapter 1, Article 3; chapter 2, section 5), and cultural issues such as language, rituals, and customs. More specifically, ethnic minorities were provided the "freedom to foster the growth of their spoken and written languages, and to preserve or reform their own customs or ways (Article 3)," the right to use their own language in court proceedings (Article 77), and the state's soft obligation (the chosen term was *should*) to "assist the various national minorities in their political, economic and cultural development" (Article 72). I will begin with an overview of the more general reactions to these issues, and then turn to groups defined by the state in primarily religious terms (Hui, Catholics, Protestants, and Buddhists) and finally to ethnic minorities, most of them in the southwest. To the best of my knowledge, this is the first in-depth accounting of how individuals from these groups responded to the 1954 Constitution, even in specialized studies of the PRC's relationship to minorities and religious adherents.[19] Like other groups examined in this book, they tended to view the constitution as an exercise designed to sow discord, jealousy, uncertainty, and fear—all emotions the CCP likely intended to invoke (and knew about) by writing a constitution and then discussing it in a politically fraught atmosphere. These views of the constitution, I suggest, were also commentary on what they had experienced in the years prior to it—in other words, they assessed the Communist Revolution itself.

Distrust, Mockery, and Critique

Like the reporting on other groups involved in the constitutional discussion, open-source discourse about religious groups and minorities (in publications for mass consumption) stressed their enthusiasm, as did the beginning paragraphs of internal CCP bureaucratic reporting, particularly for the clauses about ethnic equality and the CCP's apparent receptiveness to religion despite its reputation to the contrary.[20] Underlying this, however, was bountiful skepticism among lay commentators and people deemed more sympathetic to the regime—the "religious circles" the CCP was co-opting. In particular, many questioned the sincerity of the CCP's constitutional commitment to protect the freedom of religious belief. In Taiyuan in Shanxi, for example, an office worker wondered, probably with a dose of sarcasm, whether the CCP would allow the performance of shamanic trance dances (*tiaoshen*), which were associated with Buddhism and Daoism, under the provision of freedom of religious belief.[21] In Heilongjiang, in an area that did not have any Buddhist monks or Daoist priests and had only a few Christians, CCP propagandists wrote, "Citizens have religious freedom in China" under a drawing of a monk, a priest, and Jesus Christ on a cross, but this raised many people's suspicions about what was really happening. An "old lady" was recorded asking, "This Communist Party also believes in Buddha now?"[22] In Shanghai, people questioned the CCP's ability to differentiate between religion as a matter of belief and "popular customs" as a reflection of those beliefs, and between nonreligious local customs that appeared religious and standard religion. They asked whether the CCP would respect Buddhist monks who burn joss sticks to brand their heads as exercising their freedom of religious belief or Catholics who oppose cremation. They were equally concerned about the CCP's use of the word *reform* vis-à-vis religion, pointing out that there were some rituals and customs that absolutely cannot be reformed (*juedui bu neng gaige*). Any change, they said, should come from within groups and be voluntary rather than imposed.[23] Among religious adherents in Fuzhou in Fujian Province, some asked why, if the constitution provided for the freedom of religious belief, the government opposed and restricted religion in practice.[24]

Like other groups that carefully read the draft constitution and called it a textually cunning document, religious adherents also located words that sounded good while disguising repression. In Shanghai, for example, the exclusive focus on "belief" in Article 88 generated not a few objections, with some calling it a fake door (*zhuang men mian*). They asked whether freedom covered thought as well as religious activities and ceremonies, and how long freedom of thought would be protected. Some questioned the very possibility of freedom of religious thought in the absence of the freedom to perform rituals and ceremony. Since the CCP "severely restricted" such activities, this arrangement was impractical without adding clauses to the constitution.[25] Others in the city also noted the gap between thought and ritual and between constitutional promises and the reality on the ground. In the face of CCP restrictions on religious activities even as Article 88 proclaimed freedom of religious belief, it was important to "make sure that Article 88 is enforced and not interfered with anymore [*bu jia ganshe*]."[26]

Limiting Article 88 to belief was not the only wily turn of phrase in the draft constitution. Another was Article 3, giving minorities the freedom to "preserve or reform" their customary practices. This dichotomous choice, certainly deliberately chosen, provoked internal dissension. "Except for some activists," one report noted, "most were not happy with this." These activists, like many younger people in China, probably chafed under the authority of their elders and welcomed the opportunity to prove their revolutionary credentials, but the majority, probably older, argued, "If you believe, you believe; if not, don't." In this view, reform was impossible because it would remove the essence of faith.[27]

These honest and reasonable objections—the CCP's targeting of temples was hardly a secret, nor were its long-standing views about religion—either were ignored or produced a backlash on the part of state officials, as well as those who (like the activists above) articulated a far more secularized vision of modern China. Liu Shaoqi's brief explanation of various changes between the draft and final versions of the constitution noted that the National Draft Constitution Committee agreed to include the suggested revision "All the nationalities have the freedom to use and foster the growth of their spoken and native languages"—*to use* was not in the draft—but said nothing about the "preserve and reform" issue in the very same clause, which was the more irksome phrase during the discussion.[28] More aggressively, in Shanghai, officials conveniently used the constitution to rebut a constitution-based claim for rights. These religious figures, they claimed, "only wanted to talk about rights, not obligations." This focus, they argued, was a product of "selfishness generated by tradition" (*chuantong de zisi zili sixiang*).[29] In Jiangxi Province, people's representatives seemed exasperated by this apparent flip-flop in party policy: "From early on we've been told to destroy [*dapo*] superstition and now freedom of religious faith is allowed again?" They worried that this provision would embolden rural monks and Daoist priests to spread superstition, cheat people out of their money, and influence agricultural production under the protection of the constitution.[30] Ordinary people, some of whom surely included officials, had their illiberal say too. Writing to the National Draft Constitutional Discussion Committee, they suggested that the final version "prohibit religion from interfering in marriage freedom" and grant the freedom to "cast off religion" and "do away with superstition."[31] Others wanted the new constitution to include an obligation for citizens to report reactionary sects and secret societies to the authorities; asked that freedom of religious belief not include Buddhism, Daoism, and Catholicism; and requested an explicit stipulation that "religious faith will be reformed."[32]

These themes—disbelief verging on mockery, critiquing language and contradictions, constitutionally induced dissension, and illiberal secularist backlash—can be seen in the discussion about the draft constitution that took place among these groups. Below I drill a bit deeper to listen in on some of these conversations, beginning with the Hui.

The Hui

As noted earlier, the CCP had little reason to expect that its Leninist-modernist vision of the future would find many adherents among Hui communities or individuals.[33] Nevertheless, the strategic significance of Muslim-majority provinces such as Xinjiang and Qinghai, the definition of China as a multiethnic republic, and the small but significant presence of Muslims in many cities incentivized the CCP to find allies within the faith in order to detect and deter potentially subversive religion-based activism. The 1954 Constitution was integral to this effort, offering up carrots like autonomous regions, marriage freedom, and legal and gender equality and reform to some, while also warning, through the same concept of reform, that the CCP had only a limited zone of tolerance. To what extent did this work? Evidence shows that while some Hui praised the constitution, many—led by Muslim elites—saw the constitution as an effort to sow discord within the faith and weaken their hold on its adherents.[34]

Article 88, which gave citizens the right to freedom of religious belief, proved the most contentious among those who participated in the discussion of the draft constitution. A report on the reactions of Muslim leaders in the city of Linxia in Gansu Province noted that while they supported equality between ethnicities, minority autonomous districts, and religious freedom, they still had many fears: that Article 88 would make it more difficult for them to control who believed and who did not, which would result in daily reductions of donations to mosques; that leaders would not be able to intervene if people "reneged on their faith" (*panjiao*) or could not do anything about it if they did; and that their leadership status would become increasingly insecure. Like the businessmen discussed in chapter 2, report writers described them as anxious and suspicious because the words "United Front" were mentioned only once in the preamble but not in any of the other articles. Their suggestions for revision included adding an article about the CCP's commitment to the United Front.[35] Hui leaders in Inner Mongolia voiced similar concerns, that once people stop believing in Islam they "will no longer be Hui" and that these nonbelievers, attracted by the promise of freedom, would "destroy minority unity."[36] In Chongqing, imams noted the upside of the constitution's labeling their beliefs as "faith" ("Now that the constitution affirms faith, it can no longer be said that Islam is superstition") while also warning that even in the context of religious freedom, "the faithful still cannot violate religious law—in the end faith requires faith." Like their counterparts in Gansu and Inner Mongolia, they directed their ire toward Hui who abandoned the faith and "eat pork."[37] Lay Muslims shared this concern. In Harbin, they asked whether the CCP, in giving legal sanction to Muslims who had married Han and ate pork, contradicted the constitutional prohibition of "acts that undermine the unity of the nationalities."[38]

Some evidence suggests that Muslim CCP officials, most of whom were more secular than Muslim leaders, were at the forefront of this conflict because they had married Han women. Even though such marriages were sanctioned by the 1950 Marriage Law, they probably encountered some level of opposition from fellow Muslims. This prompted a Hui official in Rehe Province to ask why there was no specific provision in the constitution for intermarriage between ethnic groups. Fearing such limitations, he asked if future marriages between them "will require the approval of the State Council."[39] In the city of Jinlin, Hui officials married to Han wives were said to be "very dissatisfied with the constitution" for a different reason. In their view, Article 96 was too liberal because it did not limit "marriage freedom" in cases of intermarriage. Some may have felt that their Han wives would take advantage of the constitution to initiate divorce proceedings against them.[40]

Further inflaming intra-Hui tension was the question of "preserving or reforming" religious traditions. In Jinlin, Hui representatives immediately recognized the danger of assimilation in these terms, calling Article 3, where this issue was raised, "an excuse for those of wavering faith to oppose the religion" (*fanjiao*). With "so-called reform," they argued, "if all members of the minority group are willing do this it's OK, but if someone wants to casually change their religious beliefs, that [article] will violate the interests of the minority group."[41] In Xi'an, by contrast, the primary threat of the word *reform* was not the gradual decline of the Hui people through assimilation but rather the text-based essence of Islam. The Koran, they said, was holy, not mere "habit and custom" as it was articulated in the draft constitution. How could a sacred text be reformed?[42] For those who objected to certain elements of Sharia, however, reform of the Koran, holy as it was to some, might have been a welcome endeavor.

Worries about the future of religious identity and practice were central to Islamic adherents' reactions to the constitution, but not the only ones. Religious space was another concern. Islam, like Judaism, does not require fixed sacred spaces, but mosques were still central to community solidarity and identity, both of which were under Communist siege. With the constitution announcing the gradual elimination of the private property system, people in Qinghai were "mainly concerned" with what would happen to mosque property in this event.[43]

The CCP's increasingly radical policies during the mid-1950s and 1960s proved that many of these fears were justified. While often described as a gradual shift from United Front policies toward antireligious extremism, the discussion around the draft constitution demonstrates that Islamic leaders and ordinary practitioners had always been quite skeptical of CCP rhetoric and law, choosing to judge it by the actions of local officials and everyday experience. The constitution, however, was more than a reflection of the state of CCP-Islamic relations. By generating tensions within the faith, it helped prepare the ground for the broader assault on religion later in the decade, rendering them more easily exploitable.[44]

Christians

Such stressors were mild compared with those experienced by Christians. While certainly on the defensive, Islam had a longer history in China, was more indigenized, and, perhaps most importantly, was not directly implicated in imperialism. Below I turn to examine how Christians responded to articles dealing with the freedom of religious belief, private property, and "reform" of their traditions and customs. Reflecting the CCP's internal assessment about which branches of Christianity were the greatest threat, most of the material below focuses on Catholics. During the Civil War, the CCP confiscated Catholic churches, and religious personnel were "harassed, imprisoned, or even killed"; after 1949, it pressured the church along multiple fronts, including taxation, school curricula, and co-optation of religious practice through the "Three Self-Patriotic Movement," which was seen by many Catholics as a direct attack on their church.[45] Catholics' responses to the draft constitution largely reflected these experiences, much as the Five Antis Campaign shaped the perspective of commercial elites.[46]

Most reports about faith adherents who participated in the discussion of the draft constitution rarely balanced statements of enthusiastic support with those that were more critical; the antagonism between the CCP and religious organizations was too deep and well-known to be sugarcoated with the sort of "empty talk" about cordiality and support in official discourse. This animosity also produced more silences than among women, workers, and even businessmen. But even among the religious leaders CCP officials deemed "very backward" and "reactionary," the CCP harbored special ire toward Catholics. Aware of this, many feared participating in the constitutional discussion, and once gathered in small groups, "were afraid of talking about religion at all."[47] Some did not want to read the constitution or, having read it, openly called it militarist (*junguo zhuyi*) and deceitful, particularly its promise ("just talk," they said) not to violate citizens' personal freedom (Article 89), positions the CCP classified as "completely resisting" the draft constitution.[48] In a report from Jing'an District, Catholics were also described as hostile toward the document, unconvinced the CCP would uphold any promises in it.[49]

While much of this suspicion toward the constitution was rooted in recent history, at least some was based on the constitutional text itself, particularly its carefully worded ambiguity. Perhaps reflecting greater familiarity with Western constitutions, Catholics worried about the silence surrounding constitutional interpretation. That is, if the constitution provided for freedom of religious belief, who would be the arbiter of what constituted belief? "Are different views about this admissible," they wondered, or "is it that you see what you want to see—the benevolent see benevolence and the wise see the wise?"[50] In the absence of a higher level of constitutional authority, some were convinced that local officials would act with impunity.[51] This was already happening. In Hunan, a Protestant asked, "The 106 Articles of the Constitution are all good, but will they be implemented?" noting that in "Hengyang and other places there are restrictions on religious activities in place."[52] In Shanghai, Catholics complained that non-Catholics came to their churches during prayer and photographed them, laughing as they clicked away, without intervention of the authorities.[53]

The constitution's sole focus on belief was also an issue, as it was among the Hui. Catholics pointed out that the constitution's protection of belief excluded "religious life, ritual, and faith-based activities," all of which had been severely restricted.[54] The anxiety generated by this constitutional omission was further compounded by state silence about which religious practices might be tolerated under Article 88. For example, Shanghai Catholics asked whether it was now permitted to bow in front of pictures of deceased individuals, including Sun Yatsen, and what burial practices would be allowed.[55] Owing to these problems, some proposed revisions that would prohibit disrespecting religion, or perhaps a public notice that would "prohibit interference with religious freedom."[56]

Outside Shanghai, Catholics registered similar disbelief about the sincerity of the CCP's constitutional commitment to freedom of religious belief. In Inner Mongolia, some religious leaders were said to be "satisfied" with Article 88, but a Catholic priest was having none of this, arguing that speech and action were umbilically connected concepts. According to two reports about this person, he read the constitution until Article 88 and then stopped, saying there was no point reading any further: "Freedom of religious belief, huh? Can I go out on the street and proselytize and do missionary work?"[57]

The word "reform" in the text of the constitution agitated Catholics even more.[58] While this might trace back to the association of the concept *reform* with violence (e.g., land reform), Catholics reported a different source of their fear. In their view, the constitution's wording was not to be taken literally but rather read though its projected implications: the PRC encourages reform *within faiths*. This stance vis-à-vis religion, they predicted, will "create tension in each religion between those who favor reform and those who do not, and these two groups will then fight it out," thereby splintering the faith.[59] Competition to be "pro-reform" also increased the stress on the already-fraught relationship between Protestants and Catholics: "Catholics are stubborn and will not reform," said some Protestants.[60]

Beyond intra- and interfaith politics was the larger theological question that was highlighted by Muslim leaders as well: What exactly does reform imply in the context of faith? Christianity, of course, was no stranger to reform during its long history, most notably in the Protestant Reformation, but reform to satisfy an atheist regime was quite another matter. Since the CCP did not specify which elements of faith should be reformed, Catholics were forced into a difficult position. While some rituals "absolutely cannot be reformed," they conceded that "others should change."[61] In Hunan, a Protestant linked the concept "reform" (*gailiang*) in Article 3 to the word "transform" (*gaizao*) in Article 10, which dealt with CCP policy toward capitalists, arguing that they were fundamentally identical: the CCP wanted to "utilize, restrict, and transform" them all. The party, in his view, "utilized religion policy because of the international situation, restricted religion by limiting religious activity, and transformed it by requiring that religious adherents undergo education."[62]

Beyond theological questions, Catholics had many other practical concerns, most of which were situated at the intersection of recent history and the ambiguities in the constitution and religion policy. For example, many forms in the PRC required filling out a box for "class status," but Chinese converts to Catholicism were not informed what their status was. Given the recent persecution of fellow faith members, the chances of getting assigned a good status ("ordinary city person," "worker") were not favorable. They asked officials how they should fill out forms for school registration and other documents, but do not appear to have received an answer.[63] Others were very concerned about property and financial issues. Neither administrative policy nor the draft constitution clearly stated which "property system" church property belonged to. Were churches private property that could be constitutionally protected, at least for the short term, or were they collectively owned? Given widespread discrimination against Catholics, they wondered how church and individual properties would be protected or bequeathed.[64] They also asked how the church could maintain its properties when the government restricted fundraising to legally registered organizations, thereby rendering them supplicants for need-based assistance.[65] They thought that the Vatican might be a possible source, but the CCP had deemed it an imperialist state, a designation some priests rejected by citing the "principle of foreign policy in the draft constitution" that China could have relations with peace-loving peoples around the world.[66] In Chongqing, some Catholics had an even longer-shot hope. Article 2, which gave "all power to the people," and Article 3, which protected ethnic minority rights—not religious ones—might "allow us to get church land back in the countryside."[67] Jobs and benefits were another practical concern. Clergy, already worried about state-sponsored discrimination and their livelihood under Communist rule, asked constitutional educators whether their work in monasteries and churches qualifies them as laborers "who will be able to get rights and avoid social discrimination."[68]

None of these faint hopes for constitutional intervention came to pass. Some Catholics' original assessment of the constitution as "just words" proved accurate not only for the early 1950s but for the entire Mao era, as well as for many years in the post-Mao period. This bleak assessment of the efficacy of rights protection in the constitution, however, does not suggest that Christians ceased religious activity and religion-based protests. Indeed, the very same facets of the constitution that worried Christians in 1954 could occasionally work to their advantage, especially its ambiguity and lack of enforcement. For example, in Guangdong Province, a Baptist leader urged officials to "respect their right of worship" and refrain from "interfering in their spiritual affairs," both nonexistent rights. Elsewhere in the province, alongside overt repression of important church leaders as well as extensive collaboration between them and the CCP (which was the dominant pattern of interaction), there also were reports of large-scale Christmas celebrations among Catholics and Protestants as late as 1958 and 1959. Whether because officials themselves were unsure about what sort of religious activities were rights (as was likely the case), personal relationships with the faithful, gift-exchange opportunities, the common administrative practice of avoiding trouble or more important priorities such as agricultural production, many turned a blind eye to religious activities.[69] The constitution's vagueness gave ample room for (nearly always ineffectual) protest based on religious rights, as well as for state crackdown on them.

From the standpoint of the CCP, whether these activities could be sanctioned by the constitution or encouraged by them was less important than what I have identified as the constitution's primary role: instilling fear, anxiety, and jealousy through ambiguity and sowing divisions within faiths and between them. In other words, the constitution helped weaken the organizational basis for broader action against the CCP, an important step in the eventual eradication of religion altogether. With this accomplished, Christians' constitution-based rhetorical barbs were a piddling matter.

Buddhists

In contrast to Chinese Christians, Buddhists were untainted by association with Western imperialism or its practitioners' connections to Western countries and institutions, or to the Vatican. Because of this, internal CCP publications, including *Neibu cankao*, invested fewer resources investigating their views about the 1954 Constitution. Nonetheless, the PRC state, like its predecessor, could not remain aloof from their affairs.[70] While there is disagreement among historians about the role of Buddhism in inspiring various rebellions, including the famous Boxers, there is virtually no argument that, ideologically speaking, the CCP considered Buddhism part of China's feudal past that did not have a legitimate place in atheist socialist modernity.[71] In the early 1950s, it accused clerics of being parasites engaged in superstitious activities as well as members of banned sects and compelled Buddhist leaders to undertake a "self-cleansing campaign" in 1951.[72] As with other religious organizations, the CCP combined brute force (confiscating temple land and monasteries and taking control over Tibet) with the incorporation of some practitioners, particularly leaders and youth, into its New Democracy framework.[73] In Shanghai, for example the Young Buddhist Association, which began its existence in 1946, not only survived the Communist takeover but became the "most active and influential grassroots Buddhist organization in the early PRC" until it was denounced as a counterrevolutionary organization in 1955.[74] Far away in distance and status, the head monk of the Buddhist monastery in Xishuangbanna in Yunnan was appointed deputy head of the state-run Chinese Buddhist Association. When asked about the draft constitution, he reportedly raised no objections, noting that it included a provision for freedom of religious belief.[75]

The CCP's official narrative about Buddhists, more so than with Islam and Christianity, has emphasized their relatively peaceful incorporation into the new state, a position largely echoed by J. Brooks Jessup, who argues that at least in the case of the Young Buddhist Association, "political incorporation rather than coercive eradication" was the primary way they "experienced Communist governance" between 1949 and 1955.[76] The Buddhist discussion surrounding the 1954 draft constitution, an event rarely mentioned in the existing scholarship, and even then only pointing out their "enthusiastic support," adds more nuance to this story.[77] Asked to comment about the religious provisions of the draft constitution, how did Buddhists respond?

Perhaps reflecting the nature of the sources (which tend to focus on problems more than happy events), many Buddhists, like their Muslim and Christian counterparts, had a more pessimistic, and as 1955 showed, clear-eyed view about how their faith would fare than co-opted organizations like the Young Buddhist Association or Buddhist leaders such as Juzan (巨赞; 1908–84), a leading monk considered sympathetic to the CCP (he called the constitution the "great dharma" that Chairman Mao was granting to the Chinese people). They reached these views based on a close textual analysis of the draft constitution, particularly its lack of clarity about belief, freedom of speech, publishing, and property rights, as well as recent political experiences under the CCP. During the discussion some were blunt, predicting that, under the CCP, religions have "no future" and even calling out the CCP for its hypocrisy in using the Roman calendar system while simultaneously denouncing cultural imperialism ("Isn't that a contradiction? Shouldn't that change?").[78]

As was the case with Islam and Christianity, Article 88 rarely received laudatory comments among many Buddhists, at least judging by their skeptical, borderline mocking hypothetical questions. Some asked whether religious publishing, such as the classic *Yijing*, is a right protected by Article 87, which covered freedom of the press, pointing out, "Now it's not protected—will it be in the future?" Others, perhaps in jest or perhaps seriously, wanted to know if Buddhists had the right to "reject [Marxist] materialism."[79] Whereas these questions appear to have been asked with the negative response in mind, others seemed genuinely perplexed about the scope of freedom of religious belief; to get answers, they posted letters to Buddhist leaders for more information. Some of these also raised objections to the work of the (state-run) Chinese Buddhist Association.[80]

Protection of property—or the lack thereof—was another source of discontent, much as it was in other faiths thanks to several years of CCP confiscations. In Nanjing, a Buddhist noted that in the French and Polish constitutions there was an "enlightened provision" for the legal protection of religious properties, but in China the draft constitution lacked such a rule "even though the status of religion has gotten better" in the document. He hoped that the central government would consider this further and include it in the final version.[81] In Inner Mongolia, a monk called out the CCP, incorrectly, for claiming that the constitution "protects property" (*baohu caichan*) but not returning his temple's confiscated property.[82]

Finally, Buddhists were keenly aware of the fact that law is only as good as the people enforcing it. Many officials were wary of Article 88, fearing that it would open space for "feudal" and counterrevolutionary activities. As noted in a report from Guangdong, city and provincial-level officials opposed the article because it would encourage the revival of superstitious practices such as fortune-telling and using horoscopes.[83] In Shanghai, Buddhists complained about wide variation in how religion policy was enforced (noting that the situation in Tibet was better than in other areas), that officials did not treat monks well and had forced their way into private homes.[84]

From this perspective, there were only slight shades of difference between the CCP's relationship to Buddhists from the early years of the PRC to the designation of the Young Buddhist Organization as counterrevolutionary in 1955. In the eyes of many CCP officials, Buddhists were not as dangerous as Catholics but still suspicious as believers of feudal superstition who had the capacity to organize. From the perspective of many Buddhists, the CCP was an organization that illegally confiscated their properties, took over Tibet, and deliberately failed to offer meaningful protections for religious practices in the draft version of the constitution. In short, the evidence shows more continuity than change over the course of the early to mid-1950s.

Ethnic Minorities

For the CCP, ethnic minorities were a significantly greater challenge than Christians, Muslims, or Buddhists. Owing to their concentration in sensitive border regions, distinctive languages, and practice of forms of religion long derided as superstition, they potentially threatened China's territorial integrity and modernist aspirations. At the same time, minorities were also central to Chinese leaders' claim to represent China as a multiethnic unitary republic, not only the Han majority. In contrast to imperial precedent that focused more on order than on identity (allowing minority groups substantial autonomy in governance, ritual practice, language, and culture), as well as pre–World War II quasi-ethnofederalist Leninist and KMT formulations that would have given minorities full autonomy as well as the right of secession, the CCP adopted the concept zhonghua minzu (中华民族) to express the "multi-cultural composition of the Chinese 'nation' which worked to fold all ethnicities, faiths, and folk practices together into a single pan-national community." This was justified on the grounds that foreign imperialists were plotting to separate Tibet, Taiwan, and Xinjiang from China.[85]

At least in terms of its language, the 1954 draft constitution was a grab bag of approaches, including conciliatory provisions such as self-governing autonomous regions, where minorities would enjoy more latitude to adjust national policies to local conditions as well as to preserve their language and culture, in addition to not-so-veiled threats of state-imposed reform. Propaganda authorities unsurprisingly emphasized the former, arguing that ethnic minorities would gain more extensive rights than during the KMT era, be liberated from "Han chauvinism," and have better lives than ethnic minorities in capitalist countries, particularly Blacks in the United States.[86]

During the constitutional discussion, however, many people, including CCP officials, ordinary Han citizens, and minorities, criticized pre-1954 minority policy as well as the draft constitution for being either overly accommodating or insufficiently so. As far as ethnic minorities were concerned, the document not only reflected previous antagonisms between Han and minorities but also, by bringing them out into the open, exacerbated them. Since the CCP leaders knew about these tensions and did not revise the wording of the constitution to relax them, we can reasonably conclude that widening the rift between the Han majority and minority groups was at least acceptable to them.

CCP officials in different regions and at multiple levels of the party hierarchy raised several objections to the key "liberal" policies in the draft constitution. At least in the material I have read, the most prominent concern focused on minority autonomous regions.[87] In Taiyuan, for example, officials feared that such entities could lead to minority areas "separating from China," and in Jiangxi Province, where minorities were more common, some believed—erroneously according to the report-writers—that autonomous regions meant de facto "independence" that would result in the creation of a foreign state.[88] In Shanghai, officials in the Public Security Bureau questioned why minorities even deserved self-governance, arguing that they lacked culture, were backward (because they "ate with their hands" and danced in unappealing ways), and were demographically insignificant. They also worried about minority police forces backing calls for political independence, which would put the government in a difficult position.[89] Local officials were perplexed why Outer Mongolia was independent and not a part of China and why Mongols could gain independence but other minorities such as Manchus could not.[90]

Some officials were more concerned about allowing minority culture to "develop" than political independence. In the CCP's East China Bureau, "suppressing the savage minorities" was seen as the best way to deal with them, and in Jiangxi Province officials said that there was no need to develop minority language at all and that they should use Chinese instead.[91] These stereotypically "Han chauvinist" views were moderated by other perspectives. Officials in Guangdong, for instance, said that party members and many ethnic minorities had religious beliefs, some whose values resembled "a Communist view of life," not barbarism.[92]

Such views were in the minority. The Han chauvinism criticized in reports dealing with officials' views more or less represented the larger illiberal public from which they emerged to become party members during the revolution and after the establishment of the PRC. A statistician who worked at a car manufacturer in the northeast China region asked if, under the constitution, ethnic minorities have the right "not to obey us [Han]" because they had the "right to preserve or reform" their customs and had freedom of religious faith.[93] In Shanghai, people wanted to know why minorities should be allowed to develop their native languages (maintaining them would be enough) and why their "backward customs" should be preserved.[94] At Jiaotong University, faculty and staff griped that the CCP cared too much about minorities' interests, gave them undeserved privileges, and treated them with too much flexibility, particularly on language issues.[95] Like officials, some did not want autonomous regions at all, contending that there was a basic contradiction between their existence and a "unified state."[96] Since so much policy in the early 1950s focused on revolutionizing politics, economics, and society, the CCP's willingness to tolerate a gradualist approach toward reforming ethnic minorities, in contrast to capitalists, also stuck in their collective craw, especially among workers (some of whom argued that "in the past, sexual diseases were very prevalent among minorities").[97] Reaching back into Chinese history and literature, others mentioned the "minority policy" of Zhu Geliang (181–234), the famous statesman and general in the 14th-century historical novel *Romance of the Three Kingdoms*, who they understood to have pacified southwestern "barbarians" (*manren*) by capturing and then releasing their leader Meng Huo on seven occasions.[98] Generally speaking, noted a report on Shanghai workers, "they do not understand why there is a policy [of accommodation] toward minorities; to varying degrees, they are Han chauvinists."[99]

Reading the same document as Han respondents, did minorities understand the draft constitution as accommodating their interests and providing a potential basis for ethnonationalism? Reporters for *Neibu cankao* filed only three reports on minority groups—on the Dai (Thai) and Lahu in Xishuangbanna in southwestern Yunnan Province, the Mongols in the North, and on Tibetans so it is not possible to provide a comprehensive answer to this. However, the available evidence suggests that Han concerns were alarmist, in large part because they tended to see minorities as collectivities with shared interests in opposition to them rather than as normal societies with internal conflicts, some that were about the Han and some not. The discussion about the constitution mostly reflected these tensions, not demands for independence or even more cultural autonomy. If anything, rifts generated by arguments about power, status, and rights may have weakened whatever forces that existed that favored independence from China. As far as the CCP was concerned, this outcome, intended or not, was positive.

A report on the Xishuangbanna Dai supports this assessment. Following the script of centuries of Han rule over the Dai (albeit not consecutively), the CCP co-opted ethnic leaders thought to be sufficiently sympathetic by appointing them to official positions and then gradually acculturating them into the new rules and norms of the regime; the constitutional discussion was part of this educational process. Nonetheless, the draft constitution, with its conflicting articles and vague language, did not make it easy to maintain elite identity and solidarity, let alone govern. For example, the chairman of the Xishuangbanna Autonomous District, Dao Chengzong, stated in general terms that he supported the constitution but complained that by billeting PLA soldiers in the homes of ordinary people the CCP violated Article 90, which granted freedom of residence and changing residence. Others complained about blows to their aristocratic status (arguing that after the constitution, they would no longer be able to reap the benefits from governing or "eating their domains" (*chi guanzu*) and about CCP discrimination against their beliefs, claiming that the CCP only provided freedom of religion, not faith. But some were more supportive, albeit not in the way the CCP anticipated. One said that constitutional support for minority languages and customs would generate more unity among minorities, and as a result they "would no longer have to listen to the CCP's slander [*huaihua*]" against them, a far cry from the ethnic nationalism that worried the Han.[100]

Non-elites among the Dai, however, seemed less concerned about Han rule than the privileges enjoyed by their own upper class, which the constitution also addressed in sections not dealing with minority issues. Effectively pitting commoners against elites, the draft constitution's language of reform—closely associated with campaigns such as those for land reform, democratic reform, and marriage reform—gave rhetorical ammunition to lower-status groups, much as it did during the Marriage Law Campaign in the Southwest.[101] One of the Dai "masses," a man surnamed Shi, said that it was unreasonable that "the draft constitution stipulates that landlords have to reform, but our landlords still control land." Another took issue with constitutional "respect" for minority customs by arguing, "We Dai have bad customs," but he was unsure if these could be reformed, presumably by the CCP. Marriage was also a source of frustration. In one meeting, a Dai farmer said that although the draft constitution was "good article-by-article," it should have included a marriage provision. Many women, he complained, were "demanding too many things" so that "even middle peasants cannot afford to marry."[102]

The draft constitution seemed to have a similar splitting effect among the Lahu in Xishuangbanna. Internally, the constitution's language of "eliminating exploitation," understood locally as land reform, intensified disputes between

ordinary people and lower-level Lahu leaders who were very supportive, and
elites who either opposed it or recognized its inevitability and requested that
it be slow and gradual. Religion was another contentious issue. Although
many were relieved that KMT propaganda about the CCP's desire to eradi-
cate religion proved incorrect (at least temporarily), some said that "other
things can be reformed, just not religion" without pointing out which reforms
could be next in the docket. Interethnic relations between the Dai and Lahu
seem to have taken a turn for the worse thanks to the CCP's discretionary
power over the allocation of minority autonomous districts. Unlike the more
well-known Dai who received one, the Lahu had not, and they told propaganda
officials that they would like one as well.[103]

On the other side of the country on its north-south axis, Inner Mongolian
elites reacted to the draft constitution in a somewhat different way. Unlike the
southwest where the CCP devoted most of its attention to clan leaders, in Inner Mongolia it distinguished between ethnic Inner Mongolians who were
members of China's democratic parties (many of whom were educated) and
those whose primary identity was religious such as the Hui. These Inner Mongolian "democratic personages" (*minzhu renshi*), whether out of genuine con-
viction or the need for a politically correct performance, began praising Mao,
CCP policies toward minorities, and minority-related constitutional articles,
especially self-governing autonomous districts. However, their assigned identity as non-Hui Inner Mongolians deterred them from offering comments or
concerns about religion or ethnic policy. As members of the social upper class,
their eyes, much like those of the Han bourgeoisie and capitalists, were drawn
more toward chapter 1 ("General Principles") than toward shared ethnic minority concerns. Noticing the absence of the "national bourgeoisie" in Article 1 (in which the CCP identified itself only with workers in alliance with
peasants), they were anxious about the CCP's intentions with regard to its
United Front policy: "Will it change?" "Will it include the bourgeoisie?" "Does
'people' include the bourgeoisie or not?" They also fixated on the word "base,"
the Marxist notion that the nature of the economy produces politics and culture, and tried to figure out what this meant for them. Another Mongol, the
head of the Research Institute of Culture and History, expressed his concern
about the wording for the CCP's constitutional commitment to protect capitalists' ownership of the "means of production and other capital" (Article 10),
pointing out that it deployed the loophole "according to law." "What if law
changes?" he asked.[104]

The reaction of Tibetan elites to the draft constitution provides the final
data point supporting the argument. Tibet had been invaded by the PLA
roughly four years earlier but had yet to experience full-blown political and

social revolutions represented by land reform and the Marriage Law. In late July 1954, constitutional educators convened a meeting of selected Tibetan leaders who included CCP officials, officials-in-training, and intellectuals who were classified as ethnically Tibetan. Unlike the discussion among Catholics, Hui, and Buddhists that featured many people of faith, only one monk participated. Reflecting their secular modernism, CCP leaders preferred to view Tibetans as an ethnic group not defined by their religious identity, and probably hoped that these "leaders," whose status was entirely dependent on the CCP, would provide strong statements of support. However, even among this relatively sympathetic crowd, the constitution was problematic on account of its vagueness, internal contradictions, and fearsome words and associations. For example, a government official in the autonomous district worried that the Tibetan language would not be preserved, a concern prompted by grammatical problems in the transliteration of the draft into Tibetan and its binary choice of preserving or reforming language and customs. The one lama in the discussion wondered whether this clause meant that those monks who had already left the faith (huansu) or planned to would be required to undergo "reform." Political reform also stirred anxiety. An intellectual who worked in the Government Translation Office wondered if the tusi (native chieftain) system would be preserved or changed within autonomous regions because the draft constitution (in Article 67) left the form of autonomy up to the majority of local inhabitants. Officials smelled violence in the air. One noted that the draft constitution stipulated that all forms of exploitation would be "eliminated" (xiaomie). If this were the case, he wondered, "how would tusi exploitation be eliminated?" Another stated that Tibetan-area tusi were the same as landlords in Han-dominated areas. China's interior had already reformed, he noted, so "why haven't we?" They also wanted to know why these Tibetan leaders were being allowed to "arrest people they want to" given that the constitutional draft "prohibited arbitrary arrests without court authorization."[105]

As was the case throughout the country, extremely few of these questions were answered, but all proved prescient. As noted earlier, the National Draft Constitution Committee did not alter the problematic (and by then well-documented) "preserve or reform" issue in their subsequent deliberations. The PRC government, as is well known, did not tolerate Tibetan authority for very long after 1954, and moved slowly but surely to diminish the role of Tibetan language, religion, and culture. While the PRC government would have moved in this direction without a constitution, the constitution, with its crafty use of language, provided more than enough legal cover to justify its actions. More than this, the document itself helped to widen rifts within Tibetan society—between religious adherents subject to reform and those not, between officials interested in cultural preservation and those who wanted to move in a more radical direction, and surely others—thus facilitating its eventual takeover.

As China moved farther to the radical left from the mid-1950s until the early reform period, and as Mao specifically disavowed the constitution, what role, if any, did the constitution play in Chinese political life after 1954? I turn to this question in the next chapter.

CHAPTER 6

Constitutional Afterlives

In *What Is History?* the late British historian E. H. Carr analogized historians' task to a fishing expedition for facts. Which facts they catch, he suggested, depends on the body of water they choose to fish in (area of interest), chance, methodologies (bait) they select, and their perspective on the world, which will determine which fish/facts are tossed overboard. "By and large," he writes, "the historian will get the kind of facts he wants."[1] Up to this point in this book, the draft constitutional discussion of 1954 might be imagined as an artificial lake teeming with Carr's very unlucky fish—rather than being naturally occurring, it was the state that produced the context within which millions of people were encouraged to say something about the constitution (a comment, a question, a quessertion [putting forward an idea while stressing that it questionable], a suggestion for revision). The post-1954 period is best analogized as a trickling stream, more natural to be sure but less bountiful in its supply of information, particularly when it comes to evaluating ordinary people's perspective on the constitution. The only river-like body in post-1954 constitutionalism is state education about it, one of the topics in Jennifer Altehenger's *Legal Lessons*.

The relative paucity of information about the constitution's afterlife is easy enough to explain. In the Mao era, the state authored nearly all constitution-related documents. When the CCP was concerned about constitutional matters, as it was in 1954, it filled our proverbial lake. When it turned its attention elsewhere, there was a corresponding, often dramatic, decline in available data. Until the end of the Mao era, the water could not be replenished by research conducted by law school faculty or political scientists, the disciplines that traditionally demonstrated the most interest in constitutional matters. This changed considerably in the 1980s, but even then, most constitutional topics were shaped by statist concerns.

The correlation between the level of state attention and the quantity of documentation has created a parallel development in how scholars assessed the role of law more generally and the constitution specifically. Most have suggested that beginning with the 1955 Sufan Campaign (targeting so-called hidden counterrevolutionaries, most of whom were former KMT personnel, "bad class" individuals, and intellectuals) and culminating in the Cultural Revolution, the CCP rejected law as a mode of governance, and this, in turn, minimized the role the constitution played in politics and society.[2] A comparison between the early years of the PRC, which witnessed the promulgation of the 1950 Marriage Law, the 1950 Land Reform Law, and the 1954 Constitution (producing extensive documentation) among others, with the decades-long legislative drought after 1954 and the attacks on drafters of the 1954 Constitution in the Anti-Rightist Campaign, appears to justify the conventional wisdom that the CCP turned off law soon after the highpoint of 1954, flipping it back on again only after the Mao era concluded.

This broad narrative of law getting switched off and on is not entirely the product of disinterested scholars unable to find many legal documents to consume after 1955. Not entirely coincidentally, it also has been the CCP's party line about law during the reform era, which many legal scholars have to account for.[3] Peng Zhen, perhaps the most important architect of post-Mao China's legal architecture and a key figure in the drafting of the 1982 Constitution, claimed that the CCP took the constitution seriously for three years (1954–57) but changed its position to "rule by man" (renzhi) during 1957–58 (the Anti-Rightist Campaign), at which point neither the constitution nor law was considered important.[4] This narrative served multiple purposes: it conveniently gave the CCP a pass on the 1955 Sufan Campaign, helped delegitimize the Cultural Revolution period as "lawless" (wufa wutian), while legitimizing the reform era as "law-full."

This study, as well as recent scholarship on law by PRC historians, demonstrates that this official chronology is problematic. We have seen that even in 1954 many people, including officials, understood the constitution largely through the prism of politics, not law, noticing its loopholes, tricky and loaded language, and class war mongering. Looking at the continuities between the legal system in the Mao and reform eras, many of the essays in Daniel Leese and Puck Engman's edited volume *Victims, Perpetrators, and the Role of Law in Maoist China: A Case Study Approach* (2018) "question the prevalent assumption that the Cultural Revolution constitutes a radical break in adjudication practices and that with the arrest of the 'Gang of Four' China returned from 'lawlessness' to the path of socialist legality."[5] "Although destruction of a certain degree cannot be negated in some areas," noted Xu Lizhi, other parts of the pre–Cultural Revolution legal system not only continued but were even strengthened during the Cultural Revolution.[6] In the post-Mao era, many have highlighted the glaring weaknesses in "rule by law" (not to mention "rule of law"), emphasizing weak enforcement, the lack of judicial independence, and extremely high levels of legal decentralization (what Donald Clarke has called "legal polycentricity").[7]

Much like more general assessments of China's legal system, the constitution has also been criticized for not living up to its billing. In part, this is because some formal institutions, such as the National People's Congress, do not quite fulfill the roles assigned to them in the constitutional text (and people are aware of this, much as they were in 1954). But perhaps more importantly, it is because the citizens' rights enshrined in the 1982 constitution, like their 1954 counterparts, have remained unenforceable except in rare and unpredictable occasions. Disappointment with the constitution, especially when it comes to rights issues, has inspired much scholarship on the document and the tone of disillusionment about it.

This chapter, which addresses the afterlives of the 1954 Constitution, takes a different tack. Rather than asking questions about whether the constitution has fulfilled its stated and expected functions (or does it matter at all?) or focusing on enforcement as the critical stepping-stone toward some larger goal (rule of law, constitutional governance, etc.), I examine in an open-ended fashion how the constitution, as both text and subject of discussion, has been invoked and used over the years by state officials high and low as well as by ordinary citizens. Looking at the constitution as both text and talk, how has it been understood and tactically played by people in a range of political and social contexts? Shifting attention from claims to constitutional rights to smaller acts such as symbolic gestures, questions, comments, insinuations, or even constitutional utterances is a more productive approach because most people lacked the knowledge, confidence, and opportunity to mount sustained legal or constitutional arguments about their rights, and not many officials were capable of justifying their actions in constitutional terms. This sort of legal discourse was largely confined to the official press (journals and newspapers), which I will also consider.

This historical, semitextual, and nonevolutionary approach has other advantages. First, in contrast to most studies that focus on postreform developments, it allows for a finer-grained comparison of constitutionalism within the Mao era (1954 and after) and, as Leese and Engman have wisely advocated, between the entirety of the Mao era and the period following it.[8] Second, by pursuing the question of constitutional acts in an open-ended manner and without considering if they matter, we can avoid the binary and historically inaccurate narratives of law getting turned off and on or law that ignites hope but is followed by disappointment. Finally, it places us in a better position to thickly describe the complicated role of the constitution in Chinese law, politics, and society rather than deduce these from the useful but insufficiently descriptive concept of instrumentalism. We will see that for some people the constitution was a target of attack because of its complicity in revolutionary politics; for others, a source of information about politics; not a few used it as a broad platform from which they could complain about politics, jobs, and other problems (what I call the "constitutional bandwagon"); there were also those who saw it as an opportunity to comment on political changes. On occasion it was invoked to defend individual interests and collective beliefs and practices. For officials, on the other hand, it was a mechanism to enforce compliance, assuage and cause fear, explain away social problems, offer and deflect criticism, attack and defend critics, get out of political trouble, stir up social tensions, and distribute rewards, among other functions. Few took the constitutional text seriously as an important source of law. It was widely recognized as legal bullshit, but it remained useful bullshit nonetheless.[9]

The Immediate Afterlife: 1955–1970

In the immediate postconstitution period, agricultural collectivization and the state takeover of rural marketing networks in the so-called unified grain purchasing and sale policy, both of which generated widespread resistance and violence, also provided the impetus for oppositional acts against the constitution.[10] That document was perceived, usually accurately, as both intensifying repressive state actions and giving local officials more authority to act with impunity. *Neibu cankao*, with its typical focus on security threats, emphasized the class basis of this opposition but also did not shy away from alerting officials to discontent among its favored classes. In Liling County in Hunan Province, for example, reporters told leaders about rich peasants, a group of people who learned from the constitution and other sources that they would be "gradually eliminated" in the socialist economy, who used "honey traps" to bribe officials into allowing them to enter cooperatives. According to the somewhat salacious report, two women, both daughters of rich peasants, reportedly slept with twenty-four officials and activists for the purpose of "hiding grain during unified purchasing." If officials allowed them to join cooperatives, their thinking allegedly went, this subversion would be less likely to be noticed.[11] From Pingshun County in Shanxi, *Neibu cankao* pointed an accusatory finger at landlords and rich peasants, some of whom expressed their opposition to the CCP by secretly erasing the blackboard that had the draft constitution on it and then "smearing excrement over the sign of the local government." One former landlord, excluded from a cooperative, stood in front of Mao's picture and said, "If it weren't for you I wouldn't be living like this!" and then tore Mao's eyes out.[12]

Since *Neibu cankao*'s mandate was to alert the leadership about all manner of problems, it did not limit itself to the counterrevolutionary subversions perpetrated by the enemy classes. In reports about rural dissatisfaction spreading to workers, reporters in Guangdong and Hunan Provinces, for instance, informed leaders about hungry villagers who left their communities to search for food in cities, sought their urban relatives' assistance, or sold produce in return for food ration coupons. Some told their relatives, not a few of whom worked in urban factories, about their dissatisfaction with the food shortages caused by unified purchasing or penned letters to the government about this. Workers were said to be quite upset about rural conditions and "suspicious" about the CCP's "worker-peasant alliance," an important topic in their constitutional education in 1954: "In the past the party said that it wanted to solidify the worker peasant alliance," they noted in Guangdong, "but now it's the case that peasants are no longer wanted." Others were blunter. During a factory meeting someone asked, "Are we still having a meeting! How is it that we produce well but my family doesn't have anything to eat? Whatever you say is fake [*jia de*]. Nowadays even having money is useless. [If the CCP] continues like this, peasants will starve to death, and you still say stuff about the worker-peasant alliance?"[13]

If some people invoked concepts in the constitution to criticize the negative impact of collectivization or to sabotage its text, officials continued to find it helpful pushing forward these same unpopular policies. In Rehe Province, for instance, officials competed to see who could get more people into collectives. According to reporters, they applied squeeze: whoever refused would be denied their grain supply or payments for their produce and crafts. In a statement invented out of whole cloth, officials pressured villagers by asking, "The constitution requires you to go in, so why aren't you in yet?"[14]

Beyond pushing recalcitrant villagers into collectivization, the 1954 Constitution served other purposes, such as convincing anxious domestic audiences about the CCP's seriousness about the United Front with the national bourgeoisie, and international audiences about its commitment to popular constitutionalism. In December 1955, for instance, propaganda authorities in Shanghai and Beijing authorized the publication of a public letter of sorts by Liu Xianzhou (刘仙洲) detailing the reasons he joined the CCP.[15] Born in 1890, Liu participated in the 1911 Revolution as a member of Sun Yatsen's Revolutionary Alliance, studied at Beijing University, and became an engineer and an authority on agricultural mechanization; after 1949, he served as the first vice president of Qinghua University in Beijing. Presenting himself as a nonpolitical figure whose main interest was to "save China" by means of improving its education, Liu recounted the various experiences leading up to his decision to join the CCP, including participating in meetings about the use of waterwheels (1950), joining the Hebei Provincial Government (1950), admitting to excessive focus on his own career during "thought reform" (1953), and professing his emotional response to Stalin's death that same year. But it was the process of promulgating the 1954 Constitution that convinced him to join the party despite previous reservations about the worrisome definition of the PRC as a "people's democratic dictatorship." Impressed by the "democratic" nature of the discussion, Liu pushed back against the claims, advanced by capitalist countries, that the constitution was a CCP diktat: "They don't know that everyone in China who was able to participate did so in the discussion."[16]

Beyond its propaganda function, officials also invoked the constitution to explain (alleged) crime, respond to political criticism, and attack people who deployed it. In an example of crime, Shanghai mayor Chen Yi, in a speech delivered to midlevel city officials in 1958, noted that some police officials attributed many acts of counterrevolutionary sabotage to the promulgation of the constitution in 1954.[17] Faced with a population willing to use the constitutional text in defense of rights or, probably more accurately, pretend that they believed that it did this, policemen blamed the constitution for limiting their ability to respond to subversion. In a 1955 meeting of Public Security officials, leaders critiqued cops who complained that the constitution was a "bother" (mafan) because it tied their hands or provided citizens with language to contest their power. Instead, security personnel should understand its usefulness (zuoyong) as a weapon that "protects people and attacks enemies."[18]

Two years later, in May 1957, minister of public security Luo Ruiqing showed just how this could be done. In a summation speech to leaders of "five-person small groups" (who had been responsible for implementing the Sufan Campaign), Luo rejected criticism that the campaign was an "organized, state-led, large-scale violation of the constitution" by citing its Article 19, the catch-all loophole that stipulated that the PRC "safeguards the people's democratic system, suppresses all treasonable and counterrevolutionary activities and punishes traitors and counterrevolutionaries," as well as by noting that the CCP did not initiate the campaign but was merely "concretely implementing a National People's Congress resolution." Individual officials who had engaged in practices such as corporal punishment, entrapment, and "conveyor belt" (*chelun zhan*) interrogations were acting incorrectly and violating policy, but it was inappropriate to conclude that the Sufan Campaign was a constitutional violation.[19]

Unlike officials who could be promptly forgiven for constitutional violations, less powerful people caught up in the Sufan Campaign found out that charges of opposing or questioning the constitution could be a chapter of the proverbial book the state threw at them. In the final verdict issued against Han Yueshun (born in 1935 in Shen County, Hebei, allegedly to a landlord family), his superiors accused him of stating that the unified purchasing policy would not be welcomed in the countryside and might become a rationing policy not dissimilar from Japan's during its occupation of Northeast China. During the constitutional discussion, Han, like many others, was said to have expressed skepticism about the CCP's commitment to citizens' rights: "The constitution is just talk, but the reality is quite different—only if you follow the CCP will you be OK."[20]

While this is the only case I have found in which comments during the draft constitutional discussion were used to prosecute someone, it does point to a broader trend: officials of all sorts, not only those involved in purges, prosecutions, and their rationalizations, were familiar with at least some words, phrases, and articles in the document. While evidence suggests that these could be deployed as offensive weapons, the CCP could do little to prevent them from being used to defend party members accused of political crimes. In 1955, for example, the CCP mounted a withering attack on Hu Feng, a prominent literary theorist who articulated a more liberal perspective on the role of art in politics. Accused of being a member of a counterrevolutionary "anti-Party clique," he was arrested in July 1955. *Neibu cankao* reporters found that among some officials in Changchun and Wuhan, skepticism about his arrest abounded. Some wondered how a writer and literary expert could be a counterrevolutionary, a concept associated in their minds with armed struggle. Others noted that Hu had devoted his life to the CCP, did what he was asked, and was now being treated like a mule killed after finishing grinding the wheat. Familiar with internal CCP politics, some attributed the purge to personal revenge on the part of Zhou Yang, the minister of culture, because Hu was critical of the CCP-controlled press. They also raised a constitutional concern: Hu's critical essay, they argued, was "expressing his personal opinion, and the constitution says there's freedom of speech."[21]

While *Neibu cankao* was more likely to highlight such oppositional or defensive mentions of the constitution, the more public official media continued to use the constitution to rebut some intellectuals' claims that the CCP routinely violated constitutional rights, particularly freedom of speech and the press. In an article in *Xueshu yuekan* (*Academic Monthly*), for example, one Dai Shubai rejected such complaints as a misunderstanding of the origins of the term *freedom*. Freedom, he argued, is in the superstructure and therefore a class issue dependent on the mode of production at a given time. In classic Soviet propaganda fashion, he maintained that various freedoms in capitalist countries supported the bourgeois political, social, and economic order and did nothing for the working class, something that "rightists" failed to understand when they claimed that there were relatively more rights in capitalist countries.[22] In the United States, where freedom of the press was often lauded, printing presses, paper factories, and all the necessary machinery to produce media were owned by the rich. Rather than using the press to help the poor, capitalists were behind the Ku Klux Klan and other White power organizations that oppressed American workers, students, and writers. In contrast, China's constitution not only had rights such as freedom of the press, assembly, and demonstration but also required (in Article 18) that state officials "obey the constitution and law and strive to serve the people." Dai also trotted out the 1954 discussion of the draft constitution, pointing out that during the two months of discussion, people from all over the country proposed "not a few" suggestions for revisions and supplemental text, and the National Draft Constitution Committee revised the final text based on these.[23]

Marxist-based invocations of the constitution and the history of the 1954 constitutional discussion may have been common in the rarefied world of legal journals but were hardly typical of how ordinary officials made use of the constitutional text in the mid-1950s and 1960s. Whether deemed bourgeois or Marxist, constitutional rights could be marshaled to avoid unpleasant tasks or to wriggle out of political trouble. According to a report on 1962–63 training sessions at the Macheng County Party School in Hubei Province, participating officials had several incorrect perspectives and viewpoints, among them the issue of religion and its relationship to superstition—the same topics that befuddled officials in the mid- to late 1950s. Rather than accepting the CCP's view that superstitious beliefs, as part of the superstructure, could be eradicated by changing the economic base and education, attendees argued that they were thousand-year-old customs and therefore could not be changed. But they also made a constitutional case for avoiding this knotty issue. The "government's constitution," they contended, includes a provision for freedom of religious belief, which is like "wanting people to believe in superstition."[24]

An investigation into the causes of the rising death toll during the Great Leap Forward in Henan Province's Shangcheng County reveals how an official tried to use just a snippet of constitutional knowledge to avoid accountability. In March 1959, Xu Xuefu, a CCP member and PLA veteran, attempted to send urgent messages to Premier Zhou Enlai about over one hundred villagers, "mostly poor peasants," who died of starvation within one month in two brigades (Guanmiao and Wang Qiao) because the mess halls set up during the Leap stopped serving food. He stated in his message that he reported this situation to a man surnamed Liu at the Xinyang Prefectural Government but did not receive a response. If top leaders did not dispatch someone to investigate, he warned, "over a thousand people will die of starvation." To convince Zhou of his honesty, he offered to be "punished by law" if what he said was untrue.[25] In official correspondence, Xu's confidence was attributed to the fact that he was a firsthand witness of these events, but it was also the case that his actions were not unusual among PLA veterans.[26]

When this urgent message was received by officials at the State Council's Letters and Visits Reception Office on March 28, they ordered the Henan Party Committee to investigate. The committee, in turn, noted that provincial authorities were already aware of starvation-related deaths around the province but efforts to prevent these had not been implemented well in several areas. When the Henan Party Committee received the call about problems in Shangchang County, the committee "did not understand the nature of the situation" and instructed Xinyang Prefecture to order the county to investigate. However, the county official who answered the call claimed that their food supply problem had been resolved and that those who died since last winter were elderly men and women who died of illness, not starvation. Perhaps finding this unconvincing, Xinyang authorities mounted their own investigation, which focused on the actions taken by, and against, the veteran Xu.[27]

In their investigation, Xinyang recounted Xu's actions, warnings about impending deaths, and the subsequent inquiries during March and early April by the State Council, prefecture, and county governments. What Xu had reported, they concluded, was correct: people starved to death. They found that for over a month after the mess halls closed, little food could be found. Facing starvation, some villagers survived by eating edible wild herbs, green rape, and water lettuce leaf; others managed to sell their food to the city to buy rice. Those who could not muster the energy, however, had died.[28] Despite these deaths, it was Xu's willingness to alert national leaders that created the greatest sense of urgency among county officials. Faced with his accusations about the closed mess halls, several county officials, among them the head of the propaganda department and the county chief, "made his life difficult" and prevented the local telegraph office from forwarding his messages—which he paid for himself—to the center for twenty days before getting released. During the month authorities were in the dark about the situation, fifty people had died; of these, fifteen passed away from illness, ten from starvation, eleven because of starvation-caused illness, twelve because of illness caused by others' death, and two because of "cadre behavior."

In assessing culpability for these deaths, investigators blamed the usual suspects in the Great Leap Famine, primarily local officials who failed to report grain shortages lest they get labeled "rightists," falsified reports about high agricultural yields, and ransacked homes searching for hidden grain. But these actions did not make the deaths inevitable. Had Xu's telegrammed warnings been allowed to move up the chain of command, some could have been prevented. The county chief, Xiong Manyin, was harshly criticized for ordering a subordinate to haul Xu in for questioning, accusing him of being a rightist, and telling others that "if the reality is not as he describes, Xu should write a confession and be struggled against." Yu Zhongyu, the head of propaganda, led the (failed) search to detain Xu and was later uncooperative with the investigation. The person who had seized the two telegrams addressed to Zhou Enlai, CCP party secretary Wang Hanqing, was also uncooperative but constitutionally savvy. Unlike propaganda chief Yu, who remained unrepentant, he claimed that his actions were not a violation of the constitution because it "only stipulated freedom of correspondence by mail [tong xin], not telegrams [tong dian]" and that his main motive for stopping them was to "not bother the Center." Perhaps because he accurately cited the constitution—the word was "letter" (信)—and confessed to a motive the higher authorities could appreciate, Wang only received a disciplinary warning. Least satisfied were the families of the victims (who only received a mandated official apology and expressions of sympathy) and Yu Zhongyu, the county propaganda chief, on whose head the ax fell swiftest as the point person responsible for closure of the mess hall.

Even though this case involved obscure officials in a county along the Henan-Anhui border, its opportunistic style of "constitutional utterance" was not unusual. In a far more prominent case, during the Cultural Revolution (August 1967), no less of an authority than state president Liu Shaoqi, who authored the final report on the deliberations of the National Draft Constitutional Discussion Committee and then served as chairman of the Standing Committee of the National People's Congress (1954–59), cited the constitution to evade serious political trouble as part of a "throw anything" approach to personal defense. In doing so, Liu committed an extremist act of constitutional bullshit—chutzpah beyond measure—since he, of all people, knew quite well that its rights provisions would not apply to him; not only had Liu stated that "law can only serve a referential purpose when getting things done" (*falü zhi neng zuo wei banshi de cankao*), he and his senior colleagues did not afford the same courtesy to millions accused of political crimes throughout the 1950s and early 1960s.[29] According to a report on the struggle session conducted by Qinghua University Red Guards, Liu brandished a copy of the constitution, but his first appeal to the Red Guards was not legalistic; instead, he demanded that the students recognize his personal status ("How do you treat me like this?") and then beseeched them to be concerned about China's international reputation ("You are humiliating the country by behaving like this"). When this failed, he turned to the institutional arrangements established in the constitution (in chapter 2) dealing with removal from office, pointing out that "only the National People's Congress" could remove the state president. But much like prefectural-level officials in Henan in the case above who avoided all state institutions for dispensing justice such as courts (using internal CCP processes instead), Red Guards, acting on Mao's behalf, also did not see themselves as bound by the constitution. Liu then turned to three arguments extracted from chapter 3. Rather than emphasize his political high status, he posited that he was "also a citizen," implying that according to Article 85, he should be treated equally before the law and allowed to exercise his fundamental rights. Despite knowing the answer to this question, he nevertheless asked his tormentors, "Why are you not allowing me to speak?" and reminded them that "the constitution guarantees that citizens' person cannot be violated" (conveniently ignoring the many loopholes for this protection). When these constitutional invocations failed, he donned his Leninist hat, warning Red Guards that "those who violate the constitution will be subject to legal sanction" (*falü zhicai*)—even though he knew the CCP had never established a mechanism to prosecute constitutional violations. In the end, as is well known, Liu suffered the same fate as many of those he and his colleagues persecuted over the years, some of whom tried, similarly unsuccessfully, to appeal to the constitution to call attention to abuses of power and to protect themselves from it.[30]

Officials low and high were not alone in using this opportunistic approach to the constitution; far less powerful people did the same. Take for instance the negative reactions among staff at the Southwest Institute for Politics and Law to the 1955 purge of Hu Feng. In addition to cutting quessertions that doubted the party's claim to speak for the people ("If the masses trust Hu Feng, is he still considered a counterrevolutionary?"), people also asked how the CCP managed to obtain the highly private nature of the evidence against him: "Where did these letters come from?" If they had been found through a search, doesn't this jeopardize (*fanghai*) the constitutional guarantee of privacy in correspondence? As had been the case in 1954 when such questions went unanswered, so too did this. Instead, the *Neibu cankao* reporter huffed that bad elements were using the constitution to "wage legal struggle against us."[31]

A similar approach can be seen in intellectuals' airing of grievances during the Hundred Flowers Campaign. Repeating their critiques from 1954, they called the CCP's restriction of rural migration a violation of a constitutional right. Someone even wrote a 10,000-character letter to Chairman Mao about this issue ("In fact, we have not given any of the peasants the freedom to change their residence to a city . . ."). [32] But in the typical bandwagon approach, they also charged the CCP with violating human rights, which was not covered in the constitution or other documents, alongside correct constitutional violations, such as interrogations and arrests during previous campaigns: "an untold numbers of citizens throughout the country were detained by the units where they were working . . . a great many of them died because they could not endure the struggle."[33] In a June 1, 1957, article in *Guangming Daily*, Zhong Yizhun, a faculty member at Zhongshan University in Guangdong, recalled that during the Campaign to Suppress Counterrevolutionaries, many innocent men were wrongly convicted but never offered any compensation, as was stipulated in the constitution. But what irked Zhong even more, perhaps because he did not expect the CCP to fulfill its constitutional obligations, was the absence of human feeling in how restitution was offered (similar to the "spiritual compensation" someone asked about in 1954). Much like in the Great Leap Forward case in Henan, Zhong noted that officials' apologies were half-hearted, then "followed by some such lame explanation as 'the authorities have changed their line of approach' and so on."[34]

Like officials and intellectuals, ordinary citizens also used (or more accurately, continued to use) the constitution as a launching pad from which to hurl critiques at CCP policies and officials and to defend themselves against wrongful accusations. Many of these focused on forced relocation, which was interpreted as a violation of Article 90, which granted citizens the freedom to choose their own residence. For instance, in August 1955 some Shanghai factories were ordered to relocate to the interior. In a meeting in Hongkou District, several residents pushed back much as Liu Shaoqi had, with a panoply of arguments, including constitutional (the policy violated the constitution), historical (the KMT "never did anything like this"), and familial (encouraging dependents to go to the countryside will encourage divorce).[35] In another incident, over two dozen unemployed Shanghainese who had been sent to Jiangxi Province to reclaim land marched on the city's Labor Bureau to demand household registration in Shanghai, also on the basis of Article 90: "The constitution guarantees freedom of movement, so why can't we move our registration?"[36] Two years later, during a protest against a factory's relocation to Wuhan, a worker (naturally said to be a "troublemaker") "pulled out a copy of the constitution" to contest their union's acquiescence to management demands.[37] During the Cultural Revolution, an essay published in the *Mountain Eagle*, a paper published by rusticated urban youth, claimed that freedom of residence was a basic right granted in the constitution.[38] The constitution was also cited in defense of the freedom to demonstrate. During the Hundred Flowers Movement, workers in some Shanghai factories distributed flyers in a protest that called for "democracy and equality." When the police detained them, some argued that their arrest violated the constitution.[39] Just how genuine were these constitutional claims? That is, did people think the constitution would help their cases? I consider this improbable. As we have seen, in 1954 many understood the constitution as legal bullshit, and the CCP's subsequent actions could not have been encouraging. Still, many felt compelled to say *something* oppositional, and given even greater unfamiliarity with criminal law and administrative policy, the constitution was as good a platform as any.

Chucking a chunk of constitutional text when dealing with affronts to their persons (and sometimes others') and livelihood can also be seen in an early 1959 dispute involving a mine on the Guizhou/Sichuan border. According to a document from a Guizhou archive, Zhang Youcun, the party secretary of Dashan Commune in Sichuan Province, organized a large group to forcibly take over a mine, injuring the Guizhou-based workers there and confiscating their equipment. To justify this occupation, Zhang claimed that the mine belonged to a Sichuan mining entity and that the Guizhou workers were engaged in a rogue operation. The leader of the Guizhou miners explained to Zhang that they received authorization from several local authorities in Guizhou, but Zhang shrugged off these arguments and started to work the mine. In their letter of complaint, the Guizhou workers pushed back on multiple fronts, describing how Zhang and his group beat them, illegally confiscated their equipment, forcibly occupied the mine shaft, and schlepped away the iron ore. These actions, they argued in the throw anything fashion, constituted a "violation of human rights, the country's constitution, party unity, and the friendship and cooperation between neighboring counties." These intolerable breaches of party discipline and state law and the need to "protect human rights and workers' lives," they pleaded, required intervention from higher authorities.[40]

Given that the 1954 constitutional discussion penetrated urban and suburban areas more deeply than rural ones, and the remote countryside in particular, it should not be surprising that the Guizhou workers could refer only in general terms to human rights, the constitution, and state law rather than to a specific article, as was sometimes the case among intellectuals, students, workers, and rusticated youth. Another group fitting the pattern of more targeted references were ethnic minorities and religious groups (or groups that were defined by both, such as the Hui). In a 1955 report about the Hui in Baotou and Hohhot in Inner Mongolia, for example, some complained that Mao's religion policy was progressive but often violated in practice. In particular, local officials sometimes refused to allow primary schools to teach Arabic, which made it far more difficult to sustain their language skills as they aged. The Hui were particularly upset because they heard about a private school in Beijing that taught Arabic and continued doing so after it became public, but Baotou officials refused to authorize any such establishment. In a reprise of arguments Hui leaders had made in the debates over the KMT constitution, they correctly argued that the constitution "says that China will help minorities develop their languages."[41]

There were also tensions between CCP officials and Christians. Writing ominously in *Neibu cankao* about the religious situation in Liaoning Province, Shen Junhai (沈俊海), an ethnic Manchu who worked as a senior editor for Xinhua's Heilongjiang Branch among other media posts, accused church leaders of engaging in illegal activities by claiming they were constitutionally permissible. But since experience told them that they could not rely on the constitution for protection, church leaders tried other rhetorical tactics, such as comparing the church's relationship with its followers to the CCP's with its own adherents: "The CCP expands its membership; we proselytize." In the city of Luda, one leader was said to have encouraged his followers with these words: "We don't have to be afraid. We have freedom of religious belief. If the government interferes, we can just reason with them." However, he grew his membership not by citing constitutional protection but through personal and family networking ("using relatives to attract relatives" [*yiqin yinqin*]).[42]

There were, however, instances where bits of constitutional knowledge, even when incorrectly learned, proved effective in pushing back against state policies. A 1955 archival report from Rui'an, Zhejiang Province, called attention to local officials who were overly accommodating of Christians who refused to work on Sunday by citing the "religious freedom of the Common Program," not the constitution. Like some of their counterparts, these officials understood the constitution as a higher form of law that the CCP takes seriously. Fearing committing a political mistake by forcing the faithful out of church (while pressured from above to crack down on religion), and apparently unaware of or confused about which higher law was currently in place (in 1954 the new constitution was described as "the development of" the Common Program, not its replacement), the officials "could only stare at them angrily" and "had to hold in their rage."[43]

All these reports dealing with threats—less productive workers, violence in border regions, and emboldened Protestants and Catholics—were more typical of internal party communications reporting than how the constitution was invoked in more ordinary circumstances. Since the CCP was less concerned with what happened inside individual households than inside organizations, it is far more difficult to get a sense of the constitution in everyday life. A small glimpse of this, but one that might be more typical of the constitution's role after 1954, can be seen in an obscure semiannual summary report from 1957 on "Letters and Visits" work in the city of Zigong in Sichuan Province. According to this report, most letters and visits were made by the unemployed, many of whom were described as deeply frustrated and disillusioned by the gap between the CCP rhetoric of having established a new society and their own inability to succeed in it. One compared his desperation to a child who could not find his mother; he was so worried he could not sleep. Those who came to city officials to plead for work either "spoke in tears or made a big scene," refusing to leave until their problems were solved. Some wrote multiple letters or visited on several occasions. Among some of these stressed-out families, law trickled in. According to the report, youth who graduated from junior high school but could not find employment were battered by harsh, legally inflected, parental criticism: "I still have to support you? The Marriage Law says you're an adult, so why can't you find work? What an idiot! The constitution says you have the right to work, so why don't you go to the government to raise a racket?"[44]

Going to the government to loudly complain about poor job prospects was hardly the state's intention when it granted constitutional rights, but this outcome should not have been surprising. Having put rather grandiose promises to paper and then educating millions of people about them, the CCP should have anticipated that some people would put them to some use. While the CCP easily swatted away popular constitution-based arguments with its own interpretations, or, more commonly, ignoring them, it could do little to stop the everyday *mafan*, or bother, that came with citizens using snippets of the document to press them on everyday matters.

Late Mao and Early Reform-era Constitutional Discussions

Roughly three years after Liu Shaoqi waved his copy of the 1954 Constitution at the throng of Red Guards and four years after Lin Biao, Mao's heir apparent, was shot down trying to escape to the USSR by airplane, the CCP leadership, now firmly in the grip of Maoists, decided to conduct two constitutional discussions (1970 and 1975). In 1982, roughly four years after the post-Mao leadership consolidated power, the CCP mounted yet another wide-ranging discussion, also in conjunction with the promulgation of a new constitution, which remains in force today (with many amendments). On all these occasions, "local governments repeatedly made urban residents read, discuss, and comment on constitutions and other laws."[45] In the sheer quantity of constitutional discussions, the PRC easily surpassed the USSR, which conducted another one in 1977, and other socialist states.

Although scholars uniformly associate greater awareness of rights or rules with the reform period and not its Maoist counterpart, from the vantage point of constitutionalism, "statist" or conservative perspectives have become ever more pervasive and influential, albeit not without widespread pushback by ordinary officials and citizens.[46] During this period, largely as the result of the lessons learned from the broad critique of the CCP in 1954, the backlash against the lawlessness (in practice and ideology) of the Cultural Revolution, and the fear of social unrest, the space for constitutional critique has progressively narrowed though by no means disappeared.[47] As we will see in the next chapter, this constriction of constitutional space stands in marked contrast to Vietnam and the USSR. Perhaps most emblematic of this has been the undisguised annulment of constitutional rights in the 1982 Constitution. Article 51 bluntly announced that "the exercise by citizens of the People's Republic of China of their freedoms and rights may not infringe upon the interests of the state, of society and of the collective, or upon the lawful freedoms and rights of other citizens." Since Article 51 is hardly a secret, those calling for "constitutional governance" or "constitutional rights" based on the 1982 Constitution have been engaged in the same game of legal bullshit as the CCP has been in proclaiming these rights in the first place. But it has been useful bullshit for both nevertheless, for many of the same reasons we have seen throughout this book.

The draft constitutional discussion in 1970 was particularly noteworthy for this quality because their talk did not even result in a constitution—this would have to wait until 1975. Containing only thirty articles, officials—much as they had done in 1954—read the draft out loud in public places.[48] Given the sixteen-year gap between the two discussions, it is unlikely that 1970 constitutional propaganda officials knew much about the 1954 experience, but they soon found out that as far as the public was concerned, constitutional discussions, even in the context of political terror, remained a relatively open political space in which legal matters could be but one item on the agenda. For example, as in 1954, participants in the 1970 discussion were wary of the CCP's hot romance with legal obscurantism, asking why the draft excluded any mention of how delegates to the National People's Congress were to be elected.[49] They also sought greater clarity about confusing changes in policy announced in the constitution. In the 1970 draft, for example, workers were given the right to strike, but how did this make sense in the context of the "Great Proletarian" Cultural Revolution when workers in not a few cities gained prominence?[50] "Wouldn't this be similar to making a weapon against ourselves?" some asked.[51] Like 1954, they also called out the CCP for impractical language and policy inconsistency, noting, for example, that the provision "He who does not labor, neither shall he eat" was "only realistic in the countryside, not in the city" because in Shanghai many had quit their jobs, had retired, or could not work. "What would they eat?" they asked.[52] And much like the 1954 discussion provided a relatively safe space to recall traumatic personal experiences during the Five Antis Campaign, so too did the 1970 discussion with respect to the Cultural Revolution. Three years after Red Guards physically assaulted and raided the homes of so-called capitalists, former landlords, teachers, the bourgeoisie, and others, people took advantage of Article 9, which dealt with ownership rights and the state's role in safeguarding them, to query whether capitalists and homeowners would get their property back and what would happen to the savings of those who had died.[53]

Owing to various political complications, the 1970 draft disappeared soon after the discussion period but was then revived as the basis of the 1975 Constitution, which has been closely associated with the so-called Gang of Four, radical Maoist leaders purged soon after their patron Mao died in September 1976. Like its predecessors, it included a brief discussion period that was characterized by not a small amount of explicit and implicit political critique wisely disguised in the form of questions. For example, continuing threads of popular constitutionalism noted in chapter 3, people wanted to know why the document did not include more specific legal provisions and why certain concrete benefits did not apply to them. For example, in their January 1975 discussion, women in Shanghai's Luwan District, likely because they were dissatisfied with the enforcement of the Marriage Law, wanted to know why the constitution lacked a stipulation regarding the legal age of marriage, as well as why it omitted any mechanism to close the "three big differences" (between classes, urban and rural areas, and intellectual and manual labor). According to the report, they were also upset about their low salaries but reluctant to haggle about money, as well as disappointed by the constitution because they wanted it to "improve material conditions . . . especially for local cadres and disabled people." But not all reviews were bad. They praised the constitution for providing the right to strike (soon to be removed), noting, incorrectly, that such a right did not exist in capitalist countries and that, unlike China, reactionary governments feared workers.[54]

Three years later, as part of the process of promulgating another state constitution, the CCP once again mobilized its constitutional education apparatus, albeit with a narrower scope. Unlike 1954 but like 1975, the state conducted its discussion after the constitution was promulgated, not before. It also limited the time made available to talk. After announcing the new constitution in March, in May the government announced plans for only one week of constitutional propaganda and the "general task for the new period." Following the decades-long script of legal education but with newer technology, television-watching stations were set up, schools and universities were told to set aside time to read editorials and hold seminars, activists hoisted large banners in public venues, and people were presented with slide shows, pictorial exhibitions, and theatrical productions. Shanghai People's Art Press published some 150,000 copies of *Illustrated Explanations of the PRC Constitution*, which included images and "some basic explanatory text."[55] Such displays, however, rarely came off without a hitch, and the list of officially permissible subjects was notably short.[56] Propaganda teams were instructed to focus discussions on three sections: the preamble, General Principles, and the rights and obligations of citizens. In some places, officials decided to talk about the CCP's "general task" without mentioning the constitution at all, considering it repetitive (having done this in 1975) and boring "empty talk," a view apparently shared by ordinary citizens as well.[57]

Notwithstanding such restrictions, officials and ordinary people took advantage of this opportunity to express their worries about a variety of issues, most of which went beyond official talking points, the constitutional bandwagon effect. As was the case in 1954 when police officials were alarmed at the institutionalization of prosecutorial procedures and dissemination of knowledge of legal rights, in 1978 policemen expressed their concern that the constitution, by establishing an upper limit to how long they could detain suspects, restricted their ability to fight crime and extract confessions, especially when offenders knew the law.[58] Constitutional propagandists also found themselves in the same dilemma as their 1954 counterparts: a citizenry better educated in law could ask better questions about it, but few of them were able (or, more importantly, authorized) to answer them.[59] Not long after this brief constitutional discussion, for example, the government used the trial of Wei Jingsheng, an activist during the Democracy Wall protests of 1978–79 who had the temerity and courage to call Deng Xiaoping a dictator, as an opportunity to teach people about why it was important to disseminate law. Propaganda officials were told to link the case against Wei with "local cases of petty crime."

But citizens took advantage to ask probing questions: Why had Wei only been charged now given that the felony of supplying military evidence had happened months earlier? Why had his alleged accomplices not been charged? Officials also found conversations about Democracy Wall difficult to navigate. How were they supposed to respond to citizens who said that they "only wanted democracy but did not want state centralization" or to others who told them they only wanted freedom and "thought discipline" was pointless?[60]

Tensions between officials who sought to use legal texts and the conversations about them to enhance their control and citizens who wanted to use these as opportunities to express grievances, some legal but many not, are more easily discerned in the larger-scale and better-documented accounts of the promulgation of China's 1982 Constitution. Although chaired by Ye Jianying, this latest iteration of constitutional revision is generally understood to have been the handiwork of its deputy chair, Peng Zhen, whose hardline Leninist views on law and order have been well documented by Pitman Potter.[61] A longtime ally of Liu Shaoqi, Peng came under attack during the Cultural Revolution. From the new leadership's perspective, generating new laws and legal institutions and educating people about their significance were bulwarks against the return of the sort of political and social chaos epitomized by the Cultural Revolution. The 1982 Constitution was a symbolic break from the "lawlessness" of the Mao era as well as a critical piece of the package of new laws designed to enhance state power against those who would seek to subvert it by illegitimately claiming various freedoms. According to Peng and other framers, although the Cultural Revolution was initiated by Mao, all Chinese were complicit in the breakdown in order and needed to be educated in law to avoid such scenarios in the future.[62] There were, to be sure, many dissenters within the CCP about this approach. Some officials wondered why yet another constitution was necessary, and others "doubted just how effective control via law would be," worrying that it could "damage party authority when implementation was slow or people thought that laws were nothing more than another attempt . . . to assert its power on paper."[63] Such critiques, however, were quickly sidelined.

This top-down approach to law was reflected in how the discussion proceeded. Taking place between April, when the first draft was circulated among party officials, activists, and various model citizens, and September 1982, official accounts, per the standard playbook, emphasized the democratic nature of this discussion. In November 1982, for example, *Beijing Review* kvelled to foreign audiences that "opinions were canvassed from all walks of life, and the draft was repeatedly discussed and revised," estimating that roughly 80 percent of the nation's adults as well as overseas Chinese and "compatriots" in Hong

Kong and Macao participated in discussion, and "many of their opinions have been drawn into the present draft of the revised constitution."[64] One foreign observer rather uncritically cited a comment by Ye Duyi (叶笃义), the general secretary of China's Democratic League, an organization controlled by the CCP's United Front Department, who implausibly claimed on the basis of his personal experience (which included being attacked as a rightist in 1957 and imprisoned between 1968 and 1972 during the Cultural Revolution) that the 1982 national discussion was "broader and deeper" than its 1954 predecessor.[65] From a media perspective, it certainly had many of the hallmarks of a broad campaign. The journal *Zhengzhi yu falü* (Politics and Law), for example, published a helpful glossary of many terms in the constitution, including "United Front," "autonomous region," "economic system," "national system" (*guoti*), "basic law," and "administrative institution." It also republished a piece from *People's Daily* on the flag because "some cadres," seemingly reprising questions from 1954, were still unsure about why the flag had five stars.[66]

Such nods to democratic participation and disseminating legal knowledge notwithstanding, the political space opened by the 1982 national discussion was decidedly smaller than its Mao-era counterpart, perhaps unsurprisingly given the context of widespread social and political trauma people experienced during the Cultural Revolution. Whereas in 1954 the CCP could position itself as the solution to China's problems, by 1982 it was harder to credibly blame imperialism and the KMT for the devastation caused by the Great Leap Forward and Cultural Revolution. Fear—another important element in the CCP's constitutional practice—also constricted this space. Ye Duyi's praise aside, Zhao Zukang, another member of CCP-allied democratic parties, noted that his members had to "overcome our worries" to participate before repeating the party line that the constitution was a necessary response to violations of rights during the Cultural Revolution.[67]

In official circles, few were in the mood for constitutionally grounded criticism. In discussions taking place in late spring at the Shanghai Politics and Jurisprudence Association, for example, the gathered officials proposed abolishing the right to participate in processions and demonstrations, which even this conservative constitution did not do, because they were associated with striking, "which there is no longer a right to do"; like many of their security-first-minded 1954 predecessors, they also proposed that the right to free speech should not include "spreading counterrevolutionary speech" and expressed support for restrictions on religious activity. Not a few also wanted the article dealing with family planning to be in the obligations section of the constitution, since it would be taken more seriously that way.[68] At the May 30 discussion at the Nanjing People's Congress Standing Committee in the auditorium at City Hall, authorities limited the topics for discussion to "rights and obligations cannot be separated," "all power belongs to the people," and "elections produce delegates to exercise power and organize the government to manage the state."[69]

In contrast to 1954, when many officials felt secure enough to offer candid assessments of what they understood as major flaws or contradictions in the constitution, in 1982 their critiques were generally mild and supported the political goals articulated in the constitution. In a discussion at a Shanghai lightbulb factory, for example, they spoke out in favor of the now-abolished right to strike but couched it in terms of protecting themselves from "egregious behavior" on the part of other officials. As noted by Altehenger, this view meshed with the goal of law propaganda of getting people to "identify economic crimes and call out cadres and factory owners if they detected cases of 'violations of law and discipline.'"[70]

Public media reporting on the 1982 discussion, both in terms of whose voices were allowed into print and what topics were brought up, did not allocate much space for critical or dissenting views (as had been the case in 1954 as well); those that made it into print served the CCP's goal of delegitimizing the Cultural Revolution and promoting the new, supposedly more lawful, leadership. *People's Daily*, reflecting the CCP's new perspective on written law as a useful mechanism for political and social control, published a serial column titled "Everyone Discusses the Draft Constitution." Among officials, the published letters adhered to the standard formula of offering praise and downplaying criticism. For example, Ma Huaide, who worked at the Family Planning Office in Shenyang Military Region, praised the constitution for including family planning; another, working in Civil Affairs, lauded it for paying attention to state care for military dependents, disabled people, and the deaf and blind—populations that were not included in the 1954 Constitution whose omission raised some ire.[71] Wang Tianxi, an ethnic Yi who served on the National People's Congress' Ethnic Affairs committee, wrote that he was very pleased that the constitution included the stipulation that citizens have a legal obligation to support "ethnic unity."[72]

More so than officials, ordinary people writing to the column were willing to make provocative comments, but even these largely aligned with the effort to discredit the past, or were edited for this purpose. A man who worked in the motor pool in the industrial sector in Longxi District, Fujian Province, wrote that he was pleased that "anti-bureaucratism" was now in the constitution because officials did not take this very seriously in the past. Such officials should be punished, he offered, implying that they were not currently.[73] Official misconduct was also the subject of a letter penned by Zheng Yuke, a villager in

Qishan County, Shaanxi Province. Zheng was particularly irate that letters of complaint about official misconduct were often dismissed, sometimes for years. He praised the constitution for stipulating that state institutions "must investigate and responsibly handle" such complaints but, in the familiar pattern of popular constitutionalism, also requested more specifics: the revised draft should include "a deadline, either firm or rough, for responding" so that officials no longer could pass the buck.[74] A medical researcher in the city of Tianshui in Gansu Province complained about officials' "arbitrary and personalistic intervention in scientific research," which the constitution (on record in support of the advance of scientific freedom and the Four Modernizations) would hopefully rectify.[75] In another example of popular constitutionalism, others used the opportunity of the constitutional discussion to request benefits. For instance, disabled people asked for dedicated factories, supplemental funds for hardships, and cultural entertainment facilities.[76]

Not a few articles about the constitutional discussion in *Nanjing Daily* appeared to take an even harder line about rule by law as a solution to the excesses of the Cultural Revolution. Not bothering to include critiques of the document, or suggestions for revision based on its omissions, the newspaper seemed keen to give the loudest megaphone to conservative voices in the party-state, including intellectuals aiming to join its ranks after having been declared "mental workers" and thus a segment of the proletariat. For example, Li Peiguang, a faculty member at Jinling Vocational College, proposed that the constitution explicitly stipulate that family planning should be "uniformly enforced" except for minority areas, most likely in response to local resistance to it. In a comment that can be taken either as strongly statist or liberal (but given intellectuals' desire to prove their credentials probably the former), Tian Jun, a faculty member at Nanjing University Law School, argued that constitutional violations should be dealt with harshly to ensure that the constitution will be implemented.[77] In an interview with a reporter, Zhang Youyu (张友渔), the deputy director of the Chinese Academy of Social Science who also became a delegate to the National People's Congress, also veered right, making the party line argument that during the Cultural Revolution people took advantage of their rights to curtail the rights and freedoms of others. Emphasizing that "citizens' rights and duties cannot be separated," he publicly concurred with the giant loophole that was Article 51.[78] He also spoke out against the right to strike, calling it "the product of China's ultra-leftist thought."[79] Another Nanjing group that suffered during the Cultural Revolution, so-called Overseas Chinese, also registered broad support for the constitution, including removing the right to strike, because they suffered under the "extreme leftism" of that period. Like other vulnerable groups, they were careful readers, scanning for any evidence of their political status. Noticing that there were now three separate clauses protecting them in Article 47, "more than before," they were pleased. At the same time, they pointed out that in at least one respect they were not well protected: authorities were still arbitrarily opening their mail. They hoped that the new constitution would help resolve this problem.[80]

In contrast to these public media sources, archives and inner-party documents painted a somewhat different picture than widespread support tempered by mild critiques but still within the confines of a relatively short, tightly managed, top-down legal education campaign.[81] As noted by Altehenger, officials were expected to explain that the constitution was good because it eliminated leftist mistakes during the Cultural Revolution, because it combined "all the good parts" of the previous three constitutions, and because it was the only way to administer the lives of a billion people. Focusing on the big picture, they did not want to indulge popular constitutionalism that took the form of pointed inquiry because "residents whom [they] knew would want to ask specific questions that would only distract from discussion." "Splitting hairs," they argued, is of no "concern to a foundational law such as the constitution." Similarly, the questions propaganda authorities were to pose to people were relatively innocuous and drew on familiar patterns: Should the constitution be expanded or shortened, and what specific changes should be made?[82]

But given a pinhole of an opening, participants wordsmithed. While expressing appreciation that the new constitution moved the section on rights and obligations from next to last to closer to the beginning, taking this as a possible indicator that rights would be taken more seriously than during the Cultural Revolution, not a few criticized its length—138 articles—and wordiness, which made it "difficult to remember," a critique that was also leveled at the shorter 1954 version.[83] There was also considerable debate about the right to strike. In addition to those speaking out for and against it, some called it out for the bullshit it was, arguing that it had no place in the constitution because "they would not be allowed to make use of this right" anyway.[84] Nanjing legal officials were said to be pleased that law would become more important because "young workers, influenced by Cultural Revolution anarchism, did not know what 'law' was, not to mention 'abiding by law,' and solved problems on the basis of emotion and anger."[85] As was the case in 1954, they also critiqued the CCP for creating unrealistic expectations by giving people the right to work when employment opportunities were still limited. Probably envisioning large numbers of unemployed people claiming this right in a protest, they worried how they would enforce public order. They also proposed adding a clause that would "prohibit harming someone else's family and abandoning children," both troublesome issues from a legal perspective.[86]

Nanjing intellectuals also mixed praise with critique. According to a report compiled by the General Office of the Standing Committee of the People's Congress, they interpreted the constitution through the lens of their travails during the Cultural Revolution, viewing it as the "nail in the coffin of leftism" and a signal of optimism that "from here on in China is on road to democracy and law, China has a future, and there is hope for the Four Modernizations." They were also pleased that the CCP retained the clause "equal under the law" from the 1954 Constitution because "during the Cultural Revolution people could struggle against whoever they wanted to, even Liu Shaoqi," as well as "more protections" which allowed them to talk to people from abroad, especially those with whom they had long lost connection. But their questions came close to outright asserting that the CCP was bullshitting when it proclaimed its intention to rule the country by law. Was equality under the law a mere slogan? Was law or power more important? What is the relationship between law, policy, and (making policy through leaders') speeches? This skepticism was born of experience. The 1954 Constitution, they argued in a politically correct manner, was cast aside "when the Cultural Revolution started" (and not a decade before this during the Sufan Campaign). They were similarly dubious that a single propaganda campaign would be enough: "Given the absence of law during the chaos of the Cultural Revolution it will take a lot of effort for the constitution to be useful." Their suggestions for revision, like those of legal officials, also seem to have been partially motivated by trauma and were decidedly illiberal, a notable change from 1954, when their experiences with state terror inclined many toward an emphasis on rights. They favored stronger centralized power, state planning, eliminating the right to demonstrate, and family planning as a constitutional obligation. In a somewhat more liberal vein but still consistent with favoring high levels of state intervention, they wanted the government to make education compulsory and arrange work for the blind and deaf. In what was perhaps a reaction to threats to their status due to market reforms as well as to widespread atrocities against intellectuals in the Cultural Revolution, they proposed adding the phrase "respect teachers" (zunshi) to Article 22 (in the section dealing which what the state promotes) and revising the constitution so that there would be a specific article stipulating that intellectuals were members of the working class.[87]

Legal officials and intellectuals were not the only ones who may have tried to use the constitution to protect their status (and possibly benefits) and promote more conservative viewpoints. Unlike party officials and intellectuals, worker unions often gained power and prestige during the Cultural Revolution. The sudden inclusion of intellectuals into the politically venerable category of "worker" was not always welcome. For example, Li Liren, the union chair at Factory Number 3521, suggested that the state constitutionally commit itself to "oppose bourgeois liberalism" after the clause about the government giving freedom to artistic creation and other activities.[88] In a store in Nanjing's Xuanwu District, someone insisted that intellectuals would gain too much power at their expense, and that person recommended that the final draft of the constitution include the phrase "intellectuals should be concerned about the party and state affairs and support the policy of red and expert," referring to the Mao-era criterion of considering both merit and class origins.[89] Elsewhere in the city, a worker fretted that the constitutional text did not make it crystal clear that the working class was the leading class because it was only mentioned in the chapter on the General Principles. Their class status already threatened by the growing number of university students and technical school graduates, some hoped that the constitution would remain a conservative bulwark preventing its further erosion.[90]

Conservative positions also prevailed regarding family planning and morality issues. Some Nanjing workers strongly opposed the relatively loose language around the one-child policy, arguing that the word "promote" was too vague. Apparently, some had heard about people who cited the constitution to have more children ("not allowing two children is only a local policy"). They were also suspicious of religion. The chair of the union at a provincial-level factory suggested that the CCP add a clause stipulating the freedom to propagandize the theory of evolution immediately after the article about freedom of religious belief, as well as include the phrase "oppose feudal superstition activities" after the clause "no one can use religion to conduct counterrevolutionary activities."[91] Workers at a city department store also offered illiberal views on law, seeking constitutional articles that would stipulate that "parents have the responsibility of raising and educating their children" and that would "oppose immoral activities in courtship and marriage."[92]

In more anonymously submitted suggestions for revision, strongly statist, conservative views also abounded. In a compilation edited by the Standing Committee of the Nanjing People's Congress, a writer proposed that the private sector of the economy should "accept state management and supervision" (in Article 11). Someone else, apparently worried about the post-Mao decline of the status of the People's Liberation Army, wanted the constitution to clearly articulate its status as a "pillar" of the people's democratic dictatorship and that the PLA is "made up of the sons of the Chinese people." Another person wanted Marxism-Leninism and Mao Zedong Thought to be included in the constitution as the "guiding thought" of the CCP. A strict law-and-order type wanted the constitution to include a citizen's right to report and expose "bad people and things" to the authorities. Only one suggestion limited state power. In what was probably another reaction to the Mao era, someone suggested that Article 14, which stipulated that the state protects legal income, savings, and property, also include the phrase "no one can violate this."[93]

These mostly conservative views, however, existed alongside widespread apathy and cynicism about the CCP's broader constitutional project and specific constitutional articles. Indifference to and confusion about the constitution, elements of popular constitutionalism we observed in the 1950s as well, were attributed to the rapid succession of constitutions from 1975–82 and the demands these placed on people who might be called on to discuss them ("Yet another constitution!"), as well as to the correlation between leadership changes and new constitutions. If yet another group of leaders were to emerge in several years, people reasoned, the time they spent learning about the current version would have been wasted. Echoing their 1954 counterparts, not a few claimed they were too busy to participate or that constitutions did not matter to them personally, "as long as they lived their lives honestly, took a wage, had enough to eat, and did not do anything illegal."[94] Apathetic officials in Nanjing asked, "What's the point of discussion if the draft is already done and we're not experts? What kind of suggestions can we make? All we have to do is avoid doing anything improper or saying anything different."[95] Nanjing workers, said to be "confused to varying degrees," also mentioned their lack of expertise to explain their disinterest ("What could we add?").[96]

Some people, however, were too annoyed by the constitution to remain apathetic, another reaction in 1954 that we observed. In Jiangsu, discussion members praised the constitution for being well written but argued that in the end, "it's just a piece of paper." History was too close to reach any other verdict. The 1954 Constitution, they noted, "was also very good, but in the Cultural Revolution was useless; many innocent people were arrested in the middle of the night, and not even the state president [Liu Shaoqi] could escape." The new post-Mao emphasis on rule by law, they argued, was more of an ideal than any reflection of reality; power is stronger than law.[97] If even Liu could be "taken down by one big character poster," someone else skeptically wondered, how could ordinary people expect to be protected by law if they lacked power?[98] Others were cynical because of the mismatch between the nice-sounding words in the constitution and what they observed in their everyday lives, because they suspected that the heart of the constitution was an effort to control ordinary people while leaving the higher-ups free to go about their business (*guan xia, bu guan shang*), or because it "will not be enforced."[99] Some even had the courage to say that the constitutional text should not include any freedoms (affirmative rights) because "citizens were not going to be able to do this in practice anyhow, even if they had rights on paper." In a similar vein, the constitution should also remove the phrase "everyone is equal before the law" because it was unrealistic. [100]

Many other comments and questions, nearly all of which were implicit assertions about the way Chinese politics worked in practice, were far more specific, ranging from administrative issues to rights, official behavior, the status of intellectuals, and even the national anthem. In Shanghai, some noted the historical irony of including the position of state chairman in the constitution because Mao had opposed it in the previous constitution, and they pondered aloud whether the slot was created to give someone a job who was otherwise expendable.[101] In Nanjing, someone proposed including a specific clause about "freedom of mobility" in Article 35 (where rights such as the freedom of procession, speech, press, and assembly were articulated) as well as more specific state policies about education. Rather than a general commitment to it, the state should increase elementary school education in rural areas and secondary education in cities. Noting the vagueness of the right to religious freedom, some suggested that the final draft stipulate that the state will "protect *the places* where normal religious activities are conducted."[102]

People also used the constitutional discussion to complain, sometimes vociferously, about everyday politics. Many focused on the exceedingly high level of local discretion in the CCP's governance system. In Nanjing, for example, people sought an additional clause in Article 17 that would prohibit extortion and blackmail by work units and individuals "for any reason," as well as adding a clause to Article 26 requiring officials to "seek truth from facts, investigate, accept people's supervision with all their heart, serve the people and genuinely be public servants."[103] Others requested an article that would specifically protect people who filed accusations against officials and, "in order to prevent retaliation," end the practice of sending letters of complaint back to local authorities.[104] Some workers requested that the final draft include more precise language about their participation in factory-level worker representative committees, arguing that "in many enterprises it's 'whatever the leader says goes' and worker committees have no say."[105]

There was, however, one area of concern that transcended personal and class-oriented frustrations with politics. Interestingly, it was the very same issue that united people in 1954 as well: the absence of a national anthem in the constitution. Having brushed aside this suggestion in 1954, in 1982 the leadership again demurred. Like their 1954 counterparts, people asked that the new constitution designate the "March of the Volunteers" as the official anthem, arguing that the document "would be incomplete" without it. To bolster their case, they drew on international comparisons, noting that every state has one and that France, Germany, and the USSR under Stalin all used "traditional tunes." Despite such popular support, it took the CCP until 2004 to include the "March of the Volunteers" in the constitution (via an amendment).[106]

Constitutional Surveys

Constitutional discussions were not the only politically approved channels for people to express their opinions about the constitution. The revival of law schools and the field of public administration in the reform period, together with the official mandate to disseminate legal knowledge and to use social scientific methods to understand public opinion, produced a small but significant literature on "constitutional consciousness" and "constitutional knowledge." Whether because scholars accepted the long-standing Western view of constitutions as a source of limitation on executive power or because they found it more convenient, most of these surveys focused on the level of constitutional knowledge among party officials rather than among occupational groups (workers, farmers, etc.) or by gender, as was often the case in the constitution discussions. For instance, many respondents in the influential 1985 Chinese Academy of Social Sciences survey (led by Yan Xiansheng) on citizens' constitutional consciousness had close links to the party or lived or worked in districts that were "already established centers of legal learning" or "model districts," such as Haidian in Beijing, far from a representative sample of Chinese citizens.[107] Even a survey conducted in the western region of Hunan Province in 2000 (n = 690), rural residents represented just 1 percent, in contrast to officials (20 percent) and teachers and students (24 percent).[108]

Despite this shortcoming and the very different settings, many of Yan's findings are broadly consistent with what we have seen during the constitution discussions: confusion and skepticism about the status and function of the constitution in relation to rights, state policies, and class as well as strong support for political accountability if rights are violated. In Yan's survey, for example, in a question about freedom of speech, only 10 percent responded that you could say whatever you think, while 61 percent said this right could be enjoyed "if it did not violate the law"—a wide zone of uncertainty—and 14 percent that freedom of speech would not be protected in real life. Roughly 8 percent indicated that they were unclear about the question and 3 percent that "rights had no relation to their lives."[109] As had been the case historically, very few had read the constitution systematically (12 percent), with nearly 60 percent admitting that they had read it through once, leafed through it, or read parts; 18 percent copped to not reading it at all.[110] Echoing rural sentiments decades earlier, a villager in the Beijing suburbs wrote to the researchers, "I don't understand what the constitution is, only that it's a law."[111]

Subsequent surveys revealed similar confusion about what the constitution articulated and how it operated in relation to other policies, another long-standing source of misunderstanding. In a survey of 230 mid- to high-ranking officials in Hunan Province in 2003–4, for example, Liu Dan found that their constitutional knowledge was scattered (*lingsan*) and not much better than that of ordinary people. Only half could answer most questions correctly (which was slightly better than other questions about law), only 60 percent could correctly identify China as a "Socialist People's Democratic Dictatorship," and, perhaps most surprisingly given the extensive publicity surrounding it, a mere one-third knew that the 1982 Constitution was the one currently in force. The notion that the constitution was a manifestation of class interests, a decades-old propaganda talking point, remained lost on nearly everyone (only 14 percent of respondents knew this). Many were also confused about whether their behavior should be guided by law or policy and admitted that when these came into conflict, they sought further guidance from their superiors.[112]

In Deng Shibao's 2010 study of procurators (n = 107) in 17 provinces and cities, roughly three-fourths of whom were CCP members who held bachelor's degrees, the majority of respondents understood the constitution primarily in terms of its role in "administering affairs of state and ensuring national security" (*zhiguo anbang*), but, somewhat contradictorily, simultaneously believed that the constitution was not used to control ordinary people and limited their prosecutorial actions. Like their Hunan counterparts, they did not understand the constitution in the Marxist sense of class domination. How the constitution mattered in terms of their everyday, practical work was also unclear, much as it was among public security officials in 1954 who sometimes feared that citizens might use it to enforce rights and make their life difficult but otherwise did not understand how it was relevant to them. In the survey, roughly 46 percent said that the constitution was not very relevant (36.4 percent) or had no relevance (2.8 percent) or could not say (6.5 percent)—that "with or without the constitution," their work would be the same. This view was not because they read and understood the constitution, pondered its implications, and then decided that much of it was irrelevant. Instead, they blamed their confusion on the constitution itself for not being clear about the precise functions of the procurator's office in relation to other institutions.[113] But, as we have seen in this book, a hallmark of CCP constitutionalism was deliberate ambiguity, which served to keep both officials and ordinary citizens somewhat fearful of the consequences of their actions and leaving the CCP with maximum flexibility.

This approach has encountered some pushback. In contrast to the early 1950s when CCP officials grew accustomed to virtually unlimited despotic power and worried about limitations to it, the Hunan officials surveyed by Liu Dan indicated that they were dissatisfied with the lack of enforcement. They attributed this to the absence of institutions that could investigate constitutional violations and hold those who violated it accountable. Nearly 60 percent supported the creation of an independent, specialized institution for constitutional enforcement (but one-fifth considered this unrealistic in Chinese politics) and 73 percent thought that both government documents and official behavior should be subject to legal sanction if appropriate.[114] Likewise, nearly 80 percent of Deng Shibao's procurators thought that the primary function of a constitution should be to restrain state power.[115] These official views, more similar to Western views of constitutionalism than those traditionally practiced by the CCP, coincided with (or maybe fed off) a surge of legal activism among law school faculty and ordinary citizens in the late 2000s and between 2010 and 2012, in what has become known as the "rights defense" (weiquan) movement. But neither these views nor this form of activism would survive the Xi Jinping era. Coming to power two years after Deng Shibao's survey, Xi would soon reassert a more Maoist understanding of law and constitutionalism (characterized by repression, uncertainty, and anti-institutionalization). Ordinary citizens, on the other hand, continued to use the constitution much as they had previously—as a platform to critique and mock the CCP, the state, and a plethora of other problems, many of which were nonlegal.

China's Last Constitutional Discussion?

Not long after his ascension to the post of CCP general party secretary in 2012, Xi Jinping gave a major speech on the occasion of the thirtieth anniversary of the 1982 Constitution. Intended or not, this event provoked another constitutional discussion. Allegedly inspired by Xi's call for "full implementation" of the constitution so that it would have "life and authority" and be the "legal weapon for people to defend their own rights," liberal scholars and their conservative rivals argued about the meaning of the constitution in politics (domestic and international), law, and society.[116] Lasting roughly eight months (late 2012 to mid-2013, with pauses), it ended, unsurprisingly given what we have seen thus far in the reform era, with a conservative victory.

According to the recently established narrative of this latest discussion, Xi's comments on the occasion of the 1982 Constitution anniversary (as well as another speech in which he stated that "power must be locked up in the cage of regulation") inspired several prominent intellectuals to organize a meeting in a Beijing hotel to strategize how to push for reform; during this meeting "constitutionalism was a major topic of discussion," and by the end of 2012, seventy-one reformers had signed an initiative authored by Zhang Qianfan, a well-known liberal legal scholar.[117] According to *New York Times* reporters Edward Wong and Jonathan Ansfield, these intellectuals, their hopes "ignited" by Xi, urged the CCP "simply to enforce the principles of their own constitution," a reform tactic that they felt was a "moderate stance" because it did not invoke Western constitutionalism as a model for China.[118] Xi's role as a spark for this debate was also noted in an interview with He Weifang (贺卫方), one of China's most famous constitutional law professors, in the Singaporean newspaper *Lianhe zaobao*.[119]

Discussions about the constitution heated up in early 2013. In its New Year headline, the magazine *Nanfang zhoumo*, riffing on Xi's slogan of the "Chinese Dream" of national rejuvenation, called on the leadership to achieve the "dream of constitutional government" (*xianzheng*). Unhappy with this clever repurposing, censors ordered the editors to remove the headline as well as all seventeen mentions of the word *xianzheng*.[120] In response, small-scale, short-lived, and occupationally limited demonstrations (mostly involving journalists) in support of freedom of the press, characterized by Wong and Ansfield as a "nationwide outcry," emerged in several cities. Over the next several months and peaking in August 2013 after a relatively quiet summer, the term *xianzheng* could not be searched on microblogs, Zhang Qianfan's initiative was scrubbed from many internet sites, and multiple CCP media outlets in China and abroad—but not the authoritative *People's Daily*—published dozens of anti-*xianzheng* essays whose authors ranged from constitutional scholars to a retired PLA colonel working at a mysterious think tank.[121] Their arguments against constitutional governance covered familiar ground. Authors contended that having a constitution does not entail constitutionalism, that constitutionalism is a political doctrine produced by capitalist systems, and that the campaign for constitutionalism was a "Western conspiracy to reject China's developmental path and subvert the rule of the CCP."[122] Despite being overwhelmed in traditional media outlets, pro-*xianzheng* articles continued to appear, but mainly on the Internet.[123]

But the CCP was having none of this. In the context of what Sarah Biddulph has called China's broader "push back against so-called 'Western' ideas, including liberal democratic versions of the rule of law," in April 2013, the top item in the CCP's Central Committee's "Communiqué on the Current State of the Ideological Sphere" (also known as Document Number 9) charged those intellectuals and journalists "promoting Western constitutional democracy" with nothing less than "attempt[ing] to undermine" party leadership[124] In PRC official media, "the word 'constitutionalism' and the ideas with which it is associated" were subjected to withering attacks.[125] In 2014, the CCP inaugurated Constitution Day. Commemorating the promulgation of the 1982 Constitution every December 4, it has been used as a cudgel to enforce political and military discipline (CCP officials and PLA personnel must swear an oath of allegiance to it every year) and promote more conservative views of constitutionalism (court officials often lead propaganda efforts on the holiday).[126] Predictably, this reverence for the constitution has not helped the scores of human rights lawyers detained during Xi's rule or Uyghur detainees.[127] Even as Xi Jinping forced the National People's Congress to remove term limits for president and installed Wang Qishan, who had already retired, as the new vice president, all senior officials stood in front of the delegates and swore their "allegiance to that constitution." During his 2018 swearing-in ceremony, after "soldiers goose-stepped up to the lectern, one carrying a copy of the constitution," Xi recited the oath of office in white-gloved hands, his left hand on the constitution, his right hand in a closed-fist salute.[128]

Inasmuch as the CCP has sent out signals that it takes the constitution (and law more generally) seriously, there is little evidence that popular views toward it—a mix of political critique, calls for greater legal protection from injustice or improved policy enforcement, apathy, fear, confusion, and irreverent mockery—have changed all that much. In 2004, for example, journalism professor Jiao Guobiao, in his "Declaration of the Campaign against the Central Propaganda Department," listed the "fourth illness" infecting the department as "the assassination of the constitution." Surely knowing that the CCP had never implemented freedom of speech, and certainly not in the context of propaganda, he nevertheless accused the propaganda authorities as being "the worst infringer and the spiritual butcher of the freedom of speech that is guaranteed by the constitution."[129] Invoking basic protections and noting the gap between law and social reality can be discerned in Australia-based writer Sang Ye's account of mothers whose children had been stolen. "According to the Constitution," they noted correctly, "marriage, families and children are protected by the state." But perhaps to make their case stronger, they also threw in the "Decision on the Strike-Hard Campaign against Wrongdoers," supposedly passed by the NPC's Standing Committee. "With all these laws and stipulations to protect us," they complained, "why are so many children still being stolen and sold?"[130] Similarly, in the documentary film *Shangfang* (Petition), a woman being hauled away from Tiananmen Square asked, "Why is the constitution trampled on?" without referring to any specific right.[131]

But perhaps most representative of "unofficial" China today, appearing mainly in blogs and online posts, are outright mockery and a willingness to call out the constitution as legal bullshit. Han Han, an irreverent blogger in his youth, hit the nail on the head when he called attention to the CCP's penchant for linguistic acrobatics about political words. The government, he wrote on his blog, "is always coming out with some verb or noun but never explains what that word means. You're not to be counterrevolutionary, it says, for instance, without defining *counterrevolutionary*. You can't be a hooligan, it says, but it won't tell you what a *hooligan* is."[132] Not bothering to even pretend that the constitution was meaningful law, he argued that its Article 1 was, "If we say you're guilty, you're guilty" and that law more generally was likely to be used against those who contest the status quo and to protect the powerful ("when people in power want to do something, laws are not going to stop them, whereas if you infringe on the privileges of the people in power you'll find that the laws are very stringent").[133] If we can assume that such views were at least somewhat widespread—Han Han, after all, had very broad readership—why were liberal legal scholars so inspired by Xi's call for full implementation of the constitution? Was this Hundred Flowers redux? That is, did the rise and fall of the constitutional discussion replicate the typical pattern of political opening, critical and irreverent dissent, and crackdown?

This study places us in a good position to reassess the 2012 brouhaha over the constitution. The documentation of widespread official and popular skepticism about constitution-based rights throughout the Mao and reform eras, in addition to survey data showing that even officials were dubious that anything resembling a separation of powers or independent judiciary could be realized in China, suggests that we should not take at face value the claims that liberal scholars were inspired by Xi's understanding of the constitution. Such scholars are often sophisticated political players and could not have been that naïve. To use Harry Frankfurt's formulation in *On Bullshit*, what were they up to? What was their larger enterprise? In my assessment, these scholars were bullshitting about what they expected from him and the constitution and instead were using the constitution pretty much as they usually have, as a platform for complaints about a variety of issues. As careful readers, it surely could not have been lost on legal experts that Xi's comments about "people's rights and freedoms" being at risk "if we ignore the constitution or disrespect the constitution" noted in the same sentence that this risk also applied to "the party and state's affairs." Furthermore, it was hardly a secret that the 1982 Constitution was less about the expansion of citizens' rights than a conservative backlash, which included not a few intellectuals, against the disorder of the Cultural

Revolution and was recognized as such at the get-go. Its Article 51 was crystal clear about this point. *This* was the Han Hanesque "always coming out with some verb or noun but never explain[ing] what that word means" form of constitutionalism that Xi believed required better enforcement. Since liberals surely were aware of this enduring obscurantism, why would they still recommend using the constitution as a basis for political reform?

Part of the reason was that any discussion of the constitution was a ready-made platform, or cover, to talk about problems that were otherwise quite sensitive, as was the case in 1954. In what seems to be a longstanding pattern in Chinese constitutionalism, constitutional talk is often more important than the constitutional text because of the relatively open political space it can provide. Indeed, many of the issues raised in 2012 were extraconstitutional from a textual perspective. In the open letter signed by seventy-one liberal intellectuals that was triggered by Xi's "implementation" remark, the authors threw in everything, identifying centralization of decision making within the party, insufficiently well-institutionalized intraparty election mechanisms, and the lack of separation between the party and state as major problems resulting in abuses of power, corruption, unrest, disaffection, and arbitrary rule. Their solutions, such as expanding democracy, deepening market reforms, "respecting" freedom of association and expression, and instituting judicial independence, could hardly be incorporated within the constitution as everybody understood it for the past sixty years unless they pretended otherwise. Similarly, in *Nanfang Zhoumo*'s controversial 2012 New Year's message, editors proclaimed that constitutionalism would do nothing less than make China strong and wealthy, allow the people to "become truly formidable," make possible the "striv[ing] for national sovereignty abroad even better," "safeguard the freedom of the nation," and "strive even harder for civil rights."[134]

Given that during PRC history the CCP tolerated not a small amount of constitutional critique and even mockery and that not a few of the *Nanfang Zhoumo* comments were well within the legitimate boundaries of Chinese legal and nationalist discourse, why did the CCP snuff out this constitutional discussion almost immediately after it got underway? If Xi emboldened hopes for constitutional reform among liberal intellectuals, why did their response— in Hundred Flowers and Anti-Rightist Campaign fashion—trigger the crackdown? As noted but insufficiently stressed by the legal scholar Rogier Creemers, what was politically subversive was their use of the word *xianzheng*, which did not appear as a legitimate topic of discussion in any previous constitutional discussion and was not part of the "carefully manicured Party political lexicon."[135] While Han Han wittily and correctly noted that an important feature of Chinese constitutionalism is its linguistic ambiguity, the CCP also takes umbrage when others try to reduce it by suggesting clarifications (which they have tried to do since 1954) or speak frankly (or stop bullshitting) about what they want the constitution to do politically. The CCP is in its comfort zone with hard-to-pin-down, highly flexible phrases such as "socialism with Chinese characteristics" or "ruling the country according to the constitution" (which can also mean tough discipline) and reacts harshly when words actually say what they mean—in this case (as correctly identified by conservative legal scholars and Document Number 9), overthrow of the CCP-led political system. It is entirely possible that this conservative countermobilization would not have taken place had intellectuals avoided the word *xianzheng* and deployed previous generations' methods of political critique—questions, concrete suggestions for revision, quessertions (putting forward an idea while stressing that it is questionable), and implicit critique.

Conclusion

The Meanings of the Constitution
and Comparative Perspectives

So what, at long last, have we learned about the meaning of the Chinese constitutions and, by implication, the Chinese revolution? If some of my older relatives were still alive, they surely would have asked, "*Nu* [so, said impatiently in Yiddish-inflected English]—what's all this been about?"

My answer is simple and complicated. Starting with the simple, the evidence in this book demonstrates that Chinese constitutions did not contribute to legitimacy, and this was well-known to the state leaders who read citizens' comments about these documents during national discussion periods. But if constitutions did not serve the purpose of legitimization—often the primary role ascribed to them in the literature—what roles did they serve? This is where it gets more complicated and difficult to capture in neat one- or two-word descriptors (such as *instrumentalism* or *authoritarian legality*). Evidence shows that for many state officials the constitution and the discussions about it were governing practices or useful tactics to exercise power by way of inducing feelings of uncertainty, jealousy, apathy, helplessness, fear, frustration, and confusion. Both the text and the talking also served to remind people who had power and who did not, to create a certain impression of political power, to sow and intensify social divisions, and to distribute symbolic and selective material rewards. Even though many officials did not understand what exactly a constitution was or what it was supposed to do, it was interpreted as both a higher form of law and a convenient text from which even inaccurately cited nuggets could be excavated to give them leverage to push through unpopular policies.[1] To complicate things further, all this was context dependent: timing, location, biographical attributes (age, gender, ethnicity), history, and what policies, directives, and guidelines happened to be in place had significant impact on how the constitution would be understood within the state apparatus. In this respect, Radway's analysis of readers of romance novels, which emphasized the importance of taking context into account, has much to teach scholars of popular constitutionalism. Similarly, Rogiers Creemers's helpful suggestion that "scholarly models of Chinese law would gain more explanatory power if they understood its context- sensitivity and fluidity as features of the system, rather than as aberrations" applies to the case of the constitution as well, with the added proviso that history is also very important.[2]

We have also seen that the constitution was not only a vertical relationship between officials and citizens but also a horizontal one among officials. Like ordinary citizens, they experienced constitutionally induced stress, worrying about the constitutional implications of committing a political error or being confronted with legally knowledgeable citizens. While some were diehard Leninists, seeking to impose discipline on various people who seemed to threaten the preferred social order, others were enamored of Western constitutions, particularly the United States', for its limits on executive authority, separation of powers, an independent judiciary, and political rights. Many knew that the rights provisions in Chinese constitutions were legal bullshit, and they said as much; at the same time, this bullshit demonstrated its usefulness on many occasions.[3] This helps explain why the CCP has been quite willing to accept the reputational costs of promulgating constitutions that provide a juicy target for critics' rhetorical darts.[4] More than this, proceeding despite this mockery was a way for the CCP to demonstrate its "power to proclaim and promulgate a falsehood."[5] It is as if the CCP has been saying, "We can bullshit all we want and there's nothing you can do about it."

Ordinary people, for their part, also understood the constitution as useful bullshit. Confronted at the get-go by the large gap between what the constitution said on paper and what they experienced in life—about not only rights but also institutions that did not function as stipulated—they proved quite willing to "call BS" when given this opportunity, sometimes explicitly but more often through the mechanism of questions and what H. P. Grice called quessertions. When citizens today invoke the 1982 Constitution in support of demands for political reform and a plethora of other rights, they, too, are engaging in the same enterprise of bullshit because nothing in Chinese history suggests that this is a viable course of action. But this does not mean that constitutions were useless. As we have repeatedly seen, people used the texts and discussions about them as platforms to raise serious questions about the nature of CCP rule, its governance practices, interpretation of history, and understanding of class and their role in the new polity. They were also a way to request or defend material benefits, ideological position, and religious and ethnic status, as well as complain about all sorts of issues, many nonlegal in nature, in a sort of bandwagon approach. Constitutional discussions also provided space to play "gotcha" with sometimes clueless officials, mock, ridicule, critique, and rebut. In the often deployed "throw anything" tactic, people could chuck constitutional words at officials along with other tidbits of knowledge about rules, laws, and policies and do the same with family members and coworkers. The constitution also offered support to those holding more illiberal views, particularly about religion, ethnicity, and political rights.

How does this book contribute to broader theories about constitutionalism, particularly in authoritarian states? First, it confirms that PRC leaders, like their late Qing and Republican predecessors, understood the constitution in broadly "instrumentalist" terms (mainly as a mechanism for strengthening the state). Second, many of the constitutional functions in authoritarian regimes that were noted by Tom Ginsburg and Alberto Simpser, such as providing a manual and blueprint for establishing state institutions, a billboard for announcing policies, a tactic for demoralizing opponents, and window dressing for despotism, can be found in the PRC at different points in its history.[6] Third, I agree that the concept *popular constitutionalism* is helpful in capturing nonofficial voices about the meaning of the constitution.

Beyond these general "theory confirming" arguments, this book's primary contribution has been in the realm of data and specifics, illustrating how constitutional concepts and categories were understood and practiced over the course of PRC history. That is, it is one thing to deductively assert, usually based on legal texts, that the Chinese state holds a certain perspective on law or constitutions (billboard, blueprint, etc.) or that there can be a discrepancy between official and popular perspectives, and it is another to inductively demonstrate that such perspectives exist. In the absence of such specification and thick description, the study of constitutions, and law more generally, too easily veers into arid abstraction. For example, if it is argued that China approaches constitutions, or law more generally, in an instrumental fashion, what, exactly, was so useful, and what did officials in charge of this instrumentalism say about this? Did citizens accept the view that constitutions were important normative documents? Here I have identified instilling fear, stroking egos, pouring accelerants on social tensions, causing confusion, and gaining greater ability to credibly lie about its core provisions in order to implement unpopular policies as critical to understanding Chinese official and popular interpretation. High-level officials knew that constitutions were having these effects thanks to constitutional discussions and extensive media reporting in *Neibu cankao*.

Relatedly, but lower down the social hierarchy, this book has provided a more fleshed-out and "peopled" understanding of popular constitutionalism than almost all constitutional scholarship to date. Most studies of popular constitutionalism in China (as well as Vietnam) have focused on highly educated people, often law professors and political dissidents, as representatives of "the people." What those lower down the social hierarchy have thought and advocated and the ways in which they have tried to make the constitution useful to them for liberal and conservative objectives have rarely come under the purview of scholars even when data became available. Moreover, such scholarship has focused on the reform period and on unrepresentative constitutional moments in which elites happen to star, such as the outpouring of support for a former university student who died in police detention (the Sun Zhigang case), a liberal petition (Charter 08), and the 2013 call for constitutional governance. Methodologically, this book suggests that constitutional studies would significantly benefit from a more pluralistic approach to periodization and source materials than is currently practiced by most constitutional scholars. Rohit De's *The People's Constitution: The Everyday Life of Law in the Indian Republic*, which also relies on archival materials (from the Supreme Court) that reveal the voices of marginalized people's understanding and use of the constitution, is a good example of how the field should change.[7] However, as noted by Ran Hirschl, the legal training of most constitutional scholars (most of whom congregate in law schools) which emphasizes the exegesis of appellate court decisions and the incentive structure of that field (and the fact that many publish in journals that are not peer-reviewed) does not leave much room for optimism that many will adopt this methodology.[8]

The approach used in this book—looking at the constitution over a longer period and exploring data that uncover a multiplicity of voices within the CCP, government, and society—not only captures the many meanings of the constitution in China but also puts us in a better position to assess the second primary question: What do constitutional questions and comments tell us about the legitimacy of the Chinese Communist Revolution? I have argued that from the perspective of people's reactions to multiple constitutions, the CCP's legitimacy was precarious, socially narrow, disputed, and at points nonexistent.[9] This should not be surprising. The CCP came to power as a rural insurgency based largely in north China, initiated a multiyear reign of terror (1949–52, 1955, 1957–61, and 1966–68) that produced a death toll and incarceration in the millions, and implemented unpopular policies (unified purchasing, collectivization, the Great Leap

Forward, and the Cultural Revolution, among others). The limited constitutional discussion in 1954 (which did not involve many villagers) and the increasingly restricted nature of the post-1954 constitutional discussions surely reflected the CCP's awareness that it would not be politically prudent to open a wide political space for people to discuss history and politics. The longer view of constitutional discussions shows the CCP, despite its notable economic and public health accomplishments, to be increasingly scared of its own people.

This take on the CCP's legitimacy gains some support by comparing China's constitutional discussions with those of two other Marxist-Leninist regimes, the USSR and Vietnam, both of which have been extensively studied by historians and legal scholars. In 1936, the USSR promulgated a new constitution, widely known as the "Stalin Constitution," but before doing so held a national discussion about its draft "seeking to harness popular enthusiasm and participation to further strengthen and stabilize the Soviet state."[10] By several measures, it was more politically pluralistic than its PRC counterpart. Looking at official media, *Izvestia*, edited by Nikolai Bukharin, was "consistently and openly critical" of local officials, in contrast to *Pravda* and *Trud*, which, like *People's Daily* in China, emphasized the positive elements of the draft. According to Ellen Wimberg, *Izvestia* reporters "consistently put local officials on the spot," and its editors featured an almost daily column alongside highly critical reports, something that is difficult to find in China even in the 2010s.[11]

Second, the Soviet's "all-union" discussion was larger in scope than in the PRC, particularly in its inclusion of children (whose questions were sometimes quite uninhibited) as well as the countryside.[12] Soviet villagers, like their PRC counterparts, were excluded from constitutional perks (such as free vacations, health care, and pensions) that were conferred on "workers."[13] However, in contrast to China, Soviet villagers made extensive complaints about this (to no avail).[14] In fact, the most common suggestion for revision was to have the constitution provide social benefits to collective farmers. As J. Arch Getty put it, peasants wanted "benefits as workers" and were "brave enough to speak up about it."[15]

They also wrote. Soviet archives document intensive activity by the countryside, including thousands of letters written by villagers about various abuses and suggested revisions.[16] To the consternation of propaganda officials in one region, "in a great number of instances, collective farmers began reading and discussing the draft constitution themselves, without waiting for the Party organizations."[17] A resident of the village of Tatarovo, for example, essentially called out the constitution as bullshit: "You say that our constitution is the most democratic in the world but according to our constitution you can't say a single word. If you do say something and wound our leaders, then they pick you up by the scruff of your neck and throw you in jail. That's democracy for you. It would be better if we didn't have that kind of democracy."[18] In China, in contrast, the CCP appears to have struggled to organize village and township officials for constitutional study sessions that went beyond the very superficial or hold question-and-answer meetings with villagers who were busy with their work. Higher illiteracy rates among officials and villagers in China may have further limited the impact of the campaign since the constitution, more than an ordinary policy document, used particularly complex and unfamiliar terminology and was quite long.

As a result of the extensive constitutional discussion in the USSR, Soviet scholars, unlike their PRC counterparts, stress their constitution's long-term impact even as they recognize that the discussion was tightly controlled.[19] According to Lewis Siegelbaum and Andrei Sokolov, the Soviet constitution served as "the starting point for resistance to illegalities, abuses of power, deprivation of rights, and arbitrary rule. Attempts to reform the system began, as a rule, with appeals to the constitution."[20] Similarly, Petrone argues that the rhetoric of democracy in the constitution "destabilized the status quo between local Soviet officials and Soviet citizens in many parts of the Soviet Union," a claim that scholars of PRC constitutions rightly avoid.[21]

Finally, the style of oppositional speech was somewhat bolder in the USSR. In the PRC, implicit and insinuative critiques of the CCP by way of questions, some of which were surely instances of feigned ignorance, were common during constitutional discussions, and there were satiric and mocking comments. In the USSR, constitution-focused satire appears to have been more widespread, at least in published sources: "Where did all the butter go? It must have melted 'in the bright rays of the Stalin Constitution'"; "Before the introduction of the Stalin Constitution the joyous Soviet citizens asked one another incredulously: Have we reached socialism yet or will it get even worse?" After learning about the coat of arms of the USSR, some workers "thought over what they had learned: Hammer to the left, sickle to the right, our coat of arms is quite a sight. Do you want to hammer? Do you want to reap? You're fucked either way, so don't utter a peep."[22] This appears to be consistent across political media. As Altehenger notes in her study of *Manhua* magazine (which published political cartoons), Chinese illustrators—unlike their Soviet counterparts who wrote for *Crocodile [Krokodil]* magazine, on which *Manhua* was modeled—could only publish inoffensive satire. Whereas *Manhua* closed in 1960, *Crocodile* enjoyed the freedom to publish on international affairs and domestic problems such as the misconduct of party officials and local leadership until the fall of the USSR.[23]

We should not exaggerate the openness of the Soviet Union to political critique and satire, however. Like China after 1954, the USSR, owing to the large number of unanticipated responses to the invitation to talk about politics, never again asked the population to "participate in open political discussion" and in contemporary Russia young people are taught that individual rights are "less important than a citizen's duties and responsibilities to the regime."[24] Nevertheless, in comparative terms, post-1936 discussions were still more extensive and open than in China. The draft constitution of 1977 was reportedly discussed by 140 million people (more than four-fifths of the adult population at the time) over the course of four months and led to the amendment of one hundred articles and the addition of a new one.[25] Even populations considered more politically sensitive were permitted to use the constitutional discussion to demand improved rights. Veterans, for example, requested that a special status for them be written into the constitution, insisted that "respect" toward them be a major goal of government and society alike, and asked for legislation that would provide an enormous range of legal privileges, demands to which Brezhnev soon agreed.[26] In China, the government did not even seek out veterans' opinions in the 1954 discussion or any subsequent one, let alone permit them to complain about their relatively low status.

The Vietnamese experience of relatively unconstrained constitutional discussions provides another illustrative contrast to the PRC. For example, the constitutional amendment process in 2001–2, though party led and managed, provided a platform for views that were wide ranging, where debate was robust and inclusive of groups that lacked any significant voice in China, such as overseas nationals, retired officials, and Vietnam's Peasant Union (the union called for constitutional recognition of its role as representative of Vietnamese peasants). Citizens proposed revisions that would have made the constitution a mechanism to increase social justice (emphasizing the duty of the state to protect the poor, unemployed, elderly, and others who suffered in Vietnam's reform era), constrain legal institutions ("Legal institutions should not belong to the executive system. . . . The organization of the court system is inappropriate"), and strengthen the role of the constitution. Although the Communist Party ultimately managed to control the constitutional revision process and the "sweeping constitutional dialogue" it produced, and the party only revised one article in the original draft, it was nonetheless a struggle.[27]

A constitutional debate in 2010 was also more open than its PRC counterparts. Media coverage of it "successfully conveyed an intellectual environment that seemed supportive of a separation-of-powers structure," debate became bolder, and intellectuals sought to use the constitutional revision process to push for more radical reform. No less a figure that the former president of the National Assembly, Nguyen Van An, gave an online interview which was widely discussed and cited by bloggers. In it, he "offered a frank and liberal view on the revision process," arguing that people should have the power to approve the constitution, "as things should be in a 'Republic.'"[28]

But even these open, blunt, and inclusive constitutional discussions paled in comparison to the constitutional mobilization that took place three years later, particularly when set against the backdrop of the crackdown against *xian-zheng* (constitutional government) in China that same year. As recounted by Vietnamese legal scholars such as Bui Ngoc Son, Giao Cong Vu, Kien Tran, and Bui Hai Thiem, the 2013 constitutional amendment drafting process involved an increasingly large number of actors who spoke out forcefully in discussion forums and online (including Facebook) on a broad array of issues, many politically sensitive. Although I disagree that such discussions can be characterized as popular constitutionalism since most participants were legal, political, and social elites who lived in cities, the topics they broached cut across class, religious, occupational, and ethnic divides.[29]

For example, in scenarios that are difficult to imagine taking place in China, Dr. Nguyen Dinh Loc, a constitutional law scholar and former minister of justice, submitted Petition 72 to Vietnam's Constitutional Amendment Committee; the petition aimed to trigger a national constitutional dialogue, particularly among young people. Another group, called "Let's Draw Up the Constitution" was founded by two Vietnamese scholars at the University of Chicago (a mathematician and a physicist), a scholar at Harvard's Kennedy School of Government, a retired party member, and several legal scholars from Vietnam National University–Hanoi School of Law. Their work included creating a public forum for constitutional dialogue, a "means of digesting public opinion on the draft constitution, and offering constitutional suggestions." Such a "dialogical space," notes Bui, had never existed in Vietnam aside from the official government website through which citizens can submit formal comments.[30] According to official sources, there were more than 20 million public consultation memoranda and reports submitted to the Drafting Committee of the 2013 Constitution, as well as thirty thousand official conferences, meetings, or seminars held to discuss and comment on its provisions.[31]

Beyond its wide scale, the topics raised in the 2013 Vietnamese constitution discussion grew larger as the space for relatively open discussions narrowed in China. In contrast to their counterparts in the PRC for whom discussions about human rights in the context of constitutionalism has become taboo after 2013, a growing number of scholars and activists in Vietnam have directly challenged the longtime statist view that "human rights can only emanate from the laws of the state," arguing instead that human rights are "natural and fundamental, not depending on the whims and fancies of the state." During the constitutional discussion, provisions regarding human rights and citizens' rights constituted the majority of amendments and received the most public attention (28 percent of all suggestions made to the Amendment Committee). These efforts bore fruit: many rights that were problematically considered citizens' rights in the 1992 Constitution are now recognized as human rights that are no longer bestowed or gifted by the state.[32] Equally important, organizations involved in various areas involving human rights (such as women's rights, LGBT rights, and minority rights) have experienced rapid growth and "significantly influenced" implementation, the opposite of what has happened in China under Xi.[33]

What accounts for these differences between China and the USSR and China and Vietnam? We could easily imagine reasons neither of these countries would want to provide relatively open political spaces for extensive constitutional discussions. Prior to their constitutional discussions, both the USSR and Vietnam experienced foreign and civil wars, rural collectivization, and political repression of class enemies. And their pretensions to legitimacy aside, the Bolsheviks did not have a popular mandate to rule when they seized power; in Vietnam, southerners were effectively conquered by the Communists, not liberated (many former Republic of Vietnam officials, military personnel, and collaborators were sent to reeducation prison camps).[34] Yet both had constitutional discussions that were more open, longer lasting, and more influential than their PRC counterparts.

Part of the explanation surely lies in the more cosmopolitan political and legal cultures that had taken root prior to the consolidation of what might be called "hard-core" Leninism. In contrast to the PRC, where both the KMT and the CCP accepted the core tenets of Leninism in the early 1920s (not long after the collapse of the Qing Dynasty in 1911 and the emergence of warlordism), Russia experienced several decades of urbanization, broad and deep intellectual engagement with the West, and relative political pluralism before the Bolsheviks took power.[35] In Vietnam, Ho Chi Minh's ideas about the role of the constitution were shaped by Leninism as well as Western constitutional concepts such as limiting the state's despotic power and protecting democratic rights. The 1946 Constitution "was not a socialist document," according to Bui Ngoc Son, drawing primarily on French and American constitutional experiences such as popular sovereignty, popular constitution-making powers, political pluralism, fundamental liberal rights, and a Montesquieuian tripartite government with an independent judiciary. Bui notes that Ho, unlike Mao in 1954, sought to "socialize the new-born DRV into the civilized world and gain more international acceptance, especially from Western powers like the United States and France." Only in 1959 did North Vietnam's constitution fully adopt

Communist terminology.[36] This more liberal legacy can been seen in many other contrasting features to contemporary China besides constitutional discussions, such as greater checks and balances and intraparty democracy, more diverse stakeholders in the policy process, a greater willingness to incorporate international best practices in the field of human rights, a more respectful approach to voices from civil society, a more activist labor sector and vibrant religious community, and a more independent lawyers' bar association.[37]

Historical legacy, broadly understood, is not the only critical difference between the USSR and Vietnam on the one hand and the PRC on the other. I would argue that state legitimacy is also critical in explaining the diverging trajectories in constitutional development, contemporary political practices, and reform possibilities.[38] The Chinese Communist Party is understandably more afraid of opening up constitutional discussions because it is fully aware of its own history of massive political terror, violence, genocidal-scale death, and unprecedented persecution of intellectuals in the Mao era and the massacre of students and workers in the post-Mao period (Tiananmen in 1989), events without parallel in Vietnam. The death toll from mass persecution and ideologically driven policies (such as the Great Leap Forward) in China far exceeds that of the USSR as well, and is closer in historical memory.[39]

Moreover, unlike Ho Chi Minh and the Vietnamese Communist Party, the CCP cannot credibly claim to have defeated the Japanese in World War II (which it does nonetheless, while stifling alternative accounts) or, unlike Stalin, winning a war against a regime as powerful and bloodthirsty as the Nazis. Even when it sought to defend Chinese sovereignty against the United States during the Korean War, the CCP experienced tremendous difficulty drafting soldiers.[40] Equally important, the CCP, which tracks public opinion, surely knows that people would have a lot to say—much of it difficult to hear—about their political experiences and memories should they be allowed a broad platform for doing so.[41] To be sure, Vietnamese leaders are worried as well and similarly strive to control and manage constitutional discussion, but not to the same extent.[42]

In short, the severe limitations on constitutional discussion in China, and the CCP's fear of embracing civil society (even during the 2020 COVID-19 crisis that undid years of effort in building soft power and resulted in thousands of deaths), are, at least in part, a reflection of the problematic nature of CCP legitimacy and the regime's awareness of this.[43] A regime more confident in its legitimacy would not be as fearful. One can attribute other forms of state repression, such as tight restrictions on historical research and the Internet (far more than Russia and Vietnam), as well as expensive measures that incentivize pro-CCP political participation (paying people to post positive comments about the CCP on social media platforms) to the problematic nature of CCP legitimacy.[44]

This book's interpretation of Chinese constitutionalism, like all similar studies, has been shaped by its source material. Relying primarily on archival sources as well as some lesser-known studies of constitutionalism in the reform era, I have worked mostly "with the grain" of these materials—that is, contesting not their truthfulness but rather their tendency to emphasize certain problems and how these were resolved by party officials. Whether one accepts my interpretations or not, our understanding of how people have interacted with the constitution is significantly more colorful than most previous studies.

That said, this analysis is far from comprehensive. When one relies heavily on one source, others fade into the background whether because of lack of resources or bias toward what one holds near and dear. I acknowledge both deficiencies. For example, with more energy, time, money, and inclination, I could have researched dozens of provincial newspapers or, in a similar vein, conducted a thorough analysis of constitutional discussions as they surfaced in *People's Daily* since 1949. Certainly, there is more room for studies of official understandings of constitutionalism as they appeared in the media. In an ideal world, I would have liked to interview participants in the 1954 discussion, as well as subsequent ones, a labor-intensive task that was also well beyond my resources as a liberal arts college professor.[45] I hope that others take this up before it is too late. But whether future research will rely on new archival sources, provincial-level sources, or interviews, I hope that future constitutional scholars do their best to supplement text-based exegesis of constitutions with how these are interpreted by ordinary people as well as curtail the tendency to rely heavily on the accounts of unrepresentative rights defense activists, lawyers, dissidents, and quickly repressed petitions or movements, all of which amount to cherry-picking data. The numerous studies, often repetitive, of the Sun Zhigang case is a primary example of this sort of excess. As noted by Creemers, even in the Sun case social actors did not drive policy change.[46] From my vantage point, constitutional scholarship in the China field would do well to delve into archives like legal historians do, and perhaps more promisingly, learn from legal anthropologists whose perspective on what constitutes popular is closer to the ground. I strongly endorse Ran Hirschl's call for law school–based scholars to learn more from social scientists about research design and methodology as a complement to appellate court–centered analysis.[47]

From a more theoretical and comparative perspective, researchers should try to avoid thinking about Chinese constitutionalism using measures or benchmarks for progress drawn from Western legal history or asking questions implying that China is somehow deficient when it does not meet a certain standard. Like my political science colleague William Hurst in his study of law in China and Indonesia, I would enjoin scholars to avoid using the "standard rule of law template" in reference to China or, in many cases, to Western governments as well (unless as a Weberian "ideal type").[48] Chinese constitutionalism, this book has shown, has been shaped by the Chinese Communist Party's revolutionary history more than Western notions of law even though it often uses the language of the latter.[49] Moreover, unlike Vietnam, where constitutional debate is alive and well, the PRC is moving even farther away from Western ideals. Capturing constitutionalism as it is experienced and interpreted by ordinary people rather than in reference to long-fading hopes to implement rule of law or democracy could lead us in more interesting directions.

The recent treatment of Hong Kong seems to be a case in point. The ways in which the CCP has deployed its constitution shares many features with its takeover of Hong Kong, culminating in the June 2020 crackdown by way of a draconian National Security Law. China's formal agreement with the United Kingdom to maintain Hong Kong's autonomy (including a legal system known for its impartiality) for fifty years was, in hindsight, the same sort of useful bullshit the constitution has been, sharing many hallmark features: United Front–style divide and rule (in particular, developing strong ties to local tycoons), stigmatization of opponents, the distribution of particularistic benefits to supporters, broad and vague definitions of crimes (in the National Security Law these include "secession," "subversion," "terrorist activities," and "collusion with a foreign country or with external elements") that allow maximum space for political discretion, using the security forces to engage in extensive surveillance, and propaganda about maintaining rule of law.[50] The promise of half a century of autonomy was unlikely a lie (since it was unlikely the intention) but rather, as Frankfurt put it, only "pertinent to [their] interest in getting away with" what was most surely the original design to envelop Hong Kong in CCP rule as soon as possible.[51] In more ordinary times, the CCP would have had more difficulty pulling this off, but as the world was distracted by the coronavirus and Black Lives Matter protests, the CCP saw its opportunity and pushed its advantage to the maximum (which is, as Heilmann and Perry argue, a distinguishing feature of "guerrilla-style" policy making), plunging in the legal knife much as the 1954 Constitution did with the bourgeoisie. That these revolutionary tactics could be effectively deployed in the twenty-first century against one of China's most modern and Western-oriented cities makes learning more about their origins especially relevant. To be sure, verification of these arguments awaits the collapse of the Chinese Communist Party and unrestricted access to its Central Archives (much like what happened in the former USSR), but until this happens, I offer them as historically grounded and reasonably plausible scenarios as well as food for thought.

NOTES

Introduction

1. According to the Chinese constitutional scholar Han Dayuan, roughly 88 percent of the 1982 Constitution is either identical or closely related to the 1954 Constitution. See *1954 nian xianfa yu xin zhongguo xianzheng* (Changsha: Hunan renmin chubanshe, 2004), 546. "Rule of law" generally means that powerful people acknowledge law as an independent source of authority above them; "rule by law" refers to officials following laws without recognition that laws have higher status. Chinese officials usually understand law in the rule-by-law sense. Xiaowei Zheng, for example, argues that in republican political culture in China, popular sovereignty, not law, was enshrined as the "fundamental principle," and modern constitutional concepts, such as the separation of powers and limited government, were "not implemented in any serious fashion." See *The Politics of Rights and the 1911 Revolution in China* (Stanford, CA: Stanford University Press, 2018), 9. For another account of the limitations of constitutionalism in the early republic, see Andrew J. Nathan, *Peking Politics, 1918–1923: Factionalism and the Failure of Constitutionalism* (Berkeley: University of California Press, 1976).

2. As noted by Rogiers Creemers, "the impotence of China's constitution is well recognized at a more general level." See "China's Constitutionalism Debate: Content, Context, and Implications," *China Journal* 74 (2015): 92.

3. This focus on emotions builds on a well-developed literature on emotions in the context of Chinese history and politics. See, for example, Haiyan Lee, *Revolution of the Heart: A Genealogy of Love in China* (Stanford, CA: Stanford University Press, 2006); Elizabeth J. Perry, "Moving the Masses: Emotion Work in the Chinese Revolution," *Mobilization* 7, no. 2 (Summer 2002): 111–28; and Yu Liu, "Maoist Discourse and the Mobilization of Emotion in Maoist China," *Modern China* 36, no. 3 (2010): 329–62.

4. For example, some Chinese leaders might have read in the July 2, 1954, issue of *Neibu cankao* (Internal Reference) that the Indian media were skeptical of Chinese constitutional arguments (pp. 26–7). Anne Applebaum made a similar point about Soviet propaganda posters: they were about the party's "power to proclaim and promulgate a falsehood, not to convince people of a falsehood." See "History Will Judge the Complicit," *Atlantic*, July/August 2020. https://www.theatlantic.com/magazine/archive/2020/07/trumps-collaborators/612250/.

5. As noted by the legal scholar Bui Ngoc Son, "the comparative scholarship on participation has focused mainly on democratic constitution-making, particularly in post-conflict societies." See *Constitutional Change in the Contemporary Socialist World*

(Oxford: Oxford University Press, 2020), 51. In the case of China, for example, Frederick Teiwes, writing in the *Cambridge History of China* on "regime consolidation," mentions the strong influence of the Soviet Union on the PRC constitution but nothing of the months of discussion about it. See his "Establishment and Consolidation of the New Regime," in *The Cambridge History of China*, vol. 14, *The People's Republic*, pt. 1: *The Emergence of Revolutionary China, 1949–1965*, ed. Roderick MacFarquhar and John King Fairbank (Cambridge: Cambridge University Press, 1987), 104. Hua-yu Li, also focusing on the Soviet role, briefly mentions the "so-called national discussion" of its draft. See "The Political Stalinization of China: The Establishment of One-Party Constitutionalism, 1948–1954," *Journal of Cold War Studies* 3, no. 2 (Spring 2001): 43–44. The size of the 1954 discussion of the constitution was roughly 150 million. See Han Dayuan, *1954 nian xianfa*, 774.

6. Christopher Rea, *The Age of Irreverence: A New History of Laughter in China* (Berkeley: University of California Press, 2015), 160–62; Yu Hua, *China in Ten Words*, trans. Allan H. Barr (New York: Anchor Books, 2011), 186–87.

7. For this definition, see Scott Gordon, *Controlling the State: Constitutionalism from Ancient Athens to Today* (Cambridge, MA: Harvard University Press, 1999), 5; and Chris Thornhill, *A Sociology of Constitutions: Constitutions and State Legitimacy in Historical-Sociological Perspective* (Cambridge: Cambridge University Press, 2011), 2. The importance of at least some form of popular participation in constitutional drafting in sustaining democracy has been noted by Gabriel L. Negretto and Mariano Sánchez-Talanquer's "Constitutional Origins and Liberal Democracy: A Global Analysis, 1900–2015," *American Political Science Review* 115, no. 2 (2021): 522–36. They argue that new constitutions "are likely to support liberal democracy when they emerge through a plural agreement among political elites with distinct bases of social support" (522). On the limits of formal constitutional rules, the legal scholar Tim Wu has pointed out that under former president Donald Trump it was not the separation of powers formalized in the constitution that prevented him from stealing the 2020 election but rather an "informal and unofficial set of institutional norms upheld by federal prosecutors, military officers and state elections officials"—our "unwritten constitution." See "What Really Saved the Republic from Trump?," *New York Times*, December 10, 2020. For a more scholarly treatment of norms as the soft guardrails of democracy see Steven Levitsky and Daniel Ziblatt, *How Democracies Die* (New York: Penguin Books, 2018), chap. 5.

8. Quentin Skinner, "Meaning and Understanding in the History of Ideas," *History and Theory* 8, no. 1 (1969): 22.

9. Gerring notes that describing the social world is widely accepted in the natural sciences, as well as in many other social science disciplines, with mainstream political science a notable outlier. See John Gerring, "Mere Description," *British Journal of Political Science* 42, no. 4 (2012): 731–32.

10. For some examples, see Melissa Ann Macauley, *Social Power and Legal Culture: Litigation Masters in Late Imperial China* (Stanford, CA: Stanford University Press, 1998); Matthew H. Sommer, *Polyandry and Wife-Selling in Qing Dynasty China: Survival Strategies and Judicial Interventions* (Berkeley: University of California Press, 2015); Margaret Kuo, *Intolerable Cruelty: Marriage, Law, and Society in Early Twentieth Century China* (Lanham, MD: Rowman & Littlefield, 2012). The best study of the United States Constitution that relies on the voices of ordinary people—but still relatively elite—is the late

historian Pauline Meier's *Ratification: The People Debate the Constitution, 1787–1788* (New York: Simon and Schuster, 2010). William Hurst, who conducted an in-depth study of legal regimes in China and Indonesia, including local court cases, notes that "studying legal regimes cannot get us inside the heads of individuals (or collectively of social groups) to let us see what they think about the law or how they perceive their relations to or within the legal system. Many questions that are central to much of the law and society literature may remain out of reach." This book attempts to do all these things and put answers to the law and society questions within reach. See *Ruling before the Law: The Politics of Legal Regimes in China and Indonesia* (Cambridge: Cambridge University Press, 2018), 253.

11. To the best of my knowledge, the only other work to take advantage of these sources on the constitution is Jennifer Altehenger's *Legal Lessons: Popularizing Laws in the People's Republic of China, 1949–1989* (Cambridge, MA: Harvard University Asia Center, 2018). She includes material on the promulgation of the 1954 draft constitution, but her book focuses on "how the CCP regime was involved in shaping what people heard, read, and saw about laws, rather than what people actually knew about laws" (252), which is the primary focus here.

12. A bit deeper into the weeds, Chinese discussions were organized by lower-level branches of the National Draft Constitutional Discussion Committee. These ad hoc units—disbanded after September—gathered materials from meetings of occupational groups and institutions (businessmen, officials, factory workers, journalists, university faculty, farmers, youth, women, overseas Chinese, ethnic minorities) or other forms of identity the Communist Party considered important. After talking with attendees over the course of several hours (sometimes in one day, sometimes over the course of several), meeting leaders filed reports to their superiors with varying levels of descriptive detail and ideographical clarity (such as typed, neatly handwritten, or scribbled minutes).

13. Mao and other leaders were regular readers of *Neibu cankao*. Citing an MA thesis by Huang Zhengkai (2006), Feng Chen noted of Mao: "I skim the news in newspapers, but I must read *Neibu cankao* every day." He relied heavily on it "to know what was going on outside the gates of Zhongnanhai." Given that reporting about the draft constitution lasted for several months, we can reasonably infer that at least some articles on the topic reached leaders' eyes. See Feng Chen, "Against the State: Labor Protests in China in the 1950s," *Modern China* 40, no. 5 (2014): 491. Knowing that their reports were being read by top leaders, *Neibu cankao* reporters were probably deterred from blatantly lying in them.

14. Citing an essay by Mao in his *Selected Words* (vol. 5, 142), the US-based legal scholar Kam Wong argues that the discussions produced "overwhelming popular support" that "reflected common experience and registered collective concerns." See "Human Rights and Limitation of State Power: The Discovery of Constitutionalism in the PRC," *Asia-Pacific Journal on Human Rights and Law* 1 (2006): 6n21, 6n20. Zhang Qianfan, a leading constitutional scholar in China, claims that the 1954 Constitution "was generally well-received." See *The Constitution of China: A Contextual Analysis* (Oxford: Hart Publishing, 2012), 45. No evidence is cited to support this assessment.

15. For many examples of this positive assessment see Han Dayuan, *1954 nian xianfa*, 293–94, 303–4.

16. See Andrew Nathan, *Chinese Democracy* (Berkeley: University of California Press, 1986), 107; Peter Zarrow, *After Empire: The Conceptual Transformation of the Chinese State, 1885–1924* (Stanford, CA: Stanford University Press, 2012); David Strand, *An Unfinished Republic: Leading by Word and Deed in Modern China* (Berkeley: University of California Press, 2011), esp. chap. 5.

17. See "Introduction: Constitutions in Authoritarian Regimes," in Tom Ginsburg and Alberto Simpser, eds., *Constitutions in Authoritarian Regimes* (Cambridge: Cambridge University Press, 2014), 1.

18. Liang argued that "a constitutional form of government can never suffer from disorder" and that a constitution that provided for popular participation would "strengthen the state." See Nathan, *Chinese Democracy*, 54–55.

19. Stuart R. Schram, Timothy Cheek, and Nancy Hodos, eds., *Mao's Road to Power: Revolutionary Writings, 1912–1949*, vol. 7 (New York: Routledge, 2015), 497. Cheng Jie (程洁) also calls attention to the formative role of pre-1949 CCP base areas in shaping post-1949 legal developments. See *Zhidao yu zhiquan: Zhongguo xianfa de zhidu fenxi* (Beijing: Falü chubanshe, 2015), 139–50.

20. Leading roles were assigned to Li Weihan and Hu Qiaomu, but Mao, Zhou Enlai, and others offered many suggestions and criticisms of the draft.

21. Hua-yu Li, "Political Stalinization of China," 40. Mao, she writes, "did not really care" whether China had a constitution.

22. On Stalin's critical role see Han Dayuan, *1954 nian xianfa*, 53–57; Liu Shanying (刘山鹰), "Cong 'gongtong gangling' dao wusi xianfa," *Yanhuang chunqiu* 9 (2014): 50, 53.

23. Altehenger, *Legal Lessons*, 127–28.

24. Zhihua Shen and Yafeng Xia, *Mao and the Sino-Soviet Partnership, 1945–1959: A New History* (Lanham, MD: Lexington Books, 2015), 122. Chen Jian notes that 1954—the year the constitution was promulgated—was the high point of friendly relations, in part the result of Soviet support during the Korean War. See *Mao's China and the Cold War* (Chapel Hill: University of North Carolina Press, 2000), 62. Sheila Fitzpatrick notes that the Chinese constitutional discussion was "an apparent analogue to the Soviet 'popular discussion' of their new constitution twenty years earlier." See "Popular Opinion under Communist Regimes," in *The Oxford Handbook of the History of Communism*, ed. Stephen A. Smith (Oxford: Oxford University Press, 2014), 376. According to Arunabh Ghosh, the four years starting in 1954 "represented the high tide of Soviet experts in China. As many as 11,000 visited China to share their technical expertise and experience." See *Making it Count: Statistics and Statecraft in the Early People's Republic of China* (Princeton, NJ: Princeton University Press, 2020), 77.

25. CCP leaders in the original "small group" drafting the constitution in the spring of 1953 included Mao, Chen Boda, Li Weihan, Tian Jiaying, and Hu Qiaomu. The larger (33-member) drafting committee included nearly all top CCP leaders at the time. Their reading materials included three Soviet constitutions (1918, 1924, and 1936), constitutions from several Soviet satellite states in Eastern Europe, Chinese constitutions and those of the United States and France. See *Zhongguo xianfa jingshi*, ed. Cai Dingjian (蔡定剑) (Beijing: Zhongguo minzhu fazhi chubanshe, 1996), 16–17; Glenn Tiffert, "Epistrophy: Chinese Constitutionalism and the 1950s," in *Building Constitutionalism in China*, ed. Stephanie Balme and Michael Dowdle (New York: Palgrave Macmillan, 2009), 60. Jerome Cohen called the 1954 Constitution "essentially a foreign product,"

borrowed from East European people's democracies and the USSR. See "China's Changing Constitution," *China Quarterly* 76 (December 1978): 798. This view is confirmed by PRC scholars. See Han Dayuan, *1954 nian*, 774; Liu Jianping, "Sugong yu Zhongguo gongchandang renmin minzhu chuanzheng lilun de queli," *Lishi yanjiu* 1 (1998): 78–96.

26. Yang Su, *Collective Killings in Rural China during the Cultural Revolution* (Cambridge: Cambridge University Press, 2011), 161.

27. Liu Shanying, "Cong 'gongtong gangling,'" According to Liu, Stalin thought that the more moderate Common Program should become the constitution, whereas Mao pushed toward socialist ownership policies.

28. These are among the functions of authoritarian constitutions in Ginsburg and Simpser, *Constitutions in Authoritarian Regimes*, 6–8.

29. The word *xiaomie* was used once in the Common Program (Art. 7), referring to reactionaries, feudal landlords, and bureaucratic capitalists.

30. In scope, the PRC constitution was more ambitious than its more famous US counterpart, which initially mentioned very few citizen rights.

31. Dong Chengmei, one of the original drafters, noted in his memoirs that the discussion was based on [our] "consulting the all-people's discussion of the 1936 Soviet Constitution," but offers no further details. See Dong Chengmei (董成美), "Zhiding woguo 1954 xianfa ruogan lishi qingkuang de huiyi," *Faxue* 5 (2000): 2–4.

32. On return graphic loan words see Lydia H. Liu, *Translingual Practice: Literature, National Culture, and Translated Modernity* (Stanford, CA: Stanford University Press, 1995), 302, 310. *Kanji* refers to Chinese characters in Japanese (but pronounced differently than the former). On Japan's linguistic legal influence see Dan Fenno Henderson, "Japanese Influences on Communist Chinese Legal Language," in *Contemporary Chinese Law: Research Problems and Perspectives*, ed. Jerome Alan Cohen (Cambridge, MA: Harvard University Press, 1970), 171,

33. In 1955 the illiteracy rate in China (around 80 percent) was roughly comparable to that of the USSR circa 1929. By 1939, 81.2 percent of people in the USSR were deemed literate. See Glen Peterson, *The Power of Words: Literacy and Revolution in South China, 1949–1995* (Vancouver: University of British Columbia Press, 1997), 77; Lenore Grenoble, *Language Policy in the Soviet Union* (New York: Kluwer, 2003), 157. For a useful summary of one major forum where key thinkers discussed the form of the post-1917 state, see Robin Aizlewood, Ruth Coates, and Evert van der Zweerde, "Introduction," in *Landmarks Revisited: The Vekhi Symposium One Hundred Years On*, ed. Robin Aizlewood and Ruth Coates (Brookline, MA: Academic Studies Press, 2013), 20–31. I thank my colleague Alyssa DeBlasio for this reference and fruitful discussions about this issue.

34. Chen Jian, *Mao's China and the Cold War*, 61.

35. Liu Shanying, "Cong 'gongtong gangling,'" 53.

36. Sebastian Heilmann and Elizabeth J. Perry, "Embracing Uncertainty: Guerilla Policy Style and Adaptive Governance in China," in *Mao's Invisible Hand: The Political Foundations of Adaptive Governance in China*, ed. Sebastian Heilmann and Elizabeth J. Perry (Cambridge, MA: Harvard University Press, 2011): 1–29.

37. On controlled polarization in China, see Chen Yung-fa, *Making Revolution: The Communist Revolution in Eastern and Central China, 1937–1945* (Berkeley: University of California Press, 1986). On late 1940s Poland, see Czesław Miłosz, *The Captive Mind*

(trans. Jane Zielonko) (New York: Vintage International, 1990), 194. In contrast, Michael Dutton writes that the 1954 Constitution was "more of a symbol of political unity than the legality of the state." See *Policing Chinese Politics: A History* (Durham, NC: Duke University Press, 1995), 201.

38. He Jia (何佳), "Quanmin taolun xianfa xiugai cao'an de yiyi he zuoyong," *Zheng-zhi yu falü* 1 (1982): 23. The citation is from Mao Zedong, *Mao Zedong xuanji*, vol. 5, (Beijing: Renmin chubanshe, 1977), 126. For a good description of the mass line see Kenneth Lieberthal, *Governing China: From Revolution through Reform* (New York: W.W. Norton, 1995), 64. Mao Zedong summed up the mass line as "from the masses, to the masses."

39. See Xiaocai Feng, "Counterfeiting Legitimacy: Reflections on the Usurpation of Popular Politics and the 'Political Culture' of China, 1912–1949," *Frontiers of History in China* 8, no. 2 (June 2013): 202–22.

40. Fitzpatrick, "Popular Opinion," 373.

41. In their introductory essay in *Constitutions in Authoritarian Regimes*, Ginsburg and Simpser note that "the document called 'constitution' often enjoys a privileged normative status in the minds of the public, independent of the content of such document" (10). While certainly possible, how can this be known in the absence of data about the "minds of the public"?

42. For a review and analysis of these perspectives, see Joseph W. Esherick, "Ten Theses on the Chinese Revolution," *Modern China* 21, no. 1 (1996): 45–76.

43. See Jeremy Brown and Paul Pickowicz, eds., *Dilemmas of Victory: The Early Years of the People's Republic of China* (Cambridge, MA: Harvard University Press, 2010), 7–8; Jeremy Brown and Matthew D. Johnson, *Maoism at the Grassroots: Everyday Life in China's Era of High Socialism* (Cambridge, MA: Harvard University Press, 2015), 5, 15.

44. Elizabeth J. Perry, "The Promise of PRC History," *Journal of Modern Chinese History* 10, no. 1 (2016): 114.

45. In some respects, this book is similar to Rohit De's *The People's Constitution: The Everyday Life of Law in the Indian Republic* (Princeton, NJ: Princeton University Press, 2020), 2. De noted that "we have little idea of how Indians understood and experienced the new order marked by a constitution." This bottom-up view of popular constitutionalism is quite different from most accounts of this concept in the West, which understands "popular" as any elected branch (legislative or presidential) limiting judicial supremacy over constitutional meaning.

46. In Guangzhou (Canton) in Guangdong Province, "over half a million" people participated in the constitutional discussion, representing roughly one-third of the city's population according to the 1953 census. See *Guangzhou shi zhi*, vol. 1 (Guangzhou: Guangdong renmin chubanshe, 1998), 365–66. In Shanghai "those who heard a report and participated in discussion" came to over two million. See "讨论宪法草案" on the website of the municipal gazetteer (www.shtong.gov.cn). Accessed March 16, 2020.

47. In the Shanghai area, the gazetteers of Qingpu, Baoshan, and Changshu all mention the discussion of the draft (with Qingpu's *Annals* noting that it trained 2,134 people to educate about the constitution). See *Qingpu xianzhi* (Shanghai: Renmin chubanshe, 1990), 29; *Baoshan xianzhi* (Shanghai: Renmin chubanshe, 1992), 36; *Changshu shizhi* (Shanghai: Renmin chubanshe, 1990), 35, 551. For Tong County outside Beijing, see *Tong xianzhi* (Beijing: Beijing chubanshe, 2003), 563. For the Beijing Communist Youth League, see "Beijing shi zhi: qingnian zuzhi zhi" (北京市志: 青年组织志) at

www.bjdfz.gov.cn, 142–43. Sometimes the constitution was mentioned only in the context of other campaigns occurring at the time, such as Suppressing Counterrevolutionaries, the Marriage Law, and Land Reform. See, for example, in Eastern Inner Mongolia, *Zhaluteqi zhi* (Beijing: Fangzhi chubanshe, 2001), 413.

48. See "Zhiding woguo 1954 xianfa." These comments were collated into the *Xianfa cao'an chugao taolun yijian huiji* (Beijing: Zhonghua renmin gongheguo xianfa qicao weiyuanhui bangongshi, 1954). The plurality of these (44.89 percent) focused on the preamble and chapter 1 ("General Principles"). Some 30 percent focused on the state's administrative apparatus and nearly 20 percent on rights and obligations. For Shanghai, see "参与宪法讨论" on the city's municipal gazetteer's website www.shtong.gov.cn. Last accessed March 16, 2020.

49. Elsewhere, Feng Xiaocai and I have argued that the conventional chronology of popular critique should be revised based on the 1954 materials. See Neil J. Diamant and Xiaocai Feng, "China's First National Critique," *China Journal* 73 (2015): 1–37.

50. Harry G. Frankfurt, *On Bullshit* (Princeton, NJ: Princeton University Press, 2005). The book was on the *New York Times* bestseller list for twenty-seven weeks, including several at number one.

51. Frankfurt, 38, 47, 46. Italics in the original.

52. Frankfurt, 54, 23, 54.

53. Frankfurt, 56.

54. For good examples of this, see Jason Webb Yackee and Susan Webb Yackee, "A Bias toward Business? Assessing Interest Group Influence on the U.S. Bureaucracy," *Journal of Politics* 68, no. 1 (February 2006): 137; Susan Webb Yackee, "Participant Voice in the Bureaucratic Policymaking Process," *Journal of Public Administration Research and Theory* 25 (2014): 428.

55. This theory is sometimes called "Reader-response criticism." I am grateful to my colleague Siobhan Phillips for alerting me to Radway's study.

56. Janice A. Radway, *Reading the Romance: Women, Patriarchy, and Popular Literature* (Chapel Hill: University of North Carolina Press, 1984), 7–8. Emphasis in original.

57. Radway, 61.

58. This point has been made by Ran Hirschl, a scholar of constitutional law, but not at the level of readers or officials responsible for enforcing a constitution. He writes that constitutions' "import cannot be meaningfully described or explained independent of the social, political, and economic forces, both domestic and international, that shape them." No evidence in the book is presented about "import" among ordinary people. See *Comparative Matters: The Renaissance of Comparative Constitutional Law* (Oxford: Oxford University Press, 2016), 152.

59. Mitchell Green, "Speech Acts," *Stanford Encyclopedia of Philosophy* (Winter 2017 Edition), ed. Edward N. Zalta, https://plato.stanford.edu/archives/win2017/entries/speech-acts/.

60. J. L. Austin, *How to Do Things with Words* (Oxford: Oxford University Press, 1975), 99–100. Italics in the original.

61. Austin, 100.

62. Austin, 101.

63. For example, at a beer factory in Shanghai, people who were placed under "supervision" for various offenses were afraid of saying anything lest they be criticized. See Shanghai Municipal Archives (SMA) A51-1-182, 134.

64. Austin, *How to Do Things with Words*, 98; Paul Grice, *Studies in the Way of Words* (Cambridge, MA: Harvard University Press, 1989), 297.

65. Green, "Speech Acts." See Elisabeth Camp, "Insinuation, Common Ground, and the Conversational Record," in *New Work on Speech Acts*, ed. Daniel Fogal, Daniel W. Harris, and Matt Moss (Oxford: Oxford Scholarship Online, 2018), 43–44. https://doi.org/10.1093/oso/9780198738831.001.0001. In Chinese history, Patricia M. Thornton has noted that Confucian elites learned to frame critiques in a variety of safer forms. See "Insinuation, Insult, and Invective: The Threshold of Power and Protest in Modern China," *Comparative Studies in Society and History* 44, no. 3 (2002): 606. In the USSR, Serhy Yekelchyk also found that criticisms were framed as questions. See *Stalin's Citizens: Everyday Politics in the Wake of Total War* (Oxford: Oxford University Press, 2014), 159, 155.

66. Grice, *Studies in the Way of Words*, 44.

67. See Hans Steinmüller, "The State of Irony in China," *Critique of Anthropology* 31, no. 1 (2011): 21–42.

68. I thank my philosopher colleague Chauncey Maher for this point.

69. The flag has five stars. Four small ones represent the classes aligned with the Communist Party (peasant, worker, petty bourgeoisie, national bourgeoisie). All face the big star, symbolizing the party.

70. As succinctly summarized by the historian Arunabh Ghosh in his study of statistics in the PRC, "My approach to these questions [about how statistics came to be formulated and practiced] is directly shaped by the sources I was able to consult." See *Making it Count*, 7.

71. Fitzpatrick, "Popular Opinion," 372. See Sarah Davies, *Popular Opinion in Stalin's Russia: Terror, Propaganda, and Dissent, 1934–1941* (Cambridge: Cambridge University Press, 1997), 11.

72. There were other examples in the socialist world. For example, in East Germany eleven million people out of a total of 17.1 million "took part in the discussion of the 1968 Constitution" and suggestions made by citizens "led to 118 changes in the original draft." See Veniamin Chirkin, *Constitutional Law and Political Institutions* (Moscow: Progress Publishers, 1985), 240; Altehenger, *Legal Lessons*, 250. In 1975, Cuba had a discussion that lasted two months and involved six million people. See Marta Harnecker, *Cuba: Dictatorship or Democracy?* (Westport, CT: Lawrence Hill, 1980), 45.

73. Alexander C. Cook, ed., *Mao's Little Red Book: A Global History* (Cambridge: Cambridge University Press, 2014).

1. Officials Read the Draft Constitution

1. Jon Elster, "Constitutionalism in Eastern Europe," *University of Chicago Law Review* 58, no. 2 (Spring 1991): 465; Giovanni Sartori, "Constitutionalism: A Preliminary Discussion," *American Political Science Review* 56, no. 4 (December 1962): 861.

2. Graham Maddox, "A Note on the Meaning of 'Constitution,'" *American Political Science Review* 76, no. 1 (December 1982): 806.

3. Beau Breslin, *From Words to Worlds: Exploring Constitutional Functionality* (Baltimore: Johns Hopkins University Press, 2009), 15–16. I am grateful to my former Dickinson colleague Douglas Edlin for alerting me to Breslin's work. Chris Thornhill, *A Sociology of Constitutions: Constitutions and State Legitimacy in Historical-Sociological Perspective* (Cambridge: Cambridge University Press, 2011), 7.

4. As noted by Ran Hirschl, "the ever-expanding political salience of constitutional courts" and scholars and activists' "preoccupation" with rights claims has led to a "juridification" of the comparative study of constitutions. Today, he argues, owing to the "appropriation" of comparative constitutional studies by law schools, much of comparative constitutional law scholarship has a "court-centric focus." See *Comparative Matters: The Renaissance of Comparative Constitutional Law* (Oxford: Oxford University Press, 2016), 164, 157.

5. In this chapter and throughout this book I will be using the term *official* for those people who work on behalf of the state rather than *cadre*, whose meaning is less well-understood.

6. On this process, see Zhang Jishun, "Thought Reform and Press Nationalization in Shanghai: The *Wenhui* Newspaper in the Early 1950s," *Twentieth Century China* 35, no. 2 (2010): 52–80.

7. Pauline Maier, *Ratification: The People Debate the Constitution, 1787–1788* (New York: Simon and Schuster, 2010).

8. In Taishan County in Guangdong Province alone, propaganda authorities distributed 10,280 copies of the draft constitution to officials. See Guangdong Provincial Archives (GPA hereafter) 235-1-339, 15.

9. Mao claimed that in capitalist countries "the president (*zongtong*) can dissolve the legislature, but our chairman cannot dissolve the National People's Congress; on the contrary, the National People's Congress can dismiss the chairman." See *Zhongguo xianfa jingshi*, ed. Cai Dingjian (蔡定剑) (Beijing: Zhongguo minzhu fazhi chubanshe, 1996), 19. Perhaps Mao was thinking of premiers in parliamentary systems. There also could have been an error in transcription somewhere along the line.

10. Some evidence presented in this chapter appears in my article "What the [Expletive] Is a Constitution?! Ordinary Cadres Confront the 1954 Draft Constitution," *Journal of Chinese History* 2 (Fall 2017): 1–22.

11. The 1953 Marriage Law Campaign was a precedent, but it was relatively narrow in scope compared with the constitution. The Marriage Law also had far fewer articles.

12. *Neibu cankao* (*NBCK* hereafter), April 28, 1954, 286.

13. *NCBK*, July 24, 1954, 397.

14. Shanghai Municipal Archives (SMA hereafter) B2-2-62, n.p.

15. *NBCK*, July 22, 1954, 353.

16. *NBCK*, June 30, 1954, 369–70. There is no evidence that such complaints resulted in increased supply of rations. Unlike the Soviet constitutional experience of 1936, official malfeasance and corruption were not part of the CCP's agenda in 1954. The Three Antis Campaign, which targeted these problems, occurred only three years earlier.

17. *NBCK*, July 7, 1954, 107.

18. *NBCK*, July 31, 1954, 518.

19. SMA A22-2-1525, 4.

20. GPA 225-2-29, 2.

21. *NBCK*, July 3, 1954, 44.

22. SMA B2-2-57, 21.

23. SMA B2-2-63, 28.

24. SMA B2-2-58, 14.

25. SMA A80-2-309, 34.

26. SMA A79-2-381, 7; Huangpu District Archives (HDA hereafter) H20-1-182, 30.

27. HDA H202-1-182, 30.

28. SMA A71-2-973, 27; Songjiang District Archives (SDA hereafter) 7-1-6, 37.

29. *NBCK*, July 31, 1954, 520.

30. According to Jennifer Altehenger's analysis of the 1950 Marriage Law, convey-ing the spirit of a law was "the most important purpose" of propaganda. See *Legal Lessons: Popularizing Laws in the People's Republic of China, 1949–1989* (Cambridge, MA: Harvard University Asia Center, 2018), 96–97.

31. *NBCK*, August 18, 1954, 255.

32. SMA A71-2-974, 33–4; *NBCK*, June 26, 1954, 315; GPA 235-1-399, 18–19.

33. SMA A71-2-974, 33.

34. SMA A71-2-974, 101.

35. SMA A71-2-974, 81.

36. SMA A71-2-974, 120.

37. GPA 225-2-29, 75.

38. *NBCK*, June 29, 1954, 350; *NBCK*, June 26, 1954, 314; SMA A22-2-1531, 93; GPA 235-1-399, 8.

39. See David Strand, *An Unfinished Republic: Leading by Word and Deed in Early Twen-tieth Century China* (Berkeley: University of California Press, 2011), 125; *NBCK*, July 10, 1954, 161–62; *NBCK*, July 24, 1954, 403.

40. SMA B2-2-57, 19.

41. SMA A71-2-974, 126. This report, like many issued by local governments or the Discuss the Draft Constitution Committee, did not include names of the report writers.

42. SMA A71-2-975, 24.

43. *NBCK*, July 31, 1954, 521.

44. SMA A79-2-381, 7.

45. SMA B2-2-61, n.p.

46. HDA 48-2-113, 29.

47. SMA A71-2-975, 24.

48. *NBCK*, August 19, 1954, 265; *NBCK*, August 26, 1954, 385; *NBCK*, July 24, 1954, 402.

49. *NBCK*, August 19, 1954, 265.

50. As noted by Daniel Leese and Puck Engman, "the CCP came to govern with a bare minimum of laws and without a clear normative hierarchy to determine the re-lationship between Party rules and state decrees; even political speeches and newspa-per editorials could have the force of law." See "Introduction," in *Victims, Perpetrators, and the Role of Law in Maoist China: A Case Study Approach*, ed. Daniel Leese and Puck Engman (Berlin: De Gruyter Oldenbourg, 2018), 10. https://doi.org/10.1515 /9783110533651-001.

51. *NBCK*, July 31, 1954, 519; *NBCK*, June 29, 1954, 351; *NBCK*, July 22, 1954, 353.

52. *NBCK*, August 5, 1954, 77. The constitution was *lao da* (老大), the Labor Law *lao er* (老二), and the Marriage Law *lao san* (老三). Chronologically, the laws should have been in reverse order. *Liberation Daily* admitted to "very many" mistakes and in-adequacies. Citizens sometimes sent in letters to the editor requesting clarifications. See SMA A73-1-174, 2.

53. *NBCK*, July 31, 1954, 519.

54. *NBCK*, June 29, 1954, 350; SMA A38-2-144, 13–14; SMA A79-2-381, 10.

55. *NBCK*, June 29, 1954, 350; GPA 235-1-399, 21; SMA A71-2-974, 166.

56. SMA A38-2-144, 13–14.

57. *NBCK*, July 31, 1954, 518; GPA 225-2-29, 75; *NBCK*, June 29, 1954, 350.

58. SMA A38-2-144, 14.

59. Yangpu District Archives (YDA hereafter) 16-25-4, 6.

60. SMA B2-2-61, n.p.; SMA A71-2-975, 23.

61. Wang Housheng (王厚生) argued that local officials were afraid because they were always blamed for errors, whereas the center never admitted any. Wang was an anti-Communist legal scholar who left China and lived in Taiwan and the United States. See *Zhonggong zhixian pinglun: Cong zhixian kanzhong zhonggong zhengquan* (Jiulong: Wenhui chubanshe, 1955), 73.

62. GPA 225-4-104, 14; GPA 235-1-399, 16.

63. *NBCK*, August 21, 1954, 300.

64. SMA A42-1-12, 35.

65. SMA A22-2-1531, 55.

66. SMA A38-2-144, 2. For the suburbs, see SMA A71-2-975, 209.

67. SMA A71-2-974, 166.

68. SMA A71-2-974, 166; SMA A71-2-974, 62; SMA A71-2-974, 125; GPA 225-2-29, 117; *NBCK* July 31, 1954, 519; SMA A71-2-975, 209; SMA A71-2-974, 81; *NBCK*, July 31, 1954, 518; SMA B2-2-61, 4.

69. SMA B2-2-61, n.p.

70. As noted by Susan Shirk, "the post-Mao institutionalization of leadership politics had not proceeded far or deeply enough to prevent a leader as ambitious as Xi from restoring personalistic dictatorial rule. Certain norms and precedents were followed, but this minimal institutionalization failed to stop Xi from grasping power." See "The Return to Personalistic Rule," *Journal of Democracy* 29, no. 2 (April 2018): 33. Xi's behavior challenges arguments that constitutions in authoritarian regimes might not protect citizens' rights very well but can regulate relations within the state elite and specify the restraints placed on the head of state by other state elites. In a claim that is now outdated, Anne Meng argued that in China "the state constitution is considered the highest law—its authority stands above the leader and the ruling party." See *Constraining Dictatorship: From Personalized Rule to Institutionalized Regimes* (Cambridge: Cambridge University Press, 2010), 5.

71. GPA 204-3-43, 114. These officials were municipal level and above.

72. SDA 5-6-32, 127–30. In these guidelines the main rationale for the constitution was to "write in the victories of the revolution and the rights people already have so that they are fixed in law and no one can take them away" (128).

73. *NBCK*, August 21, 1954, 298.

74. SMA A38-2-144, 28.

75. SMA A71-2-974, 166.

76. SMA A79-2-381, 2, 6; SMA A80-2-74, 99.

77. *NBCK*, June 26, 1954, 315.

78. *NBCK*, August 26, 1954, 385.

79. Altehenger, *Legal Lessons*, 159.

80. *NBCK*, June 30, 1954, 367.

81. GPA 225-2-29, 3, 130, 134.

82. SMA A71-2-974, 81.

83. SMA A71-2-974, 39.

84. SMA A48-1-287, 2; SMA A79-2-381, 7.

85. SMA B2-2-65, 2.

86. GPA 225-2-29, 91.

87. On rural dissatisfaction with CCP politics during this period, see Elizabeth J. Perry, "Rural Violence in Socialist China," *China Quarterly* 103 (September 1985): 414–40.

88. The most comprehensive work to date on Chinese police remains Michael Dutton, *Policing Chinese Politics: A History* (Durham, NC: Duke University Press, 1995). His source materials from the 1950s, however, do not allow him to write about ordinary policemen's perspective, only their alleged behavior (such as accepting bribes, acting arrogantly, etc.). For the Republican period, see, for example, David Strand, *Rickshaw Beijing: City People and Politics in the 1920s* (Berkeley: University of California Press, 1989), chap. 4; Zhao Ma, *Runaway Wives, Urban Crimes, and Survival Tactics in Wartime Beijing, 1937–1949* (Cambridge, MA: Harvard University Asia Center, 2015); Frederic Wakeman Jr., *Policing Shanghai, 1927–1937* (Berkeley: University of California Press, 1995). For recent work on PRC policemen, see Suzanne Scoggins and Kevin J. O'Brien, "China's Unhappy Police," *Asian Survey* 56, no. 2 (2016): 225–42. For Taiwan, see Jeffrey T. Martin, *Sentiment, Reason, and Law: Policing in the Republic of China on Taiwan* (Ithaca, NY: Cornell University Press, 2019).

89. SMA A79-2-381, 3; SMA A71-2-974, 80.

90. *NBCK*, July 24, 1954, 403. Scoggins and O'Brien note that low pay remains an issue: "The work is hard and the pay is too low. . . . My girlfriend wishes I had never become a policeman." Wearing a "sharp uniform" is still an attractive part of the job. See "China's Unhappy Police," 231–32.

91. *NBCK*, July 24, 1954, 397, 403.

92. SMA A22-2-1525, 17; SMA B2-2-61, 121.

93. GPA 204-3-43, 114–15; SMA A79-2-381, 2.

94. *NBCK*, July 7, 1954, 106; SMA A79-2-381, 3; *NBCK*, August 19, 1954, 264–65.

95. HDA H202-1-182, 30.

96. On these campaigns, see Julia Strauss, "Paternalist Terror: The Campaign to Suppress Counterrevolutionaries and Regime Consolidation in the People's Republic of China, 1950–1953," *Comparative Studies in Society and History* 44, no. 1 (2002): 80–105.

97. *NBCK*, June 23, 1954, 281; SMA A71-2-975, 65.

98. GPA 225-4-104, 32; GPA 204-3-43, 114.

99. SMA A71-2-974, 80; SMA A79-2-381, 4.

100. SMA A22-2-1531, 55.

101. *NBCK*, July 22, 1954, 352.

102. SMA A71-2-975, 209.

103. *NBCK*, June 23, 281.

104. SMA B2-2-62, 2.

105. SMA A22-2-1525, 17.

106. SMA B2-2-62, 2; SMA A22-2-1525, 17.

107. SMA B2-2-62, n.p.

108. SMA A22-2-1525, 15.

109. SMA A22-2-1525, 17.

110. SMA A79-2-381, 2.

111. SMA B2-2-62, 4.

112. SMA A26-2-304, 41.

113. For instance, many high-ranking CCP officials married highly educated urban women even though they had problematic political backgrounds. See my *Revolutionizing the Family: Politics, Love and Divorce in Urban and Rural China, 1949–1968* (Berkeley: University of California Press, 2000), chap. 1.

114. *NBCK*, July 24, 1954, 403; SMA B2-2-62, n.p.

115. *NBCK*, July 3, 1954, 43.

116. On views of the poor, see Janet Y. Chen, *Guilty of Indigence: The Urban Poor in China, 1900–1953* (Princeton, NJ: Princeton University Press, 2012).

117. GPA 225-2-29, 91.

118. SMA A22-2-1525, 17.

119. SMA A79-2-381, 3.

120. SMA A79-2-381, 7.

121. SMA B2-2-58, 34.

122. SMA B2-2-63, 26.

123. SMA A22-2-1531, 92.

124. HDA 48-2-113, 22.

125. SMA A79-2-381, 2; SMA B2-2-61, n.p.

126. SMA B2-2-63, 28.

127. SMA B2-2-63, 26.

128. SMA B2-2-61, n.p.

129. SMA A71-2-974, 46.

130. *NBCK*, July 24, 1954, 398; SMA A79-2-381, 2.

131. GPA 235-1-399, 8.

132. SMA A79-2-381, 133.

133. SMA A79-2-381, 173.

134. SMA A71-2-973, 28.

135. SMA B2-2-63, 26; *NBCK*, June 29, 1954, 350–51.

136. SMA B2-2-63, 27.

137. SMA B2-2-61, n.p. Sixty people in attendance raised this issue, which appears to have been the second most common question after "How will the rich peasants be eliminated?" The document does not provide the total number of questions.

138. SMA A79-2-381, 2.

139. *NBCK*, July 31, 1954, 519.

140. SMA A71-2-974, 80.

141. SMA B2-2-66, 83; GPA 225-2-29, 32.

142. *NBCK*, August 19, 1954, 264. In a rural region in the USSR, this exclusion of peasant rights was "by far the most contentious issue raised" during its constitutional discussion. See Samantha Lomb, *Stalin's Constitution: Soviet Participatory Politics and the Discussion of the 1936 Draft Constitution* (London: Routledge, 2018), 97.

2. The Draft Constitution in China's Business Community

1. Yang Kuisong notes that "right from its establishment, in common with all other communist parties, the CCP . . . regarded the bourgeoisie as the enemy." The wartime United Front policy could only be temporary. After the KMT had been defeated, he argues, "it was just a question of time before they would once again regard the Chinese national bourgeoisie as their political enemy." See "The Evolution of the Chinese

Communist Party's Policy on the Bourgeoisie(1949–1952)," *Journal of Modern Chinese History* 1, no. 1 (August 2007): 13, 16.

2. As colorfully argued by Parks Coble Jr., "relations between Nanking and the Shanghai bourgeoisie were characterized by government efforts to emasculate politically the urban elite and to milk the modern sector of the economy." See "The Kuomintang Regime and the Shanghai Capitalists, 1927–1929," *China Quarterly* 77 (March 1979): 1–2.

3. For an excellent study of diverging paths within families, see Sherman Cochran and Zhengguang Xie, *The Lius of Shanghai* (Cambridge, MA: Harvard University Press, 2013); many of the essays in Sherman Cochran, ed., *The Capitalist Dilemma in China's Communist Revolution* (Ithaca, NY: Cornell East Asia Series No. 172, 2014); Joseph W. Esherick, *Ancestral Leaves: A Family Journey through Chinese History* (Berkeley: University of California Press, 2011).

4. After a trip to Tianjin, Liu Shaoqi argued that "today, the exploitative nature of capitalism is not evil, but is making contributions to our country." See Yang, "Evolution," 18–19.

5. In Shanghai, until 1952 deputy mayor Pan Hannian tried to convince some capitalists who were shuttling between Shanghai and Hong Kong to send capital and equipment back to Shanghai, but the entrepreneurs "returned only occasionally and temporarily." Following events on the mainland, they were disappointed and left for good. See Marie-Claire Bergère, *Shanghai: China's Gateway to Modernity*, trans. Janet Lloyd (Stanford, CA: Stanford University Press, 2009), 352–53. As documented by Bruce Dickson, relations between the CCP and capitalists (and the private sector more generally) remain a point of debate within the party in the reform era as well. In the 2000s many party members objected to allowing capitalists to join the CCP under the "Three Represents" policy, enshrined in the CCP (not state) constitution. Under Hu Jintao and Xi Jinping, setting up party committees in private enterprises was an important priority. See *Red Capitalists in China: The Party, Private Entrepreneurs, and Prospects for Political Change* (Cambridge: Cambridge University Press, 2003), chap. 4.

6. As noted by Marie-Claire Bergère, the opportunities offered by the United Front policy to capitalists "were eagerly seized by those who accepted being controlled as well as accommodated." See "China in the Wake of the Communist Revolution: Social Transformations, 1949–1966," in *China's Communist Revolutions: Fifty Years of the People's Republic of China*, ed. Werner Draguhn and David S. G. Goodman (Hoboken, NJ: Taylor and Francis, 2012), 104. For more information on this, see Yang Kuisong, "Evolution of the Chinese Communist Party's Policy," 14.

7. Yang Kuisong, 14. For a summary of events in Shanghai, see Bergère, *Shanghai*, 360–62.

8. Feng Xiaocai, "Between Class Struggle and Family Loyalty: The Mobilization of Businessmen's Wives and Children during the Five Antis Movement," *European Journal of East Asian Studies* 13 (2014): 299.

9. See Xiaohong Xiao-Planes, "'Buy 20 Years': Li Kangnian, Class Identity and the Controversy over the Socialisation of Private Business in 1957," and Chen Zhengqing, "Socialist Transformation and the Demise of Private Entrepreneurs: Wu Yunchu's Tragedy," in *European Journal of East Asian Studies* 13 (2014): 214–39, 240–61.

10. Bergère, "China in the Wake," 99. Emphasis mine. The same holds for her broader overview in *Shanghai*.

11. See, for example, "Shanghai Industrial and Commercial Circles Enthusiastically Support Draft Constitution," *Selections of the Mainland Chinese Press,* no. 842, 30. The report quoted Liu Hongsheng, vice chairman of the Shanghai Municipal Federation of Commerce and Industry, who was a well-known businessman before the revolution.

12. Shanghai Municipal Archives (SMA hereafter) C1-1-62, 29–30; Yangpu District Archive (YDA hereafter) 21-1-71, 138. Although stored in the Yangpu Archive, the report is from Yulin District.

13. SMA C48-2-702, 5.

14. SMA C48-2-702, 1.

15. SMA C48-2-702, 3.

16. SMA C48-2-702, 17.

17. *NBCK,* May 6, 1954, 58–59.

18. SMA A79-2-381, 9.

19. SMA B2-2-63, 148.

20. *Neibu cankao* (*NBCK* hereafter), April 28, 1954, 285.

21. *NBCK,* July 24, 1954, 404. A similar use of *xian* as the homophone for *restrict* was also noted in Beijing. See Jennifer Altehenger, *Legal Lessons: Popularizing Laws in the People's Republic of China, 1949–1989* (Cambridge, MA: Harvard University Asia Center, 2018), 141.

22. *NBCK,* June 30, 1954, 370–71.

23. *NBCK,* July 24, 1954, 404.

24. SMA C48-2-702, 17.

25. *NBCK,* May 26, 1954, 386.

26. SMA C48-2-702, 18.

27. SMA C48-2-702, 18.

28. SMA A22-2-1531, 58.

29. *NBCK,* July 24, 1954, 399.

30. *NBCK,* June 25, 1954, 300; *NBCK,* July 24, 1954, 404.

31. SMA A79-2-381, 9; SMA A79-2-381, 148.

32. SMA B2-2-58, 25.

33. *NBCK,* July 28, 1954, 465.

34. Businessmen's anxiety, as distinct from fear and terror, was initially explored in Neil J. Diamant and Xiaocai Feng, "Textual Anxiety": Reading (and Misreading) the Draft Constitution in China, 1954," *Cold War Studies* 20, no. 3 (Summer 2018): 153–79.

35. *NBCK,* June 25, 1954, 300.

36. SMA A22-2-1525, 59. In late 1940s Poland there were similar reactions. As described by Czesław Miłosz, "small contractors and merchants trembled at the knowledge that they were destined to be exterminated as a group." See *The Captive Mind* (trans. Jane Zielonko) (New York: Vintage International, 1990), 166.

37. SMA C1-1-62, 29.

38. SMA C48-2-702, 5.

39. YDA 21-1-71, 137.

40. SMA B2-2-63, 141.

41. SMA B2-2-63, 147.

42. *NBCK,* June 25, 1954, 298.

43. SMA C1-1-62, 4, 30. "Courtesy" as a well-planned deception was central to Communist parties prior to and after World War II. In Poland, for example, Miłosz notes

that "it was politic to show that even rightists and Catholics had joined forces with the government." See Miłosz, *Captive Mind*, 188.

44. SMA B2-2-61, n.p.; for the sense of relief in Beijing, see *NBCK*, June 23, 1954, 284.

45. SMA C48-2-702, 19.

46. *NBCK*, June 29, 1954, 352.

47. *NBCK*, May 5, 1954, 49.

48. *NBCK*, June 30, 1954, 368.

49. *NBCK*, June 25,1954, 299.

50. *NBCK*, July 24, 1954, 399–400.

51. SMA C48-2-702, 17.

52. SMA 103-4-158, 7.

53. *NBCK*, July 7, 1954, 106.

54. Guangdong Provincial Archives (GPA hereafter) 225-4-104, 24.

55. *NBCK*, July 24, 1954, 396.

56. *NBCK*, July 2, 1954, 22.

57. SMA A22-2-1525, 8. I am grateful to Sebastian Heilmann and Zhang Jishun for pointing out the "ways of killing" translation.

58. GPA 235-1-399, 4.

59. SMA A51-1-182, 25, 135–36.

60. In his mid-1980s research on the city of Magnitogorsk, Soviet historian Stephen Kotkin wrote that "how much people consciously thought through the inconsistencies they saw and the affronts they suffered is difficult to gauge." In these Chinese materials, it is clear many did, in fact, do this. In Kotkin's terms, the Chinese business community probably was learning how to "speak Bolshevik." Such speech, Kotkin notes, was often context dependent, and a performance of sorts. In the USSR, "a person could 'speak Bolshevik' one moment, 'innocent peasant' the next, begging indulgence for a professed inability to master fully the demanding new language and behavior." See Stephen Kotkin, *Magnetic Mountain: Stalinism as a Civilization* (Berkeley: University of California Press, 1995), 229, 220.

61. *NBCK*, June 29, 1954, 351–52.

62. SMA C48-2-702, 6.

63. SMA B2-2-58, 24.

64. SMA B2-2-63, 158.

65. Huangpu District Archives (HDA hereafter) 48-2-113, 21.

66. *NBCK*, July 7, 1954, 110.

67. *NBCK*, June 30, 1954, 367.

68. SMA S104-4-24, 37; SMA B2-2-58, 24, 49.

69. SMA B2-2-63, 147.

70. *NBCK*, May 21, 1954, 315; *NBCK*, June 25, 1954, 300.

71. SMA C1-1-62, 6, 32.

72. For evidence of such coercion, see my *Embattled Glory: Veterans, Military Families, and the Politics of Patriotism in China, 1949–2007* (Lanham, MD: Rowman & Littlefield, 2009), 130–31.

73. SMA C1-1-62, 5; also see SMA A22-2-1531, 59.

74. See Articles 85, 6, 8, 9, 12, 13, 18, and 19.

75. SMA B2-2-63, 155.

76. *NBCK*, May 26, 1954, 384.

77. *NBCK*, July 5, 1954, 64.

78. SMA A22-2-1531, 58-59; SMA C1-1-62, 29; SMA B2-2-63, 162.

79. SMA B2-2-58, 50.

80. *NBCK*, June 23, 1954, 285.

81. SMA C1-1-62, 6, 32.

82. SMA B2-2-63, 162.

83. HDA 48-2-113, 22.

84. SMA A22-2-1531, 58.

85. *NBCK*, July 5, 1954, 64.

86. SMA C48-2-702, 14.

87. *NBCK*, June 23, 1954, 284–85.

88. SMA A22-2-1531, 93.

89. SMA A79-2-381, 148; SMA C48-2-702, 20.

90. SMA B2-2-63, 155. In the reform era, this argument would not be controversial. In Jie Li's *Shanghai Homes*, her "aunt Treasure," a former Maoist, embraced materialistic desires: "Workers would be out of jobs without capitalists. Your uncle might make ten times more money than his employees, but he also works twenty times as hard." See Jie Li, *Shanghai Homes: Palimpsests of Private Life* (New York: Columbia University Press, 2014), 135.

91. SMA A22-2-1531, 60.

92. *NBCK*, June 23, 1954, 284.

93. SMA A42-2-85, 18–19.

94. SMA B2-2-58, 15.

95. SMA B2-2-58, 47.

96. SMA A71-2-974, 101; *NBCK*, July 24, 1954, 399.

97. SMA B2-2-58, 24; SMA C48-2-702, 19.

98. SMA C48-2-702, 2.

99. SMA C48-2-702, 1–2.

100. *NBCK*, June 25, 1954, 299.

101. SMA C48-2-702, 19.

102. Wang Housheng (王厚生) made a similar point, noting that the CCP used exaggerated descriptions about the enthusiasm of elites (not a few of whom were handpicked by the party) and that much of the praise for the constitution was fake and coerced. See Wang Housheng, *Zhonggong zhixian pinglun: Cong zhixian kanzhong zhonggong zhengquan* (Jiulong: Wenhui chubanshe, 1955), 71, 75.

103. *NBCK*, August 9, 1954, 135–36.

104. SMA C48-2-702, 2.

105. SMA B2-2-63, 155.

106. SMA A79-2-381, 14.

107. *NBCK*, June 30, 1954, 369.

108. HDA 48-2-113, 22.

109. SMA C48-2-702, 19.

110. SMA B2-2-61, n.p.

111. SMA A22-2-1525, 7–8, 59.

112. *NBCK*, July 10, 1954, 163; SMA B2-2-58, 16.

113. See Han Dayuan's interview with Dong Chengmei in *1954 nian xianfa yu xin zhongguo xianzheng* (Changsha: Hunan renmin chubanshe, 2004), 779; Han was provided

with some of the transcripts of the deliberations among the key drafters as well, surely as part of a legitimating project. Also see Altehenger, *Legal Lessons*, 144–45; *Zhongguo xianfa jingshi*, ed. Cai Dingjian (蔡定劍) (Beijing: Zhongguo minzhu fazhi chubanshe, 1996), 19. Cai notes that the CCP's drafting committee discussed the draft "article by article and sentence by sentence."

114. See "饶彰风在中共广东省第一市, 镇委书记会议的发言" (December 1955) in Song Yongyi, ed., *Database of the Chinese Political Campaigns in the 1950s: From Land Reform to the State-Private Partnership, 1949–1956* (Cambridge, MA: Fairbank Center for Chinese Studies, Harvard University, 2014).

3. Popular Constitutionalism

1. For Marriage Law propaganda, see Jennifer Altehenger, *Legal Lessons: Popularizing Laws in the People's Republic of China, 1949–1989* (Cambridge, MA: Harvard University Asia Center, 2018).

2. See, for example, Robert Culp, *Articulating Citizenship: Civic Education and Student Politics in Southeastern China, 1912–1940* (Cambridge, MA: Harvard University Asia Center, 2007); David Strand, *An Unfinished Republic: Leading by Word and Deed in Early Twentieth Century China* (Berkeley: University of California Press, 2011); Xiaowei Zheng, *The Politics of Rights and the 1911 Revolution in China* (Stanford, CA: Stanford University Press, 2018). In *Building Constitutionalism in China*, Stéphanie Balme and Michael Dowdle use the term *popular constitutionalism* to capture "a discourse that clearly takes place outside the reach of the state elite" and involves "bottom-up articulations" of constitutional ideas but ordinary people do not feature prominently in this volume. Instead, activist lawyers, who represent "social diversity" and can be distinguished from "the elite," play starring roles. See "Introduction: Exploring for Constitutionalism in 21st Century China," in *Building Constitutionalism in China*, ed. Stephanie Balme and Michael Dowdle (New York: Palgrave Macmillan, 2009), 19.

3. Lydia Liu identifies *citizen* and *society* as return graphic loans, but *congress* is also in this category. See *Translingual Practice: Literature, National Culture, and Translated Modernity* (Stanford, CA: Stanford University Press, 1995), 308, 336. In the case of *citizen*, Xiaocai Feng notes that "only rarely did average people use this term to describe the everyday connection between themselves and political power. Thus, it is doubtful that most pronouncements containing the new word 'citizens' actually represented popular political participation or the will of the people." See "Counterfeiting Legitimacy: Reflections on the Usurpation of Popular Politics and the 'Political Culture' of China, 1912–1949," *Frontiers of History in China* 8, no. 2 (2013): 205.

4. See Czesław Miłosz, *The Captive Mind*, trans. Jane Zielonko (New York: Vintage International, 1990), 60.

5. See Neil J. Diamant, "Policy Blending, Fuzzy Chronology and Local Understandings of Policy Initiatives in Early 1950s China," *Frontiers of History in China* 9, no. 1 (2014): 83–101.

6. Marc Galanter, "The Radiating Effects of Courts," in *Empirical Theories about Courts*, ed. Keith O. Boyum and Lynn Mather (New York: Longman, 1983): 117–42.

7. *Neibu cankao* (*NBCK* hereafter), July 31, 1954, 522.

8. *NBCK*, July 24, 1954, 396.

9. *NBCK*, June 23, 1954, 282.

10. *NBCK*, July 6, 1954, 85; *NBCK*, July 2,1954, 25–26; Shanghai Municipal Archives (SMA hereafter) A22-2-1525, 3.

11. *NBCK*, August 18, 1954, 256.

12. *NBCK*, July 7, 1954, 106; *NBCK*, July 24, 1954, 399; *NBCK*, July 22, 1954, 353.

13. *NBCK*, July 28, 1954, 465.

14. *NBCK*, July 14, 1954, 230.

15. *NBCK*, July 24, 1954, 391.

16. *NBCK*, June 23, 1954, 283.

17. *NBCK*, June 30, 1954, 371.

18. *NBCK*, August 5, 1954, 78. In contrast, *People's Daily* glowingly reported that in the Beijing suburbs villagers enthusiastically participated in the discussion despite being fatigued from working in the fields. See "Bejing shi jieshu taolun xianfa cao'an ge jie renmin jiji tichu xiugai he buchong yijian," *People's Daily*, September 10, 1954.

19. *NBCK*, August 26, 1954, 385.

20. *NBCK*, July 28, 1954, 466.

21. *NBCK*, August 21, 1954, 298.

22. *NBCK*, June 30, 1954, 371.

23. SMA A79-2-385, 4.

24. SMA A48-1-287, 129; Baoshan District Archives (BDA hereafter) 9-6-1, 3.

25. SMA B2-2-63, 171.

26. *NBCK*, July 7, 1954, 110.

27. *NBCK*, June 30, 1954, 368; *NBCK*, July 22, 1954, 350.

28. *NBCK*, July 22, 1954, 349.

29. *NBCK*, July 7, 1954, 107.

30. *NBCK*, July 3, 1954, 44.

31. *NBCK*, July 2, 1954, 21.

32. *NBCK*, July 24, 1954, 397.

33. Yu Xingzhong argues that "if the concept of citizenship is to be effectively incorporated into Chinese political life and discourse, conceptual difficulties such as the confusion between the terms 'people' and 'citizens' and the leading-led mentality must be resolved." See "Citizenship, Ideology, and the PRC Constitution," in *Changing Meanings of Citizenship in Modern China*, ed. Merle Goldman and Elizabeth J. Perry (Cambridge, MA: Harvard University Asia Center, 2002), 306.

34. See Xiaocai Feng, "Political Labels and Societal Reactions: The 'People' and 'Nationals' in the Early Years of the People's Republic of China," paper presented at the Annual Meeting of the Association of Asian Studies, Toronto, Canada (March 2017), 14.

35. SMA A79-2-381, 157; SMA B2-2-58, 52.

36. Guangdong Provincial Archives (GPA hereafter) 235-1-399, 3.

37. See, for example, BDA 9-6-1, 2; SMA A71-2-974, 200; *NBCK*, July 22, 1954, 350; GPA 225-2-29, 40; SMA A26-2-304, 64; *NBCK*, June 23, 1954, 283; *NBCK*, July 13, 1954, 212; *NBCK*, July 7, 1954, 107.

38. SMA A48-1-287, 128.

39. SMA A26-2-304, 36.

40. See, for example the "Report Card" (*baogao ka* 报告卡) of one such discussion. Among topics listed under "Content" was "What is a Constitution?" and "Why have a Constitution?" "Xiang gongren xuanchuan xianfa cao'an de jianghua cankao cailiao," SMA (copied without file number), July 30, 1954, 169.

41. SMA A79-2-381, 10.

42. Yangpu District Archives (YDA) 16-25-4, 6; SMA A71-2-974, 166. The "report card" cited earlier noted that results were unsatisfactory because the propaganda official could not be heard well, and his dialect was not understood.

43. GPA 235-1-399, 15.

44. SMA B2-2-61, 3.

45. SMA A38-2-144, 25.

46. SMA A71-2-975, 2.

47. *NBCK*, September 15, 1954, 213.

48. *NBCK*, September 15, 1954, 214.

49. *NBCK*, July 28, 1954, 466.

50. As summarized by Leese and Engman, "for Mao, law and courts constituted a weapon that, along with the procuratorates and the public security apparatus, fulfilled the fundamental function of detecting, investigating, and sentencing individuals or groups posing a threat or inflicting harm on society." See "Introduction" in *Victims, Perpetrators, and the Role of Law in Maoist China: A Case Study Approach*, ed. Daniel Leese and Puck Engman (Berlin: De Gruyter Oldenbourg, 2018), 5. https://doi.org/10.1515 /9783110533651-001.

51. *NBCK*, June 23, 1954, 283–84.

52. Huangpu District Archives (HDA hereafter) 3055-1-14, 38; *NBCK*, July 7, 1954, 107; GPA 225-4-104, 42; SMA A26-2-304, 64; SMA B2-2-61, n.p.; *NBCK*, June 23, 1954, 283.

53. SMA B2-2-61, n.p.

54. GPA 235-1-399, 2; SMA B2-2-66, 71; SMA A71-2-973, 73; SMA A26-2-304, 33; GPA 235-1-399, 2.

55. *NBCK*, July 22, 1954, 349.

56. SMA B2-2-66, 74.

57. *NBCK*, July 7, 1954, 107. "Nationalities" refers to ethnic minority groups.

58. *NBCK*, July 6, 1954, 86.

59. SMA A26-2-304, 36; SMA A79-2-381, 157; SMA A71-2-973, 79; SMA A71-2-974, 200.

60. SMA B2-2-58, 31–32.

61. SMA A71-2-973, 73.

62. SMA A79-2-381, 133.

63. *NBCK*, July 31, 1954, 522.

64. SMA B2-2-61, n.p.; BDA 9-6-1, 4.

65. SMA A51-1-182, 11.

66. HDA N7-1-455, 95; SMA A26-2-304, 66.

67. *NBCK*, July 6, 1954, 86.

68. SMA A71-2-975, 87. In Shanghai's Dongchang District a report noted that "very many people do not understand Northern dialect."

69. *NBCK*, July 31, 1954, 522.

70. *NBCK*, June 23, 1954, 280.

71. *NBCK*, September 15, 1954, 213.

72. SMA B2-2-58, 9. Perhaps they spoke a similar dialect.

73. SMA July 24, 1954, 397.

74. *NBCK*, July 24, 1954, 402.

75. SMA B2-2-61, 3.

76. SMA S104-4-24, 34.

77. SMA B2-2-66, 87.

78. SMA B2-2-61, 3, 31–32.

79. SMA A38-2-144, 3.

80. *NBCK*, July 31, 1954, 522; SMA A71-2-974, 63.

81. *NBCK*, July 24, 1954, 400.

82. *NBCK*, July 10, 1954, 163; *NBCK*, July 24, 1954, 402.

83. GPA 235-1-399, 16, 21.

84. SMA B2-2-58, 9.

85. GPA 235-1-399, 21.

86. SMA A71-2-974, 124.

87. *NBCK*, June 23, 1954, 281.

88. *NBCK*, July 10, 1954, 163.

89. *NBCK*, September 15, 1954, 213.

90. GPA 235-1-399, 21. As noted by Frederic Wakeman Jr., "Somehow, Northerners always think of the Cantonese as eating something ungodly, such as newborn rats ('honey peepers'), raw monkey's brains, fried snake, or sauerkraut of buffalo curd." See *Strangers at the Gate: Social Disorder in South China, 1839–1861* (Berkeley: University of California Press, 1966), 57.

91. GPA 235-1-399, 22. In the report this was "宪法, 宪鬼, 宪马养, 连唐呀, 鱼呀都无得吃, 有什么好宪法." Similarly, in Shanghai, workers in Luwan District asked officials, "If peasants' land rights are protected, why can't you buy bean cake in the countryside?" and "If the state protects labor why are peasants forced to sell excess grain to the state?" See SMA B2-2-61, n.p. In another report, family members of workers in a cotton mill were upset about the state's unified purchasing policy. During the discussion, they complained about a clause in Article 8 ("The state guides and helps individual peasants to increase production"): "What's all this about increasing production? Peasants don't have enough oil and you can't buy fertilizer." See SMA A22-2-1525, 3.

92. See Ran Hirschl, *Comparative Matters: The Renaissance of Comparative Constitutional Law* (Oxford: Oxford University Press, 2016), 152.

93. In the sources, many omissions appeared in the collection of suggested revisions published by the National Draft Constitutional Discussion Committee (*NDCDC* hereafter). See multiple volumes of *Quanguo renmin taolun xianfa yijian huibian* (全国人民讨论宪草意见汇编) (Beijing: 1954). Unfortunately, copies of this volume that I received through interlibrary loan only included pagination, not volume number.

94. *NBCK*, July 22, 1954, 346.

95. *NBCK*, July 24, 1954, 391.

96. *NBCK*, July 22, 1954, 355; SMA A71-2-973, 51; SMA B2-2-66, 68.

97. *NBCK*, July 22, 1954, 347.

98. *NBCK*, July 24, 1954, 391; *NBCK*, July 22, 1954, 355.

99. *NDCDC*, 83; SMA B2-2-61, n.p.; SMA B2-2-58, 49.

100. As noted by Elizabeth J. Perry in the context of rural North China, "losses at the gambling table were a potent motivation for the move to open banditry." See *Rebels and Revolutionaries in North China: 1845–1945* (Stanford, CA: Stanford University Press, 1980), 53.

101. *NDCDC*, 184.

102. *NDCDC*, 184.

103. *NDCDC*, 10, 184.

104. See my *Embattled Glory: Veterans, Military Families, and the Politics of Patriotism in China, 1949–2007* (Lanham, MD: Rowman & Littlefield, 2009), chap. 7, for problems in CCP policy toward military families.

105. SMA A71-2-973, 28.

106. *NBCK*, May 26, 1954, 385.

107. *NBCK*, June 16, 1954, 210.

108. Strand, *Unfinished Republic*, 179–81. Political cartography was critical to give people the tools to "imagine China."

109. *NBCK*, July 2, 1954, 21.

110. *NBCK*, August 9, 1954, 136; *NBCK*, June 23, 1954, 283.

111. GPA 235-1-399, 2–4.

112. SMA A22-2-1525, 17; SMA A26-2-304, 32; SMA A71-2-975, 108; SMA A71-2-973, 83; SMA A79-2-381, 1–2.

113. Liu Shao-chi, *Report on the Draft Constitution of the People's Republic of China* (Peking: Foreign Languages Press, 1954), 60–61. Liu's cherry-picked topics formed the basis of this section of his widely circulated report (Part 3), which in turn became an important source for PRC scholarship on the 1954 national discussion. See, for example, *Zhongguo xianfa jingshi*, ed. Cai Dingjian (蔡定剑) (Beijing: Zhongguo minzhu fazhi chubanshe, 1996), 21–23; Han Dayuan, *1954 nian xianfa yu xin zhongguo xianzheng* (Changsha: Hunan renmin chubanshe, 2004), 300–303.

114. The star represents the "national bourgeoisie," not the "bureaucratic bourgeoisie." However, state policy toward these groups was often unclear to people, so they were lumped together as targets of elimination.

115. *NBCK*, July 7, 1954, 111; *NBCK*, June 23, 1954, 282; GPA 225-4-104, 51; SMA A22-2-1525, 17; SMA A79-2-381, 133, 157; SMA A71-2-974, 102; SMA B2-2-58, 53; SMA B2-2-66, 86; SMA A26-2-304, 36; SMA C48-2-702, 1; SMA S103-4-158, 7; HDA 3055-1-14, 37.

116. See, for example, *NBCK*, July 7, 1954, 111; *NBCK*, July 2, 1954, 25; *NBCK*, July 13, 1954, 212; *NBCK*, July 22, 1954, 351; *NBCK*, July 8, 1954, 126; GPA 225-2-29, 40; SMA A26-2-304, 36; SMA A71-2-975, 65; SMA B2-2-62, 4; SMA B2-2-63, 68; BDA 9-6-1, 3; SMA A79-2-381, 4, 165; SMA A71-2-975, 65; SMA B2-2-58, 10; SMA B2-2-61, n.p.; SMA B2-2-66, 86; SMA B2-2-65, 4.

117. *NDCDC*, 11–12. For this debate, see Wu Haiyun, "Flower Power: Understanding China's National Flower Debate." https://www.sixthtone.com/news/1004596/flower-power-understanding-chinas-national-flower-debate. Accessed April 1, 2020.

118. *NBCK*, July 6, 1954, 86; *NDCDC*, 232; GPA 225-2-29, 32; GPA 225-4-104, 51; SMA A71-2-973, 81. For Republican-era discussions, see David Strand, "A High Place Is No Better than a Low Place: The City in the Making of Modern China," in *Becoming Chinese: Passages to Modernity and Beyond*, ed. Wen-hsin Yeh (Berkeley: University of California Press, 2000), 100–101.

119. *NBCK*, July 6, 1954, 86; GPA 225-2-29, 32; SMA B2-2-66, 66.

120. *NDCDC*, 232.

121. *NDCDC*, 11–13.

122. *NBCK*, August 19, 1954, 264.

123. *NBCK*, July 2, 1954, 25. These officials worked in institutions under direct provincial administration.

124. *NDCDC*, 184.

125. *NDCDC*, 182.
126. *NDCDC*, 10, 182, 205; SMA B2-2-58, 49.
127. *NDCDC*, 205.
128. *NDCDC*, 206.
129. *NDCDC*, 206.
130. SMA B2-2-58, 9.
131. *NDCDC*, 206, 210.
132. *NDCDC*, 191, 193, 210.
133. *NDCDC*, 13, 217, 219.
134. SMA A26-2-304, 64.
135. *NDCDC*, 191.
136. SMA B2-2-66, 85.
137. SMA B2-2-63, 158.

4. Reading about Rights and Obligations

1. Shanghai Municipal Archives (SMA hereafter) A22-2-1525, 95–96.
2. SMA C1-1-62, 35.
3. Jennifer Altehenger, *Legal Lessons: Popularizing Laws in the People's Republic of China, 1949–1989* (Cambridge, MA: Harvard University Asia Center, 2018), 84; Guangdong Provincial Archives (GPA hereafter) 225-4-104, 42, 50.
4. SMA C1-1-62, 35.
5. SMA B2-2-61, 27.
6. Andrew J. Nathan, *Chinese Democracy* (Berkeley: University of California Press, 1986), 125.
7. For a discussion of this "populist" conception, see Elizabeth J. Perry, "The Populist Dream of Chinese Democracy," *Journal of Asian Studies* 74, no. 4 (November 2015): 903–15.
8. SMA B2-2-63, 174. Making rights dependent on *obligations* is a more accurate description than a more generic notion of rights based on behavior, as argued by Pitman B. Potter. See *From Leninist Discipline to Socialist Legalism: Peng Zhen on Law and Political Authority in the PRC* (Stanford, CA: Stanford University Press, 2003), 124.
9. SMA B2-2-58, 33.
10. *Neibu cankao* (*NBCK* hereafter), July 31, 1954, 520–21.
11. SMA A71-2-974, 126.
12. SMA B2-2-61, 3.
13. GPA 235-1-399, 15. On the publication and marketing of constitutional materials, see Altehenger, *Legal Lessons: Popularizing Laws in the People's Republic of China, 1949–1989* (Cambridge, MA: Harvard University Asia Center, 2018), 84.
14. SMA A51-1-182, 134.
15. SMA A51-1-182, 135.
16. On these efforts, see Jennifer Altehenger, *Legal Lessons*, chap. 3.
17. See Neil J. Diamant, *Revolutionizing the Family: Politics, Love, and Divorce in Urban and Rural China, 1949–1968* (Berkeley: University of California Press, 2000), chaps. 2–4.
18. SMA B2-2-58, 7–8.
19. SMA A71-2-975, 2; SMA A71-2-974, 51.
20. SMA B2-2-58, 31.

21. Songjiang District Archives (SDA) 1395-6-32, 141.

22. SMA B2-2-58, 34, 41–43; SMA B2-2-63, 173; SMA C1-2-234, 10.

23. SMA B2-2-61, 24; SMA A48-1-287, 131–34, 138–39.

24. GPA 225-2-29, 93; GPA 235-1-399, 11.

25. SMA A26-2-304, 31; SMA B2-2-61, 24.

26. SMA A79-2-381, 15.

27. SMA B2-2-58, 26.

28. *NBCK*, June 25, 1954, 300.

29. *NBCK*, June 30, 1954, 367.

30. SMA B2-2-58, 9.

31. SMA B2-2-58, 25.

32. *NBCK*, June 29, 1954, 351; *NBCK* July 22, 1954, 350.

33. SMA B2-2-62, 12.

34. SMA A26-2-304, 36.

35. Huangpu District Archives (HDA hereafter) N7-1-455, 95; SMA B2-2-61, n.p.

36. SMA A42-2-86, 40.

37. SMA B2-2-61, 33.

38. SMA A26-2-304, 44; SMA A42-2-86, 42; SMA B2-2-61, n.p.

39. SMA A71-2-973, 80. Also see *NDCDC*, 134.

40. GPA 225-2-29, 32.

41. *NDCDC*, 209.

42. *NDCDC*, 214, 10. On this issue of exhaustion because of high birth rates, see Gail Hershatter, *The Gender of Memory: Rural Women and China's Collective Past* (Berkeley: University of California Press, 2011).

43. *NDCDC*, 107.

44. *NDCDC*, 134, 182, 215.

45. SMA B2-2-58, 26.

46. *NDCDC*, 214–15.

47. On different patterns of elite domination outside of the classical education route, see Joseph W. Esherick and Mary Rankin, eds., *Chinese Local Elites and Patterns of Dominance* (Berkeley: University of California Press, 1990).

48. For more information on China's education system and the Civil Service examinations, see Benjamin Elman, *A Cultural History of Civil Examinations in Late Imperial China* (Berkeley: University of California Press, 2000); and Elman, *Civil Examinations and Meritocracy in Late Imperial China* (Cambridge, MA: Harvard University Press, 2013). On the belief on the superiority of Chinese civilization vis-à-vis "barbarians," see Joseph R. Levenson, *Confucian China and Its Modern Fate* (Berkeley: University of California Press, 1965).

49. At least in the United States, Chinese Americans are often viewed as "model minorities" partly because of their academic success. The popularity of books purporting to teach non-Chinese the secrets of academic success, such as Amy Chua's *Battle Hymn of the Tiger Mother* (New York: Penguin, 2011), speaks to this widespread view.

50. On CCP efforts to recruit educated people into its ranks through large-scale registration campaigns, see Eddy U, *Creating the Intellectual: Chinese Communism and the Rise of a Classification* (Oakland: University of California Press, 2019), chap. 4.

51. Chen Yung-fa, *Making Revolution: The Communist Revolution in Eastern and Central China, 1937–1945* (Berkeley: University of California Press, 1986), 301–2. On the

role of education in attracting workers to the Communist Party in the early years, see Elizabeth J. Perry, *Anyuan: Mining China's Revolutionary Tradition* (Berkeley: University of California Press, 2012), 51–57.

52. See Glen Peterson, *The Power of Words: Literacy and Revolution in South China, 1949–95* (Vancouver: University of British Columbia Press, 1997), 32.

53. They observed that "dictators may also use the gap between promise and reality to demoralize internal opponents: the false promise is a costly signal of one's intent to crush opponents." See Tom Ginsburg and Alberto Simpser, eds., *Constitutions in Authoritarian Regimes* (Cambridge: Cambridge University Press, 2014), 8.

54. When "political mobilization" does occur, it is usually on the state's terms. See Juan L. Linz, "An Authoritarian Regime: Spain," in *Cleavages, Ideologies and Party Systems: Contributions to Comparative Political Sociology*, ed. Erik Allardt and Yrjö Littunen (Helsinki: Academic Bookstore, 1964), 304.

55. SMA A22-2-1525, 95–96; SMA C1-1-62, 36.

56. SMA A48-1-287, 129.

57. SMA A71-2-974, 81.

58. *NBCK*, July 7, 1954, 110.

59. GPA 204-3-43, 114. For a compelling account of this crisis, see Peterson, *Power of Words*, chap. 2.

60. *NDCDC*, 208–9.

61. SMA A38-2-144, 7; SMA B2-2-66, 85.

62. SMA A22-2-1531, 56.

63. SMA C1-1-62, 36.

64. *NBCK*, July 31, 1954, 521.

65. SMA B122-2-31, 18.

66. SMA B2-2-58, 9; SMA B2-2-58, 12.

67. SMA A22-2-1525, 8.

68. SMA C48-2-702, 20.

69. HDA 48-2-113, 22.

70. SMA B2-2-63, 154–55.

71. Yangpu District Archives (YDA) 21-1-11, 139.

72. SMA B2-2-63, 159.

73. SMA A26-2-304, 36. Emphasis mine.

74. SMA B2-2-63, 154.

75. SMA B2-2-63, 173.

76. SMA B2-2-61, n.p.

77. *NBCK*, July 13, 1954, 213.

78. See Benjamin Schwartz, *China and Other Matters* (Cambridge, MA: Harvard University Press, 1996), 117.

79. Jeremy Brown, *City Versus Countryside in Mao's China: Negotiating the Divide* (Cambridge: Cambridge University Press, 2012), 30–34.

80. SMA A26-2-304, 40.

81. See Timothy Mitchell, "The Limits of the State: Beyond Statist Approaches and Their Critics," *American Political Science Review* 85, no. 1 (March 1991): 90. He writes that "the power to regulate and control is not simply a capacity stored within the state, from where it extends out into society. The apparent boundary of the state does not mark the limit of the processes of regulation. It is itself a product of those processes."

82. Anne Applebaum, "History Will Judge the Complicit," *Atlantic*, July/August 2020. https://www.theatlantic.com/magazine/archive/2020/07/trumps-collaborators/612250/.

83. According to Han Dayuan's interview with Dong Chengmei, it also was subject to vigorous debate at the elite level. Mao opposed the right, arguing that people cannot be allowed to go wherever they want to, but was overruled by his colleagues who thought it was necessary. See Han Dayuan, *1954 nian xianfa yu xin zhongguo xianzheng* (Changsha: Hunan renmin chubanshe, 2004), 778. This explanation is at odds with what is known about Mao's interactions with his colleagues in both domestic and international politics (such as the decision to intervene in the Korean War); that is, Mao could not be overruled. However, Mao's commitment to the constitution was not exactly strong, and since this was a relatively low-stakes affair, compromising on this matter might not have been very difficult. After his unpopular Korean War decision, it might have also helped repair relationships.

84. SMA A22-2-1525, 95–96.

85. SMA A26-2-304, 64.

86. GPA 225-4-104, 51.

87. SMA A71-2-974, 39.

88. SMA B2-2-61, n.p.

89. SMA B2-2-58, 53.

90. SMA A26-2-304, 35–36.

91. *NBCK*, August 19, 1954, 265–66.

92. SMA A79-2-381, 3.

93. SMA B2-2-61, n.p; B2-2-66, 83; SMA A26-2-304, 36.

94. GPA 225-4-104, 51.

95. *NBCK*, August 19, 1954, 265.

96. Han Dayuan, *1954 nian xianfa*, 79. On an early draft of the constitution Mao wrote "it's better not to write it" (不写为好). His view did not prevail, however.

97. Accepting the inevitability and universality of contradictions (the disparity between facts and theory) was central to Hegel's understanding of dialectics, but given the low education levels of most CCP officials, it is unlikely that this was a cause of their toleration of citizens noting this phenomenon.

98. Recent scholarship estimates that as many as two million were killed during the CCP's land revolution, occurring from the late 1940s to roughly 1952. Adding approximately 712,000 killed during the Campaign to Suppress Counterrevolutionaries (1950–53) would bring the total to nearly three million. See Brian J. DeMare, *Land Wars: The Story of China's Agrarian Revolution* (Stanford, CA: Stanford University Press, 2019), 161–62. For the 712,000 figure see Yang Kuisong, "Reconsidering the Campaign to Suppress Counterrevolutionaries," *China Quarterly* 193 (March 2008), 120.

99. GPA 225-4-104, 50.

100. *NBCK*, July 22, 1954, 353.

101. SMA A22-2-1525, 95–6; SMA C1-1-62, 36.

102. SMA A22-2-1525, 15.

103. SMA A71-2-975, 108.

104. SMA B2-2-62, n.p.

105. SMA A26-2-304, 35.

106. SMA C48-2-702, 20.

107. *NBCK*, July 24, 1954, 397.

108. *NBCK*, July 24, 1954, 398.

109. SMA B2-2-66, 82.

110. SMA C1-1-62, 36.

111. *NBCK*, July 31, 1954, 519.

112. GPA 225-4-104, 50.

113. SMA B105-5-2046, 8.

114. SMA C1-1-62, 36; SMA B105-5-2046, 8.

115. SMA S103-4-158, 13.

116. The 1947 Republican Constitution (Art. 16) provided the right to lodge complaints and submit petitions but did not specifically include demonstrations or processions.

117. SMA A42-2-85, 19.

118. HDA 202-1-182, 30.

119. *NBCK*, June 23, 1954, 285.

120. SMA B2-2-66, 82.

121. SMA C1-1-62, 36; SMA A22-2-1525, 95–96.

122. SMA A26-2-304, 35.

123. *NBCK*, June 23, 1954, 283.

124. On these efforts, see Rebecca Nedostup, *Superstitious Regimes: Religion and the Politics of Chinese Modernity* (Cambridge, MA: Harvard University Asia Center, 2010).

125. SMA A26-2-304, 40.

126. SMA B2-2-61, n.p.

127. SMA B2-2-66, 83.

128. GPA 225-4-104, 50.

129. GPA 225-2-29, 32.

130. SMA B2-2-63, 104, 165.

131. *NBCK*, August 26, 1954, 385.

132. GPA 204-3-43, 114.

133. SMA B2-2-66, 83.

134. *NBCK*, July 2, 1954, 25–26.

135. GPA 225-2-29, 117.

136. SMA A26-2-304, 36.

137. SMA A71-2-975, 108.

138. SMA B2-2-66, 73.

139. SMA A71-2-973, 79.

140. SMA A38-2-144, 4. Young workers were said to disparage their own status, fearing that they could not get married if women saw them wearing their uniforms. The split in the Shanghai workforce between skilled and unskilled labor and the different politics this engendered were explored in Elizabeth J. Perry, *Shanghai on Strike: The Politics of Chinese Labor* (Stanford, CA: Stanford University Press, 1993).

141. SMA B2-2-65, 2. Workers advanced the same logic to ask why people "under state supervision" use labor to reform themselves. See SMA B2-2-66, 73.

142. SMA A79-2-381, 133.

143. SMA A22-2-1531, 57; SMA B2-2-61, 4.

144. SMA B2-2-61, 32.

145. SMA B122-2-31, 18.

146. *NBCK,* July 24, 1954, 397.

147. *NDCDC,* 203.

148. GPA 225-2-29, 130.

149. GPA 235-1-399, 7–8.

150. GPA 235-1-399, 4.

151. *NBCK,* June 30, 1954, 368.

152. *NBCK* July 24, 1954, 405.

153. SMA A26-2-304, 44.

154. SMA A26-2-304, 64.

155. SMA A22-2-1525, 96.

156. SMA A22-2-1531, 56.

157. SMA B2-2-63, 155.

158. *NDCDC,* 203.

159. *NDCDC,* 200.

160. *NBCK,* July 2, 1954, 23; *NBCK,* June 23, 1954, 283.

161. *NBCK,* August 18, 1954, 255; *NBCK,* June 23, 1954, 283.

162. SMA B2-2-58, 26.

163. Jeremy Brown, "When Things Go Wrong: Accidents and the Legacy of the Mao Era in Today's China," in *Restless China,* ed. Perry Link, Richard P. Madsen, and Paul G. Pickowicz (Lanham, MD: Rowman & Littlefield, 2013), 11–36.

164. SMA B2-2-61, n.p. Elizabeth J. Perry notes that the implementation of labor insurance was seen by some workers as the urban equivalent of land reform in the countryside: "In the villages, the CCP attacked the landlords during land reform and now they are using the labor insurance law to bring their struggle to the factories." See *Patrolling the Revolution: Worker Militias, Citizenship, and the Modern Chinese State* (Lanham, MD: Rowman & Littlefield, 2007), 104.

165. SMA A71-2-973, 79; SMA B2-2-66, 84. On the wide variety of temporary laborers in this era, see Philip C. C. Huang, "Misleading Chinese Legal and Statistical Categories: Labor, Individual Entities, and Private Enterprises," *Modern China* 39, no. 4 (2013): 351.

166. *NBCK,* August 19, 1954, 264.

167. SMA B2-2-61, n.p.; GPA 225-2-29, 33.

168. SMA A26-2-304, 41.

169. For example, in Meiji-era Japan (1868–1912), "Japanese workers . . . were neither keen on taking orders nor enthusiastically committed to their jobs, and persuading them to submit to the discipline of factory labor was not an easy task; it was far from accomplished by the turn of the century." See Andrew Gordon, *The Evolution of Labor Relations in Japan: Heavy Industry, 1853–1955* (Cambridge, MA: Council on East Asian Studies, Harvard University, 1985), 27.

170. SMA A38-2-144, 6, 36.

171. SMA B2-2-61, 32; SMA B122-2-31, 18–20.

172. SMA A22-2-1531, 57; also, SMA B2-2-61, n.p.

173. SMA B122-2-31, 18; SMA A38-2-144, 3; *NBCK,* June 26, 1954, 314.

174. SMA B2-2-61, 4.

175. *NBCK,* July 6, 1954, 86.

176. GPA 225-2-29, 4, 32.

177. *NBCK,* July 31, 1954, 522.

178. *NBCK*, June 25, 1954, 300.

179. SMA A26-2-304, 31.

180. SMA A71-2-975, 65.

181. SMA A42-2-86, 42; Baoshan District Archives (BDA) 9-6-1, 3; *NBCK*, June 29, 1954, 351; SMA A79-2-381, 165; SMA B2-2-66, 85.

182. SMA C48-2-702, 20.

183. *NBCK*, July 24, 1954, 398.

184. *NBCK*, July 6, 1954, 86.

185. *NBCK*, July 10, 1954, 162.

186. *NBCK*, June 23, 1954, 282; *NBCK*, July 7, 1954, 110.

187. *NBCK*, July 22, 1954, 353.

188. GPA 235-1-399, 22.

189. *NBCK*, July 24, 1954, 400.

190. *NBCK*, June 23, 1954, 282.

191. SMA A22-2-1525, 8, 15.

192. SMA B122-2-31, 18.

193. *NBCK*, July 6, 1954, 86; *NBCK*, July 10, 1954, 162.

194. SMA A71-2-974, 101.

195. SMA A71-2-974, 99; SMA A79-2-381, 4.

196. SMA B2-2-61, 4; SMA A26-2-304, 41.

197. SMA B2-2-65, 4; *NBCK*, June 29, 1954, 351.

198. *NBCK*, July 2, 1954, 24.

199. *NBCK*, July 6, 1954, 86.

200. *NBCK*, July 2, 1954, 26.

201. SMA B122-2-31, 18; SMA A22-2-1531, 56; SMA B2-2-65, 4.

202. SMA A22-2-1525, 59.

203. GPA 225-4-104, 51; GPA 225-2-29, 32, 101.

204. *NBCK*, July 13, 1954, 212; SMA A26-2-304, 44.

205. SMA A71-2-973, 28.

206. SMA B2-2-58, 7.

5. Christians, Buddhists, and Ethnic Minorities

1. The division between "ethnic minority" affairs (*minzu*) and issues dealing with "religion" are uneasily disentangled as a matter of practice. Almost all *minzu* had some form of religious belief (Islam in the case of the Hui, for example). Later in this chapter, I follow the PRC's rough categorization as it manifested during the constitutional discussion, with *ethnic group* assigned to groups along China's frontiers in the southwest, with "mainline" faiths—Christianity, Islam, and Buddhism—designated matters of religion. I am, of course, aware that ethnicity and religion can overlap.

2. Raphael Israeli, *Islam in China: Religion, Ethnicity, Culture, and Politics* (Lanham, MD: Lexington Books, 2002), 243.

3. Vincent Goossaert and David A. Palmer, *The Religious Question in Modern China* (Chicago: University of Chicago Press, 2011), 154, 158.

4. Elizabeth J. Perry, *Rebels and Revolutionaries in North China, 1845–1945* (Stanford, CA: Stanford University Press, 1980) and *Anyuan: Mining China's Revolutionary Tradition* (Berkeley: University of California Press, 2012); Chen Yung-fa, *Making Revolution: The*

Chinese Communist Movement in Eastern China, 1937–1945 (Berkeley: University of California Press, 1986).

5. On *jimi*, see Evelyn Rawski, "Chinese Strategy and Security Issues in Historical Perspective," in *China's Rise in Historical Perspective*, ed. Brantly Womack (Lanham, MD: Rowman & Littlefield, 2010), 66–67.

6. Goossaert and Palmer, *Religious Question*, 57.

7. Goossaert and Palmer, 57.

8. Goossaert and Palmer, 58. Emphasis mine.

9. Goossaert and Palmer, 61.

10. Z. Hale Eroglu Sager, "A Place under the Sun: Chinese Muslim (Hui) Identity and the Constitutional Movement in Republican China," *Modern China* (2020): 3, 14. https://doi.org/10.1177%2F0097700420915430.

11. Xiaoxuan Wang, *Maoism and Grassroots Religion: The Communist Revolution and the Reinvention of Religious Life in China* (Oxford: Oxford University Press, 2020), 85.

12. Goossaert and Palmer, *Religious Question*, 154.

13. Unknown to Catholics at the time, one year later the CCP would arrest pro-Vatican Catholic leaders and replace them with pro-government leaders in the Chinese Catholic Patriotic Association. This association was run by lay Catholics, not clergy. See Goossaert and Palmer, 158.

14. On this campaign, see Julia Strauss, "Paternalist Terror: The Campaign to Suppress Counterrevolutionaries and Regime Consolidation in the People's Republic of China, 1950–1953," *Comparative Studies in Society and History* 44, no. 1 (2002): 90; Yang Kuisong, "Reconsidering the Campaign to Suppress Counterrevolutionaries," *China Quarterly*, no. 193 (March 2008): 120. https://doi.org/10.1017/S0305741008000064. Among those arrested, 380,000 guilty of minor crimes were released "after receiving education."

15. Goossaert and Palmer, *Religious Question*, 140, 148–49. By the end of 1953, the campaign against sects resulted in legal action against 4,000 leaders and registration of over 10,000 members. Over 320,000 renounced their membership. See J. Brooks Jessup, "Beyond Ideological Conflict: Political Incorporation of Buddhist Youth in the Early PRC," *Frontiers of History in China* 7, no. 4 (December 2012): 566–67. https://doi.org/10.3868/s020-001-012-0032-9.

16. *Shanghai shi gong'an zhi* (Shanghai: Shanghai shehui kexueyuan chubanshe, 1997), 108, 105.

17. S. A. Smith, "Redemptive Religious Societies and the Communist State, 1949 to the 1980s," in *Maoism at the Grassroots: Everyday Life in China's Era of High Socialism*, ed. Jeremy Brown and Matthew Johnson (Cambridge, MA: Harvard University Press, 2015), 345. He found that in Jiangsu Province between 1954 and 1960, the Public Security Bureau claimed to have uncovered 217 acts involving the societies trying to restore the older order (precollectivization), 88 of them in 1958. This involved 1,385 sect leaders, 401 alters, and 16,363 followers (346).

18. Goossaert and Palmer, *Religious Question*, 154.

19. Goossaert and Palmer, for example, note that the mission of the Religious Affairs Bureau was to "implement the *policy* of religious freedom" rather than its true legal source in the constitution (152). Christie Chui-Shan Chow and Joseph Tse-Hei Lee's study of Christianity in 1950s coastal China also does not mention the constitution. See their "Covert and Overt Activism: Christianity in 1950s Coastal China," *Fron-*

tiers of History in China 11, no. 4 (2016): 579–99. https://doi.org/10.3868/s020-005 -016-0034-9. J. Brooks Jessup's discussion of Shanghai Buddhists from the late 1940s to the mid-1950s also omits the 1954 Constitution. See Jessup, "Beyond Ideological Conflict." Likewise, Xiaoxuan Wang's exhaustive, archive-based study, *Maoism and Grassroots Religion*, does not include material on the 1954 Constitution. Holmes Welch's *Buddhism under Mao* (Cambridge, MA: Harvard University Press, 1972) is similarly silent on this topic.

20. For positive reporting, see, for example, "People of All Walks of Life Write to Support Draft Constitution," *Selections from Mainland Chinese Press*, no. 834, 6. Based on New China News Agency, June 21, 1954. For enthusiastic early paragraphs, see Shanghai Municipal Archives (SMA hereafter) A79-2-381, 133.

21. *Neibu cankao* (*NBCK* hereafter), July 7, 1954, 110.

22. *NBCK*, August 5, 1954, 78.

23. SMA B2-2-63, 173–74.

24. *NBCK*, June 30, 1954, 368.

25. SMA C1-1-62, 34–35.

26. SMA B2-2-63, 173.

27. SMA C1-1-62, 34.

28. Liu Shao-chi, *Report on the Draft Constitution of the People's Republic of China* (Peking: Foreign Languages Press, 1954), 50.

29. SMA B2-2-63, 174.

30. *NBCK*, August 19, 1954, 265. In Jishui County, the following article was proposed instead: "The state adopts the policy of gradually educating those who believe in religion until it is eradicated bit by bit."

31. National Draft Constitutional Discussion Committee (*NDCDC* hereafter), 192–93.

32. *NDCDC*, 193.

33. Owing to the limitation of source materials on the constitution, this discussion cannot capture the diversity of identity and experiences of Hui in China, as documented in several pioneering studies of the Hui. See, for example, Dru C. Gladney, *Muslim Chinese: Ethnic Nationalism in the People's Republic* (Cambridge, MA: Council on East Asian Studies, Harvard University, 1991), 21–36; more recently, and with a legal focus, see Matthew S. Erie, *China and Islam: The Prophet, the Party, and Law* (Cambridge: Cambridge University Press, 2016). Hui, unlike Uyghurs who are concentrated in Xinjiang Province, are geographically dispersed. They trace their origins to Persian and Arab merchants who came to China beginning in the Tang Dynasty (618–907 AD). See Erie, 10.

34. SMA B2-2-58, 17.

35. *NBCK*, July 30, 1954, 502–3.

36. *NBCK*, July 28, 1954, 464.

37. *NBCK*, July 24, 1954, 404.

38. *NBCK*, July 24, 1954, 401. Although unstated, this critique probably referred to the Marriage Law's protection of "marriage freedom" or the constitutional protection of marriage in Article 96.

39. *NBCK*, July 7, 1954, 111. Rehe Province, in China's northeast, ceased to exist as an administrative unit from 1955.

40. *NBCK*, July 5, 1954, 63.

41. *NBCK*, July 5, 1954, 63.

42. *NBCK*, July 22, 1954, 349.

43. *NBCK,* July 24, 1954, 405.

44. Here I disagree with Paul Mariani's assessment of the constitution as a "showcase of united front strategy, designed to rally as many people as possible to the new regime, and to present a benign face to the outside world." See Paul P. Mariani, *Church Militant: Bishop Kung and Catholic Resistance in Communist Shanghai* (Cambridge, MA: Harvard University Press, 2011), 31.

45. Mariani, 32–40, 56.

46. Mariani's account of the Shanghai Catholic Church is the most extensive to date but does not address these responses, only noting briefly (citing the missionary source *Bamboo Wireless*) that "in July and August there were indoctrination sessions in Shanghai about the new Constitution" (140).

47. SMA C1-1-62, 34.

48. SMA C1-1-62, 35.

49. SMA A79-2-381, 172.

50. SMA B2-2-63, 171.

51. *NBCK,* June 26, 1954, 314.

52. *NBCK,* August 9, 1954, 135.

53. SMA B2-2-63, 175.

54. SMA A22-2-1531, 62.

55. SMA B2-2-63, 165.

56. SMA B2-2-63, 175.

57. *NBCK,* June 30, 1954, 371; *NBCK,* July 28, 1954, 464.

58. SMA A22-2-1531, 62.

59. SMA C1-1-62, 34.

60. SMA B2-2-63, 173–74.

61. SMA B2-2-63, 165.

62. *NBCK,* August 9, 1954, 135.

63. SMA B2-2-63, 168.

64. SMA C1-1-62, 35.

65. SMA B2-2-63, 173.

66. SMA C1-1-62, 35.

67. *NBCK,* July 24, 1954, 405.

68. SMA C1-1-62, 35.

69. Christie Chui-Shan Chow and Joseph Yse-Hei Lee, "Covert and Overt Activism," 582–83. For evidence of similar confusion among officials in Zhejiang Province, see Xiaoxuan Wang, "The Dilemma of Implementation: The State and Religion in the People's Republic of China, 1949–1990," in *Maoism at the Grassroots: Everyday Life in China's Era of High Socialism,* ed. Jeremy Brown and Matthew Johnson (Cambridge, MA: Harvard University Press, 2015), 261, 268.

70. On the KMT's efforts vis-à-vis Buddhists, see Rebecca Nedostup, *Superstitious Regimes: Religion and the Politics of Chinese Modernity* (Cambridge, MA: Harvard East Asian Monographs 322, 2010), 124–26.

71. For a succinct review of some of these debates about the Boxers, see Paul A. Cohen, *History in Three Keys: The Boxers as Event, Experience, and Myth* (New York: Columbia University Press, 1997), 38–39. While there were Boxers who claimed that "on account of the Protestant and Catholic religions the Buddhist gods are oppressed" (84),

it is far less clear that Boxers were inspired by Buddhism directly. There is extensive documentation of repression of Buddhists. For an early account, see Welch, *Buddhism under Mao*, 42–144. Jan Kiely argues that in the early 1950s the CCP was "not simply engaged in further extending preexisting modes of state control over Buddhist institutions but rather was enacting a crucial initial stage in the winnowing down of Buddhism for the sake of a 'new China' imagined, in time, to be free of religion." See "The Communist Dismantling of Temple and Monastic Buddhism in Suzhou," in *Recovering Buddhism in Modern China*, ed. Jan Kiely and J. Brooks Jessup (New York: Columbia University Press, 2016), 217.

72. Welch, *Buddhism under Mao*, 46–47; Kiely, "Communist Dismantling," 216; J. Brooks Jessup, "Beyond Ideological Conflict: Political Incorporation of Buddhist Youth in the Early PRC," 567. This campaign was designed to "clearly distinguish and dismiss from Buddhism those heterodox teachings (*waidao xieshuo*) and reactionary sects (*fandong daomen huimen*) that rely on, attach themselves to, and mix among [us]."

73. For an excellent local account of this process in Suzhou between 1949 and 1952 (based on archival materials), see Kiely, "Communist Dismantling," 228–31, 235–36.

74. Jessup, "Beyond Ideological Conflict," 554.

75. *NBCK*, July 29, 1954, 485. On the early history of the Chinese Buddhist Association, see Welch, *Buddhism under Mao*, 18–25.

76. Jessup, "Beyond Ideological Conflict," 551.

77. See Xue Yu, "Buddhist Efforts for the Reconciliation of Buddhism and Marxism in the Early Years of the People's Republic of China," in Kiely and Jessup, *Recovering Buddhism in Modern China*, 202. Such enthusiasm was noted among "progressive" Buddhists; those who were less progressive (that is, not CCP supporters) were not mentioned.

78. SMA A79-2-381, 172; SMA B2-2-63, 165.

79. SMA B2-2-63, 175; SMA C1-1-62, 35.

80. SMA B2-2-63, 175.

81. *NBCK*, May 26, 1954, 384.

82. *NBCK*, July 28, 1954, 464. The draft constitution did not include any general provision for the legal protection of property, only noting in Article 12 that it protects the right of citizens to inherit private property "according to law."

83. Guangdong Provincial Archives (GPA hereafter) 204-3-43, 114.

84. SMA B2-2-63, 173–75.

85. See Vivienne Shue, "Party State, Nation, Empire: Rethinking the Grammar of Chinese Governance," *Journal of Chinese Governance* 3, no. 3 (2018): 275. https://doi .org/10.1080/23812346.2018.1488495.

86. See, for example, SMA A26-2-304, 30.

87. SMA B2-2-67, 7. Among religious groups, Article 88 (about religious freedom) attracted the most attention, but in the articles dealing with minorities autonomous regions, usually separate from culture, produced more questions.

88. *NBCK*, July 7, 1954, 106; *NBCK*, August 19, 1954, 266.

89. SMA B2-2-62, n.p.; SMA B2-2-63, 2.

90. SMA A79-2-381, 4.

91. SMA B2-2-65, 2; *NBCK*, July 22, 1954, 353.

92. GPA 225-2-29, 92–93.

93. *NBCK*, July 7, 1954, 110.

94. SMA A22-2-1525, 17; SMA B2-2-61, n.p.

95. SMA B122-2-31, 18; SMA A26-2-304, 33; SMA B2-2-61, n.p.; SMA C1-1-62, 2.

96. SMA A48-1-272, 13; SMA B122-2-31, 18.

97. SMA B2-2-61, n.p.

98. SMA B2-2-61, n.p. (This was the "七擒孟获的方法.")

99. SMA B2-2-61, n.p.

100. *NBCK,* July 22, 1954, 354.

101. Neil J. Diamant, *Revolutionizing the Family: Politics, Love, and Divorce in Urban and Rural China, 1949–1968* (Berkeley: University of California Press, 2000), 152–54.

102. *NBCK,* July 22, 1954, 354.

103. *NBCK,* July 29, 1954, 484.

104. *NBCK,* July 28, 1954, 463–64.

105. *NBCK,* July 26, 1954, 427–28.

6. Constitutional Afterlives

1. Edward Hallett Carr, *What Is History? The George Macauley Trevelyan Lectures Delivered in the University of Cambridge, Jan.–March 1961* (New York: Knopf, 1962), 26.

2. For a summary of this argument, see Xu Lizhi, "Beyond 'Destruction' and 'Lawlessness': The Legal System during the Cultural Revolution," in *Victims, Perpetrators, and the Role of Law in Maoist China: A Case Study Approach,* ed. Daniel Leese and Puck Engman (Berlin: De Gruyter Oldenbourg, 2018), 25. https://doi.org/10 .1515/9783110533651-001. For problems implementing Sufan in the Shanghai region, where there were quite a few people who supported the KMT, see Julia C. Strauss, *State Formation in China and Taiwan: Bureaucracy, Campaign, and Performance* (Cambridge: Cambridge University Press, 2020), 166–67.

3. Xu Lizhi, "Beyond 'Destruction' and 'Lawlessness,'" 26. He writes, "After the end of the Cultural Revolution, the official negation of the movement, as well as the emphasis on showcasing its destructive impact on existing structures and the public order, has had a major influence on scholarship."

4. Liu Zheng, "1954 nian xianfa shixiang sannian hou weishenme bei zhujian qifei," *Zhongguo renda* 14 (2002): 43; also see Pitman B. Potter, *From Leninist Discipline to Socialist Legalism: Peng Zhen on Law and Authority in the PRC* (Stanford, CA: Stanford University Press, 2003).

5. Daniel Leese and Puck Engman, "Introduction," in *Victims, Perpetrators, and the Role of Law in Maoist China: A Case Study Approach,* ed. Daniel Leese and Puck Engman (Berlin: De Gruyter Oldenbourg, 2018), 8.

6. Xu Lizhi, "Beyond 'Destruction' and 'Lawlessness,'" 42. In addition to this volume, a recent study on inheritance law in the PRC noted continuities between the Mao and post-Mao eras: "the Succession Law of 1985 was not a departure from the previous 'lawless' Mao era, but the completion of PRC judges' long process of amending the 'incomplete' 1956 draft." See Byungil Ahn, "Searching for Fairness in Revolutionary China: Inheritance Disputes in Maoist Courts and Their Legacy in the PRC Law of Succession," *Modern China* 47, no. 1 (January 2021): 50.

7. According to Clarke, there are "many Chinese legal systems, each with its own jurisdiction, hierarchy of authority, and way of operating." See "How Do We Know

When an Enterprise Exists? Unanswerable Questions and Legal Polycentricity in China," *Columbia Journal of Asian Law* 19, no.1 (2005): 64.

8. For instance, taking a longer view, is it the case that "the legalistic aspect of workers' mobilization is new and a product of the reform era's emphasis on law," as Mary E. Gallagher has argued? See *Authoritarian Legality in China: Law, Workers, and the State* (Cambridge: Cambridge University Press, 2017), 36.

9. For the remainder of the Mao era, I will be looking at sources such as *Neibu cankao*, records of meetings, and archival material as well as more traditional materials such legal journals. Many of the nontraditional materials are contained in CD-ROM databases of materials from the Mao era (Song Yongyi, editor-in-chief), including the *Database of the Chinese Political Campaigns in the 1950s: From Land Reform to the State-Private Partnership, 1949–1956* (Cambridge, MA: Fairbank Center for Chinese Studies, Harvard University, 2014); *The Chinese Anti-Rightist Campaign Database (1957–)* (Hong Kong: Universities Service Centre for China Studies, The Chinese University of Hong Kong Press, 2010); *The Chinese Great Leap Forward/Great Famine Database, 1958–1962* (Cambridge and Hong Kong: Fairbank Center for Chinese Studies, Harvard University and the Universities Service Centre for China Studies, the Chinese University of Hong Kong, 2013). Reflecting the greater openness of the reform era toward legal scholarship, I will take advantage of several surveys of constitutional understanding and awareness that appeared in Chinese legal journals from the 1980s through the 2010s, newspapers, archival data, and secondary sources.

10. Xiaoxuan Wang notes that these policies encountered "fierce resistance," including riots, as well as an "exodus from collective farms." See *Maoism and Grassroots Religion: The Communist Revolution and the Reinvention of Religious Life in China* (Oxford: Oxford University Press, 2020), 86; also see Elizabeth J. Perry, "Rural Violence in Socialist China," *China Quarterly*, no. 103 (September 1985): 421–22.

11. "醴陵县有一些富农以美人计的方法打互助合作组织," *NBCK*, November 18, 1954. Song Yongyi, ed., *From Land Reform to the State-Private Partnership Database*.

12. "平顺县今年发生的有关破坏互助合作案件超过以往任何一年," *Neibu cankao (NBCK* hereafter), February 3, 1955, Song Yongyi, ed., *From Land Reform to the State-Private Partnership Database*.

13. "广东省有一些农民对购粮的不满情绪已波及到工人," *NBCK*, April 7, 1955, Song Yongyi, ed., *From Land Reform to the State-Private Partnership Database*.

14. "热河省少数区村建社中有急躁冒进偏向," *NBCK*, September 18, 1954, Song Yongyi, ed., *From Land Reform to the State-Private Partnership Database*.

15. Whether these represented his genuine beliefs is, of course, difficult to ascertain. Was he truly attracted to the "New Faith" like a moth to a candle, as Miłosz notes of some Eastern European intellectuals? Was it purely pragmatic given his circumstances? For an interesting typology of intellectuals' choices in Eastern Europe, see Miłosz, *The Captive Mind*, trans. Jane Zielonko (New York: Vintage International, 1990), 4.

16. See "我为什么加入中国共产党," *Wenhui Bao*, December 10, 1955. Originally published in *People's Daily*.

17. See "陈毅同志在专, 市, 处, 局长会议上关于制定今后逮捕反革命分子及其他犯罪分子初步计划的总结报告," 1958, Song Yongyi, ed., *Anti-Rightist Database*.

18. "中共公安部关于须严格遵守宪法和法律的指示," January 30, 1955. The original source was "公安会议文件选编, 1949–1957," Song Yongyi, ed., *From Land*

Reform to the State-Private Partnership Database. For more information on public security officials, see Jennifer Altehenger, *Legal Lessons: Popularizing Laws in the People's Republic of China, 1949–1989* (Cambridge, MA: Harvard University Asia Center, 2018), 160. Many thought that teaching people about the constitution was "asking for trouble."

19. "罗瑞卿在各省,市,自治区党委五人小组负责人会议上的总结," May 23, 1957, Song Yongyi, ed., *Anti-Rightist Database.*

20. "韩悦顺的肃反结论," February 1, 1956, Song Yongyi, ed., *From Land Reform to the State-Private Partnership Database.*

21. See "黑龙江, 吉林等地群众对胡风反革命集团存在的错误认识," *NBCK,* June 28, 1955; "武汉市机关干部和高等学校师生对胡风反革命集团问题存在一些糊涂思想," *NBCK,* June 24, 1955. Song Yongyi, ed., *From Land Reform to the State-Private Partnership Database.*

22. This perspective can be seen in a 1950 document titled "How to Understand the United States." Readers were told that "the people enjoy neither freedom to vote nor any freedom of speech, publication, meeting, or association. The secret police rule everything. . . . American publishing houses and newspapers are almost entirely in the hands of the few big capitalists." See R. David Arkush and Leo O. Lee, eds., *Land without Ghosts: Chinese Impressions of America from the Mid-nineteenth Century to the Present* (Berkeley: University of California Press, 1989), 248–50.

23. Dai Shubai (戴树柏), "Jianlun ziyou," *Xueshu yuekan* 12 (December 1957): 24–30.

24. "中共麻城县委党校党员轮训中暴露出的一些观点," January 1963, Song Yongyi, ed., *Great Leap Forward/Great Famine Database.* In Chinese this was "这是要人信迷信."

25. "许学富关于河南商城 群众断粮死人事件第二次致周恩来总理加急电," March 28, 1959, Song Yongyi, ed., *Great Leap Forward/Great Famine Database.*

26. In previous work I explored the role of veterans as whistleblowers. Like many whistleblowers around the world, they were often subject to retaliation. See *Embattled Glory: Veterans, Military Families, and the Politics of Patriotism in China* (Lanham, MD: Rowman & Littlefield, 2009), 111–18.

27. "关于商城县越美公社观庙, 汪桥管理区因生活安排不好发生饿死人情况的检查处理报告," May 31, 1959, Song Yongyi, ed., *Great Leap Forward/Great Famine Database.*

28. For a vivid description of such survival strategies in a Henan village, see Ralph A. Thaxton Jr., *Catastrophe and Contention in Rural China: Mao's Great Leap Forward Famine and the Origins of Righteous Resistance in Da Fo Village* (Cambridge: Cambridge University Press, 2008), 199–214.

29. Cited in Xu Lizhi, "Beyond 'Destruction' and 'Lawlessness': The Legal System during the Cultural Revolution," 33.

30. Liu Zheng, "1954 nian xianfa shixiang sannian hou weishenme bei zhujian qifei," 43.

31. "武汉市机关干部和高等学校老师生对胡风反革命集团问题存在一些糊涂思想," *NBCK,* June 24, 1955, Song Yongi, ed., *From Land Reform to the State-Private Partnership Database.*

32. Roderick MacFarquhar, *The Hundred Flowers Campaign and the Chinese Intellectuals* (New York: Praeger, 1960), 94.

33. MacFarquhar, *Hundred Flowers Campaign,* 94.

34. MacFarquhar, 111.

35. Shanghai Municipal Archives (SMA hereafter) B168-1-233 (August 25, 1955). I am grateful to Nara Dillon for this reference, as well as the next two.

36. SMA B-54–2, May 20, 1955.

37. SMA B54–4, August 13, 1957.

38. Yiching Wu, *The Cultural Revolution at the Margins: Chinese Socialism in Crisis* (Cambridge, MA: Harvard University Press, 2014), 166.

39. Feng Chen, "Against the State: Labor Protests in China in the 1950s," *Modern China* 40, no. 5 (2014): 505. The original source was *Neibu cankao*, June 7, 1957.

40. "对古岭县大山公社党委书记张有村及石亮河铁厂矿山车间主任熊仕彬无辜捆绑打签署工人侵犯人权的控告," April–May,1959, Song Yongyi, ed., *Great Leap Forward/Great Famine Database*.

41. On the Republican-era arguments, see Z. Hale Eroglu Sager, "A Place under the Sun: Chinese Muslim (Hui) Identity and the Constitutional Movement in Republican China," *Modern China* (2020): 15. The PRC data are from Shao Canhua (邵灿华), "呼和浩特, 包头两市伊斯兰教的情况和问题," *NBCK*, February 11, 1955, Song Yongyi, ed., *From Land Reform to the State-Private Partnership Database*.

42. Shen Junhai (沈俊海), "宪法颁布后辽宁省宗教界的上层分子活动情况," *NBCK*, February 8, 1955, Song Yongyi, ed., *From Land Reform to the State-Private Partnership Database*.

43. See Xiaoxuan Wang, *Maoism and Grassroots Religion*, 92. This sort of rebuttal, however, would not be effective beyond 1957 given the crackdown on CCP critics in the Anti-Rightist Campaign and the rush to communism during the Great Leap Forward.

44. "市委秘书处关于半年来人民来信工作情况的报告," July 13, 1957, Song Yongyi, ed., *Anti-Rightist Database*.

45. Altehenger, *Legal Lessons*, 173.

46. Altehenger similarly notes that the national discussion of the constitutional draft in 1954 was the "apogee of law propaganda while Mao was alive." See Altehenger, 166.

47. During the Cultural Revolution, "bourgeois lawfulness" was associated with the activities of "capitalist roaders" in the CCP. Praising lawlessness, Mao ordered attacks on the police, procuratorate, and legal sector. See Altehenger, 166.

48. Altehenger, 174. Unlike 1954, the public discussion was limited to the second and third drafts, not the first.

49. Altehenger, 175.

50. For perhaps the most prominent example, see Elizabeth J. Perry and Li Xun, *Proletarian Power: Shanghai in the Cultural Revolution* (Boulder, CO: Westview, 1997).

51. Altehenger, *Legal Lessons*, 175. Similar arguments were made in late 1940s Poland: "Against whom are they to strike? Against themselves? After all, the means of production belong to them, the state belongs to them." See Czesław Miłosz, *The Captive Mind*, 196.

52. Altehenger, *Legal Lessons*, 176.

53. Altehenger, 176.

54. Huangpu District Archives (HDA hereafter) 42-1-70, 40, 42–43.

55. Altehenger, *Legal Lessons*, 180.

56. Altehenger, 183.

57. Altehenger, 182.

58. Altehenger, 196–97.

59. Altehenger, 195.

60. Altehenger, 195.

61. See *From Leninist Discipline to Socialist Legalism: Peng Zhen on Law and Political Authority in the PRC* (Stanford, CA: Stanford University Press, 2003), 107.

62. See Altehenger, *Legal Lessons*, 167, 198, 172.

63. Altehenger, 198, 173.

64. *Beijing Review*, November 15, 1982, 5.

65. On Ye's history, see Joseph W. Esherick, *Ancestral Leaves: A Family Journey through Chinese History* (Berkeley: University of California Press, 2011), 116. Ye had been declared a rightist in 1958 and rehabilitated in 1960. See http://www.chinavitae.com/biography/Ye_Duyi/bio. Last accessed November 24, 2020. For the "broader and deeper" assessment, see Constance Johnson, "The 1982 Constitution of the PRC: One Small Step for Legal Development," *Journal of Chinese Studies* 2, no. 1 (April 1985): 89.

66. See "关于国旗的答问," and "宪法名词解释," *Zhengzhi yu falü*, no. 1 (1982): 93–104.

67. "人民宪法全民讨论," Jiangsu Provincial Archives (JPA hereafter), file number not supplied.

68. "人民宪法全民讨论," 3–5.

69. "关于组织学习和讨论宪法修改草案的安排意见," JPA 3002-5-15.

70. Altehenger, *Legal Lessons*, 201.

71. *People's Daily*, May 31, 1982; *People's Daily*, June 2, 1982.

72. *People's Daily*, June 2, 1982.

73. *People's Daily*, May 28, 1982.

74. *People's Daily*, June 21, 1982.

75. *People's Daily*, June 21, 1982. The Four Modernizations included reforms to agriculture, industry, national defense, and science and technology.

76. *People's Daily*, July 11, 1982.

77. "Wo shi zhengfa keji wenjiao jie renshi taolun xianfa xiugai cao'an," *Nanjing Ribao*, June 24, 1982.

78. "Zhang Youyu jiu xianfa xiugai cao'an dajizhe wen," *Nanjing Ribao*, May 12, 1982.

79. Zhang Youyu, (张有渔), "Guanyu xiugai xianfa de jige wenti," *Faxue yanjiu* 3 (1982): 1–9.

80. Wang Yong'an (王永安), "Yiqie quanli shuyu renmin: Quanguo qiaolian taolun xianfa xiugai cao'an pangting ji," *Nanjing Ribao*, May 14, 1982.

81. In Nanjing, constitutional educators at the district and county levels were expected to propagandize the constitution's "basic content and spirit" to officials and ordinary people. According to one report, over 80 percent received a "one-time education in socialist democracy and law." See *Xuanchuan gongzuo jianbao*, no. 9 (August 10, 1982), JPA 4009-5-105, 86.

82. Altehenger, *Legal Lessons*, 199.

83. Altehenger, 199–200.

84. Altehenger, 201.

85. *Xuanchuan gongzuo jianbao*, no. 9, JPA 4009-5-105, 87.

86. JPA 3002-5-15, June 25, 1982.

87. JPA 3002-5-15, 16, 63–66; JPA 3002-5-15, 16.

88. JPA 6001-5-302, 26–28.

89. JPA 6001-5-302, 27.

90. JPA 6001-5-302, 29.

91. JPA 6001-5-302, 26–28.

92. JPA 6001-5-302, 28.

93. JPA 3002-5-15, 16–18.

94. Altehenger, 203–4.

95. *Xuanchuan gongzuo jianbao*, no. 9, JPA 4009-5-105, 89–90.

96. JPA 6001-5-302, 29.

97. *Xuanchuan gongzuo jianbao*, no. 9, JPA 4009-5-105, 89–90. In Shanghai, some said that propaganda claims that law is greater than power, but in real life if you have power, "you can write laws and change laws, regulations, and decrees." See Altehenger, 203.

98. JPA 6001-5-302, 28.

99. Altehenger, *Legal Lessons*, 203; JPA 6001-5-302, 28–29.

100. Altehenger, *Legal Lessons*, 202.

101. Altehenger, 202.

102. JPA 3002-5-15, 16–17.

103. JPA 6001-5-302, 26; JPA 3002-5-15, 17.

104. JPA 6001-5-302, 29.

105. JPA 6001-5-302, 26.

106. JPA 3002-5-15, 20.

107. See Altehenger, *Legal Lessons*, 217–18.

108. Li Weidi (李伟迪), "Xueli, nianling he zhiye yu xianfa yishi: Xiangxi diqu de diaocha yu sikao," *Huaihua xueyuan xuebao* 22, no. 1 (February 2003): 20–23.

109. Yan Xiansheng (严显生), "Gongmin xianfa yishi wenti de diaocha baogao," *Beijing daxue xuebao*, no. 4 (1985): 66.

110. Yan, 63.

111. Yan, 69.

112. Liu Dan (刘丹), "Lingdao ganbu xianfa yishi wenjuan diaocha yu shizheng fenxi," *Guojia xingzheng xueyuan xuebao* (May 2004): 66–68.

113. Deng Shibao (邓世豹), "Dangdai zhongguo jiancha guan xianfa yishi de shizheng fenxi," *Lingnan xuekan*, no. 4 (2010): 71–75.

114. Liu Dan, "Lingdao ganbu," 67.

115. Deng Shibao, "Dangdai zhongguo," 72.

116. "If we ignore the constitution or disrespect the constitution," he argued, "people's rights and freedom as well as party and state's affairs will be at risk." See "在首都各界纪念现行宪法公布施行 30 周年大会上的讲话" (December 4, 2012). http://cpc.people.com.cn/xuexi/n/2015/0720/c397563-27331671.html.

117. They were also encouraged by Xi's takedown of political rival and quasi-/pseudo-Maoist Bo Xilai.

118. See Edward Wong and Jonathan Ansfield, "Reformers Aim to Get China to Live Up to Own Constitution," *New York Times*, February 3, 2013.

119. Qian Gang, "The Uncertain Death of 'Constitutionalism,'" *China Media Project*, posted September 2, 2013.

120. Samson Yuan, "Debating Constitutionalism in China: Dreaming of a Liberal Turn?" *China Perspectives*, December 1, 2013: 69. http://journals.openedition.org/chinaperspectives/6325.

244	NOTES TO PAGES 187–193

121. Qian Gang, "The Uncertain Death of 'Constitutionalism"; for more details on these essays, see Yuan, "Debating Constitutionalism in China."

122. Yuan, "Debating Constitutionalism in China."

123. Qian Gang, "Uncertain Death."

124. See Sarah Biddulph, "Democratic Centralism and Administration in China," in *Socialist Law in Socialist East Asia*, ed. Fu Hualing, John Gillespie, Pip Nicholson, and William Edmund Partlett, (Cambridge: Cambridge University Press, 2018), 197. For Document Number 9, see http://www.chinafile.com/document-9-chinafile-translation for the English language translation.

125. Qian Gang, "Uncertain Death."

126. On the oath swearing, see "Rules of the Party," *Economist*, November 1, 2014. For censorship of liberal constitutionalist views on Constitution Day, see Kiki Zhao, "On China's Constitution Day, Book on Constitutionalism Largely Disappears," *New York Times*, December 4, 2015.

127. Zhao, "On China's Constitution Day."

128. Simon Denyer, "China's Xi Gets Right-Hand Man, Loyal 'Firefighter,' Elected Vice President," *Washington Post*, March 17, 2018.

129. For a translation of this essay, see http://www.zonaeuropa.com/20040505_2 .htm. Accessed January 29, 2020.

130. See Sang Ye, *China Candid: The People on the People's Republic*, ed. Geremie R. Barmé with Miriam Lang (Berkeley: University of California Press, 2006), 115. I have been unable to locate this "decision." Such documents usually emerge from the State Council, not the NPC.

131. See Zhao Liang and Sylvie Blum, *Shangfang* (New York: Cinema Guild, 2009).

132. Han Han, *This Generation: Dispatches from China's Most Popular Literary Star (and Race Car Driver)* (New York: Simon & Schuster, 2012), 123. The author Yu Hua has also been a chronicler of sarcasm and mockery in this period. See his *China in Ten Words*, trans. Allen H. Barr (New York: Anchor Books, 2011), 186–87.

133. Han Han, *This Generation*, 102, 195.

134. Cited in Rogier Creemers, "China's Constitutionalism Debate: Content, Context, and Implications," *China Journal* 74 (2015): 96–97.

135. Creemers, 107.

Conclusion

1. Some of these aspects of law in China, such as its role in exploiting social divisions and the state's determination to retain maximum flexibility, have been noted by Mary E. Gallagher in her study of China's 1995 Labor Law. See *Authoritarian Legality in China: Law, Workers, and the State* (Cambridge: Cambridge University Press, 2017), 47, 49.

2. See Rogiers Creemers, "China's Constitutionalism Debate: Content, Context, and Implications," *China Journal* 74 (2015): 108.

3. The legal scholar Thomas Kellogg argues that the CCP "seeks to use the Constitution to legitimate its rule by maintaining the political fiction that China is transitioning to constitutional governance." This is an insult to fiction (or at least to decent fiction). Fiction requires internal credibility, gained by good characters, plot coherency, and plausibility within the genre, none of which characterized the constitution. See

"Arguing Chinese Constitutionalism: The 2013 Constitutional Debate and the 'Urgency' of Political Reform," *University of Pennsylvania Asian Law Review* 11, no. 3 (2016): 351. My perspective is also somewhat at odds with Mary E. Gallagher's argument that "the half-hearted and half-way adoption of legality undermines the state's goals of improved governance *by exposing the gaps between law on the books and law in reality*, by mobilizing individual workers to protect themselves, and then depriving labor, the weaker side in the employment relationship, of effective representation and the ability to harness its collective power." She calls this a "'high standards, self-enforcement' model that creates space for bottom-up mobilization as workers exploit the gap between law on the books and law in reality." Emphasis mine. In my view, at least when it came to constitution-based labor rights (she examines the 1995 Labor Law), workers had a healthy degree of cynicism and disbelief for quite some time. In this sense, the gap between reality and law was not well concealed and thus not exposed. See Gallagher, *Authoritarian Legality* 38, 31.

4. In this respect, offering unenforceable rights is not as cheap as Ginsburg and Simpser suggest. See Tom Ginsburg and Alberto Simpser, *Constitutions in Authoritarian Regimes* (Cambridge: Cambridge University Press, 2014), 7.

5. Anne Applebaum, "History Will Judge the Complicit," *Atlantic*, July/August 2020. https://www.theatlantic.com/magazine/archive/2020/07/trumps-collaborators/612250/.

6. Ginsburg and Simpser, *Constitutions in Authoritarian Regimes*, 5–7.

7. Rohit De, *The People's Constitution: The Everyday Life of Law in the Indian Republic* (Princeton, NJ: Princeton University Press, 2020).

8. See Ran Hirschl, *Comparative Matters: The Renaissance of Comparative Constitutional Law* (Oxford: Oxford University Press, 2016), 228–29. Hirschl focuses on the "limited focus on causality, inference, and explanation in comparative constitutional law," but this list can also include popular constitutionalism.

9. This does not suggest that the CCP could be more legitimate in other dimensions of governance. As I have suggested elsewhere, legitimacy is best seen in disaggregated institutional terms as well as by region and time period. See Neil J. Diamant, *Revolutionizing the Family: Politics, Love, and Divorce in Urban and Rural China, 1949–1968* (Berkeley: University of California Press, 2000), 319. That said, because the constitution covered many issue areas (ideology, institutions, policies, etc.), it enables us to assert a broader argument about legitimacy.

10. Samantha Lomb, *Stalin's Constitution: Soviet Participatory Politics and the Discussion of the 1936 Draft Constitution* (London: Routledge, 2018), 1.

11. Ellen Wimberg, "Socialism, Democratism and Criticism," *Soviet Studies* 44, no. 2 (1992): 313, 318, 320.

12. Karen Petrone, *Life Has Become More Joyous, Comrades: Celebrations in the Time of Stalin* (Bloomington: Indiana University Press, 2000), 197.

13. As J. Arch Getty notes, citizens had rights to these benefits, but only workers got them at no cost. See "State and Society Under Stalin: Constitutions and Elections in the 1930s," *Slavic Review* 50, no. 1 (Spring 1991), 23.

14. Getty, 23.

15. Getty, 26.

16. Lewis Siegelbaum and Andrei Sokolov, *Stalinism as a Way of Life* (New Haven, CT: Yale University Press), 170, 173, 178, 180.

17. Petrone, *Life Has Become More Joyous*, 177.

18. Cited in Alexander Vatlin, Seth Bernstein, and Oleg Khlevniuk, *Agents of Terror: Ordinary Men and Ordinary Violence in Stalin's Secret Police* (Madison: University of Wisconsin Press, 2016), 98.

19. Tong Jiwei, for example, argues that the 1954 Constitution had only a slight impact on actual political practice. See "China's Constitutional Research and Training: A State of the Art," in *Building Constitutionalism in China*, ed. Stéphanie Balme and Michael W. Dowdle (New York: Palgrave Macmillan, 2009), 100.

20. Siegelbaum and Sokolov, *Stalinism as a Way of Life*, 206.

21. Petrone, *Life Has Become More Joyous*, 201.

22. David Brandenberger, *Political Humor under Stalin: An Anthology of Unofficial Jokes and Anecdotes* (Bloomington, IN: Slavica, 2009), 96, 98–99.

23. Jennifer Altehenger, "A Socialist Satire: *Manhua* Magazine and Political Cartoon Production in the PRC, 1950–1960," *Frontiers of History in China* 8, no. 1 (2013): 86, 99. https://doi.org/10.3868/s020-002-013-0005-3.

24. Petrone, *Life Has Become More Joyous*, 176; on Russia under Putin see Karrie J, Koesel, "Legitimacy, Resilience, and Political Education in Russia and China: Learning to be Loyal," in *Citizens and the State in Authoritarian Regimes: Comparing China and Russia*, ed. Karrie J Koesel, Valerie J. Bunce, and Jessica Chen Weiss (Oxford: Oxford University Press, 2020), 263.

25. Veniamin Chirkin, *Constitutional Law and Political Institutions* (Moscow: Progress Publishers, 1985), 240.

26. Mark Edele, "Collective Action in Soviet Society: The Case of War Veterans," in *Writing the Stalin Era: Sheila Fitzpatrick and Soviet Historiography*, ed. Golfo Alexopoulos, Kiril Tomoff, and Julie Hessler (New York: Palgrave Macmillan, 2011), 126.

27. Mark Sidel, *Law and Society in Vietnam: The Transition from Socialism in Comparative Perspective* (Cambridge: Cambridge University Press, 2008), 19, 21, 34, 41; and Sidel, "Analytical Models for Understanding Constitutions and Constitutional Dialogue in Socialist Transitional States: Reinterpreting Constitutional Dialogue in Vietnam," *Singapore Journal of International and Comparative Law* 6 (2002): 42–89.

28. Nguyen Thi Huong, "Pursuing Constitutional Dialogue within Socialist Vietnam: The 2010 Debate," *Australian Journal of Asian Law* 13, no. 1 (2012): 1, 8, 11–12.

29. Bui Ngoc Son and Pip Nicholson, "Activism and Popular Constitutionalism in Contemporary Vietnam," *Law and Social Inquiry* 42, no. 3 (2017): 700. They argue that Vietnamese popular constitutionalism is *popular* in that "it involves the discourse and mobilization of different sectors of the public. It is not the case that it is driven by a *narrow elite.*" Emphasis mine. However, their evidence rarely includes voices of ordinary workers, farmers, migrants, policemen, or even low-level officials. Middle-class intellectuals and NGO activists feature prominently. That is, *popular* reflects a *broader* elite (but still elite) population.

30. Bui Ngoc Son, "Constitutional Mobilization," *Washington University Global Studies Law Review* 17, no. 1 (2018): 138–40. A Vietnamese student I asked to peruse the official website found mostly positive statements about the constitution.

31. Giao Cong Vu and Kien Tran, "Constitutional Debate and Development on Human Rights in Vietnam," *Asian Journal of Comparative Law* 11 (2016): 250.

32. Giao Cong Vu and Kien Tran, 251–53.

33. Giao Cong Vu and Kien Tran, 259. The difference between Vietnam and China has also been noted in a study comparing China and Cuba. Similar to Vietnam but unlike China, Cuba had "vibrant" discussions of the draft constitution from August 13 to November 15, 2018. Some constitutional petitioners demanded radical democratization. A letter critical of the draft constitution was promoted by the Cuban Observatory of Human Rights and the Damas de Blanco Association and signed by intellectuals and leaders of Cuban civil society. See Bui Ngoc Son, *Constitutional Change in the Contemporary Socialist World* (Oxford: Oxford University Press, 2020), 253.

34. The number of prisoners in these camps is not known, with estimates varying widely. One report, based on interviews with eight hundred survivors, estimated between fifty thousand and eight hundred thousand "in the first years after Communist victory." See Sonni Ephron and Thuan Le, "Haunting Tales of Vietnamese Gulag," *Los Angeles Times*, January 23, 1990.

35. For a synthesis of studies examining these trends, including the emergence of the Russian middle class, see Wayne Dowler, *Russia in 1913* (DeKalb: Northern Illinois University Press, 2010).

36. Bui Ngoc Son, "Constitutional Dualism: Socialism and Constitutionalism in Contemporary Vietnam," in *Socialist Law in Socialist East Asia*, ed. Fu Hualing, John Gillespie, Pip Nicholson, and William Partlett (Cambridge: Cambridge University Press, 2018), 166–68, 170; Bui Ngoc Son, *Constitutional Change in the Contemporary Socialist World*, 94–96.

37. Fu Hualing and Jason Buhi, "Diverging Trends in the Socialist Constitutionalism of the People Republic of China and the Socialist Republic of Vietnam," in Fu Hualing et al., *Socialist Law in Socialist East Asia*, 142–56; Benedict J. Tria Kerkvliet, *Speaking Out in Vietnam: Public Political Criticism in a Communist-Party Ruled Nation* (Ithaca, NY: Cornell University Press, 2019), 108–12; for diversity in Vietnam's online petitioning community see Jason Morris-Jung, "Vietnam's Online Petition Movement," *Southeast Asian Affairs* (2015), 412.

38. Pip Nicholson, "Vietnamese Constitutionalism: The Reform Possibilities," *Asian Journal of Comparative Law* 11 (2016): 199.

39. Bui and Nicholson also argue that "Vietnam did not the experience the repressive excesses of China's revolutionary leaders, for example, the Cultural Revolution, in such a sustained way. The Chinese focus on stability over rights . . . is less present in Vietnam." See "Activism and Popular Constitutionalism," 680–81. Collectivization in the USSR in the 1920s and 1930s resulted in significantly fewer deaths than the Great Leap Forward in China, and the roughly 682,000 deaths in Stalin's Great Purge (1937–1938) were surpassed by the PRC's land reform, the Campaign to Suppress Counterrevolutionaries, and the Cultural Revolution. On the death toll in the USSR see Massimo Livi-Bacci, "On the Human Costs of Collectivization in the Soviet Union," *Population and Development Review* 19, no. 4 (1993): 743–66; and Wendy Z. Goldman, *Terror and Democracy in the Age of Stalin: The Social Dynamics of Repression* (Cambridge: Cambridge University Press, 2007), 5.

40. See my *Embattled Glory: Veterans, Military Families, and the Politics of Patriotism in the PRC* (Lanham, MD: Rowman & Littlefield, 2009), 126–34; Masuda Hajimu, *Cold War Crucible: The Korean Conflict and the Postwar World* (Cambridge, MA: Harvard University Press, 2015), 130, 189, 193–94; Son Daekwon, "Domestic Instability as a Key

Factor Shaping China's Decision to Enter the Korean War," *China Journal* 83 (January 2020): 53.

41. Ralph B. Thaxton Jr. has shown that the legitimacy crisis that resulted from policy disasters was never redressed, resulting in numerous contentious, antistate actions. See *Force and Contention in Contemporary China: Memory and Resistance in the Long Shadow of the Catastrophic Past* (Cambridge: Cambridge University Press, 2016).

42. For a more detailed analysis of the differences between constitutional mobilization in Vietnam and China, some of which overlaps with my argument above, see Bui Ngoc Son, *Constitutional Change in the Contemporary Socialist World*, 295–97.

43. Li Yuan, "In Coronavirus Fight, China Sidelines an Ally: Its Own People," *New York Times*, February 18, 2020.

44. On limitations to historical research see item number five in the CCP's "Communiqué on the Current State of the Ideological Sphere" (also known as "Document no. 9"), which calls more objective historical research on the PRC "historical nihilism" that is doing nothing less than "trying to undermine the history of the CCP and of New China." See "Document 9: A ChinaFile Translation," November 8, 2013. http://www.chinafile.com/document-9-chinafile-translation. For an overview of censorship see Rebecca MacKinnon, "China's 'Networked Authoritarianism,'" *Journal of Democracy* 22, no. 2 (April 2011): 33–47; on social media see Jason Q. Ng, *Blocked on Weibo: What Gets Suppressed on China's Version of Twitter and Why* (New York: The New Press, 2013). The PRC also uses extremely intrusive measures to prevent petitioning and protest, such as pressuring relatives to convince petitioners to stay home. See Yanhua Deng and Kevin J. O'Brien, "Relational Repression in China: Using Social Ties to Demobilize Protestors," *China Quarterly* 215 (September 2013): 533–52.

45. Mark West's studies of law and society in Japan, combining experimental methods, extensive fieldwork, interviews, survey research, and textual analysis, are exemplary—but also cost-prohibitive for many. See Mark West, *Law in Everyday Japan: Sex, Sumo, Suicide, and Statutes* (Chicago: University of Chicago Press, 2005). On the China side, William Hurst's study of legal regimes at the subnational level in China and Indonesia is also excellent but very expensive. See William Hurst, book citation from note 48.

46. Creemers, "China's Constitutionalism Debate," 109. For another example of using cases involving famous people (including a former Minister of Culture, "celebrated dissidents," and an acclaimed journalist) to assert claims about "the interplay of legality and power in the contemporary People's Republic of China as well as authoritarian societies more generally," see William P. Alford, "Double-Edged Swords Cut Both Ways: Law and Legitimacy in the People's Republic of China," *Daedalus* 122, no. 2 (1993), 46. This sampling problem has also been noted in Ethan Michelson's interesting research on the origins and appropriation of the term *weiquan*. See "Many Voices in China's Legal Profession: Plural Meanings of *Weiquan*," *China Law and Society Review* 4 (2019): 72, 75, 95–96.

47. Hirschl, *Comparative Matters*, 186–87.

48. Hurst, Ruling before the Law, xi.

49. Sarah Biddulph, focusing on the case of state efforts to deal with wage arrears, also notes the continued importance of campaign-style enforcement of laws in the PRC. However, her periodization of this style does not mention the war years, only the "pre-reform period (between 1949 and 1978)." See "Democratic Centralism and

Administration in China," in *Socialist Law in Socialist East Asia*, ed. Fu Hualing, John Gillespie, Pip Nicholson, and William Partlett (Cambridge: Cambridge University Press, 2018), 211.

50. Edmund Cheng similarly emphasizes such tactics in the repression of protests. See "United Front Work and Mechanisms of Countermobilization in Hong Kong," *China Journal*, no. 83 (January 2020): 1–33. https://doi.org/10.1086/706603. Article 29 is an excellent example of legal ambiguity. It criminalizes (among other acts) perceived obstruction of the PRC or Hong Kong governments in setting and implementing laws and policies and any "unlawful" conduct (undefined) that provokes Hong Kong residents' "hatred" of the governments of the PRC or Hong Kong, when done with the direct or indirect support of, or in conjunction with, any overseas organization or individual. As was the case in the Mao era, the statute's vague wording, surely by design, makes it impossible to figure out exactly what speech and actions will result in harsh legal consequences.

51. Harry G. Frankfurt, *On Bullshit* (Princeton, NJ: Princeton University Press, 2005), 56. In contrast, some foreign reporting argued that the desire to do away with Hong Kong autonomy was of more recent vintage ("since last year when the protests broke out"). See Ishaan Tharoor and Eva Dou, "Why China Chose Now to Crack Down on Hong Kong," *Washington Post*, July 8, 2020. https://www.washingtonpost.com/video/world/why-china-chose-now-to-crack-down-on-hong-kong/2020/07/08/5222d6c7-0823-407c-b48d-23ca191c2a02_video.html.

GLOSSARY

anding renxin 安定人心
baogan zhi 包干制
baogao yuan 报告员
baohu caichan 保护财产
bian xifa 变戏法
bu fanfa jiuxing la 不犯法就行啦
bu jia ganshe 不加干涉
bu xingle 不行了
bu xuexiao 补学校
caofa 草法
chelun zhan 车轮战
chengban 惩办
chengfen 成分
chi guanzu 吃官族
chibuxiao 吃不消
chou zhuangding 抽壮丁
choubing 抽兵
chuantong de zisi zili sixiang 传统的自私自利思想
chulu ruhe 出路如何
chushen 出身
da tianxia 打天下
da xishi 大喜事
dafa 大法
daigeng 代耕
daiti 代替
dalu 大陆
danggang dangzhang 党纲党章
danwei 单位
dao shehuizhuyi yaobuyao wo 到社会主义要不要我
dapo 打破
dashe 大赦
dashiji 大事记
dashu ling 大赦令
diaoer langdang de 吊儿浪当的
duding 笃定
dui yi dui xianfa 对一对宪法

duifu 对付
fa laosao 发牢骚
faling 法令
falü 法律
falü zhicai 法律制裁
falü zhi neng zuo wei banshi de cankao 法律只能作为办事的参考
fandui mixin 反对迷信
fanghai 妨害
fanjiao 反教
fanshen 翻身
fanwei 范围
fanying 反映
fei renmin 非人民
fenting kangli 分庭抗礼
fubingyi 服兵役
fucong xianfa he falü 服从宪法和法律
gailiang 改良
gao shehuizhuyi 搞社会主义
gaodiao 高调
gei woni qingmi 给我伲猜谜
gejie renmin 各界人民
genben dafa 根本大法
genben fa 根本法
gongmin 公民
gongtong gangling 共同纲领
gongxiu 公休
guaihua 怪话
guan 管
guan bieren 管别人
guan bu guan 管不管
guan xia, bu guan shang 管下, 不管上
guanxin 关心
guding 固定
guohuo le 过火了
guofen 过分
guomin 国民
guoqu you, xianzai mei youle 过去有, 现在没有了
guoti 国体
guowu huiyi 国务会议
hao nongle 好弄了
haochu zai sha difang 好处在啥地方
hebi hai yao xianfa ne 何必还要宪法呢
hefa 合法
hefa shouru 合法收入
heping daolu 和平道路
houci bobi 厚此薄彼
huairen huaishi 坏人坏事

huansu 还俗
Huanxian 欢宪
huatou 滑头
huayang duo 花样多
hukou 户口
huidaomen 会道门
hunluan 混乱
huokou 活扣
hushuo badao 胡说八道
jiade 假的
jianfa 减法
jibie 级别
jiduan minzhu 极端民主
jimi 羁縻
jingkong 惊恐
jinhou dagai yao qiangpole 今后大概要强迫了
jizao 急躁
juedui bu neng gaige 绝对不能改革
junguo zhuyi 军国主义
konghuang 恐慌
kuoda minzhu 扩大民主
Lahu 拉祜
laoban 老板
laodong de quanli 劳动的权利
laodong jilü 劳动纪律
laodong shouru 劳动收入
laodongzhe 劳动者
laotouzi 老头子
linghuo 灵活
lingsan 零散
lingtu 领土
Linxia 临夏
liyong, xianzhi, gaizao 利用, 限制, 改造
luan 乱
mafan 麻烦
manren 蛮人
maodun 矛盾
meiyou shenma liaobuqi 没有什么了不起
mimi 秘密
minban xuexiao 民办学校
mingling 命令
minxiao 民校
minzhu renshi 民主人士
minzu gongdi 民族公敌
mohu 模糊
mufa 母法
nan gaole 难搞了

nao diwei 闹地位
naozi hen luan 脑子很乱
neibu 内部
Neibu cankao 内部参考
niao wutou bufei 鸟无头不飞
panghuangde lihai 彷徨得利害
panjiao 叛教
pohuai shehui gongde 破坏社会公德
qiangying 强硬
qiantu mangmang 前途茫茫
quanguo renmin taolun xiancao yijian huibian 全国人民讨论宪草意见汇编
quanmin 全民
quanmin suoyouzhi 全民所有制
quanmin taolun 全民讨论
quanquan taotao 圈圈套套
renge 人格
renmin 人民
renzhi 人治
Rui'an 瑞安
shehui gongde 社会公德
shehui liliang 社会力量
shen'ao 深奥
shensheng 神圣
shensuo 伸缩
shiquan 实权
shoufa 守法
shuo bu qingchu 说不清楚
sifa 死法
sima fenfei 四马分肥
suoyou 所有
suoyouquan 所有权
suoyouzhi 所有制
tai guangle 太广了
tai lihai 太厉害
tan cuole yao fan fa; fan fale yao pan sixing 谈错了，要犯法；犯法了，要判死刑
tanxing 弹性
tebie youdai 特别优待
teshe 特赦
teshe ling 特赦令
tianyi wufeng 天衣无缝
tiaoshen 跳神
tingbudong 听不懂
tong dian 通电
tong xin 通信
tongyi fenpei 同一分配
tongzhi jieji 统治阶级
tuguan 土官

tusi 土司
wandan 完蛋
wanquan tuifan 完全推翻
wanyi 玩意
weidao 味道
weijin fa 违禁法
weiquan 维权
wenwu guan 文物馆
wenyu 文娱
women yiqie dou wanle 我们一切都完了
wudian 污点
wufa jieshou 无法接受
wufa wutian 无法无天
wuxian guangrong 无限光荣
xiahu 吓唬
xianbing houli 先兵后礼
xianfa 限法
xianfa 宪法
xianfa yibailingliu tiaotiao shifa 宪法一百零六条条是法
xianli houbing 先礼后兵
xianshi 闲事
xianzheng 宪政
xianzhi 限制
xianzhi ren de bing 限制人的兵
xiaohu zibenjia 小户资本家
xiaomie 消灭
xiaomie pinkun 消灭贫困
xinjiao ziyou 信教自由
Xishuangbanna 西双版纳
yangyang youfa 样样有法
yanzhong 严重
yao gao shenma ne 要搞什么呢
yaowu yangwei 耀武扬威
yibu yibu si 一步一步死
yikao renmin qunzhong 依靠人民群众
yindi zhiyi yinshi zhiyi 因地制宜, 因时制宜
yingyong fendou 英勇奋斗
yiqin yinqin 以亲引亲
yiwu 义务
yizhao falü 依照法律
you falü 由法律
you meisa daguanxi 有没啥大关系
youdai 优待
yuele 悦乐
zai falü shang 在法律上
zhan zai gongmin de lichang shuohua 站在公民的立场说话
zhaogu 照顾

zhaogu zhoudao 照顾周到
zhendong 震动
zhengyong 征用
zhenya 镇压
zhiguo anbang 治国安邦
zhuabing 抓兵
zhuang men mian 装门面
zhubu 逐步
ziyuan 自愿
zongjiao jie 宗教界
zongjiao xinyang 宗教信仰
zui da de fa 最大的法
zunshi 尊师
zuo jiangshan 坐江山
zuoyong 作用

MATERIALS CONSULTED

Materials are listed by archive and by archival finding number, in alphabetical order. *Neibu cankao* is listed by date. The text *Constitution of the People's Republic of China*, adopted on September 20, 1954, is available at https://hdl.handle.net/1813/104273.

Baoshan District Archives (BDA)

"江湾区直属人民代表大会第一次会议对宪法草案所提出意见," BDA 9-6-1.

Guangdong Provincial Archives (GPA)

"广铁政治部宣传部直属机关干部高, 中级组学习人民共和国宪法草案的简单总结," GPA 204-3-234.
"市以上机关干部对宪法草案讨论情况的报告," GPA 204-3-43.
"华南歌舞团初级组宪法草案学习的综合报告," GPA 225-2-29.
"宪法草案第三, 四章学习情况报告," GPA 225-2-29.
"广东电台学习讨论宪法草案总结简报," GPA 225-2-29.
"广东, 广州人民广播电台学习宪法草案问题," GPA 225-2-29.
"南方日报中初级组讨论宪法草案所提出来的问题," GPA 225-2-29.
"关于宪法草案讨论情况的报告," GPA 225-4-104.
"宪法草案学习与讨论情况的综合报告," GPA 225-4-104.
"第三部分: 讨论宪法草案第三章, 第四章提出的疑难问题," GPA 225-4-104.
"中山大学教职员学习宪法草案的一般情况," GPA 225-4-104.
"关于宪法草案讨论情况第二次报告," GPA 225-4-104.
"台山县宪法草案学习与讨论情况汇报," GPA 235-1-339.
"江门市宪草讨论委员会第一次电话汇报," GPA 235-1-399.
"汕头市宪法草案讨论委员会第一次电话汇报," GPA 235-1-399.
"省协学会关于省统战系统讨论宪草情况报告," GPA 235-1-399.
"佛山市宪法草案学习情况," GPA 235-1-399.
"石岐市宪草讨论委员会第一次电话汇报," GPA 235-1-399.

Huangpu District Archives (HDA)

"上海市黄浦区第一届人民代表大会第一次会议代表对宪法草案所提的意见," HDA N7-1-455.
"卢湾区工商界宪法草案论支会宣传和讨论宪法草案工作总结," HDA 48-2-113.

"上海市民主妇联卢湾区办事处地区妇女群众中宣传讨论宪法草案总结,"
HDA 48-2-113.
"蓬莱区机关干部讨论宪法草案总结," HDA 202-1-182.
"宪法草案讨论中疑问," HDA 3055-1-14.
"部分妇女对中华人民共和国宪法反映," HDA 42-1-70.

Jiangsu Provincial Archives (JPA)

"关于组织学习和讨论宪法修改草案的安排意见," JPA 3002-5-15.
"关于对宪法修改草案的修改意见的报告," JPA 3002-5-15.
"南京市几次学习'草案'座谈会的情况报告," JPA 3002-5-15.
"宣传工作简报," JPA 4009-5-105.
"关于'讨论宪法修改草案'的情况报告," JPA 6001-5-302.

Shanghai Municipal Archives (SMA)

本市宪法草案讨论委员会办公室编, "简报" (1–13 期) SMA A22-2-1525.
"上海市各界讨论宪法草案中所暴露的主要思想问题," SMA A22-2-1531.
"关于最近上海报纸对中华人民共和国宪法草案宣传报道中存在几个问题
的汇报" SMA A22-2-1531.
"交通大学宪草讨论总结初稿," SMA A26-2-304.
"上海财经学院宪法草案讨论总结," SMA A26-2-304.
"关于宪法草案宣传讨论工作的总结," SMA A38-2-144.
"第九祖学习中华人民共和国宪法草案 (初稿) 总结," SMA A38-2-144.
"国营红星制车厂本厂技术员宪草讨论后思想," SMA A42-1-12.
中共上海市委重工业部宣传处 "宪法草案汇报," SMA A42-2-85.
"上海冶炼厂支会办公室宪法草案讨论情况汇报," SMA A42-2-86.
"关于一个月来本市各报宣传宪法关草案的情况报告," SMA A47-2-66.
中共上海市轻工业委员会宣传部, "关于宣传讨论宪法草案的工作总结,"
SMA A48-1-272.
中共上海市轻工业委员会宣传部, "关于宪法草案的辅导报告," SMA A48-
1-272.
"宪草讨论委员会新华印刷厂支会周报," SMA A48-1-287.
"中共华光啤酒厂支部宪法草案讨论宣传总结," SMA A51-1-181.
"宪法草案公布后思想情况," SMA A51-1-182.
"郊区宪法宣传讨论情况报告," SMA A71-2-973.
"上海市高桥区宪法草案宣传讨论总结," SMA A71-2-974.
"区级机关与乡干部对宪法草案的思想反映," SMA A71-2-974.
"本区[高桥]宪法草案第二周来的宣传讨论情况作一汇报," SMA A71-2-974.
"杨思区宪法草案宣传讨论的情况汇报," SMA A71-2-974.
"大场区机关干部宪法草案中提出的疑问," SMA A71-2-974.
"大场区干部宪法草案讨论情况," SMA A71-2-974.
"上海市新泾区关于中华人民共和国宪法草案宣传工作总结," A71-2-974.
"东昌区在群众中进行贯彻宪法草案宣传和讨论工作的总结报告," SMA A71-
2-975.
"东昌区宪法草案讨论分会一周情况汇报," SMA A71-2-975.

"东昌区七月份宪法草案宣传讨论的情况综合与八月工作意见," SMA A71-2-975.

"关于宪法草案讨论宣传工作的检查报告," SMA A73-1-174.

中共上海市静安区委员会, "情况汇报," SMA A79-2-381.

"静安区宪法草案宣传讨论里弄干部训练情况汇报, SMA A79-2-381.

"里弄群众对宪法草案公布后的反映," SMA A79-2-381.

"静安区工商界宪法草案讨论情况汇报," SMA A79-2-381.

"静安区私立小学教师讨论宪法草案情况汇报, SMA A79-2-381.

"静安区医务界静安区私立小学教师讨论宪法草案情况汇报," SMA A79-2-381.

"对宪法草案公布后某些资产阶级, 教徒的反映," SMA A79-2-381.

上海市静安区人民政府第四办事处, "关于中华人民共和国宪草宣传工作总结报告," SMA A79-2-381.

"静安区里弄居民宪法草案讨论总结," SMA A79-2-381.

"上海市民主妇女联合会宣传教育部对上海各报报道上海妇女讨论宪法草案的意见的报告," SMA A80-2-74.

"水上区妇联1954年宪法草案宣传讨论工作打算的总结," SMA A80-2-309.

"上總暨各产业工会党员干部讨论宪法草案情况汇报," SMA B2-2-57.

"上海各产业工会机关干部讨论宪法草案情况汇报," SMA B2-2-57.

上海市人民政府政治法律委员会, "关于在广大妇女群众中宣传和讨论宪法草案的通知," SMA B2-2-58.

"关于在妇女群众中展开宪法草案的宣传和讨论工作的计划," SMA B2-2-58.

"地区进行宪法草案宣传工作的情况," SMA B2-2-58.

"工商家属讨论宪法草案的反映," SMA B2-2-58.

"地区基层妇女干部讨论宪法草案情况综合," SMA B2-2-58.

"妇女群众对宪法草案第八十六条, 九十六条的感想和意见," SMA B2-2-58.

"机关支会干部宪法草案讨论所提出的疑问," SMA B2-2-61.

中共卢湾区委宣传部, "情况反映," no. 11, 13, SMA B2-2-61.

中共上海市卢湾区委, "关于各阶层人民学习讨论宪法草案中的情况和问题的报告," SMA B2-2-61.

"[卢湾区]本区机关工会干部宪法草案讨论提出来的疑问," SMA B2-2-61.

上海市公安局政治部, "思想情况简报," SMA B2-2-62.

上海市公安局, "关于组织干部学习讨论宪法草案情况的汇报," SMA B2-2-62.

"关于宪法草案学习讨论情况的汇报," SMA B2-2-63.

"上海市宪法草案讨论委员会宗教分会讨论宪法草案情况汇报," SMA B2-2-63.

"华东一级机关干部在宪法宣传公布后的一些思想反映和提出的问题," SMA B2-2-65.

中共上海市委重工业部, "关于宪法草案学习讨论情况汇报," SMA B2-2-66.

"重工业各厂职工讨论宪法草案提出的修改意见汇报," SMA B2-2-66.

"关于组织五类民主人士讨论宪法草案的情况报告 (草稿)," SMA B2-2-67.

"上海市中等学校宪法草案宣传讨论总结报告," SMA B105-5-2046.

中共上海市商业局委员会宣传部, "关于当前部分职工中存在不符合宪法要求的一些思想行为反映," SMA B122-2-31.

"关于组织上海市民主人士讨论宪法草案的情况报告," SMA C1-1-62.

"基层妇女干部和职工家属对宪法草案的反映," SMA C1-2-234.

"工业部份工商界对宪草公布总的思想情况," SMA C48-2-702.

上海市工商业联合会，"关于上海市工商界对宪法公布前后的思想情况综合报告，" SMA C48-2-702.

"上海市彩印工业同业公会委员一级宪法草案座谈会总结报告，" SMA S103-4-158.

Songjiang District Archives (SDA)

"宪法草案宣传要点，" SDA 5-6-32.

青年团叶树区委，"关于召开牌楼乡副支部会　学习宪法的基本知识教育，" SDA 7-1-6.

"松江县首国一次人民代表大会讨论宪法草案的初步总结，" SDA 1395-6-32.

Yangpu District Archives (YDA)

"榆林区宪法草案宣传讨论工作总结，" YDA 11-4-7.

"榆林区人民政府第二办事处宪法草案宣传工作总结，" YDA 16-25-4.

"上海市榆林区工商业联合会筹备会宪法草案宣传讨论工作总结，" YDA 21-1-11.

Neibu cankao (Internal Reference)

"江苏省各民主党派和工商界的上层人士对宪法草案初稿的反应，" *Neibu cankao*, April 28, 1954.

"中南区各民主党派讨论宪法草案的情况，" *Neibu cankao*, May 4, 1954.

"江苏省民主人士和资本家对宪法草案的反应，" *Neibu cankao*, May 5, 1954.

"上海资本家讨论宪法草案的情况，" *Neibu cankao*, May 6, 1954.

"重庆资本家，民主人士讨论宪法草案的情况，" *Neibu cankao*, May 21, 1954.

"南京，潘阳资本家和民主人士对宪法草案的反应，" *Neibu cankao*, May 26, 1954.

"太原各民主党派负责人对宪法草案的反应，" *Neibu cankao*, June 16, 1954.

"北京各阶层人民对宪法草案的反应，" *Neibu cankao*, June 23, 1954.

"潘阳市各阶层人民对宪法草案的反应，" *Neibu cankao*, June 25, 1954.

"天津资本家对宪法草案的反应，" *Neibu cankao*, June 25, 1954.

"上海市各阶层人民对宪法草案的反应，" *Neibu cankao*, June 26, 1954.

"吉林省一些农民和村干部在宣传宪法草案中的思想情况，" *Neibu cankao*, June 26, 1954.

"武汉，昆明机关企业干部对宪法草案的反应，" *Neibu cankao*, June 29, 1954.

"长沙资本家对宪法草案的反应，" *Neibu cankao*, June 29, 1954.

"内蒙古呼和浩持市和平地泉行政区各阶层人民对宪法草案的模糊认识，" *Neibu cankao*, June 30, 1954.

"福州，贵州等地各界人民对宪法草案存在的疑虑，" *Neibu cankao*, June 30, 1954.

"四川，江苏等地各界人民对宪法草案的反应，" *Neibu cankao*, July 2, 1954.

"印度的某些报纸曲解我国宪法草案的内容，" *Neibu cankao*, June 23, 1954.

"成都市敌对阶级分子对宪法草案进行诬蔑宣传，" *Neibu cankao*, July 3, 1954.

"重庆市有些宪法草案的报告员错误地解释宪法草案得内容，" *Neibu cankao*, July 3, 1954.

"吉林市回族的一些代表人物对宪法草案得反应，" *Neibu cankao*, July 5, 1954.

"黑龙江省部分群众对宪法草案的内容有些误解," *Neibu cankao*, July 5, 1954.

"鞍山的工人, 市民对宪法草案的反应," *Neibu cankao*, July 6, 1954.

"太原, 武汉等地各界人民对宪法草案的反应," *Neibu cankao*, July 7, 1954.

"长沙人民代表大会代表讨论宪法草案的情况," *Neibu cankao*, July 8, 1954.

"山东省民主人士和资本家讨论宪法草案的情况," *Neibu cankao*, July 9, 1954.

"潘阳市各机关, 工厂讨论宪法草案中的偏向和各阶层人民的思想动态,"
    Neibu cankao, July 10, 1954.

"浙江省各界人民在讨论宪法草案中提出了不少疑问," *Neibu cankao*, July 13,
    1954.

"湖南省平江县人民代表对选外籍人当省人民代表不满," *Neibu cankao*, July 13,
    1954.

"安徽省宪法草案宣传中的偏向," *Neibu cankao*, July 14, 1954.

"西安市各阶层人民在讨论宪法草案中提出的问题," *Neibu cankao*, July 22, 1954.

"潘阳市少数高级技职人员对宪法草案的认识模糊," *Neibu cankao*, July 22, 1954.

"江西省部分干部在讨论宪法草案中的思想情况," *Neibu cankao*, July 22, 1954.

"云南少数民族上层人士对宪法草案的反应" *Neibu cankao*, July 22, 1954.

"西安市各阶层人民在讨论宪法草案中提出的修改意见," *Neibu cankao*, July 22,
    1954.

"全国各地人民对宪法草案的反应," *Neibu cankao*, July 24, 1954.

"西康省藏族自治区藏族领神人物在讨论宪法草案中提出的问题," *Neibu cankao*, July 26, 1954.

"山西省平顺县农民在讨论宪法草案中的思想情况," *Neibu cankao*, July 28, 1954.

"内蒙民主人士和民族上层分子在宪法草案讨论的思想情况," *Neibu cankao*,
    July 28, 1954.

"云南省西双版纳傣族自治区各阶层人民对宪法草案的反应," *Neibu cankao*,
    July 29, 1954.

"甘肃省临夏市宗教上层人士对宪法草案中规定信教自由顾虑很大," *Neibu
    cankao*, July 30, 1954.

"浙江各级干部普遍不重视宪法草案的学习," *Neibu cankao*, July 31, 1954.

"河北省定县曹村宣传宪法草案的情况," *Neibu cankao*, July 31, 1954.

"无锡市各工厂对宪法草案的宣传讨论不深不透," *Neibu cankao*, July 31, 1954.

"黑龙江省部分地区在宪法草案宣传中产生不少缺点," *Neibu cankao*, August 5,
    1954.

"湖南省各界人民对宪法草案的反应," *Neibu cankao*, August 9, 1954.

"哈尔滨不少单位对宪法草案的宣传讨论重视不够," *Neibu cankao*, August 18,
    1954.

"江西省的县, 市人民代表大会的代表对宪法草案的反应," *Neibu cankao*, August 19, 1954.

"武东县七区有不少农民不了解宪法草案的意义," *Neibu cankao*, August 21,
    1954.

"黑龙江省有些地方在宣传宪法草案中有违法政策的现象," *Neibu cankao*, August 26, 1954.

"四川省有些地区农民对宪法草案的内容有误解," *Neibu cankao*, September 15,
    1954.

INDEX

age and constitutional commentary, 24
Altehenger, Jennifer, 7, 34, 157, 197,
    241n46
anthem. *See* national anthem
antipathy, 72–73. *See also* boredom
Anti-Rightist Campaign (1957), 19, 29, 158
apathy, 72–73. *See also* boredom
Applebaum, Anne, 114, 205n4
Article 3, Chinese Constitution (1954),
    140–41. *See also* Chinese Constitution
    (1954)
Article 9, Chinese Constitution (1954), 173.
    See also Chinese Constitution (1954)
Article 11, Chinese Constitution (1982), 58,
    181. *See also* Chinese Constitution
    (1982)
Article 14, Chinese Constitution (1982), 182.
    See also Chinese Constitution (1982)
Article 17, Chinese Constitution (1982), 183.
    See also Chinese Constitution (1982)
Article 19, Chinese Constitution (1954), 43,
    162–63. *See also* Campaign to Suppress
    Counterrevolutionaries (1950–53);
    Chinese Constitution (1954)
Article 22, Chinese Constitution (1982), 180.
    See also Chinese Constitution (1982)
Article 26, Chinese Constitution (1982), 183.
    See also Chinese Constitution (1982)
Article 35, Chinese Constitution (1982), 183.
    See also Chinese Constitution (1982)
Article 47, Chinese Constitution (1982),
    179. *See also* Chinese Constitution
    (1982)
Article 51, Chinese Constitution (1982), 172,
    178, 190. *See also* Chinese Constitution
    (1982)
Article 53, Chinese Constitution (1982), 130.
    See also Chinese Constitution (1982)
Article 86, Chinese Constitution (1954),
    103–8. *See also* Chinese Constitution
    (1954)

Article 87, Chinese Constitution (1954),
    117–21, 149. *See also* Chinese
    Constitution (1954)
Article 88, Chinese Constitution (1954),
    121–22, 135, 140, 142, 145, 149, 237n87.
    See also Chinese Constitution (1954);
    religious belief and freedom
Article 90, Chinese Constitution (1954),
    113–17, 153, 168–69. *See also* Chinese
    Constitution (1954)
Article 91, Chinese Constitution (1954),
    122–24. *See also* Chinese Constitution
    (1954)
Article 92, Chinese Constitution (1954), 123.
    See also Chinese Constitution (1954)
Article 93, Chinese Constitution (1954), 106,
    123. *See also* Chinese Constitution
    (1954)
Article 94, Chinese Constitution (1954), 96,
    103, 108, 109–13, 115, 125. *See also*
    Chinese Constitution (1954)
Article 96, Chinese Constitution (1954), 83,
    103–8, 143, 235n38. *See also* Chinese
    Constitution (1954)
Austin, J. L., 16, 17
authoritarian legality, 192. *See also* instru-
    mentalism

Beijing Review (publication), 175
Biddulph, Sarah, 187, 248n49
boredom, 27, 35. *See also* apathy
boundaries, national and provincial, 91–92
Boxers, 148, 236n71
Brezhnev, Leonid, 198
Brown, Jeremy, 11
Buddhism, 137, 141, 237n72. *See also*
    religious belief and freedom
Buddhist Chinese, 148–50, 237n77. *See also*
    religious belief and freedom
Bui Hai Thiem, 199
Bui Ngoc Son, 199, 200

CPSIA information can be obtained
at www.ICGtesting.com
Printed in the USA
LVHW090931171221
706366LV00024B/357/J